Courageous Past–Bold Future

Courageous Past–Bold Future

*The Journey Toward Full Clergy Rights for Women
In The United Methodist Church*

Patricia J. Thompson

General Board of Higher Education and Ministry
The United Methodist Church
Nashville, Tennessee

The General Board of Higher Education and Ministry leads and serves The United Methodist Church in the recruitment, preparation, nurture, education, and support of Christian leaders–lay and clergy–for the work of making disciples of Jesus Christ for the transformation of the world. Its vision is that a new generation of Christian leaders will commit boldly to Jesus Christ and be characterized by intellectual excellence, moral integrity, spiritual courage, and holiness of heart and life.

The General Board of Higher Education and Ministry of The United Methodist Church is the church's agency for educational, institutional, and ministerial leadership. It serves as an advocate for the intellectual life of the church. The Board's mission embodies the Wesleyan tradition of commitment to the education of laypersons and ordained persons by providing access to higher education for all persons.

Acknowledgment:
Excerpts from SEVEN STEEPLES by Margaret K. Henrichsen. Copyright © 1953, and renewed 1981 by Margaret K. Henrichsen. Reprinted by permission of Houghton Mifflin Company. All rights reserved.

Cover and book design by Laura Deck

This book is printed on acid-free paper that meets the American National Standards Institute Z39.48 standard. ∞

ISBN 0-938162-00-4

Produced by the Office of Interpretation   Manufactured in the United States of America

Contents

Chapter 5

First Women of the Southeastern Jurisdiction to Receive Full Clergy Rights 99

Chapter 6

First Women of the South Central Jurisdiction to Receive Full Clergy Rights 126

Foreword

In 2002, the General Board of Higher Education and Ministry of The United Methodist Church named the Fiftieth Anniversary Task Force for the Celebration of Full Clergy Rights for Women in the Methodist Tradition in 2006, under the direction of the Reverend Dr. Marion Jackson, director of Continuing Education for Ministry, Clergywomen's Concerns, and Spiritual Formation at the time. The purpose of the task force is to enable United Methodists worldwide to celebrate the fiftieth anniversary of the historic decision in 1956 to allow women in The Methodist Church to have full clergy rights–the same clergy rights as their male counterparts. The task force is composed of a broad spectrum of women, lay and clergy: women of color; local church pastors; a representative of United Methodist Women; a district superintendent; general agency staff; seminary faculty; and a bishop.

The task force was charged with developing a variety of resources to assist The United Methodist Church at all levels to participate in this celebration. From the outset, it was clear that there needed to be a historical statement describing the difficult and courageous journey that began with women preachers in John Wesley's time, was continued by those in predecessor denominations of The United Methodist Church, and eventually led to the final passage of the 1956 legislation. There was also agreement that the first women to be received into annual conference membership needed to be lifted up and celebrated. In the course of its deliberations, the history subcommittee of the task force recommended that an attempt be made to identify and recognize the first woman in every annual conference, the first woman in every ethnic group represented in the conference, as well as the first woman in each of the central conferences.

Due to the number of biographies that were eventually collected and the fact that the focus of the fiftieth anniversary

celebration is on those women who were the first to be received into conference membership as elders in full connection, a further decision was made not to include the first deacons to be received into full connection following the 1996 reordering of ministry, which replaced the two-step ordination process that was in effect in 1956.

When I agreed to take responsibility for writing *Courageous Past–Bold Future*, I had no idea how much new information would be uncovered. Although most of the historical information about Methodist women preachers was known by individual conferences, for the most part, this book represents the first time that all this information has been collected in a single volume.

The year 1956 did not mark the first time for women in some predecessor denominations to The United Methodist Church to receive full clergy rights. Women in both The Church of the United Brethren in Christ and The Methodist Protestant Church were granted full clergy rights in the late 1800s. I include the story of these women in chapter 1. Further, the chapter challenges some long-held beliefs about who some of our "first" women were. This may disappoint some readers. Yet it is truly exciting to uncover stories that have been long buried and in so doing to expand the understanding of our history. Regardless of whether a particular woman was the first or not, *all* these women were pioneers who struggled to live out their divine calling to preach the gospel as they experienced it–often in an environment extremely hostile to women.

I had no idea when I started the research just how difficult it would be for some annual conferences to identify their "first" women and then to gather the information from these conferences. Though I did have some notion of how difficult the journey had been for many women–especially for women of color–I was not totally prepared for the absolutely amazing stories of both pain and of faith they told. The United Methodist Church has indeed been blessed with many courageous women whose relationship with the steadfast and ever-faithful God may be the only thing that has kept them moving forward in their journeys to live out their call. The stories are sometimes humorous and sometimes hard to believe. They often reflect deep hurt, but just as often reveal heartfelt gratitude for the steady presence of God in their lives and the encouragement from those who supported them.

The biographical statements in this book are as varied as the women themselves. Indeed, to allow each woman to share the joy and pain, the struggle and the triumph of her story in her own words, I have left the stories as close to their original form as possible. Unfortunately, in cases where a woman has been deceased a long time, very little biographical information is available. For a small number of these women, no memoirs were ever published, making it difficult to collect information. No doubt, there are women who should have been included here who were not identified by their annual conferences. For the most part, I have had to rely on annual conference personnel to identify the women. I apologize to anyone who may have been overlooked. Unfortunately, a small number of women chose not to participate in this project, despite repeated contacts. I can assure the reader that whatever oversight may exist in this book, it was not intentional or due to lack of diligence in research.

I am deeply humbled and grateful to have been the person blessed to receive the stories of so many remarkable and outstanding women and to be able to present these stories to our readers. It is clear that some annual conferences have done a great deal of research on the history of women in their conferences. For other conferences, this may have been the first time to examine that history. The truth is, some annual conference commissions on archives and history are far more active than others. However, it is my hope that this project will have at least laid the foundation for a celebration of clergywomen in every annual conference in 2006.

I want to thank the many people without whose assistance this book could never have been written: staff from the General Commission on Archives and History (especially Dale Patterson, Mark Shenise, and Kevin Newburg, who did a lot of detailed work in the last weeks of the project); Brid Nicholson, PhD candidate at Drew University, who did amazing research on the Methodist Protestant women; members of annual conference commissions on archives and history; annual conference archivists; secretaries; registrars of boards of ordained ministry; clergy colleagues; and, most of all, the clergywomen themselves, who put up with my numerous requests for information, sometimes for information that got lost somewhere in the process. Special thanks to my sisters of color, who patiently guided this European American woman through her many questions.

In addition, I would like to thank the Reverend Dr. Marion Jackson, who originally convened the Fiftieth Anniversary Task Force and who, from the outset, strongly supported the publication of the book. Special thanks also to the Reverend Dr. HiRho Park, who has continued to shepherd the project since July 2005.

Finally, I would like to thank my husband, Vernon, without whose patience and support this manuscript would never have been completed.

It is my prayer that all who read this book will be as blessed by the stories as I have been.

Grace and peace,
Patricia J. Thompson

Chapter 1

"Shall She Be Allowed to Preach?"
Celebrating the Courageous History of Women Preachers in the United Methodist Tradition

At the 1956 General Conference of The Methodist Church, held in Minneapolis, Minnesota, an action was taken that would change the face of the denomination forever: the decision to grant women clergy the same rights afforded to male clergy! Such action did not come, however, without a great deal of hard work and heartache on the part of untold numbers of women, and men as well. Indeed, women had been advocating for the right to preach from the onset of the Methodist movement in England in the eighteenth century.

This chapter chronicles the history of some of these women and their call to preach–from John Wesley's day through the development of Methodism in the United States, as it unfolded through the various denominations that today compose The United Methodist Church (UMC). In this and subsequent chapters, I rely heavily on the writings of Paul W. Chilcote and Jean Miller Schmidt, both of whom have done groundbreaking work on women in the Methodist tradition. "Women helped to make the Wesleyan revival in England a powerful religious awakening. Their search for truth and justice brought vitality to the movement.... Methodist women dared to claim their rightful place within the life of the church. They challenged repressive institutions. They questioned the validity of exclusive structures. The women preachers stood on the cutting edge of this struggle for liberation."[1]

So states Paul Chilcote in the introduction to his book on the legacy of the women preachers in Mr. Wesley's day. As Chilcote notes, "Women have proclaimed the good news they discovered in Christ" from the first Easter Sunday, the day of the Resurrection.[2] However, just as the women's report of seeing Jesus alive was considered "just an idle tale," so women's call to preach the good news of Jesus Christ has been treated with raised eyebrows, scorching criticism, and worse, down to the present day. Nevertheless, sustained by their faith in the God whom they knew had called them, women have continued to live out that summons–often without the sanction of either church or society. Chilcote says of these exceptional women: "They were exceptional, not because they possessed extraordinary gifts, but because they allowed God to use fully whatever they had. God takes that which is ordinary, you see, and invests it with eternal significance and sacred power when it is offered freely for others. These women had the courage to offer Christ to their world."[3]

These words are true of the women not only in John Wesley's time but also those who heard the call of God and followed it wherever God chose to lead.

Women Preachers in the Time of John Wesley

The first woman to exert her influence on the Methodist movement was Susanna Wesley, wife of Samuel Wesley and mother of John and Charles. Susanna is well known for her organized and disciplined lifestyle. She personally educated her many children, not only in the basics of reading and writing but also in more complicated subjects such as ethics and theology.[4]

As the children became grounded in their elementary education, Susanna quite naturally began to be more concerned about their spiritual and moral development, and so she set aside an hour every evening for the purpose of developing this side of their education. During the winter months of 1710–11, when Samuel was away for long periods of time attending the Convocation of Clergy in London, she began holding prayer services on Sunday evenings for all members of the household. Gradually, some of the neighbors began to join these services until the numbers grew to around forty people. At the same time, having read an account of some Danish missionaries to the East Indies, Susanna became aware of her "pastoral" duties to her children. She wrote in her journal: "At last it came into my mind, though I am not a man, nor a minister of the gospel... I might do somewhat more than I do.... I might pray more for *the people*, and speak with more warmth to those with whom I have an opportunity of conversing. However, I resolved to begin with my own children."5

Thus, during the following winter, Susanna's evening prayer services quickly expanded into religious services, drawing not only neighbors but also folks from the nearby town. Eventually, the numbers increased to nearly three hundred people. The problem was somewhat exacerbated by the rather inept curator at St. Andrews Church, who eventually complained to Samuel Wesley. However, when Wesley wrote Susanna asking for an explanation of her actions, she quickly responded that "her labors produced specific fruit. Relationships among the townspeople improved. People were excited about their faith and desired to know more about God. She agreed with Samuel about the impropriety of a woman taking the lead in such matters. But she believed that the life of the church hung in the balance and no other course of action was left open to her."6

Samuel Wesley apparently took no further action, and John, who was around nine years old at the time, had an outstanding example of the kind of leadership women might exert in the church. This example apparently stayed with him throughout his life and would influence the role women would eventually have in the newly developing Methodist movement.

After John Wesley's "heart-warming experience" in May 1738, the Methodist movement began to grow rapidly. Since the foundation of the movement was small groups, in which all members were allowed to express themselves freely, women, in particular, were attracted. In fact, the early days saw a preponderance of women, so much so that some accused the movement of being a female sect!7

Wesley subdivided his Methodist societies into "classes" and "bands." Bands consisted of four or five people of the same sex and marital status, organized for the purpose of "intense personal introspection and rigorous mutual confession." The classes usually had twelve persons of both sexes. They met weekly for fellowship and were somewhat less intense than the band meetings.8

Wesley himself appointed the leaders of these small groups. It was in these settings that women began not only to grow in their Christian faith but to also exercise leadership roles—roles that, for some, would lead to preaching the gospel. Because there were a large number of women members and the bands were segregated, these groups offered many leadership opportunities for women. Though, generally, men led the classes, Wesley often appointed women as class leaders. Chilcote states: "The band leaders, in particular, had to be persons of spiritual depth and maturity. Special gifts and qualities were necessary for the pastoral oversight of souls. Wesley required that his band leaders have a clear understanding of God's saving grace and the way of salvation. They had to be able to communicate their own experience and knowledge to others."9

Three forms of public speaking took place in the bands and classes: public prayers, testimony, and exhortation. While each of these forms was distinctly different, says Chilcote, it was natural that they would overlap. "Not only could prayer easily become testimony, and testimony sound very much like exhortation, but any one of these means of communicating the gospel could transgress that fine line which separated them from preaching."10

For many women, public prayer was the first experience of speaking in public. Many of them became very gifted in the art of public prayer, even establishing prayer groups to expand the work of the classes and bands in which they participated. However, public prayers often led to personal testimony, with the ultimate purpose of transforming lives; and such testimony eventually "became a distinct feature of Methodist gatherings."11 It was not at all unusual for personal testimonies to follow the preaching service.

This sharing of testimony could often become an exhortation that "consisted primarily of reproving sin, pleading for the sinner to repent and be saved, and testifying to one's own experience. Exhortation took a number of forms ranging from informal conversations in intimate circles to formal addresses in assembled groups."12

To the modern reader, this may seem to be very much like our definition of preaching. However, Wesley drew a fine distinction: preaching consisted of "taking a text" and "speaking in a continued discourse."13 As women continued to become more and more experienced in leadership roles, many came very close to actually preaching. Some of them seemed to realize this and would often seek advice from Mr. Wesley. One of the first to do this was Sarah Crosby, born near Leeds on November 7, 1729. She was converted under the preaching of both George Whitefield and John Wesley in 1749 and became an established class leader by 1751. By 1761, Crosby found herself publicly exhorting before nearly two hundred persons. Worried that she might have strayed into actual preaching, she immediately sought Wesley's advice.14 Wesley responded:

My Dear Sister,
Hitherto, I think you have not gone too far. You could not well do less. I apprehend all you can do more is, when you meet again, to tell them simply, "you lay me under a great difficulty. The Methodists do not allow of women preachers; neither do I take upon me any such character. But I will just nakedly tell you what is in my heart . . ." I do not see that you have broken any law. Go on calmly and steadily. If you have time, you may read to them the *Notes* on any chapter before you speak a few words, or one of the most awakening sermons, as other women have done long ago.15

Sarah Crosby was associated with two other women, Mary Bosanquet and Sarah Ryan, who had opened an orphanage and a school at "The Cedars" in Leytonstone, where they took in the neediest people from the London streets. Crosby and Bosanquet both continued to hold midweek prayer meetings, which grew so large that they needed to be divided, thus spreading their work even further. Eventually, the women moved their ministry north to

Yorkshire and opened Cross Hall, which soon became a thriving center for Methodism.[16] Finally, in 1771, Bosanquet, having received criticism from some of the Methodist preachers, who claimed that her speaking was "unscriptural," wrote Wesley for guidance. Both Chilcote and Schmidt consider Bosanquet's letter the first significant defense of women's preaching in Methodism.[17] There are times, Bosanquet told Wesley, when God calls women to preach in *extraordinary* circumstances. This seems to have paved the way for Wesley to give limited approval to women who had an extraordinary call. His response to Bosanquet's inquiry is illuminating.

> Londonderry, June 13, 1771
>
> My dear sister,
> I think the strength of the cause rests there, on your having an *Extraordinary Call*. So, I am persuaded, has every one of our Lay Preachers [male]: otherwise I could not countenance his preaching at all. It is plain to me that the whole Work of God termed Methodism is an extraordinary dispensation of His Providence. Therefore, I do not wonder if several things occur therein which do not fall under ordinary rules of discipline. St. Paul's ordinary rule was, "I permit not a woman to speak in the congregation." Yet in extraordinary cases he made a few exceptions; at Corinth, in particular.[18]

Thus began Wesley's endorsement of those women preachers whom he judged to have an "extraordinary" call. However, each case was evaluated on an individual basis, according to Wesley's assessment of the woman's gifts, grace, and fruit. In the end, though, Wesley could not bring himself to approve of women preachers as an ordinary practice in the Methodist movement.[19]

Nevertheless, other women began to emerge. One of the best known was Sarah Mallet, who began her ministry in February 1786. Under Wesley's guidance Mallet became the first officially approved female traveling preacher in Methodism. In 1787, Wesley gave her a note of authorization from the Methodist Conference in Manchester. Chilcote says of this note: "[It] is the single most important piece of documentary evidence concerning the women preachers of early Methodism. The official authorization simply reads: 'We give the right hand of fellowship to Sarah Mallet, and have no objection to her being a preacher in our connexion, so long as she preaches the Methodist doctrines, and attends to our discipline.'"[20]

In 1781, another event took place that would become a model for many women preachers in the years ahead, especially in the United States among women in the Church of The United Brethren in Christ (UB Church), who were often married to preachers, as well. On November 12, 1781, Mary Bosanquet married the Reverend John Fletcher, Wesley's confidant and the one Wesley had pegged as his successor. Chilcote says, "John and Mary formed a unique partnership of mutual service and love, perhaps the first 'clergy couple,' so to speak, within the Methodist movement. They functioned as co-pastors, for all practical purposes, through the course of their marriage."[21] Unfortunately, this partnership would last only a short while due to Fletcher's untimely demise in 1785.

Despite the fact that Wesley accepted women preachers with an "extraordinary call," the practice still did not enjoy widespread support among the Methodist "brethren." Opposition increased after Wesley's death in 1791; and at its meeting in Manchester in 1803 the Methodist conference voted that "any woman convinced that she had 'an extraordinary call from God to speak in public' was advised to address 'her *own sex*, and *those only*.'"[22]

In the years following, many women who felt the call to preach left the Wesleyan Methodists to join groups that were more open to women preachers, such as the Primitive Methodists or the Bible Christians. Others began to emigrate to America.[23]

Women Called to Preach in Nineteenth-Century America

Unordained Traveling Preachers

Methodism spread to America in the 1760s by way of Irish immigrants and, from the outset, women were a vital part of that movement. Robert and Elizabeth Piper Strawbridge organized a Methodist class in their Maryland home as early as 1763. While Robert was traveling throughout the area preaching, Elizabeth, with the help of a neighbor, John Evans, managed the Strawbridge family farm. Evans experienced a conversion after a "serious conversation" with Elizabeth in her kitchen one day. Barbara Ruckle Heck was long known as the "Mother of American Methodism," for her role in convincing her cousin, Phillip Embury, to begin preaching in New York City in 1766.[24] Methodism spread quickly up and down the eastern seaboard and westward as immigrants began to move away from the East Coast.

In her book *Petticoats in the Pulpit*, Elizabeth Gillan Muir writes: "In the first half of the nineteenth century, Methodist women preachers from Great Britain emigrated not only to Upper Canada but also to the United States, where many of them continued preaching to mixed reactions. Generally, in spite of resistance, they made greater progress in the United States than in Canada."[25]

Although many of the early women preachers came to America from Great Britain out of a Bible Christian or Primitive Methodist background, it was not long before American-born women also heard the call to preach and lived out that call in a variety of ways. Just as in Great Britain, many women in America found themselves in leadership positions in classes and bands and began speaking publicly in these settings—first by praying, then by testifying, and eventually by exhorting.[26] And these experiences often led to preaching. Says historian Schmidt: "There were women in the Methodist denomination in this country who experienced a call to preach and became (unordained) traveling preachers as early as the 1810's and 1820's. Two of the earliest examples were Jarena Lee, a free black woman born in New Jersey, and probably the first female preacher of the African Methodist Episcopal Church, and Fanny Butterfield Newell, wife of a circuit riding Methodist Episcopal preacher in the New England Conference. From the published spiritual memoirs of these two women, we know something about how they experienced and responded to their call."[27]

Jarena Lee, born in Cape May, New Jersey, in 1783, first published her memoirs in 1836 as *The Life and Religious Experiences of Jarena Lee*. She related how she was converted at age twenty-one under the preaching of the Reverend Richard Allen, pastor of the Bethel African Methodist Episcopal Church (AME Church) in Philadelphia. A few years later, Lee felt a call to preach and approached her pastor, who told her that she could hold prayer meetings or exhort but that Methodism did not allow for women preachers.

In 1811, Jarena married the Reverend Joseph Lee, pastor of the black church in Snow Hill, New Jersey, just a short distance from Philadelphia. A few years later, her husband and four of her children died, leaving her with two infants, two years old and six months old, respectively. Lee returned to Philadelphia, where the AME Church had been officially organized with Richard Allen as its first bishop. One Sunday at a service in Bethel Church, Lee sprang to her feet and began exhorting after the regular preacher seemed to have lost his spirit. When Lee sat down and remembered Bishop Allen's earlier warning against her preaching, she feared that she might be expelled. However, recalling their earlier conversation, Bishop Allen stated that her call to preach was as valid as any other preacher's.

That was the beginning of Jarena Lee's life as a traveling itinerant preacher, starting in Philadelphia and moving into Maryland, New York, and beyond, where she preached to black and white congregations in both the North and the South.[28]

Though she seems to have received widespread acceptance, Lee occasionally encountered objections. Recalls Schmidt, "When confronted by a black male preacher in 1824 who told her it was something new for women to preach, Jarena Lee appealed to the example of earlier Methodist women preachers like Mary Bosanquet Fletcher. When he asked why she did not go to the Quakers (since they authorized women preachers), she replied simply that she was sent to the Methodists. Like the Hebrew prophets, she relied fundamentally on a God who says, 'I will send by whom I will [send].'"[29]

Unable to secure the support of the AME Church's Book Committee, Lee actually paid for the publication of her memoirs herself. The first edition appeared in 1836, followed by a second edition in 1849. Nothing is known of her activities after 1849.[30]

Lee was only the first of a number of women who felt the call to preach and who worked unsuccessfully throughout the nineteenth century for formal recognition within the AME Church. In her article, "Nineteenth-Century A.M.E. Preaching Women," Jualynne Dodson recounts the struggles of several of these women for official recognition with the AME hierarchy. The most that they were able to achieve officially, at the General Conference in 1884, was obtaining licenses to serve as local preachers. However, this same General Conference limited their right to that of serving "simply as evangelists."[31]

As noted earlier, a Methodist Episcopal woman from Maine, Fanny Butterfield Newell, also had her memoirs published. These were published posthumously by her husband, Ebenezer F. Newell, and Orange Scott, one of the founders of the Wesleyan Methodists, and went through several editions.

Fanny Butterfield was born May 12, 1793, in Sidney, Maine. According to her memoirs, she was converted in 1808 under the influence of Brother Henry Martin[32] at age fifteen.

Shortly afterward, she began to ponder the possibility of being baptized and presented herself to Brother Martin when he next offered the sacrament. She recalls the experience: "I kneeled down and was plunged forward, and when I arose, I stood some time in the water, and exhorted the numerous congregation which crowded round the shore; and I praised the Lord with loud strains."[33]

Her mind soon became preoccupied with preaching to sinners but she also questioned why this is so since she is a woman:

When awake, the subject rests upon me, and I am brought to wonder, why my mind is so much on preaching, both night and day, sleeping and waking, seeing I am but a feeble woman. At times I think I will go and join the people called Quakers or Friends, because they approbate females to preach amongst them.... Notwithstanding I have labored to collect all the objections that could be made against a woman's speaking in public, on any occasion whatever, to exercise myself, and then owning that it was my youth and ignorance that had pushed me forward, [at the time of writing, Fanny was sixteen]–after all my labor, I could not ease my conscience, or obtain peace of mind; therefore I must go in that way where I can find peace with God; for if God frowns upon me, who can appease his wrath?[34]

The following March, the circuit rider Ebenezer F. Newell asked for Fanny's hand in marriage. He must have recognized that she had a special calling for Fanny records that he wrote, "If you are convinced that the Lord has called you to this great work, and I could be so happy as to have your help, I would receive you as a tender lamb to my bosom, and by the grace of God, be a guard to you while you might labor with me in the Gospel."[35] In his own memoirs, Ebenezer notes, "I viewed it my duty to bring her gift into the more public service of the church."[36]

Fanny and Ebenezer were married in 1810 and Fanny eventually gave birth to a son, Ebenezer Butterfield, and a daughter, Olive Fanny. Shortly after the birth of her son, Fanny had a near-death experience in which she met the living Christ who told her, "Fanny, you must not come yet; thou shalt not die, but live, and declare the works of the Lord to the children of men. Go back to yonder earth." Two more times the words were repeated to her until she was reconciled to returning to this life, declaring to her husband how she had answered "I shall not die, but live, and declare the wonderful works of God to the children of men."[37]

This was Fanny's confirmation of her call to preach and she lived out that call by traveling with her husband around the circuit, exhorting and preaching as occasions presented themselves. Though from time to time she continued to struggle with her call, she continued to preach and often found acceptance in unusual places. On July 14, 1816, her husband wrote:

My amiable and true help-meet, with our little son and daughter, went round the circuit with me. One Sunday evening we held a meeting in a school house, near the residence of an old Congregational minister, who had, like other Calvinists, bitterly opposed females talking or praying in public. It being noised abroad that the preacher's wife would be there who exhorted publicly, the house was crowded, and more stood round the door. Immediately after the sermon she rose with these words–"Come and see a man that told me all things that ever I did; is not this the Christ?"–and observed that they were the words of a woman spoken publicly to all her neighbors.

After reasoning awhile in defence of women's improving in public, she warned sinners of their danger and invited them to Jesus.... The old preacher was present, hid from most of the people on a low seat in one corner. The brother with whom we stopped ran over in the morning and asked him what he thought now of a woman's talking in meeting; he replied,–"If all the women would talk as that woman did last night, I would say, speak on!" Praise God for the help of the Holy Ghost.[38]

Fanny Butterfield Newell died of "consumption" (tuberculosis) in 1824 at age thirty-one.[39]

In 1830 a group of members of The Methodist Episcopal Church (MEC) who was unhappy with the amount of authority afforded to bishops and the lack of a significant role for laypeople in the church broke away to form The Methodist Protestant Church (MPC).[40] Although there was no formal role for women preachers until the latter part of the century, at least one woman, Hannah Pearce, originally a member of the Bible Christian Church in England, was preaching regularly in the denomination as early as 1831.[41]

Hannah Pearce was born in Devonshire, England, in 1800. After she was converted in the Bible Christian Church, she worked for a time as a parlor maid for the son of Canada's first lieutenant-governor, John Graves Simcoe, until she became an itinerant preacher at age twenty-five.[42] Sometime in 1827, a friend invited William Reeves, a Wesleyan Methodist lay preacher who was opposed to women preaching, to accompany him to hear Pearce preach. Reeves was impressed by the fact that this young woman could "expand on a text for an hour without any notes." When he asked her how she was able to do this, she is reported to have replied, "Throw away your crutches and fight like a man."[43] Shortly after this encounter, Reeves traveled to America and joined the newly formed MPC. Over the next year, he corresponded with Hannah, finally convincing her to travel to America to marry him. They were married in July 1831 in Zanesville, Ohio, and worked together in the itinerant ministry for the remainder of Hannah's life.[44] Hannah became known as "the Lady Preacher." In his *Concise History of the Methodist Protestant Church*, Ancel H. Bassett mentions her in conjunction with her husband on two different occasions, always speaking positively of her work.[45]

In fact, Schmidt reports that, after having been invited to preach before the 1831 Ohio Annual Conference of The Methodist Protestant Church, Hannah was approached about the possibility of accepting her own circuit. To which she responded that all she desired "was the conference's concurrence in her labors with her husband." Hannah Pearce Reeves died November 13, 1868, at age 68.[46]

Women Evangelists in the Holiness Movement

Schmidt states, "The holiness movement was one of the ways in which the earlier Methodist tradition of religious leadership manifested itself after 1830. Nurtured in the Tuesday meeting of the 1830's and 1840's the holiness revival in Methodism flowered in the holiness camp meeting of the 1850's–1860's."[47] Phoebe Worall Palmer and Amanda Berry Smith emerged as two of the best-known female Holiness evangelists.

Phoebe Worall was born December 18, 1807, the fourth of nine surviving children born to Henry and Dorothea Wade Worall, members of the Duane St. (New York City) MEC. Phoebe was raised in a home centered on family worship and had given her life to Christ at a young age, but was bothered by the fact that she was unable to point to a specific conversion experience.[48] At age nineteen, Phoebe married a young medical doctor named Walter Clarke Palmer, an active member of the Allen St. (New York City) MEC. Three of Phoebe's six children died in the early years of the marriage. Indeed, "her commitment to evangelism dated to [the] time of her daughter [Eliza's] death, and her evangelistic ministry can, at least in part, be seen as a memorial to her dead children."[49]

After the birth of her daughter, Eliza, in 1835, Phoebe and her husband moved into a house on the Lower East Side and invited her sister, Sarah, and Sarah's husband, Thomas Lankford, to live with them. In May of that year Sarah received the blessing of "entire sanctification" that she had been seeking. At the time, she was leading women's prayer meetings at two Methodist churches. She decided to combine the meetings and began holding the meeting on Tuesday afternoons at the home she and Phoebe shared. The meeting became known as the "Tuesday Meetings for the Promotion of Holiness." It was at one of these meetings in 1837 that Phoebe was led to her own experience of sanctification. Phoebe soon began to exercise her leadership, which would, in turn, exert great influence on the Holiness movement. Such prominent Methodists as Nathan Bangs, Bishop Edmund Janes, and Leonides Hamline eventually became regular members of the Tuesday Meeting.[50]

Though at first somewhat shy about speaking in public, Palmer "believed that she would lose the spiritual gift she had received if she did not publicly testify to it." In 1840, she assumed leadership of the Tuesday Meeting when her sister and brother-in-law moved away. At the same time, as invitations to speak about holiness came from beyond New York, Palmer's sense of her calling as "a woman called to public witness" began to deepen. This call would take her through the United States, Canada, and Great Britain. In addition to a distinguished public speaking career, Palmer also witnessed to the experience of sanctification through her writing. She wrote regularly for the *Guide to Christian Perfection*, begun in 1839, with the Reverend Timothy Merritt as editor. She also published *The Way of Holiness* (1843), *Entire Devotion to God* (1845), and *Faith and Its Effects* (1848).[51]

Though receiving widespread acceptance as a Holiness evangelist, Palmer was not immune from criticism and resistance. Also, other women shared with her their stories of not being allowed to speak in public. Thus, in 1859, Palmer penned *Promise of the Father*, "a defense of women's right to preach on the basis of the gift of the Spirit to both men and women at Pentecost."[52] Nevertheless, Palmer never insisted on ordination for women. It was not that she did not consider herself suitable for ordained ministry. Rather, as Lucille and Donald Dayton point out, Palmer felt that "the whole system of ordination was unscriptural and vastly different from the New Testament church where everyone–man, woman and child–was called to preach the Gospel."[53]

Palmer continued her amazing career as a Holiness evangelist and author until she contracted kidney disease in 1872 and died "a good death" in 1874 at age 66.[54]

Another woman, Amanda Berry Smith, who became one of the "most powerful internationally known holiness evangelists of the nineteenth century," came from a background very different from that of Phoebe Palmer. Born on a farm near Baltimore, Maryland, Berry was a former slave and washerwoman. After her father purchased freedom for his family, Amanda, at age thirteen, began working as a domestic and "enjoyed the religious influences of revival meetings at the Albright Church [Evangelical Association] and then the Methodist Church."[55]

At seventeen, Amanda married Calvin Devine and had a daughter, Mazzie. Devine enlisted in the Union Army during the Civil War and never returned. Amanda later married James Smith, an ordained deacon in the AME Church, thinking she was marrying a minister. However, he did not receive an appointment at the church's annual conference.

In 1855, while near death from an illness, Smith had a dream, or perhaps a vision, in which she saw herself preaching to thousands of people at a camp meeting. She awoke much improved, believing that God had spared her for a reason. In 1856 she finally experienced a conversion and vowed to believe in God henceforth.[56]

It was not until she experienced sanctification under the ministry of the Reverend John S. Inskip, first president of the National Camp Meeting Association, that Smith had her first real contact with the Holiness movement. "This experience was also nurtured in Phoebe Palmer's 'Tuesday Meeting,' where the presence of a black tended to upset some of the 'proper' ladies in attendance."[57]

After attending a meeting of the National Camp Meeting Association and encountering some of the Holiness leaders, Smith slowly began her ministry of speaking at these meetings, despite resistance on account of her race and sex.[58] Over the next ten to fifteen years, Smith traveled to Britain, India, and Africa. She eventually settled in Harvey, Illinois, and bought land for an orphanage, which became the Amanda Smith Industrial School for Girls. Unfortunately, the school was destroyed by fire in 1918, three years after Smith's death. Schmidt reports that Smith "often suffered the hostility of both blacks and whites. When she attended the 1872 General Conference of the AME Church in Nashville, she was treated with disdain because of her 'plain Quaker dress' and with suspicion as a woman preacher because the male clergy thought she was there to fight for the ordination of women."[59]

Thus, it would seem that some women were accepted (or at least tolerated) in the role of exhorter, evangelist, and even preacher, as long as they did not apply for licenses, and ordination remained officially reserved for men only. Their numbers were relatively few; and, for the most part, the work of women in the church was limited to more subordinate roles with little chance of upsetting the authority of the male leadership. However, this was to change in the second half of the nineteenth century.

Women Preachers in The Church of the United Brethren in Christ

The first denomination in the Methodist family to give official recognition to women preachers was The Church of the United Brethren in Christ (UB Church), formally organized in Frederick, Maryland, in 1800.[60] The first known records of women applying for formal recognition of the right to preach occurred in the Scioto [Ohio] Conference in 1841 and 1843. Sister Courtland sought counsel from the conference regarding "an impression to read and comment on the Scriptures."[61] Subsequently, a committee was appointed to advise Sister Courtland.

Two years later, Louisa P. Clemens made a similar request, perhaps seeking ordination–though the records are unclear. The matter was to be referred to the next annual conference, but the proceedings for 1844 make no note of it. The General Conference convened in Circleville, Ohio, the center of the Scioto Conference, in 1845. One of the many petitions presented that year was by the Reverend J. Montgomery from the Scioto Conference on behalf of Louisa Clemens. After being reviewed by a committee appointed for that purpose, Clemens's petition was rejected because "(1) she was not a member of the church, (2) she was not a member of the annual conference, and (3) the committee felt that the Gospel did not authorize 'the introduction of females into the ministry in the sense in which she requests it.'"[62]

Despite this action, however, Charity Opheral from the White River [Indiana] Conference applied for a license to preach at its first session in January 1847. She was granted "a note of commendation to liberate to public speaking," which amounted to an exhorter's license. Historians believe this was the first license given to a woman by an annual conference in the UB Church–and the first bestowed on any woman in any predecessor denomination of the UMC.[63] Unfortunately, little else is known about Charity Opheral.

Four years later, on May 3, 1851, the Iroquois Circuit of the Illinois Conference of the UB Church granted Lydia Sexton a quarterly conference license to preach, believed to be the first ever given to a woman in the Methodist tradition, though the conference refused her an annual license. Further, in 1857, a General Conference resolution was passed that "prohibited women from even receiving a license to preach." Nevertheless, on April 2, 1859, the Upper Wabash [Indiana] Conference issued Sexton a letter of recommendation to preach.[64]

Unlike Charity Opheral, a great deal is known about Lydia Sexton, who published her *Autobiography* in 1882. Though she was born in 1799, Sexton was not converted until she was thirty-four years old and married to her third husband, Joseph Sexton. She and members of her family joined the first United Brethren class in Dayton, Ohio, and soon established an altar for family devotions. At first, Sexton was shy about speaking in public but eventually experienced a call to preach. Initially, she was restrained by her conviction that it was not proper for a woman to preach, though her call continued to grow stronger. "I did believe firmly that it was my bounden duty to preach. But oh! That man-fearing Spirit."[65]

After moving to Jasper County, Indiana, in 1843 and joining a newly organized United Brethren class, Sexton's third son became seriously ill. Since both of her two previous sons had died, Sexton made a covenant with God. If God would spare this son, she would devote her life to God to follow the divine bidding. Her preaching career commenced soon afterward and continued until 1871. Unlike Fanny Butterfield Newell and Hannah Pearce Reeves, Lydia Sexton was not married to a preacher. Nevertheless, her husband, Joseph, supported her in her work of preaching and accompanied her as much as possible. At times, she would share a pulpit with another woman in an effort to support other women who also felt a call to preach.[66]

In 1865, the Sextons moved to Kansas City, Missouri, where, five years later, Lydia was appointed as chaplain to the Kansas State Penitentiary. For roughly a year, she ministered to some 170 convicts. She resigned the post in February 1871 due to failing health. Lydia Sexton moved to Seattle in 1890 to live with her youngest son and died there December 17, 1894, at age 95.[67]

Despite the action of the 1857 General Conference, in May 1874, the Conference issued a quarterly conference license to preach to Maggie Thompson at its gathering in Pleasant View Church near New Albany, Indiana. This was the first license granted since Lydia Sexton received hers in 1859.[68] Maggie Thompson served as an evangelist for the next fourteen years. In August 1876, at the Indiana Annual Conference, Thompson's name was among a list of nine male applicants referred to a committee. The following day the conference accepted a report from the committee recommending that Maggie Thompson "receive a letter of commendation as a worthy Christian sister and a profitable laborer in the vineyard of the Lord to be signed by the Bishop of the Conference."[69]

The next year Thompson married Rev. John Elliott, a minister in the Indiana Conference. They resided in Corydon, Indiana, for nearly twelve years and moved to Illinois in 1889 when Thompson was transferred to the Central Illinois Conference.[70]

The 1889 General Conference of The Church of the United Brethren met in York, Pennsylvania, and took actions that would move the denomination into a whole new era. For many years, a debate raged between the "radicals," who resisted all change, and the "liberals," who insisted that the church adapt to changing circumstances. In an overwhelming 110 to 20 vote, the Conference instituted the proposed changes to the Confession of Faith and the Constitution. The "radicals," under the leadership of Bishop Milton Wright, withdrew and formed The Church of the United Brethren in Christ (Old Constitution).[71]

The third item of business under the changed constitution had to do with a petition for ordination from the women in the Central Illinois Conference. The Committee on Superintendency and Ministry discussed the request and brought a favorable recommendation to the floor. The proposal passed after some debate. With this action, women received the right not only to be licensed to preach but also to be ordained as elders in an annual conference.[72] In addition, the Conference approved the right of laity (both men and women) to be represented at General Conference.[73]

At its meeting in September 1889, the Central Illinois Conference conferred the license to preach on Ella Niswonger and Mrs. Maggie Elliot. The following day, upon the recommendation of the Committee on Ordination, Ella Niswonger was ordained and "received into the itinerancy," the first woman to receive this status in the UB Church.[74]

Reflecting on the events at the Central Illinois Conference over which he presided, Bishop E. B. Kephart wrote: "Two very intelligent Christian ladies were licensed to preach at this session, and the first woman ordained to elders' orders by order of an annual conference in the history of the denomination. Is the millennium dawning? God grant it."[75]

Maggie Thompson Elliot was ordained by the Central Illinois Conference the next year, followed by Visa Bell in 1891 in the Indiana Conference and Ellen Runkle King in 1892 in the East Ohio Conference. With the door to the ordination of women opened, women began to respond; and by 1901, the United Brethren ministerial directory had listed the names of ninety-seven women who had been ordained at various times, with the numbers continuing to increase.[76]

The 2004 edition of the Index to Ministerial Memoirs, published by the United Methodist General Commission on Archives and History, indicates that more than 200 women had served as ministerial members of annual conferences from 1889 until 1946, when the UB Church united with The Evangelical Church to form The Evangelical United Brethren Church (EUB Church). Thirty-four, or nearly 20 percent, of these women served in Kansas. Many of them were wives of clergymen and served in churches with their husbands. It would be interesting to know how many of these women were already members of the UB Church and how many were drawn to that denomination because of its willingness to ordain women.

One other woman deserves mention here: Minnie Jackson Goins, ordained in the Northwest Kansas United Brethren Annual Conference. She may be not only the first black woman ordained in the UB Church but also the first black woman ordained in the entire United Methodist tradition.

Jackson grew up in the Quaker settlement of Raisen Valley, Michigan. Sometime later she moved to Detroit, Kansas, where she was converted in a revival held in the Detroit United Brethren Church in 1897.

Drawn to the work of the Lord and to public speaking, she answered the call to the ministry. "She was ordained into the United Brethren ministry by Bishop Castle in the Northwest Kansas Conference in 1904, and was assigned to the position of Evangelist at Large," a post she held for the remainder of her ministry. She also "had a special interest in Christian education and children's work."[77]

After marrying James W. Goins of Sterling, Kansas, Minnie ceased working as an evangelist but remained active in her church. Listed in United Brethren *Journals* until 1942, Minnie Jackson Goins died in 1945.[78] She was a wonderful role model for her African American sisters, who would follow in her footsteps.

Women Preachers in The Methodist Protestant Church

The Methodist Protestant Church (MPC) was officially organized in 1830 after a decade of controversy with the MEC over the issues of the power of bishops and presiding elders (now district superintendents) and lay representation at all conferences.[79]

Like the UB Church, the MPC began ordaining women in the late 1800s. For many years, scholars thought Anna Howard Shaw, ordained in 1880 at the New York Annual Conference in Tarrytown (after being refused ordination by the MEC), was the first woman ordained in the Methodist tradition. However, this is not the case. At the August 1866 session of the Wabash [Indiana] Annual Conference, a woman named Helenor Alter Davisson was ordained a deacon, thus making her the first woman to be ordained in the United Methodist tradition.

Until recently, little was known about the life of Helenor Davisson. However, a recent article by Christopher M. Shoemaker in the journal *Methodist History* sheds significant light on this remarkable woman. Helenor Alter was born in Pennsylvania in 1823, the oldest daughter of John and Charity VanAusdall Alter. In 1834 Helenor's father, John, himself a preacher, moved his family west to Indiana. Shortly after their arrival, Charity Alter died, leaving Helenor responsible for caring for the home and seven siblings. John eventually remarried twice more, while Helenor married John Draper in 1842 and began to work with her father in the ministry. A history of the UMC in Remington, Indiana, mentions the Reverend John Alter and his daughter, Mrs. Helenor Draper, traveling "on horseback through miles of open prairie, tall grass, ponds, and sloughs and stay[ing] in an occasional hunter's cabin or settler's crude shanty. In 1849, they organized a Methodist Protestant Church at Alter's Grove."[80]

Helenor Davisson's name first appears in the official Methodist Protestant records in the October 3, 1862, minutes of the Bradford Circuit of the Wabash Annual Conference. Her name is listed just below that of her father, both as ministers in the circuit. She was presented to be received and have her license renewed June 6, 1863. On July 25, 1863, it was moved and approved to recommend Helenor to the annual conference "to preach the gospel or at least a small work."[81]

We do not know what happened to Helenor's first husband, but we know she married Thomas H. Davisson, the son of Moses E. Davisson, who was ordained at the same time as Helenor. "The record of the Third Quarterly Conference," of the Grand Prairie Circuit, June 4, 1864, "shows Helenor's last name as Davisson for the first time." The next year, Helenor was recommended for deacon's orders at the Quarterly Meeting of the Grand Prairie Circuit, held at Burnes Schoolhouse on July 29, 1865. Then, in August 1866, at the twenty-first session of the Wabash Annual Conference, held in the Alter family home, she was ordained deacon. Shoemaker notes that it was at this point that Helenor Davisson apparently became the first ordinand in American Methodism.[82]

However, a year later, at the twenty-second session of the Wabash Annual Conference (the name was changed to North Indiana Conference during the session), the Reverends T. H. Lancaster and A. H. Widney presented the following resolution: "Resolved that the election of females to orders is incompatible with the teachings of Holy Scriptures, and not in accordance with our book of discipline."[83] The matter was referred to the next General Conference, to be held in 1871. Reverend Lancaster moved that Sister Davisson be allowed to carry on as a deacon until General Conference had decided the

issue. Thus, during the meeting of the 1871 General Conference, held in Pittsburgh, May 17-27, a study committee considered the question of female ordination. The majority, strongly in favor of the ordination of women, brought a report on "female ordination," while the minority report opposed "the ordination of ladies." The minority report prevailed by a vote of 46 to 17.[84]

Interestingly enough, this same General Conference, which decided against ordaining women, may nevertheless have been the first to permit a woman to address a General Conference! According to William Noll, "'Sister M. A. Bradford' led a worship service at the conference and spoke on the ordination issue. Who she was and what she said are not recorded."[85] Following her address, however, a resolution was presented "that each Annual Conference shall have power to authorize females to preach the Gospel in the Methodist Church."[86] The published edition of the Conference minutes does not record whether the resolution passed, but apparently it became the practice over the next few years. Further, there appears to be no record that Helenor Davisson's ordination was ever revoked. Shoemaker notes that the last mention of Davisson's name in the Grand Prairie Circuit Register occurs on August 4, 1874, where she is listed on the roll beneath her father's name, above the list of preachers. The Reverend Helenor M. Davisson died October 9, 1876, followed seven days later by her father.[87]

In his history of Iowa Methodism entitled *Between the Rivers*, John A. Nye confirms the presence of women in the ministry of the MPC. The Iowa Conference received a Mrs. Pauline Martindale into membership in 1872, making her the only woman minister in the state.[88] Although Nye offers no further information on Martindale, a review of the *Minutes of the Iowa Conference of the Methodist [Protestant] Church* led to some amazing discoveries. Pauline Martindale was first mentioned in 1870, noting that she conducted religious services. The following page, listing the item-by-item adoption of the report of the Committee on Itinerancy and Orders, contains this entry: "Report favorably upon the following named, for Itinerancy: M R Hixon, R Miller, George Swonston, Phoebe [sic] M Martindale, John Davis."[89] It appears that approval for the itinerancy equaled receiving a license to preach. Pauline was married to John A. Martindale, also a pastor in the conference. According to the 1870 census for Iowa, Pauline and John resided in Clayton Township in Taylor County, with their two-year-old daughter Luella. Both Pauline and John were listed as ministers.[90] The 1871 minutes of the Iowa Conference further note: "Bros. McFadden, J F Crouze, J W Martindale, P W Martindale, B F Pearman, examined in Character and passed."[91] Page 10 of the minutes features a report of the Conference Steward in which J. A. and P. W. Martindale are listed as pastors for the Union Circuit. In the list of appointments for 1871, J. A. and Pauline Martindale are appointed to the Montezuma Circuit for the following year and are included under the conference roll of "Minister's Names."[92] In the Conference minutes for 1872, we read, "Examination of character resumed. J A Martindale called, and on motion, referred to a committee consisting of Bros M R Hixon and J R Pershall," while "Sister Pauline E W Martindale passed."

However, on page 12, John A. and Pauline E. Martindale are left without appointment at their own request.[93]

The minutes of the 1873 Annual Conference record resumption of the examination of character. Sister Pauline E. Martindale was called and referred to committee in the case of John A. Martindale. There is no explanation of the issues with which the committee dealt. However, the next day a "Communication from John A and Pauline E Martindale was read and referred to committee on communications." At the close of the annual conference, "it was ordered that in the case of J A and Pauline E Martindale…the Committee, after mature deliberation and proper investigation, shall find no cause of complaint, their characters pass, and their request be granted, namely; [sic] transferred to Kansas Conference." In the Roll of Conference Itinerants for that year, the Martindales are listed as serving in Louisville, Pottawattamie, Kansas. Apparently, they had already begun serving in Kansas.[94]

Then comes the surprise. A review of The Minutes of the Kansas Methodist (Protestant) Church reveals that at its 1875 session in Americus, Kansas, on Thursday morning, September 30, the Committee on Itinerancy and Orders "report the name of Sister P. W. Martindale as a proper person to be elected to Elder's Orders.…On motion report rec'd and Sister P. W. Martindale was elected to Orders."[95] The minutes give no indication that this action was unusual. Thus, on Sunday morning, October 3, 1875, while meeting in the local Methodist Episcopal church, Sister P. W. Martindale, along with four men, was ordained as an elder in the Kansas Conference of the Methodist [Protestant] Church, apparently making Martindale the first woman in the United Methodist tradition to be ordained as an elder in full connection.[96] There is no evidence that John A. Martindale ever applied for ordination.

Pauline Martindale seems to have served in the Kansas Methodist Protestant Conference with no difficulties until the early 1880s. Something must have occurred in 1881, because "charges [were] preferred" against Pauline Martindale. In 1882, she was referred to the President for Trial, while her husband, John, was placed on the "unstationed" list. Soon after, the Martindales disappeared from the official record.[97]

Apparently, the two-step ordination process (deacon, then elder) in the MPC was eliminated sometime between 1866 and 1871, since no mention seems to have been made in the Iowa or Kansas minutes regarding Pauline Martindale's election to deacon's orders. As noted earlier, up to this point it has been the belief that Anna Howard Shaw was the first woman in the Methodist tradition to have been elected to elder's orders in the MPC, in 1880. But research for this project has proved that to be incorrect.

Furthermore, in addition to Pauline Martindale, a woman named Maggie Ritchie Elliot (not to be confused with Maggie Thompson Elliot of the UB Church), along with her husband, Charles B. Elliott, was ordained elder by the Missouri MPC on October 19, 1877, three years before Anna Howard Shaw was ordained.[98] Both Maggie and Charles were appointed to LeRoy, Missouri, the same year. In 1879, Charles was appointed to Lamar Circuit and Maggie to the Jasper Circuit.[99] It would appear, however, that Maggie did not have a happy experience in the MPC, for

the 1884 minutes contain the following entry:

Reports of Special Committees
a) Report of Committee on case of Elders
Maggie R. Elliott
Whereas Mrs. Maggie R. Elliott, an ordained elder of this conference of the Methodist Protestant Church, has publicly, irreligiously, informally, and spitefully proclaimed her voluntary withdrawal from this conference. Therefore, Be it resolved: That her name be stricken from the roll of the conference.
W.A. Fogle
W.V. Tunstall
S.W. Bliss[100]

Maggie Elliott may have left The Methodist Church, but she did not leave the ministry. She joined the Congregational Church in Wisconsin in 1891.[101]

This information raises the question: Why have these two women not been identified before? In the case of Elliott, according to Missouri Conference archivist John Finley, the reason may simply be that the conference minutes have apparently never been published. Add to that the fact that Elliott's tenure in the MPC was relatively brief. The relevant Kansas conference minutes too apparently have never been formally published–they are still in handwritten form. Since Martindale apparently left the ministry under some doubtful circumstances, perhaps there was no need for their names to be raised. This is a story for another day.

This brings us at last to Anna Howard Shaw, whose story is one of the best known in Methodist circles, primarily because of her relationship to Boston University, as well as her work with the National Woman's Suffrage Association, which eventually led to the passage of the Nineteenth Amendment, guaranteeing women the right to vote.

Anna Howard Shaw was born in Newcastle-on-Tyne, England, on February 14, 1847. When she was four years old, her family moved to America, eventually settling in Michigan when Anna was a young teenager. Even at that age Anna "preached to a congregation of listening trees." Unlike many other early women preachers in the United States, however, Anna actually had a female clergy mentor, the Reverend Marianna Thompson, a Universalist minister, who encouraged her to pursue an education if she really wanted to be a pastor.[102]

In 1873, Anna Shaw met the Reverend H. C. Peck, presiding elder of the Big Rapids District, who suggested that she become a local preacher and assisted her in obtaining a local preacher's license. Shaw was admitted to Albion College, attended for two years, and then transferred to Boston University School of Theology, where she became the second woman to graduate. Anna Snowden Oliver was the first woman to graduate from the theological school in 1876, and the first woman in the United States to graduate with a bachelor of divinity degree.[103] During her final year at Boston University, Shaw pastored the Methodist Episcopal Church of Hingham, Massachusetts.[104] Following graduation she was invited to pastor the Wesleyan Methodist Church in East Dennis, Cape Cod, Massachusetts. Six months later, the Congregational Church in Dennis asked her to be its interim pastor. She served these churches for six and a half years, though not without some difficulties. For example, at the Wesleyan Church Shaw had to ask a Captain Sears to leave the church. "Several weeks later he came back to confess that in all the years he had been a member of that congregation, he had never seen the pulpit occupied by a minister with enough backbone to uphold the discipline of the church.... After that victory the congregation was often heard to brag about the 'spunk' of its young female pastor."[105]

At this same time that Shaw was pursuing her career in the ministry, another young woman named Anna was traveling a similar road–Anna Snowden Oliver, who had graduated from Boston University School of Theology two years before Shaw. The full story of Oliver's and Shaw's attempts to be ordained in the MEC will be chronicled in the section on the MEC. Suffice it to state here that Oliver had been granted a license to preach from the Jamaica Plain, Massachusetts, Quarterly Conference in 1876.[106] Both women decided to apply for deacon's orders at the 1880 session of the New England Conference. When Bishop Andrews, the presiding bishop, refused to accept their names when they were presented, the two women appealed the decision to the 1880 General Conference of the MEC, meeting in Cincinnati, Ohio. When that General Conference not only refused to grant the women deacon's orders but also repealed the right for women to be granted even a license to preach, Shaw decided to look elsewhere for ordination.

In October 1880, Shaw's name was presented for ordination at the New York Annual Conference of the MPC, held at Tarrytown. Miss Shaw was initially refused ordination because she had failed to transfer her membership to the MPC. Nevertheless, Shaw was supported by the pastor of the Tarrytown church, Lyman Davis, who called a late-night meeting of his trustees and received Shaw as a member. Her case was then raised again on Monday and, after extensive questioning, Anna Howard Shaw was approved for ordination in a special service–since the regular ordination had been held the day before.[107]

Schmidt records, "When Shaw returned to her East Dennis parish in time for church the following Sunday morning, she found the communion table set with a beautiful new communion service purchased during her absence."[108] To this day, the congregation proudly displays the Communion set.

Not everyone in the MPC supported Shaw's ordination. An appeal was brought to the 1884 General Conference, which voted that "the act (was) unauthorized by the law of the Church, and that she is not entitled to recognition as an Elder in the Methodist Protestant Church." Yet this General Conference was the first to seat women within the bar of the conference.[109] One might wonder why questions about the other two women's ordination as elders were not also raised at the same time. Pauline Martindale had apparently left the ministry, and Maggie Elliott had withdrawn from the MPC during this same year. It is possible, of course, that a part of Elliot's frustration with the MPC was her knowledge that this issue was indeed to come before the General Conference and that her ordination as well as Shaw's would be called into question.

Despite the decision of the 1884 General Conference, the New York Annual Conference continued to recognize Shaw's ordination. Eventually a beautiful stained-glass window was installed in the Tarrytown Methodist Protestant Church that depicts Mary Magdalene meeting the angel at the empty tomb and that bears the inscription: "Commemorating the Brave Strong Christian Stand of the Church in Ordaining to the Ministry, October 12, 1880, Anna Howard Shaw, whom other churches Persistently Refused to Recognize as a Christian Minister." Today, that window hangs in the stairwell of Boston University School of Theology on the way to the women's center that bears Anna Howard Shaw's name.

In 1885, after serving churches on Cape Cod for seven years, Rev. Shaw resigned to devote herself full-time to the struggle for women's suffrage and temperance.[110] It would be in great part due to Shaw's leadership in the fight for women's suffrage that women were given the right to vote.

At the same time that women in the MPC were advocating for the right to be ordained, laywomen too were fighting for their right to be recognized. Noll says, "Among Methodist denominations in America the Methodist Protestant Church was unique in that it granted women the right to be ordained as ministers more or less concurrently with granting full laity rights. The story of the struggles and achievements of Methodist Protestant laywomen cannot be separated from the successful campaign of their sisters for ordination."[111]

Despite the step of the 1884 General Conference to nullify the decision by the New York Annual Conference to ordain Anna Howard Shaw, annual conferences continued to ordain women. In 1889, the Kansas Conference ordained Eugenia St. John, wife of Charles H. St. John, a minister in the MEC. Eugenia St. John had begun preaching when her husband became ill and she was asked to fill his pulpit for the two months during which he took a leave. She preached for eleven years before seeking ordination in the MPC in Kansas.[112] She was described as "a lady of middle age, prepossessing in appearance with an attractive manner and pleasant voice. She is thoroughly versed in the legal and ecclesiastical features of her case, and fully prepared to defend her position, if necessary."[113]

In 1892, Eugenia St. John was elected as the ministerial delegate to General Conference by the Kansas Conference, making her the first woman to represent an annual conference. At the same time, three laywomen had also been elected to represent their annual conferences. Although there was a lot of speculation as to whether or not the women would be seated, in the end all four of the women's credentials were recognized.[114] Schmidt concludes, "After 1892, full laity and clergy rights for women were virtually assured in the Methodist Protestant Church."[115]

Despite this fact, however, it would seem that far fewer Methodist Protestant women actually sought ordination and membership in the annual conference than did their counterparts in the UB Church. A review of the Memoirs Indexes of the General Commission on Archives and History identifies no more than thirty women who seem to have had membership in the annual conferences. Nevertheless, a handful of women did have full clergy rights at the time of the merger of the MEC, The Methodist Episcopal Church, South (MECS), and the MPC in 1939. These women had their orders recognized and served as clergy in full connection in their respective conferences.

After the merger and up until 1956, women out of the Methodist Protestant tradition who sought ordination had to be satisfied with becoming local deacons and elders until the General Conference, in 1956, finally voted to grant women full clergy rights. There were, as well, three Methodist Protestant women who were still serving in 1956 and beyond. They will be recognized in chapter 2, along with those who were received on probation that year.

The Fight for Full Clergy Rights for Women in The Methodist Episcopal Church and The Methodist Episcopal Church, South

The Right to Receive a License to Preach

Women in the Methodist Episcopal churches (North and South) had the most difficult and longest struggle to obtain full clergy rights. The year 1869 marks two significant events for the role of women in the Methodist Episcopal tradition. One stormy day, March 23, six women met to listen to Mrs. Clementina Butler and Lois Stiles Parker, wives of Methodist missionaries to India. After hearing of the plight of Indian women, these eight women determined to form the Woman's Foreign Missionary Society (WFMS) of the MEC.

By November of that same year, despite an effort by the male missionary board to control the funds, these women had made arrangements to send Isabella Thoburn and Dr. Clara Swain to India as missionaries. Dr. Swain was the first female medical doctor to be sent as a missionary to any foreign country by any denominational missionary society. The organization of the WFMS marked only the first of such societies that would be organized by women in all the predecessor denominations of the UMC. It also signaled the beginning of a new role for women in the church outside of their accepted sphere in the home.[116]

During the same month, on March 6, the Stoneridge Quarterly Conference of the Ellenville District of the New York Conference, "asked [Maggie Van Cott] to appear before the quarterly conference, and after the required examination, she was duly awarded a preacher's license, signed by [Elder A. H. Ferguson].... For many evangelists, the license to preach would have been a natural result of their efforts and activities. However, the license awarded to Maggie Van Cott, though she herself 'valued it very little,' caused a great stir within sections of the Methodist Episcopal Church."[117]

Margaret Newton was born March 25, 1830, to an Episcopalian father from England and a mother of Scottish descent. In 1847, she married a druggist named Peter Van Cott and began to assist him in his store. Forbidden to attend The Methodist Church when she was growing up, Maggie joined her husband's Dutch Reformed Church after her marriage.[118]

After experiencing a powerful conversion one day while walking past John Street MEC in New York City, Maggie began attending the Wednesday evening services at Duane Street MEC.[119] "After an experience of being 'filled with the Spirit,' she was increasingly led to testify there. Like many women before her, she then experienced in a dream her call to preach.... Shortly after her husband's death in 1866, [she] joined the Methodist Episcopal Church."[120] Because she now

had a daughter to support, Maggie initially planned to continue in her husband's druggist business; however, as she became more and more sought after, she eventually devoted all her time to evangelistic work.

Greatly moved while attending the 1867 ordination service at the New York Annual Conference, Maggie is said to have cried out, "O God, why could I have not been a man, that I could be ordained for the great work of preaching the blessed gospel of my dear Redeemer."[121] This, however, seems to be the only time that Maggie Newton Van Cott yearned to be ordained. In most instances it appears that others were more interested in giving Maggie a license than she was in receiving one.

On September 6, 1868, the Reverend Alonzo Church Morehouse signed an exhorter's license for Van Cott, from the Windham Circuit of the New York Conference. According to Van Cott's autobiography, the license was obtained without her knowledge.[122] Only a few months later she would receive her local preacher's license. A motion presented to the 1869 New York Annual Conference held at Sing Sing opposing the granting of licenses to female preachers did not succeed–and neither did a motion to censure Ferguson (the presiding elder of the quarterly conference that granted Maggie's license). But the [New York] *Times* was quoted as saying that it was secretly understood that Van Cott's license would not be renewed.[123]

The following year, in 1870, the New England Conference convened at Trinity MEC in Springfield, Massachusetts, where Van Cott had been supplying the pulpit for the pastor who had been ill. Many of the preachers in the conference heard her preach and there was some speculation that a proposal may be put forward to admit Van Cott as a probationer to the New England Conference, but nothing came of it. However, the quarterly conference of Trinity Church did vote to continue her license as a local preacher.[124]

In 1874, Maggie Van Cott traveled to the West Coast and conducted several revival meetings in California, the result of which was a recommendation from the San Francisco District Conference that she be ordained a deacon. The California Annual Conference, however, under the leadership of Bishop Stephen M. Merrill, turned down the recommendation due to the interpretation of the Board of Bishops that neither a quarterly nor a district conference had the right to grant women licenses to preach. Schmidt points out, however, that despite this understanding of the bishops, presiding elders continued to issue local preachers' licenses to women.[125] Janet Everhart reports that her limited research had uncovered fourteen other women who had been issued local preachers' licenses while Noll reports that up to seventy women may have received such licenses.[126] There does not seem to be a list of these women available, however.[127]

One of these women, Mrs. Emma Richardson, was actually licensed by the Canadian MEC in 1864, five years prior to Maggie Van Cott and eventually she continued to have her license renewed in the United States. An article in the *Northwest Christian Advocate*, for August 6, 1873, states, "At the second session of the La Crosse District Conference, held at Melrose, July 22, after a full discussion of the question, the character of the local preachers was examined, and licenses renewed. Among these was Mrs. Emma Richardson, the oldest woman local preacher in America. Sister Richardson was first licensed to preach in the M.E. Church in Canada in 1864, and hence outranks Mrs. Van Cott, and takes the lead of lady preachers."[128]

Although an appeal of Bishop Merrill's refusal to consider ordaining Van Cott and a report from the California Conference regarding the issue of local preachers' licenses for women were referred to the Committee on Revisals at the 1876 General Conference, no official action was taken.[129] Despite the fact that some presiding elders apparently ignored the attempts to prevent women from being granted licenses, others were concerned about women preaching without licenses. For example, the Reverend J. W. Robinson advocated in favor of women being licensed because he was concerned about their otherwise lack of accountability.[130] The issue would finally come to a head at the 1880 General Conference.

As noted in the section on the MPC, both Anna Howard Shaw and Anna Snowden Oliver applied to the 1880 New England Conference for ordination as deacons. Anna Snowden was born near New Brunswick, New Jersey, on April 12, 1840, and was baptized Vivianna Olivia Snowden. When she began pursuing a career in the ministry, however, she assumed the last name of Oliver so as not to embarrass her family.[131] After having received her education at Rutgers Female College in New York City, Oliver went to Georgia under the auspices of the American Missionary Association but left after only a year due to their discriminatory policies regarding salaries for female teachers.[132]

In 1870, Oliver moved to Ohio to study art and became involved in the woman's temperance crusade. It was during this time that she reluctantly began to experience a call to the ministry: "You know, I believe I was called by the Lord to study for the ministry. I told the Lord that no seminary would admit me; if one did, perhaps I would not be successful, and would only bring myself into unpleasant notoriety, and be abused by my enemies and rejected by friends. I was not anxious to be a martyr. I brought every conceivable argument against it I could find, but the Lord overturned all and bid me go on."[133]

Oliver applied to Oberlin College in Ohio, the first college to accept women. But despite assurances from President Fairchild, like Antoinette Brown before her, she met with negativism and criticism.[134] She then applied to fourteen theological schools and was accepted in three of those schools, deciding to enroll at Boston University School of Theology in 1874. Established a few years earlier, the University was coeducational from the outset and welcomed the young female theological student. She graduated in 1876, the first woman graduate of a theological school and was one of four students chosen to speak at the graduation ceremonies. Earlier that same year Oliver had been granted a local preacher's license by the Jamaica Plain Quarterly Conference of the Boston District of the New England Conference, signed by David Sherman, the presiding elder.[135]

That fall, Oliver became the pastor of a newly reorganized church in Passaic, New Jersey. Amanda Berry Smith, the Black Holiness evangelist, served as Oliver's assistant for a part of the year. "Between them," reported a local newspaper, "Passaic is having a lively time what with stirring up of sinners and Christians on the one hand, and on the other, two women in the pulpit, and one black, the buzzing grows apace."[136]

While she was pastoring in Passaic, Oliver met opposition from one of the MEC's most outspoken opponents of women preachers–the Reverend James Monroe Buckley, described by Kenneth Rowe as an "unabashed woman hater." Having heard of her success at the church in Passaic, the "stuffy" New York Preachers Meeting, a weekly gathering of New York City-area Methodist clergy, resolved to invite Oliver to deliver a sermon at one of the gatherings. At the following meeting, James Buckley led a lively discussion against such an invitation, stating, "I am opposed to inviting any woman to preach before this meeting. If the mother of our Lord were on earth I should oppose her preaching here."[137] The invitation was withdrawn. Brother Buckley would prove to be a formidable opponent for many years to come.

After only one year, as well, the Newark Annual Conference replaced Oliver with a regularly ordained male pastor. In 1879 she became the pastor of another "beleaguered" Methodist Church in Brooklyn, New York. The following year both Anna Snowden Oliver and Anna Howard Shaw decided to apply for their deacon's orders at the 1880 session of the New England Conference.[138] "As a preliminary step we were both examined by the Conference board, and were formally reported by that board as fitted for ordination. Our names were therefore presented at the Conference, over which Bishop Andrews presided, and he immediately refused to accept them. Miss Oliver and I were sitting together in the gallery of the church when the bishop announced his decision, and, while it staggered us, it did not really surprise us. We had been warned of this gentleman's deep-seated prejudice against women in the ministry."[139]

Lorenzo R. Thayer, presiding elder of the Boston District, then announced that he would appeal the decision to the upcoming General Conference and Anna Oliver was asked to address the Conference on her reasons for seeking ordination. Following her presentation, Thayer presented his resolution that was adopted by a large majority, "Resolved that our delegates to the next General Conference be and are hereby instructed to use their influence to remove all distinctions of sex in the office and ordination of our ministry."[140]

Miss Shaw continues, "After the services were over Miss Oliver and I called on him [Bishop Andrews] and asked him what we should do. He told us calmly that there was nothing for us to do but to get out of the Church. We reminded him of our years of study and probation, and that I had been for two years in charge of two churches. He set his thin lips and replied that there was no place for women in the ministry, and, as he then evidently considered the interview ended, we left him with heavy hearts."[141]

It seems fair at this point to note that the bishops of the MEC seemed to have been more conservative in their views of women in the ministry than many of the presiding elders and the pastors themselves or there would not have been women like Shaw and Oliver and others who were approved at the district level for licenses to preach and for ordination.

Although both Oliver and Shaw appealed the decision of Bishop Andrews to the 1880 General Conference, meeting in Cincinnati, Ohio, it appears that it was Anna Oliver who attended and personally led the appeal.

Although neither a clergy nor a lay delegate, Anna Oliver made the long trip from Brooklyn to Cincinnati in May for the Conference, her suitcase filled with copies of a pamphlet she had prepared for distribution at the proper moment. As the duly elected delegates took their places on the morning of Tuesday, May 17, they discovered the small eight-page pamphlet on each of their desks. It was her appeal from the decision of Bishop Andrews against her ordination and full installation as pastor of Willoughby Avenue Church in Brooklyn.[142]

Despite Lorenzo Thayer's appeal, a petition from the Willoughby Avenue Church, and strong support from other pastors, the Judiciary Committee upheld Bishop Andrews's decision as being in "accordance with the Discipline of the Church as it is." The Committee on Itinerancy and Orders, however, went even further, declaring: "They have considered the several papers referred to them in relation to the licensing of women as exhorters and local preachers, their ordination, admission to the traveling connection and eligibility to all offices of the church; and inasmuch as women are by general consent of the Church *accorded all the privileges which are necessary to their usefulness* the Committee recommends that in the respects named no change be made in the Discipline as it regards the status of women in our church."[143]

Thus, the 1880 General Conference not only denied women their right to ordination, they also revoked the right even to hold a license to preach and "declared that all local preacher's licenses issued to women from 1869 on were to be rescinded."[144]

Unlike Anna Howard Shaw, Anna Snowden Oliver stayed with the MEC, returning to her church in Brooklyn. The church, however, closed in 1883 due to financial difficulties. Though William Fairfield Warren, president of Boston University presented a memorial on behalf of Oliver at the 1884 General Conference, the Committee on Itinerancy, chaired by James M. Buckley, deemed it "inexpedient" to take any action.[145]

Little more is known about Oliver's ministerial career. She died an untimely death on November 20, 1892, in Greensboro, Maryland. The following January, the Reverend Anna Howard Shaw delivered a "moving tribute" to Anna Snowden Oliver at the American Suffrage Association Meeting in Washington, D.C.[146]

Oliver wasn't the only woman, however, whose life was deeply affected by the 1880 General Conference decisions. Schmidt relates the "little known" story of Mary A. Phillips, whose father, the Reverend Dr. Jeremiah Phillips, was pastor of the MEC in Olney, Illinois, in the 1870s. After experiencing a call to the ministry, Mary attended and graduated from Garrett Biblical Institute. Following her graduation Mary applied for ordination at the 1879 session of the Southern Illinois Conference which, unfortunately, was presided over by the same Bishop Andrews who would deny ordination to Anna Oliver and Anna Howard Shaw the following year. Mary Phillips died at her father's home on August 17, 1880, at the age of twenty-one. Her father believed her death to be the result of her shock at having been refused ordination by Bishop Andrews, whom he blamed since Andrews had met Mary while she was a student at Garrett and never gave her any indication of his disapproval of women in the ministry. Mary's headstone reads "The Rev. Mary A. Phillips."[147]

Laity Rights Granted and the Deaconess Movement Approved

The next major battle for women's rights in the MEC took place at the 1888 General Conference. While women had been applying for licenses to preach, laypeople in the MEC had been working for representation in the governing of the church at the annual conference and General Conference level. It was not until 1872 that "laymen" were finally allowed to be seated as delegates of General Conference. At the same time, the question arose as to whether or not women could be included in the lay delegations. In 1880, at the same General Conference in which women were denied even the right to obtain licenses to preach, the "General Conference 'judicially interpreted' the language of the Discipline by declaring that 'the pronouns *he, his,* and *her* when used in the Discipline with reference to stewards, class-leaders, and Sunday School superintendents, shall not be construed as to exclude women from such offices.'"[148] Thus, women as members of Quarterly Conferences were able to both vote for and be elected as members of the electoral college that elected delegates to General Conference. This, of course, eventually led to the election of women as delegates to General Conference. In 1888 the issue was "put to the test" when five annual conferences elected women as lay delegates: Angie F. Newman from Nebraska, Mary Clark Nind from Minnesota, Amanda C. Ripley from Kansas, Lizzie D. Van Kirk from Pittsburgh, and Frances E. Willard from Rock River [Illinois]. The debate regarding the seating of these women at General Conference began even before General Conference, as news of the election became known. In their Episcopal Address at the beginning of the Conference, the bishops "gave their opinion that the five women could not be seated because their eligibility as delegates had not been properly determined according to the constitution of the MEC."[149] The matter was referred to a special committee of which the powerful James M. Buckley was a member. The committee recommended against the women being seated, and the delegates, formally voting on the issue on May 7, the sixth day of the Conference, upheld the committee's recommendations. The women were dismissed. Of this action Frances Willard stated, "I confidently predict that we five women, whose election was disavowed, will have more enviable places in history than any who opposed us on these memorable days."[150]

The following year, Willard, who served as president of the Woman's Christian Temperance Union from 1879 to 1898, published *Woman in the Pulpit*, a powerful advocate for women's rights in the church. Willard's frustration at the intransigence of the men to share power is clear from her suggestion that perhaps the time had come for women to "take matters into their own hands" and form a new church in which full rights for both clergy and laity would be honored.[151] Although Willard and her supporters decided not to secede from the MEC, it would take until the 1900 General Conference before women were allowed to be seated as delegates. In 1904, twenty-four women attended the conference as lay delegates and another thirty as reserve delegates. Schmidt comments, "In gaining lay representation at the General Conference of the MEC, women had at least wrested one victory from their unremitting opponent, James M. Buckley."[152]

United Brethren had included laywomen as delegates to their General Conference in 1893. By that time, women had already had full clergy rights for four years. And it is clear that other denominations were also well aware of the influence that James M. Buckley had in the MEC. Schmidt quotes a report from the *Religious Telescope* that ends with these words: "Well, well; will not some one kindly inform Dr. Buckley that now at least two respectable denominations admit women to participation in their highest law-making departments?"[153]

While denying MEC women the right to be seated as lay delegates, the 1888 General Conference did take another action that would offer women the opportunity for service in the church, when it recognized the deaconess movement as an official ministry. One of the early leaders of the movement was Lucy Rider Meyer, who came to the work out of a grave concern that there was no school to train women for religious leadership in Christian work. After her marriage to Josiah Shelly Meyer, a secretary for the Chicago YMCA, in May 1885, Lucy Rider Meyer spoke to the Chicago MEC Preachers Meeting, seeking their support for such a training school. With their assistance, along with that of both the WFMS and the Woman's Home Missionary Society (which had been formally organized in 1880), Rider Meyer and her husband rented a home on West Park Avenue and opened the Chicago Training School for City, Home, and Foreign Missions, better known as CTS. Out of this effort grew the deaconess movement in the United States.[154]

Two petitions, one from the Rock River [Illinois] Conference and one from the Bengal Conference in India were brought before the 1888 General Conference meeting, seeking official recognition for the deaconess movement. In particular, the Bengal Conference expressed the need for "deaconesses with the authority to administer the sacraments to the secluded zenanna women of India."[155]

The General Conference approved the office of deaconess and assigned deaconesses these responsibilities: "To minister to the poor, visit the sick, pray with the dying, care for the orphan, seek the wandering, comfort the sorrowing, save the sinning and relinquishing wholly all other pursuits, devote themselves in a general way to such forms of Christian labor as may be suited to their abilities."[156]

Though there was widespread support for the deaconess movement, some questioned the motives of the General Conference delegates. In 1889 the Akron, Ohio, *Daily Beacon* reported on this action: "The Methodist Episcopal Church at its last General Conference seeing no other way to keep women still, created the office of Deaconess, and the wise men assembled went so far as to prescribe the uniform to be worn by those filling the office."[157]

The General Conference refused to approve the request to allow deaconesses to administer the sacraments, either in the mission field or anywhere else.[158] When the General Conference in 1924 granted women the right to be ordained as local deacons and local elders, however, some deaconesses were among the first to apply for the privilege. And some were already being used to fill pulpits even before Methodist Episcopal women were once again granted the right to obtain licenses to preach in 1920. One of those was Miss Edith

Porter from Maine: "Miss Porter is remembered throughout the Maine Conference in a dual capacity. She was consecrated as a Deaconess of the Methodist Church and was employed in numerous capacities across the Conference.... As a pastor, she will be remembered as a faithful shepherd, a constant visitor and one who preached the word of God with a strong evangelistic message. Her first pastorate in Maine was in 1917 when she was appointed to the Sebec Circuit serving Sebec Village Church and several churches in the vicinity."[159]

Some deaconesses were supplying pulpits in Maine even before 1917. "In 1911 Miss Audrey L. Hunt began working in the East Maine Conference as a deaconess, supplying part-time that year in Prospect Harbor and Gouldsboro. Inez Webster was assigned to the East Maine Conference in 1913. Both women worked as supply pastors during the next few years."[160] In New Hampshire, Mary Victoria Granger was appointed to Henniker as supply pastor for a number of years starting in 1917.[161] In North Montana, deaconess Florence Moore was pastor at Oswego and Frazer from 1917 to 1919, and Belle Harmon was appointed to Lehigh in 1920.[162] Many of these pastorates were in rural areas where it was difficult to recruit male pastors. In the New England Southern Conference, however, "[Miss] Kate M. Cooper, a deaconess from the Providence [Rhode Island] Deaconess Home, was appointed as a 'Supply Pastor' to the Portsmouth, Rhode Island, church in 1918, 1919, and again in 1920."[163] Most likely, there were other deaconesses, particularly in rural areas, who were supplying pulpits as well.

In 1902, under the leadership and encouragement of Belle Harris Bennett, the MECS also created the office of deaconess. Schmidt points out, however, that this office was approved only after extended and often acrimonious debate. Apparently some worried that recognizing women's ministry in the church in this official way would encourage women to seek ordination or would compete with the ministry of ordained clergy.[164]

It would not be until 1920 that women would finally be allowed the right to be granted licenses to preach in the MEC once again. According to Noll, three reasons contributed to the change in attitude opening the way for this action: 1) The ratification of the Eighteenth Amendment to the United States Constitution which ushered in the Prohibition era, and which had been spearheaded by Frances Willard and the W.C.T.U.; 2) The ratification of the Nineteenth Amendment, in 1920, mandating woman's suffrage; and 3) The organization of the International Association of Women Preachers (I.A.W.P.) by a Methodist Episcopal woman from Kansas named M. Madeline Southard.[165]

In addition, the powerful Dr. Buckley was no longer a delegate to the General Conference, having served his eleventh and final time as a delegate to General Conference in 1912.[166] But it was probably the efforts of Madeline Southard that created the greatest impetus for the changes made at the 1920 and 1924 General Conferences. Mabel Madeline Southard was born near Rock, Kansas, on July 29, 1877. Beginning in her teens she became a preacher and an evangelist, lecturing on the WCTU circuit, serving as a foreign missionary and as a local church pastor, and traveling as an evangelist.

But it was in 1917 after organizing the IAWP that she began, in earnest, to fight for the right for women to be ordained. She briefly served her first church in Moundridge, Kansas, because she "wanted people to experience how a woman could do the job effectively." She also wrote an article entitled, "Woman and the Ministry," which was published in *Methodist Review* and completed her master's thesis, "Jesus' Attitude toward Women," for her theological degree at Northwestern University.[167]

Southard then received a letter from Sena Hartzell Wallace, strongly encouraging her to prepare a memorial for the 1920 General Conference asking for ecclesiastical equality. On May 10, 1920, Southard, a lay delegate from the Southwest Kansas Conference, presented the following memorial on the floor of the General Conference:

> Whereas, Today the principle of equality of opportunity for women is being recognized in all fields of activity; and
>
> Whereas, This General Conference has gone on record as urging political equality for women by requesting the Delaware house of representatives to sign the Susan B. Anthony Amendment; therefore be it
>
> Resolved, That the General Conference approve ecclesiastical equality for women, that it remove all restrictions and limitations upon women in the service of the church, and that it instruct the proper committee to make any changes in the Discipline necessary to accomplish this end.[168]

Southard then spoke to the issue, referencing the careers of both Anna Howard Shaw and Frances Willard. She quoted Willard as saying, "My unconstrained preference would long ago have led me to the pastorate, but even my dear old mother church, the Methodist Episcopal Church, did not call a woman to her altars, and I was too timid to go on without a call."[169]

After a great deal of discussion, debate, and political maneuvering, on May 27, the following report from the Committee on Itinerancy and Orders was passed:

> 1. That the provisions of…the Discipline…bearing the title "Local Preachers," be so construed as to include women, except in so far as these provisions apply to candidates for the traveling ministry and for Deacon's and Elder's Orders….
>
> 2. That the expedience of granting to women ordination and admission to the Annual Conference be referred to a commission…with instructions to report their conclusions to the General Conference of 1924.[170]

Limited Clergy Rights Granted–1924

Although this was far less than Southard and many others had hoped for, it was at least a step in the right direction. Noll reports that as soon as the report was passed, annual conferences began to vie for the honor of licensing the first woman.[171] Winifred Willard from Trinity Church, Denver, and Witlia D. Caffray from First MEC of Wetachee, Washington, were both issued licenses by their local churches on May 27, the day that the legislation passed.[172]

As the 1924 General Conference approached, the issue of women's ordination began to be debated on both sides and another woman joined the discussion. Dr. Georgia Harkness was associate professor of religious education at Elmira College. Prior to the General Conference, she wrote an important article titled "The Ministry as a Vocation for Women," in which she referred to the church as "probably our most conservative institution." She insisted,

> To put it baldly, [the crux of the matter] is that women cannot enter a field where they are not welcome. Ordination is desirable, I believe, to put the stamp of the Church's approval upon the admission of women to its ministry. But what is needed even more is a general recognition by pulpit and pew of the legitimate place of trained women in this field. Women will never find a welcome in the ministry until the press and present religious leadership have remoulded public sentiment. Ordination is a step in this direction, but it is a step–not the final goal.[173]

In the meantime, Madeline Southard continued with her campaign, as well, keeping in touch with Bishop Stuntz, who was the chair of the Commission on Licensing and Ordination of Women. The bishop had also kept Southard abreast of the work of the Commission. Unfortunately, Bishop Stuntz died just before the 1924 General Conference and J. M. M. Gray submitted the report to the General Conference, recommending that women have the right to be ordained as local deacons and elders but not be granted conference membership.[174] There was much discussion and debate until someone moved the previous question. Noll quotes the *Western Christian Advocate* as reporting "with understated glee": "The climax came when Miss M. M. Southard, who had had difficulty in getting the floor from the rear of the auditorium, could no longer contain herself, when running to the front greatly excited, demanding that she be given the floor. She got it. Verily she did. Bishop Bristol could not do otherwise under the circumstances. She addressed the Conference in no uncertain language, which conformed to her feeling at that very moment."[175]

Like Frances Willard before her, Southard issued a strong warning. "Now I submit to you that the brilliant young women in Methodism are not going to be satisfied to be shunted into a blind alley, and submit to you, furthermore, that Methodism may lose the strength of her strongest young womanhood if it persists in turning them into a blind alley."[176] Despite her warning, the next day, May 9, 1924, the General Conference adopted the report of the Commission, granting women partial status. They could be ordained but they could not become members of the annual conference.[177]

According to research done by the General Commission on Archives and History, the first two women to be ordained as deacons under the new legislation were Belle C. Harmon and Mrs. A. L. McAlister from the Montana Conference on August 31, 1924. This appears to have been the first annual conference that was held following the 1924 General Conference.[178] Those who were ordained in 1925 were ordained a year later, in some cases, because their annual conferences had already met at the time of the 1924 General Conference, which was held at the end of May. During the following week, Gertrude L. Apel and Witlia D. Caffrey were ordained deacons in the Columbia River [Washington] Conference. Twenty-seven additional women were ordained deacons within the following month, among them Charlotte Elizabeth Jones and Mary Charlotte Hickman.[179] Hickman and Jones were among four women who served churches in the Sonoma Valley in California and who became known as the Four Fordsmen of Sonoma.[180] Noll reports that Puera Robison, a teacher at Centenary Collegiate Institute, was ordained in the Newark Conference on March 26, 1925.[181] Kendra Irons notes that M. Madeline Southard was ordained in the Kansas West Conference in 1925.[182] And a number of women from New England were ordained as well. Mabelle H. Whitney and Emma Eliza Harrison were ordained in the Maine Annual Conference.[183] Mabelle Whitney had been appointed to Pittsfield in 1920 and 1921.[184] An article in the *Portland* [Maine] *Press Herald* in August 1925, reported, "Miss Mabelle Whitney, the pastor [of the Union Church, Broad Cove, Maine] is the first woman ordained by the Methodists of Maine. She is a native of Boston and has the further distinction of being one of the first six women to be licensed as preachers in the United States."[185]

Apparently, this article is referring to the first six women to be ordained as deacons following the 1924 legislation. Though the other women are not identified, the article may have referred to the five women in the New England Conference who also received deacon's orders in 1925.[186] In addition, Kate M. Cooper and Bertha Marion Hope from the New England Southern Conference and Ruth G. Barr from the Vermont Conference were ordained in 1925 as well.[187]

These women were followed in 1926 by Georgia Harkness and Eliza Duffield in Troy, Audrey L. Hunt MacDonald and Inez Webster in Maine, and Laura J. Lange in the Lexington Conference of the Central Jurisdiction, making her the first black woman to be ordained a deacon in the MEC.[188]

However, there would be fewer women who were granted elder's orders following the required two-year period as a deacon. Belle Harmon, Gertrude Apel, Mary Charlotte Hickman, and Charlotte Elizabeth Jones were ordained as elders in 1926 along with only eight others from the original 1924 list.[189] Of those listed above who were ordained as deacons in 1925, only Mabelle H. Whitney and Kate Morrison Cooper received their elder's orders in 1927, followed in 1928 by Audrey MacDonald, Inez Webster, and Eliza Duffield.[190]

Madeline Southard did not receive her elder's orders until 1933 and Georgia Harkness not until 1939.[191] Laura J. Lange, along with Sallie M. Crenshaw, who was ordained a deacon in 1932 in the East Tennessee Conference of the Central Jurisdiction, were both ordained as local elders in 1936, making them the first two women in the Central Jurisdiction to be ordained as local elders.[192] Crenshaw would be among the first women to be received on probation after the 1956 legislation passed.

Though the 1924 General Conference ruling was only a partial victory for women, Noll notes that this General Conference "marked the culmination of the efforts of a generation of women to expand their rights and role in the Methodist Episcopal Church. The action which the conference did take, to allow for the ordination of women as clergy and pastors, ushered in a new era for Methodist clergywomen whose yearning for full equality with their clergy brothers would eventually be

heard."[193] It should be noted too that there were many women whose names will probably never appear in a history book who were pioneers in their own right and who have served and continue to serve the UMC as highly qualified local pastors, who for a wide variety of reasons, never sought membership in the annual conferences in which they have served. Some, however, did become associate members.

This partial step may have been perfectly understood by folks in 1924 and the years following for, as noted, there were a number of women across the United States who began applying for even these limited rights. In more recent years, however, this step has caused great confusion–especially as attempts have been made to identify "first" women for this project. From 1968 (the time of the merger of The Evangelical United Brethren [EUB Church] and The Methodist Church to form The United Methodist Church) onward, probationary membership and ordination as a deacon, and full membership and ordination as an elder have, for the most part, taken place in the same year–though there are exceptions as can be noted in the individual biographies in the following chapters. Thus, more recent researchers, not having knowledge of the slow process by which women in the Methodist tradition gained full clergy rights, have had difficulty understanding the status of these women ordained as local deacons and elders prior to 1956. This is due, in part, to the fact that in most other denominations, it is ordination and not conference membership that has been the ultimate goal.

Robert Kohler, assistant general secretary at the United Methodist General Board of Higher Education and Ministry explains it this way: "Methodism has always been more interested in conference membership than ordination. In some annual conferences, election to annual conferences occurred at least a year before ordination. After World War II, when hundreds of chaplains were released from the military and returned to their annual conferences for appointment, some conferences were not able to bring in new ordination classes for several years due to the surplus of ministers. During that time, they accepted students as probationary members of the conference, but did not ordain them until an appointment was available."[194]

Thus, "election to conference membership always has preceded election to ordination.... All the questions a candidate must answer are for conference membership, not ordination."[195] The exception to this policy, of course, was for those women who had been ordained as local deacons and elders and who then applied for conference membership following the 1956 ruling. Ordination was ordination and these women were never "reordained." They *were* granted membership in the annual conference that gave them the right to voice and vote at the annual conference and a guaranteed appointment. This would not happen, of course, until 1956–though the issue was certainly not forgotten in the intervening years.

Although Madeline Southard took advantage of the opportunity to be ordained a deacon immediately following the 1924 ruling, she began more and more to focus on "creating a way for women ministers to join in companionship, thereby overcoming the isolation that accompanied such pioneering work."[196] Georgia Harkness "became the spiritual leader of the movement which would gain much of its support from the leadership of the women's missionary societies, and later the Woman's Society of Christian Service."[197] Georgia Harkness was born in Harkness, New York, on April 21, 1891. After teaching at Elmira, Cornell, and Mount Holyoke colleges, she became the first woman to teach theology at a Protestant seminary in the United States. She worked as professor of applied theology at Garrett Biblical Institute from 1939 to 1950, and from 1950 until her retirement in 1961 taught at Pacific School of Religion.[198] However, it is for her efforts on behalf of full clergy rights for women that many remember her best.

Women in The Methodist Episcopal Church, South, Work for Full Clergy Rights

The next major milestone in the fight for full clergy rights for women would be the 1939 Uniting Conference of the MEC, MECS, and the MPC. Two major issues faced these three denominations as they negotiated the terms of the merger: the place of African Americans in this new church and full clergy rights for women. The first problem would be resolved with the organization of the Central Jurisdiction, which would include all of the black congregations, with the exception of a handful of churches in the Northeast and the West. The issue of clerical rights for women resulted in the status quo for women in the MEC and major changes for both MPC and MECS women.

Women of the MPC, of course, had had full clergy rights from before the turn of the century, while women in the MECS had never even gained the right to receive a license to preach. In fact, it was not until 1922 that laywomen in the MECS finally gained the right to be seated at their General Conference.[199]

Nevertheless, this had not discouraged women in the MECS from pushing for clerical rights, as well:

> Once laity rights were won…organized Methodist women increased pressure for women's clergy rights. The fact that women in the Methodist Episcopal Church won the right to be ordained as local pastors in 1924 and that women in the Methodist Protestant Church could be ordained encouraged the southern Methodist women. Starting in 1926 and continuing at every succeeding General Conference of the Methodist Episcopal Church, South, the Woman's Missionary Council submitted a memorial calling for women clergy to be granted full ordination and conference membership. The margin of defeat was narrow enough that in 1931 hopes were high that at the next conference authority would be given for full ordination and conference membership for women.[200]

Despite their efforts, however, the 1938 *Discipline* of the MECS contained this paragraph:

> Women Not Recognized as Preachers–Our Church does not recognize women as preachers, with authority to occupy the pulpit, to read the Holy Scriptures, and to preach, as ministers of the Lord Jesus Christ; nor does it authorize a preacher in charge to invite a woman claiming to be a minister of the Lord Jesus Christ to occupy our pulpits, to expound the Scriptures as a preacher. Such invitations and services are against the authority and order of our Church.[201]

And despite the fact that the MECS did not recognize women as pastors, there were, of course, women who were called to the ministry and were preaching–most often in the more accepted role of a pastor's wife. One of those was Rebecca Fisher, the wife of the Reverend Orceneth Fisher. In 1855, after serving in the East Texas Conference, Fisher transferred to the Pacific Conference. "He was appointed to Stockton, California, where his wife's courage and evangelistic labors became legendary. During their ministry there, Brother Fisher decided to hold a camp meeting. Sister Fisher would work at the tent all day feeding the people and at night would 'enter the altar' and 'point the penitents to the world's Redeemer.'"[202]

Not everyone accepted Rebecca's ministry. One night in the middle of the revival, while Rebecca was leading the meeting in prayer, someone tossed an explosive among those gathered. Instead of upsetting Rebecca, the incident only made her more resolute. Participants responded to her message with enthusiasm, leading to numerous conversions.[203]

The revival was considered to have been a great success, a new circuit was formed, and eventually a new church building and a parsonage were built. Noll states that "together they [the Fishers] can be credited with establishing the Methodist Episcopal Church, South, in the Pacific Northwest."[204]

Another woman was Carolina Austin Farías, wife of Rosario Farías who was serving the church in Mission, Texas, in the early 1900s. Rosario Farías died unexpectedly in 1920 and Carolina was asked to serve in his place. "Her effective service as her husband's co-worker and her outstanding leadership qualities prompted the superintendent to ask Carolina, who had been left with seven children, to take charge."[205] From 1920 to 1929 she was appointed as a "missionary" and for the following two years as assistant to the pastor.[206] This, most likely, makes her the first Hispanic woman to have been appointed to serve a church. Carolina A. Farías died on March 20, 1980, at the age of 97.[207]

The 1939 Union of The Methodist Episcopal Church, The Methodist Episcopal Church, South, and The Methodist Protestant Church

The question of full clergy rights for women became a bargaining chip in negotiations that led to the 1939 merger. Church leaders representing the three denominations reached agreement that women would not be eligible for full clergy rights in the newly formed Methodist Church. A memorial submitted to General Conference granting women full clergy rights–and thus full membership in the annual conference–failed. The reason given for the defeat of the measure was that "the church had enough to do regarding the merger." Thus, "women's rights would have to wait."[208] Noll points out, however, that the resolution seeking full clergy rights for women was, in fact, "defeated by a narrow margin…. After first passing by voice vote, full clergy rights for women was defeated 371 to 384"[209]–a matter of only seventeen votes.

And, of course, there was the problem of the Methodist Protestant women who already had full clergy rights. Since these women had full clergy rights in the MPC, "there was nothing else to do but to keep them enrolled in the new church and provide work for them."[210]

Given the statement that appeared in the 1938 MECS *Discipline* regarding women as preachers, it is likely that the attitude of men in the South toward welcoming women in the pulpit changed slowly. This appears to be reflected in the fact that even though women in the MECS had been advocating for full clergy rights during the years preceding the 1939 merger, there seems to be little evidence that women in the South took much advantage of the opportunity to apply for even limited clergy rights. In Arkansas, for example, despite the fact that four Methodist Protestant women came into the merger with full clergy rights, Nancy Britton states, "the unavoidable recognition of Methodist Protestant clergy-women, however, did not open the door to ordination for women in general for almost two decades."[211] And it appears from the remainder of her paper that no other women even sought to become ordained as local deacons and elders until the 1956 legislation was passed granting women full clergy rights. And, in 1956, the first year that women could be received on probation, only three women from the South would be received on trial–Myrtle Saylor Speer from Missouri, and two African American women, Sallie Crenshaw and Nora Young, from the East Tennessee Conference.

Victory at Last!

In the meantime, the fight for full clergy rights continued and the Women's Division of the Board of Mission (now the Board of Global Ministries) and laywomen from local Women's Society of Christian Service (WSCS) units became major forces in the battle. Georgia Harkness wrote:

> In the General Conference of 1952, after repeated attempts to secure full clergy rights for women in successive General Conferences had been rejected, the matter came up in its closing moments. It was passed over rapidly with the usual rejection, to the accompaniment of considerable laughter. I may be divulging some unwritten history when I say that some of the women present resolved that it was no longer to be treated as a laughing matter! The consequence was action by the Woman's Society of Christian Service which resulted in over 2,000 petitions on the subject to the General Conference of 1956; between three and four hours of vigorous debate on the floor of the Conference, mainly between men on both sides of the issue; and a vote for the full eradication of official sex discrimination in the ministry of the Methodist Church. (I purposely sat in silence, for there were able and discerning men to carry the issue, and I had long before learned that this is often the surest way to get something passed.)[212]

As Harkness points out, despite the fact that this legislation finally passed, it still did not happen without a good deal of disagreement. When the majority report of the committee was reported, it recommended that only single women and widows be allowed to apply for full clergy rights; further, it recommended that women who had previously received full clergy rights would lose those rights if they chose to marry. The minority report recommended that the status quo be maintained. One of the major objections to giving women full clergy rights seems to have been the "administrative problems" that it posed for district superintendents who would be required to guarantee an appointment to every woman who had been elected to conference membership. That is, district superintendents would be faced with appointing women to churches who did not want women pastors.[213]

After a great deal more discussion, proposed amendments, and substitutes, however, just prior to adjournment on Friday afternoon, May 4, 1956, the General Conference voted to amend Paragraph 313 of the *Discipline* to read:

> Par. 313. Women are included in the foregoing provisions, and may apply as candidates for the traveling ministry as provided in Chapter III of the *Discipline*, entitled "Traveling Preachers." Paragraphs 321-356 inclusive.[214]

What excitement must have reigned among those women *and men* who had worked so hard and for so long to bring about this victory!

Before concluding this chapter, one other item relating to full clergy rights for women needs to be clarified, as well. There has been some misunderstanding regarding the question of whether women were actually guaranteed an appointment in 1956 or whether this was, in fact, not the case until the 1968 merger between the EUB Church and the MC. Again, Robert Kohler explains it this way:

> Both men and women were guaranteed an appointment in 1956, the same year that the ordination of women was affirmed by General Conference. However, the guaranteed appointment was not viewed as the right of a clergy member of the annual conference in full connection, but as a limitation on the power of the bishop to leave a conference member without an appointment. What the *Discipline* said in 1956 in ¶ 432.9 was that "every traveling preacher, unless retired, supernumerary, on sabbatical leave, or under arrest of character, must receive an appointment." What happened in 1968 was that this statement, originally designed to limit the arbitrary use of power by bishops, was moved from the duties of the bishop to the description of the rights of those in full conference membership. Paragraph 316 of the 1968 *Discipline* simply states, "Every ministerial member who is in good standing in an Annual Conference shall receive an annual appointment by the bishop unless he is granted a sabbatical leave or a disability leave or is in the supernumerary or superannuate relation." This statement was reiterated in ¶ 332. This was nothing new. The statement was simply moved from the duties of the bishop to the rights of full members.[215]

And, as soon as the legislation was passed, there were women ready to be received into conference membership. Their stories will be told in chapter 2.

Notes
1. Paul W. Chilcote, *She Offered Them Christ: The Legacy of Women Preachers in Early Methodism* (Nashville: Abingdon, 1993), 7. Many thanks to Dr. Chilcote for permission to reproduce selections from his book.
2. Ibid., 11.

3. Ibid., 8.

4. Frank Baker, "Susanna Wesley: Puritan, Parent, Pastor, Protagonist, Pattern," in *Women in New Worlds: Historical Perspectives on the Wesleyan Tradition*, ed. Rosemary Skinner Keller, Louise L. Queen, and Hilah F. Thomas, 2:118 (Nashville: Abingdon, 1982).

5. Jean Miller Schmidt, *Grace Sufficient: A History of Women in American Methodism 1760–1939* (Nashville: Abingdon, 1999), 25. © Abingdon Press. Used by permission.

6. Chilcote, *She Offered Them Christ*, 19-20.

7. Ibid., 24-25.

8. Ibid., 35.

9. Ibid., 36.

10. Ibid., 47.

11. Ibid., 50-51.

12. Ibid., 55.

13. Ibid., 73.

14. Schmidt, *Grace Sufficient*, 29.

15. Ibid., 29-30.

16. Ibid., 68-72.

17. Chilcote, *She Offered Them Christ*, 78; Schmidt, Ibid., 30.

18. Chilcote, Ibid., 80.

19. Ibid., 81.

20. Ibid., 101.

21. Ibid., 103-4.

22. Schmidt, *Grace Sufficient*, 32.

23. Chilcote, *She Offered Them Christ*, 121.

24. Schmidt, *Grace Sufficient*, 54-55.

25. Elizabeth Gillan Muir, *Petticoats in the Pulpit: The Story of Early Nineteenth-Century Methodist Women Preachers in Upper Canada* (Toronto: The United Church Publishing House, 1991), 139.

26. Schmidt, *Grace Sufficient*, 65.

27. Ibid., 100.

28. Ibid., 100-102.

29. Ibid., 102-3.

30. Ibid., 103.

31. Jualynne Dodson, "Nineteenth-Century A.M.E. Preaching Women," in *Women in New Worlds: Historical Perspectives on the Wesleyan Tradition*, ed. Hilah F. Thomas and Rosemary Skinner Keller, 1:276-89 (Nashville: Abingdon, 1981-82). See especially, 1:286.

32. Fanny Newell, *Memoirs of Fanny Newell: Written by Herself…3rd Edition, with Corrections and Improvements. Published by O. Scott and E. F. Newell* (Springfield, MA: G. & C. Merriam, Printers, 1833), 26-32.

33. Ibid., 39.

34. Ibid., 68.

35. Ibid., 82.

36. E. F. Newell, *Life and Observations of Rev. E. F. Newell* (Worcester, MA: C. W. Ainsworth, 1847), 138.

37. Fanny Butterfield Newell, *Memoirs of Fanny Newell*, 110, 111.

38. Newell, *Life and Observations of Rev. E. F. Newell*, 184-85.

39. Ibid., 177, 192.

40. Robert J. Williams, "Methodist Protestant Church," in *Historical Dictionary of American Methodism*, ed. Charles Yrigoyen Jr. and Susan E. Warrick, 143-44 (Lanham, MD, and London: Scarecrow, 1996).

41. Muir, *Petticoats in the Pulpit*, 161.

42. Ibid.

43. Schmidt, *Grace Sufficient*, 107-8.

44. Ibid.

45. Ancel H. Bassett, *A Concise History of the Methodist Protestant Church* (Pittsburgh: James Robison; Baltimore: W. J. C. Dulaney, 1882), 195, 345.

46. Schmidt, *Grace Sufficient*, 108, 109.

47. Ibid., 133.

48. Ibid.

49. Ibid., 134.

50. Ibid., 135-36.

51. Ibid., 136, 137, 138.

52. Ibid., 142.

53. Lucille Sider Dayton and Donald W. Dayton, "'Your Daughters Shall Prophesy': Feminism in the Holiness Movement," *Methodist History* 14, no. 2 (January 1976): 74.

54. Schmidt, *Grace Sufficient*, 143.

55. Ibid., 144.

56. Ibid., 145.

57. Dayton and Dayton, "'Your Daughters Shall Prophesy,'" 81.

58. Ibid.

59. Schmidt, *Grace Sufficient*, 147.

60. Daryl M. Elliott, "Church of the United Brethren in Christ," in *Historical Dictionary of American Methodism*, 213.

61. Jim Will, "The Ordination of Women–The Development in the Church of the United Brethren in Christ," in *Woman's Rightful Place*, ed. Donald K. Gorrell (Dayton, OH: United Theological Seminary, 1980), 28.

62. Ibid.

63. "Historical Bulletin Insert No. 21," published by South Indiana Conference for the Indiana United Methodist Bicentennial 2000–2001, prepared by John R. Riggs, Archives Researcher, Archives of DePauw University and Indiana United Methodism.

64. Ibid.

65. Schmidt, *Grace Sufficient*, 110.

66. Ibid., 111.

67. Ibid.

68. "Historical Bulletin Insert, No. 21."

69. Will, "The Ordination of Women," 28.

70. Ibid, 31.

71. Donald K. Gorrell, "Ordination of Women by The United Brethren in Christ, 1889," *Methodist History* 18, no. 2 (January 1980): 137, 138.

72. Ibid., 138-42.

73. Will, "The Ordination of Women," 32.

74. Gorrell, "Ordination of Women by The United Brethren in Christ, 1889," 143.

75. Ibid.

76. Will, "The Ordination of Women," 32.

77. Ronald J. Williams, "Anecdotage," gleaned from information in the Kansas West United Methodist Archives, PO Box 65, Baker University, Baldwin City, KS 66006.

78. Ibid.

79. Robert J. Williams, "Methodist Protestant Church," in *Historical Dictionary of American Methodism*, 143.

80. Christopher M. Shoemaker, "A Small Work: The Story of Helenor Alter Davisson, Methodism's First Ordained Woman," *Methodist History* 41:2 (January 2003): 3-4, 6.

81. Ibid., 7

82. Earlier reports that Helenor was married to Moses Davisson and that they served together as a clergy couple are incorrect. See Ibid., 7, 8.

83. Ibid., 8.

84. Ibid., 9.

85. William T. Noll, "Women as Clergy and Laity in the 19th Century Methodist Protestant Church," *Methodist History* 15, no. 2 (January 1977): 110.

86. Shoemaker, "A Small Work," 10. It should be noted that in 1858 there had been a split in the MPC over the issue of slavery, with the Northern Division becoming known as the Methodist Church (MC). The two branches reunited in the 1870s.

87. Ibid.

88. John A. Nye, *Between the Rivers: A History of Iowa United Methodism* (Commission on Archives and History, Iowa Annual Conference of The United Methodist Church, 1986), 93.

89. *1870 Minutes of the Iowa Conference of The Methodist [Protestant] Church*, 5, 6.

90. 1870 Census for the state of Iowa, Clayton Township, Taylor County, 11.

91. *1871 Minutes of the Iowa Conference of The Methodist [Protestant] Church*, 2.

92. Ibid., 10, 13, 17.

93. *1872 Minutes of Iowa Conference of The Methodist [Protestant] Church*, 8, 12.

94. *1873 Minutes of the Iowa Conference of The Methodist [Protestant] Church*, 4, 5, 12.

95. *1875 Minutes of the Kansas Methodist [Protestant] Church*, 100. Many thanks to Brid Nicholson, PhD candidate at Drew University, whose careful research in the Kansas MPC records uncovered this new information.

96. Ibid., 110.

97. *1881 Minutes of the Kansas Conference of The Methodist [Protestant] Church*, 16; *1882 Minutes of the Kansas Conference of The Methodist [Protestant] Church*, no page given–last day of the annual conference. The minutes of the Iowa and Kansas Methodist Protestant Conferences can be found in the United Methodist Archives at the General Conference Commission on Archives and History, The United Methodist Church, P.O. Box 127, 36 Madison Avenue, Madison, NJ 07940.

98. *Minutes of the 1877 Missouri Conference of The Methodist Protestant Church*, 347. These minutes are in the Missouri Conference Archives at Central Methodist University, Fayette, MO 65248.

99. Ibid., 355. See also, *Minutes of the 1879 Missouri Conference of The Methodist Protestant Church*, 394.

100. *Minutes of the 1884 Missouri Conference of The Methodist Protestant Conference*, 503.

101. The Reverend Douglas Showalter, e-mail message to the author, September 10, 2004. Reverend Showalter is a United Church of Christ pastor from Falmouth, Massachusetts, who has researched early Congregational female pastors and was the individual whose research on Maggie Elliott led him to the Missouri Conference Archives.

102. Schmidt, *Grace Sufficient*, 185-86.

103. Ibid., 185-87.

104. "Historical Firsts for Women Clergy: Anna Howard Shaw (1847–1919)"; Web site for the General Commission on Archives and History (GCAH) of The United Methodist Church: http://www.gcah.org/women_ministry2.htm.

105. Schmidt, *Grace Sufficient*, 187.

106. Ibid., 188.

107. Noll, "Women as Clergy and Laity," 111-12.

108. Schmidt, *Grace Sufficient*, 194.

109. Noll, "Women as Clergy and Laity," 112.

110. Schmidt, *Grace Sufficient*, 194.

111. William T. Noll, "Laity Rights and Leadership: Winning Them for Women in the Methodist Protestant Church, 1860–1900," in *Women in New Worlds*, 1:220.

112. Noll, "Women as Clergy and Laity," 113-14.

113. Schmidt, *Grace Sufficient*, 338n37.

114. Noll, "Women as Clergy and Laity," 114-16.

115. Schmidt, *Grace Sufficient*, 194.

116. For an in-depth description of this changing role for women and the rise of the various woman's missionary societies, see Schmidt, *Grace Sufficient*, 151-78.

117. Janet S. Everhart, "Maggie Newton Van Cott," in *Women in New Worlds* (1982), 2:303.

118. Ibid., 301. See also, Schmidt, *Grace Sufficient*, 181.

119. Everhart, "Maggie Newton Van Cott," 301.

120. Schmidt, *Grace Sufficient*, 181.

121. Ibid., 181-82.

122. John O. Foster, *The Harvest and the Reaper: Reminiscences of Revival Work of Mrs. Maggie N. Van Cott, the First Lady Licensed to Preach in the Methodist Episcopal Church in the United States* (New York: N. Tibbals & Sons, 1876), 206.

123. Schmidt, *Grace Sufficient*, 182.

124. Ibid., 183.

125. Ibid., 185.

126. Everhart, 309. See also, William T. Noll, "A Welcome in the Ministry: The 1920 and 1924 General Conferences Debate Clergy Rights for Women," *Methodist History* 30, no. 2 (January 1992): 91.

127. Everhart does not include a list in her article and, in an e-mail, William T. Noll states, "I never tried to list all women local preachers of any era" (e-mail from Noll to author, April 14, 2005).

128. S. S. Benedict, "'Local Preachers' License," in *Northwest Christian Advocate* (August 6, 1873): 254.

129. Schmidt, *Grace Sufficient*, 185.

130. Everhart, 315.

131. Kenneth E. Rowe, "Evangelism and Social Reform in the Pastoral Ministry of Anna Oliver, 1868–1886," in *Spirituality and Social Responsibility*, ed. Rosemary Skinner Keller (Nashville: Abingdon, 1993), 117.

132. Schmidt, *Grace Sufficient*, 187.

133. Rowe, "Evangelism and Social Reform," 123.

134. Ibid. Antoinette Brown is considered to be the first woman to be ordained in the United States in 1853 in a small Congregational church in New York. See also, Schmidt, *Grace Sufficient*, 196.

135. Schmidt, *Grace Sufficient*, 188.

136. Ibid.

137. Kenneth E. Rowe, "The Ordination of Women: Round One; Anna Oliver and the General Conference of 1880," in *Perspectives on American Methodism: Interpretive Essays*, ed. Russell E. Richey, Kenneth E. Rowe, Jean Miller Schmidt (Nashville: Kingswood, 1993), 300.

138. Schmidt, *Grace Sufficient*, 188-89.

139. Anna Howard Shaw, *The Story of a Pioneer* (Cleveland: The William Bradford Collection edition, The Pilgrim Press, 1994), 122. Copyright © 1994 The Pilgrim Press), Reprinted by permission.

140. Schmidt, *Grace Sufficient*, 189.

141. Shaw, *Story of a Pioneer*, 123.

142. Rowe, "The Ordination of Women," 303.

143. Schmidt, *Grace Sufficient*, 191. The latter quotation contains my italics.

144. Ibid., 192.

145. Ibid., 193.

146. Rowe, "The Ordination of Women," 308.

147. Schmidt, *Grace Sufficient*, 192-93.

148. Ibid., 215.

149. Ibid., 217.

150. Ibid., 219.

151. Ibid., 195.

152. Ibid., 223-24. A list of the twenty-four female delegates appears on 224.

153. Ibid., 227.

154. Ibid., 197-200.

155. Ibid., 200.

156. Ibid., 201.

157. Patricia A. Jewett [Thompson], *The History of Maine Methodism: Through the Women's Sphere* (Maine: Maine Annual Conference Commission on the Status and Role of Women, 1984), 33.

158. Schmidt, *Grace Sufficient*, 201.

159. Jewett, *History of Maine Methodism*, 24-25.

160. Ibid., 34.

161. Charles W. Kern, *God, Grace, and Granite: The History of Methodism in New Hampshire 1768–1988* (Canaan, NH: Phoenix Publishing, 1988), 133.

162. George Harper, "Women Ministers in Montana Methodism" (two pages, typewritten, 2002), 1.

163. Carmen Dressler Ward, "Contributions of Women," in *Roots and Branches: Historical Essays on Methodism in Southern New England*, ed. Jerry O. Cook (Boston: New England Methodist Historical Society, 1989), 104.

164. Schmidt, *Grace Sufficient*, 210.

165. Noll, "A Welcome in the Ministry," 91-92.

166. Schmidt, *Grace Sufficient*, 273.

167. Kendra Weddle Irons, "From Kansas to the World: M. Madeline Southard, Activist and Pastor," *Methodist History* 43, no. 1 (October 2004): 33-34, 35.

168. Ibid., 35-36.

169. Noll, "A Welcome in the Ministry," 94.

170. Ibid.

171. Ibid., 96.

172. Schmidt, *Grace Sufficient*, 273.

173. Ibid., 274.

174. Irons, "From Kansas to the World," 38-39.

175. Noll, "A Welcome in the Ministry," 98.

176. Irons, "From Kansas to the World," 40.

177. Schmidt, *Grace Sufficient*, 274.

178. GCAH, e-mail to the author, June 2005.

179. Ibid., 1-2.

180. E-mail from GCAH, June 2005. *They Served for Love: The Story of 271 Women in Mission in the California-Nevada Conference of The United Methodist Church*, ed. Dorothy Bartell (California: The Conference United Methodist Women and The Conference Commission on Archives and History, 1990), 7, 79.

181. William T. Noll, e-mail message to author, April 14, 2005.
182. Kendra Irons, e-mail message to author, March 30, 2005.
183. Jewett, *History of Maine Methodism*, 35.
184. Charles Downer Schwartz and Ouida Davis Schwartz, *A Flame of Fire: The Story of Troy Annual Conference* (Rutland: Academy Books, 1982), 327-28.
185. Jewett, *History of Maine Methodism*, 35.
186. Jeannie M. Redstone, Charlotte Cartmill, Emma J. Davis, Annalee Stewart, and Emily B. Vance are listed in Ward, 104.
187. Ward, "Contributions of Women," 104-5. See also, Downer and Schwartz, *Flame of Fire*, 327.
188. Schwartz and Schwartz, *Flame of Fire*, 327, 330; Jewett, *History of Maine Methodism*, 36; Grant S. Shockley, gen. ed., *Heritage and Hope: The African-American Presence in United Methodism* (Nashville: Abingdon, 1991), 53. Please note that this is not meant to be an exhaustive list of women ordained deacon in 1925; it only reflects those known by the author at the time of this writing.
189. GCAH, e-mail message to author, June 2005.
190. Jewett, *History of Maine Methodism*, 36; Ward, "Contributions of Women," 104; Downer and Schwartz, *Flame of Fire*, 327.
191. Irons, e-mail message to author, March 30, 2005. See also, 1939 Journal of the Troy Conference, MC, 372.
192. Memoir for Sallie A. Crenshaw, *1987 Journal of the Holston Conference, UMC*, 228. See also, Schockley, 53.
193. Noll, "A Welcome in the Ministry," 99.
194. Robert Kohler, e-mail message to author, October 4, 2004.
195. Ibid.
196. Irons, "From Kansas to the World," 41.
197. Noll, "A Welcome in the Ministry," 98.
198. K. James Stein, "Georgia Elma Harkness," in *Historical Dictionary of Methodism*, 104. See also, Rosemary Skinner Keller, "Georgia Harkness–Theologian of the People," in *Spirituality and Social Responsibility*, 206.
199. Schmidt, *Grace Sufficient*, 227-30.
200. Alice Knotts, "The Debates over Race and Women's Ordination in the 1939 Methodist Merger," *Methodist History* 29, no. 1 (October 1990): 42-43.
201. Barbara B. Troxell, "Ordination of Women in the United Methodist Tradition," *Methodist History* 37, no. 2 (January 1999): 124.
202. Schmidt, *Grace Sufficient*, 124-25.
203. Ibid., 125.
204. William T. Noll, "'You and I Are Partners:' A Heritage for Clergy Couples in Nineteenth Century American Methodism," *Methodist History* 26, no. 1 (October 1987): 48.
205. Clotilde Falcón Náñez, "Hispanic Clergy Wives," in *Women in New Worlds*, 1:170.
206. Ibid.
207. *1980 Journal of the Rio Grande Conference, UMC*, 168.
208. Knotts, "The Debates over Race and Women's Ordination in the 1939 Methodist Merger," 43.
209. Noll, "Women as Clergy and Laity," 120.
210. Ibid.
211. Nancy Britton, "'Firsts' among Arkansas Methodist Clergy-women" (unpublished paper, n.d.), 1. A copy may be found in the Arkansas United Methodist Archives, Bailey Library, Hendrix College, Conway AR 72032.
212. Troxell, "Ordination of Women in the United Methodist Tradition," 125.
213. *Journal of the 1956 General Conference Methodist Church*, 688, 1547, 688-95.
214. Ibid., 720, 1546-47.
215. Kohler, e-mail message to author, October 4, 2004.

Chapter 2

"They Stepped Out in Faith":
The First Women to Be Received into Conference Membership
in The Methodist Church

ONE THING THAT HAS BECOME EVIDENT IN WRITING this book is how difficult it is to identify the "first" woman in almost any category. Sometimes those who have become well known as the first may have become so simply because their stories were well known, as in the cases of Anna Howard Shaw, Maggie Ritchie Elliott, and Pauline Martindale. In the cases of women ordained deacons in 1924, the first were "first" only due to the schedule of their annual conferences. *All of these early women were pioneers.* The same is true of the women who were received into conference membership in 1956.

Moreover, despite the fact that 2006 marks the fiftieth anniversary of full clergy rights for women, it is important to note here that all of the women received into conference membership in 1956 were, in fact, *received on trial* and served as probationary members for at least the required two years before being received as full members of their respective annual conferences.

Twenty-seven women from nineteen annual conferences were received on probation in 1956. The original list that was circulated for many years recorded only twenty-two women from sixteen conferences, listing the names in order of the dates of their annual conferences. The first response received for this project identified two additional women from the East Tennessee Conference of the Central Jurisdiction–Sallie Crenshaw and Nora Young–whose annual conference was held following the last conference on the original list. Jean Miller Schmidt, however, does identify these two women.[1] In addition, two women from Ohio who seemed not to have ever been identified before were reported, as well: Marie Tschappat and Jane Ann Stoneburner (Moore). The annual conference in which they were received was held just prior to

the East Tennessee Conference. There was also one Central Conference woman received: Antonia Wladar from Hungary.

Fourteen of the women, or a little more than 50 percent, were the only women in their conferences to be received that year. In three conferences there were two women, in one conference there were three women, and in the Maine Annual Conference there were four women received in 1956, where women had been supplying pulpits for at least forty years.

The Northeastern Jurisdiction had nine–or 33 percent–of the "first" women. The North Central Jurisdiction and the Western Jurisdiction each had seven women; the Southeastern Jurisdiction had only two women and the South Central Jurisdiction only one woman received on probation in 1956. In addition, there was one woman received on probation in the Central European Conference. Three of the women, one from the Northeast and the two from the Southeast, were actually received in the Central Jurisdiction. The South Central Jurisdiction, however, had two Methodist Protestant women who had been serving in full connection since 1939 and who continued to serve after 1956. The North Central Jurisdiction had one Methodist Protestant woman. The women whose biographies appear below are listed chronologically in the order they were received into conference membership as a result of the date of their annual conference in 1956. Note that many of the women had been ordained as local elders prior to 1956.

Maud Keister Jensen

Central Pennsylvania Conference (Northeastern Jurisdiction)
May 18, 1956

Ordained Deacon – 1948
Ordained Elder – 1952
Received on Trial – 1956
Received into Full Connection – 1958
Deceased – 1998

MAUD KEISTER JENSEN was born September 27, 1904, in New Cumberland, Pennsylvania. She attended her local Methodist church at an early age and, much to her parents' surprise, one Sunday when the pastor issued a call for those seeking baptism, Maud stepped to the front of the church and proclaimed herself ready. She began to teach Sunday school at the age of twelve. At a relatively young age, Jensen felt called to the ministry. As she later recalled in an interview, "I just knew that that was the thing I should do…. I had no doubt about my talents. I believe God had called me to the ministry and expected my proper response, as he [*sic*] had provided the essential qualifications." On January 25, 1929, she received her license to preach.

Maud became interested in missionary work while attending Bucknell University in Pennsylvania and was sent to Korea by The Methodist Church (MC) after her graduation in 1926. In 1928, she married Kris Jensen, whom she had met while they were both missionary candidates, and they devoted the rest of their missionary career to work in Korea.

After earning a bachelor of divinity degree from Drew Theological School in 1946, Maud applied for deacon's orders in the New Jersey Area in 1948. The bishop of that area, however, was not supportive of this request. Recalled Maud, "I remember it was quite discouraging. He wasn't interested in the least in having a woman be ordained. But since I was interested, I applied to another one and to my own conference." She was ordained a deacon in the Central Pennsylvania Conference by Bishop Charles Wesley Flint that same year. She received her elder's orders in 1952.

Thus, in 1956 Maud Keister Jensen was eligible to be received into the Central Pennsylvania Conference on probation. Since she and her husband were serving as missionaries in Korea, however, Maud was actually received in absentia, making her the first woman to be received into membership in an annual conference of the MC. In response to a wire sent from the Board of Missions, she replied, "I am deeply grateful for privilege but honor completely unexpected and due entirely to early meeting of my annual conference. Feel Georgia Harkness and other active women ministers deserved first recognition after long struggle and able contributions to church."[2]

After her death, her son Philip reported, "Being the first woman to receive full clergy rights in the Methodist Church was, for her, not the most important accomplishment of her life…. She would say that she wanted to be most remembered for her missionary work in Korea." Maud Keister Jensen died October 12, 1998, at age ninety-four.[3]

Grace E. Huck

North Dakota Conference (North Central Jurisdiction)
May 22, 1956

Ordained Deacon – 1945
Ordained Elder – 1949
Received on Trial – 1956
Received into Full Connection – 1958
Retired – 1981

GRACE ELOISE HUCK was born June 27, 1916, in Bowman, North Dakota.

"During my senior year in High School, I attended the Four Square Church for the youth group and the evening service with a friend. The youth meetings were regular worship services with a youth preaching the sermon. I began to want to do that, but since I did not 'speak in tongues,' I was not considered a Christian so was never asked.

"Then I attended the Methodist Church camp that summer. As the closing consecration service was being led by a Deaconess, she gave the invitation for us to commit our lives to Christ. She said, 'Maybe there is someone here who would like to commit his or her life as a full-time worker as a minister, missionary or deaconess.' I felt God's hand upon me. I wanted to give myself to Christ for full-time service as a preacher. I went forward and knelt at the log altar and committed my life as a full-time worker in the church. My ministerial journey began when the new minister, the Rev. Ross Hutsinpillar and wife Vernie, came to our church in Bowman, N.Dak. They recognized my call, encouraged me and led me through the steps to become an Accepted Supply Pastor in The Methodist Church. That was all I could be at that time.

"I was ordained deacon in 1945, ten years after I made my commitment to become a minister. When I came up for deacon's ordination, the committee was somewhat reluctant to grant it to me because I was a woman. But by that time I had served as a pastor quite acceptably–though not without some resistance."

The end of November, when I had been at the parish for a little more than two months, I was making calls on members and one of the ladies told me that Mr. Julian had been telling everyone what a good preacher and pastor I was. Mr. Julian was one of the leaders of the church and quite vocal. Then she laughed and told me that when Reverend Grunstead [the D.S.] had first told them he was appointing a woman as their pastor, Mr. Julian, who was a very outspoken leader of the church, had pounded the back of the pew and shouted, "There will be no skirts in this pulpit while I am alive." Of course, that had not deterred Reverend Grunstead, and I was appointed. Mr. Julian was now my firm supporter.[4]

On May 22, 1956, Grace E. Huck became the second woman in the MC to be received on trial, in the North Dakota Conference. She was, however, the first woman to be present at an annual conference and to answer the historic questions posed to all those who are to be received as members of an annual conference. She was also the first woman to receive an appointment in an annual conference as a member of the conference.

Grace served many churches in the Dakotas and also served as a missionary in the Philippines for eleven years, returning later as a volunteer. After continuing to serve churches in her retirement, Grace is still active in her local church in Spearfish, North Dakota, and has published her memoirs under the title *God's Amazing Grace*.

Grace M. Weaver

Idaho Annual Conference (Western Jurisdiction)
May 22, 1956

Ordained Deacon – 1954
Received on Trial – 1956
Ordained Elder – 1956
Received into Full Connection – 1958
Retired – 1977

GRACE MARGARET WEAVER was born September 4, 1909, in Philadelphia, Pennsylvania. In an interview at the time of her retirement from the ministry in 1977, she observed, "At [age] 12, I knew I wanted to be a missionary, minister's wife or a minister. Both my grandfathers were local Methodist preachers, and they had certificates to conduct services. As a child, the church was my home. I was there whenever the church was open. We lived three houses away."[5]

Grace's calling would be put off for fourteen years, due in part to the Depression. She attended Glassboro Normal School and taught school, never losing her desire to be a minister or a missionary. When she approached the Mission Board, however, she was told that she would not be considered without a college degree, so she began taking courses at Temple University. Her pastor, the Reverend Everett Palmer (who later became a bishop in Oregon) led her to Morningside College in Sioux City, Iowa, where she earned her degree in 1947. Going back to the Mission Board, she was then given a choice of three placements: one as a music teacher in Cuba, one at a children's home in Alaska, and one at the Highland Bay Community House in Bingham, Utah. She chose the position in Utah and from there began attending classes at Iliff School of Theology, over the mountains in Denver. She graduated in 1954, was granted her deacon's orders, and was told that there was no place for a woman deacon in Denver. The Idaho bishop, however, agreed to appoint her to the charge in Emmett, Idaho, where she was well received and loved by the congregation. Thus, when the 1956 legislation was passed, Grace was received on trial and granted her elder's orders in the Idaho Conference.

Her application to serve as a missionary had been approved by that time, as well, and Grace was sent to Alaska where she served for five years as the first woman pastor in full connection. After she returned to Idaho, she served a number of churches in the conference before retiring. It is said of her,

> In general hers was a happy and productive ministry.... Only in one church did she have any real problems when the habits of a seasoned teacher came to the fore and she disciplined a misbehaving boy whose father took exception to her methods. She only spent one year in that church. When her bishop learned of her problem he told her not to worry, he would find her another charge and he did.... The ministry was always her ambition...and her years as a minister were the happiest of her life. She feels she has lived a very satisfying and fulfilling life.

At the time of this writing, Grace resides in the Jason Lee Home in Salem, Oregon.[6]

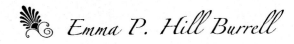 *Emma P. Hill Burrell*

Washington Conference (Central Jurisdiction)
May 26, 1956

Ordained Deacon – 1953
Received on Trial – 1956
Received into Full Connection – 1959
Ordained Elder – 1959
Deceased – 1989

EMMA P. HILL BURRELL was born August 9, 1912, in Washington, DC, the daughter of the Reverend Florence P. Simms, who was the first woman to be ordained as a local elder in the Washington Conference, and stepdaughter of Dr. William G. Simms, who was a pastor in the Baltimore Conference. Reverend Florence Simms was ordained an elder in 1939 and appointed to the Ritchie Methodist Church in Ritchie, Maryland, where she served for twenty-six years.

Her daughter, Emma, served with her at that church as assistant pastor early in her ministry. Following her mother's death in 1961, Emma then served the Ritchie Church as pastor for one year along with the Jackson-St. Luke charge, which she also served. During the seven years in which she was appointed to the Jackson-St. Luke charge, she led the two congregations in uniting and purchasing the ground for their Westphalia Union Methodist Church. She then served Mount Vernon UMC in Ivy City, Washington, DC, for seven years; Brightwood UMC, Washington, DC, for two years; and Good Hope Union UMC, Silver Spring, Md, for nine years.

When Emma was received on probation in 1956, she became the first African American woman to be received into the membership of an annual conference. Since she was not received into full connection and ordained an elder until 1959, however, she would not be the first African American woman to be received into full connection.

Prior to entering the ministry, Emma was principal of the Fauquier High School in Irwin, Virginia, for two years and taught evening and day school in Washington, DC, grades 3 through 12, and worked for several years as a government employee in the U.S. Census Bureau as supervisor and statistical clerk. In addition to her AB, BD, and MDiv degrees, Emma Burrell also held an honorary DD (doctor of divinity) degree.

Emma retired in 1981 after twenty-six years of service in the UMC. She was the widow of the late Reverend George W. Burrell, who was pastor of the Community Baptist Church, Oakcrest, Laurel, Maryland. They enjoyed and participated fully in the great fellowship of the Baptist Union and Associations. Emma Burrell died February 26, 1989, at age seventy-seven.[7]

JoLorene Miller Parker Anderson

Central New York Conference (Northeastern Jurisdiction)
May 27, 1956

Received on Trial – 1956
Ordained Deacon – 1956
Received into Full Connection – 1958
Ordained Elder – 1958
Deceased – 1997

JoLorene Miller Parker Anderson was born February 7, 1916, in Chicago, Illinois. She graduated from Chicago's Audubon Elementary School in 1929 and Lakeview High School in 1933. Thereafter, she attended Chicago's American Conservatory of Music, earning a bachelor of music degree. JoLorene taught music at several locations, including upstate New York. After returning to college in 1950, she earned an associate of arts degree in 1952 from Kendall College in Evanston, Illinois. In 1952, JoLorene experienced a call to the ministry and moved to Syracuse, New York, for study and experience in the MC, enrolling at Syracuse University. JoLorene majored in Bible while working at the nearby Phoenix Methodist Church. She received her bachelor's degree in 1955 and worked for a number of months at Vesper Church. She then enrolled at Boston University School of Theology.

When the 1956 General Conference voted to receive women into conference membership, JoLorene "scrambled" (her word) to make sure that her credentials were in order so that she might be received on probation and ordained deacon at the 1956 annual conference. While studying at Boston University, she was also called to pastor churches in the Otselic Valley in the Central New York Conference.

Following her graduation with an STB degree, JoLorene was received into full connection and ordained elder. Over the next thirty years, she remained in the Otselic Valley, bringing her unique style of ministry to half a dozen small congregations as an active pastor, a retired pastor, and a community activist. She served on the school board, was active in Eastern Star, and fought for adequate health care for the rural area she served. No one, church member or not, went unvisited in times of illness, trouble, or hospitalization. The Perryville Church, in the Valley, had a special relationship with JoLorene, as forty years earlier the church had been pastored for more than three years by Nettie Annabel, a pastor's widow and a deaconess.

JoLorene united in marriage with Charles H. Parker in 1961. After his death, she married Paul Anderson. While her political views often differed from her neighbors', no one could deny her passion for justice, her concern for those in poverty, or her devotion to her Lord and Savior, Jesus Christ, and his church.[8]

Gertrude Genevra Harris

Maine Annual Conference (Northeastern Jurisdiction)
May 27, 1956

Ordained Deacon – 1948
Ordained Elder – 1950
Received on Trial – 1956
Received into Full Connection – 1958
Deceased – 1982

GERTRUDE GENEVRA HARRIS was born December 1, 1901, in Boston, Massachusetts, the granddaughter of a Methodist preacher and evangelist. She was a graduate of Girls Latin School in Boston, earned a bachelor of science degree in chemistry from Massachusetts Institute of Technology, and a master of religious education degree from Columbia University, with much of the work done at Union Theological Seminary. She studied for three semesters at the seminary as a guest student since she was the first woman ever admitted to that institution. She worked toward a master of arts degree and completed the resident requirements toward a PhD but never received this degree.

She passed all the examinations for the office of a deaconess and hoped to become a missionary, but circumstances prevented her from doing so. She worked for a time as director of religious education in the Episcopal Church.

Gertrude was influenced greatly by reading Glen Clark's *Soul's Sincere Desire*, and she met him when she was just out of college. She felt that God had laid his hand upon her many times, and she led many people to Christ by her daily living as she practiced what she preached.

In 1946 she visited Margaret Henrichsen in Maine and became interested in rural church work of the MC. She secured a local preacher's license and took several courses in the Conference Course of Study, being ordained as deacon in 1948 and elder in 1950. In 1956, along with Margaret Henrichsen, Alice Hart, and Esther Haskard, she was admitted on trial in the Maine Conference. These four women came to be known as the 4-Hs.

After serving churches in rural Maine, Gertrude served under special appointment to the Koinonia Foundation in Baltimore, Maryland. There she worked in summer camping and as a spiritual retreat and prayer group leader. In later years she served as codirector of the retreat center at Merrybrook in Wells, Vermont. She retired in 1967.

Gertrude left a vast impression on all who knew her. She was gracious, unassuming, and truly a godly person. Gertrude died June 19, 1982, at age eighty.[9]

 *Alice Townsend Hart*

Maine Annual Conference (Northeastern Jurisdiction)
May 27, 1956

Ordained Deacon – 1943
Ordained Elder – 1945
Received on Trial – 1956
Received into Full Connection – 1958
Retired – 1971
Deceased – 1991

ALICE TOWNSEND HART was born June 13, 1889, in Newport, Maine. From the time that Alice was in high school, she had desired to become a minister, but women were not encouraged to enter the ministry then. She entered the teaching field, but she lasted only one year before entering Boston Lyceum School. After a year, Alice entered Boston University School of Religious Education where she took courses in religious work. She was not fully satisfied, however, until she began to take courses in preaching. "I was so happy doing it that I didn't mind the work…. I loved it, just loved it."[10]

Finally, in the 1940s, Alice realized her lifelong dream when she entered the ministry in the Maine Annual Conference. She was to have received her deacon's orders as a local preacher in 1942 but was not able to attend annual conference due to gas rationing. She received her deacon's orders in 1943 and her elder's orders in 1945. She was then among the first eight women to be received on trial in 1956.

From 1942 until her retirement in 1971, Alice served local churches in Eddington, North Waldoboro, Hallowell, Newport, and Portland, Washington Avenue, in the Maine Conference. Following her retirement, she needed to work to support herself. When her D.S. approached her, she said, "I would so enjoy continuing in Christian work." Her D.S. asked, "But what can a woman do?" Alice answered, "There is always work as a hospital chaplain and if the men would accept the idea I think I could do that very well." She notes that there was plenty of work to be done. While the men gave her a hard time, she simply got on with the work. She served as the chaplain at the Osteopathic Hospital of Maine for ten years.[11]

In an interview with the Rev. Donna Ivery, Alice says, "I had a great time in the ministry. I wish everybody could have as good a time as I had…. You may think I don't miss it, but I do. Ministry is the best job in the world."[12] Alice died September 11, 1991, at age 102.

Esther A. Haskard

Maine Annual Conference (Northeastern Jurisdiction)
May 27, 1956

Ordained Deacon – 1930
Ordained Elder – 1932
Received on Trial – 1956
Received into Full Connection – 1958
Retired – 1964
Deceased – 1985

ESTHER A. HASKARD was born in Bellingham, Massachusetts, on August 21, 1898. She attended Eastern Nazarene College in Wollaston, Massachusetts, for three years and then transferred to Pembroke College in Providence, Rhode Island, where she received a bachelor of philosophy degree in 1924. She completed one semester of graduate work at Boston University.

Esther remembered that, as a child, all day Sunday was spent in the Bellingham Baptist Church and it was here, at the age of seven, that she had a "born again" experience at a revival meeting. She was baptized by immersion on June 3, 1906, in Lake View, Bellingham, and received into membership in the church the following Sunday.

After her year at Boston University, Esther took a position at the Reformatory for Women in Framingham, Massachusetts. The superintendent at the time was Jessie D. Hodder, a noted reformer in the field of prisons.

Esther came to Maine in June 1925 to assume the pastorate of the MC in West Southport, which marked the beginning of a rewarding career in the ministry. She also served churches in Eastport, Rumford Center, Newfield, South Paris, West Scarborough, and the Columbia Falls Circuit, from which she retired in 1964.

In both Rumford Center and South Paris, Esther became a foster mother to some young girls needing a home. Esther served as chairman of the conference board of hospitals and homes. It was during this time that the conference voted to establish a retirement home in Rockland, Maine. The actual building began after she retired in 1964. Her efforts on behalf of the home were rewarded by having the Maine lounge dedicated in her honor.

Travel was one of her interests. In 1958 she went on Thomas Cook's "Grand Tour of Europe" and in 1972 she traveled to the Holy Land. Esther died November 6, 1985, at the age of eighty-seven.[13]

Margaret Kimball Henrichsen

Maine Annual Conference (Northeastern Jurisdiction)
May 27, 1956

Ordained Deacon – 1948
Ordained Elder – 1950
Received on Trial – 1956
Received into Full Connection – 1958
Deceased – 1976

MARGARET KIMBALL HENRICHSEN was born November 23, 1900, in New Jersey. She eventually married, and she and her husband, Christian, often traveled in Maine. Margaret's heart was touched by the many "little churches that needed paint, little churches that were not used, save for a month or two in the summer when some visiting minister held a few services."[14] After her husband died unexpectedly, Margaret writes,

> Gradually out of the resulting sense of devastation, a plan for my life was forming. I had written a good friend, a former pastor in our town, to see if he thought that anywhere in the country there might be closed churches who would like to have a woman pastor, and to find out whether he thought I could be useful in such a place.... One Sunday noon, in the house so horribly empty now, the telephone rang insistently as I returned from church. I dashed to answer it. A far-distant voice said, "Margaret? This is Vaughn. Will you come up to this District? I must have another pastor here right away." I replied, "Wait a minute. I didn't ask you for a job, I just wanted your advice." And the reply came, "Well—I asked you to come up, didn't I?" It was all the advice he ever gave me.[15]

Margaret accepted the offer and drove to Sullivan, Maine, in that area that the natives refer to as "Downeast," to become the pastor of the Schoodic Circuit, which would eventually include seven churches. "No one expected she would stay long; least of all the members of her congregation, who thought the lady parson would just fill in until the right man came along."[16] Eventually Margaret's fame spread beyond her seven steeples as, poignantly and humorously, Margaret tells her own story of those early years in Maine in a book published in 1953 entitled *Seven Steeples*.

In 1956 Margaret was among the first women in The Methodist Church to be received on trial and two years later into full connection. Then in 1967, Bishop James Matthews appointed Margaret as district superintendent (D.S.) of the Bangor District in Maine, making her the first woman to be appointed to serve as a district superintendent in American Methodism.[17]

Clarice Bowman says of Margaret's work as D.S.

> With...spunky zip and zing, she took on the huge Bangor District.... Until her accident she was ever on the road, God's magnificent circuit rider of America's northernmost district.
>
> Showing up unexpectedly on a Sunday morning to hear some student pastor, counseling with wit, creative criticism and common sense, she could be what psychiatrists call a "tough lover," cutting through phoniness and down to the core, evoking latent heroism, deeper dedication. How many are now ministering the more richly for her counsel, the chain-reacting influence going on and on. Annual Conference was for her a glorious reunion. Her presence made Conference different.[18]

Margaret's term as D.S. was cut short by injuries sustained in an automobile accident and she died March 21, 1976, at age seventy-five.

Ellen Maria Studley

North Indiana Conference (North Central Jurisdiction)
May 27, 1956

Received on Trial – 1956
Ordained Deacon – 1956
Received into Full Connection – 1958
Ordained Elder – 1958
Retired – 1970
Deceased – 1989

ELLEN MARIA STUDLEY was born May 27, 1899, in Grand Rapids, Michigan. She was active with her family in the Mishawaka First Church. She graduated from DePauw University (Phi Beta Kappa and Mortar Board), Boston University, and Union Theological Seminary.

Ellen was an educational missionary in China from 1924 until she was allowed to return to the United States in 1945 because of the War. After the War, she went back to China for several years before again returning to the States in 1951. Following her return, Ellen served for many years as the director of the Chinese Student and Alumni Services in the Midwest Area, during which time she played an important role in bridging the gap between the Chinese and American communities by creating good will between the two peoples. In 1956, after she was received into the North Indiana Conference on trial, she was given a celebration party by her Chinese friends during which a robe in the style of John Wesley's was presented to her in gratitude for the service that she had given to the Chinese community.[19]

Ellen went to Taiwan in 1964 and returned in 1966 to serve the Howe/Pretty Prairie United Methodist churches in 1968. Ellen retired in 1970 and moved to Claremont, California. In 1986, at age eighty-seven, Ellen was honored by DePauw University with an honorary doctor of humanities degree. Ellen Studley died August 11, 1989, at age ninety.[20]

Myrtle Saylor Speer

Missouri Annual Conference (South Central Jurisdiction)
June 5, 1956

Ordained Deacon, Kansas Conference, MEC – 1926
Ordained Elder, Missouri Conference, MEC – 1929
Received on Trial – 1956
Received into Full Connection – 1974
Retired – 1974
Deceased – 1981

MYRTLE SAYLOR SPEER was born January 18, 1891, in Gilmore City, Iowa. When she was ten years old, Myrtle made a major religious decision. During the Sunday morning Communion service, "it seemed to me the heavens opened, and an angelic voice said: 'Little girl, I want you to be a minister for me some day and say those beautiful words [of the Communion liturgy].'"[21] Although she was insistent about this intention, she found it difficult to obey the voice she heard from on high. "Male voices from relatively high places in the church hierarchy kept giving her other sets of instructions. In the end, however, she prevailed."[22]

Myrtle had her call confirmed in 1915 when she attended a summer Epworth League Institute at Clear Lake, Iowa. She enrolled in the Chicago Training School, as Garrett Evangelical Seminary did not receive women students in their ministerial course. Myrtle began preaching in 1917 as an evangelist in the Crawfordsville, Indiana, district of the MEC and also in the Iowa Conference.[23] In 1920, after General Conference voted to allow women to apply for licenses to preach, Myrtle's D.S. called a special session of his district in order to issue her a license, making her the first woman in Iowa to be issued a local preacher's license. Myrtle was the first woman in the Kansas Conference to be ordained deacon, in 1926, and the first to be ordained an elder, in 1929.[24]

Thus, when the legislation was passed in the General Conference in 1956, Myrtle was ready. But things did not go as expected.

> The Reverend Michael F. Hauser Winter was chairman of the Committee on Ministerial Qualifications…. When Reverend Winter told me that the committee had voted unanimously to recommend me for admission to the Conference in full connection, I was naturally pleased and felt that a dream of many years was, at long last, to be fulfilled….When [Bishop Ivan Lee Holt] saw my name on the list of those recommended for full connection, he said to Reverend Winter, "Receive her on trial." I was very surprised to hear my name thus presented…. [Reverend Winter] hastened to find me at the close of the session to explain what happened. Just what the Bishop's motive was, we have never known.[25]

Had Myrtle Speer been received into full connection in 1956, she would have been the only woman so received. Instead, she became the only woman received on trial in the United States in 1956 who was not received into full connection by 1959. Missouri West had had a change of bishops, and Bishop Frank wanted the first woman received into full connection to be a graduate of one of the Methodist seminaries. Thus, he refused to receive her into full connection despite her many years of experience and the fact that she had met the requirements that were applied to male pastors. She would not be received into full connection until 1974, the year she retired.[26]

The following year, the first National Consultation of Ordained Women in The United Methodist Church was held in Nashville, and Myrtle was the keynote speaker. Roy Larson, reporting this event, writes, "She's thoroughly delighted at what happened in Nashville this week. She has some reservations about some aspects of the women's liberation movement…but she is convinced women are at least as capable as men are of preaching and understanding theology. 'There's no sex difference in the brain,' she said. She said that with a smile—and with an air of authority, born of experience and belatedly validated by her church."[27]

Myrtle Saylor Speer died November 1, 1981, at age ninety.

Helena L. Champlin

Genesee Conference (Northeastern Jurisdiction)
June 10, 1956

Deacon's Orders – 1925
Elder's Orders – 1927
Received on Trial – 1956
Received into Full Connection – 1958
Deceased – 1988

HELENA LORRAINE CHAMPLIN was born July 7, 1896, in Roxbury, New York, the daughter of a Methodist minister. She graduated from Stamford High School at age sixteen with an advanced regent's diploma, as valedictorian of her class, and with a scholarship to Syracuse University, where she earned her bachelor of arts degree in 1917. She then enlisted in the Board of Home Missions and became a director of religious education, working in that capacity until 1924. As that was the first year that Methodist Episcopal women were able to be ordained, Helena applied for and was granted deacon's orders in 1925. She was ordained an elder in 1927 after doing graduate work at Boston University.[28] After ordination she returned to Boston to attend Boston University School of Theology, receiving her MA degree in 1927 and her master of divinity degree cum laude in 1930. In 1933 she completed all course requirements for a PhD but "never defended her (lost) doctoral papers on 'Why We Call God *Father*.'"[29]

Helena decided at that time to devote her life to pastoral ministry rather than teaching in the university setting. She remained a scholar and maintained her interest in education all of her life. She was a true pioneer for women in ordained ministry, but her high standards, professionalism, and devoted life remain an inspiration to the many persons of both genders she touched in her years of ministry.

Helena served the Board of Home Missions, and North Gainesville, Jasper, Avoca and Wallace, Springwater and Canadice, Konona, Wheeler and Towelsville, Andover, Dalton, Prattsburg and Pulteney, Wyoming and Covington, Gainesville, and East Otto charges with distinction. Larry R. Baird, who wrote her memoir, stated, "She also had a profound influence on this pastor's life, ministry, and spiritual discipline."[30]

Helena L. Champlin died November 17, 1988, at age ninety-two. She "is the only Western New York clergywoman to 'make' Conference Patriarch. Not until the next year was the official list adjusted to consist of 'Conference Patriarchs and Matriarchs.'"[31]

Ruth Marion Ellis

Northern New Jersey Conference (Northeastern Jurisdiction)
June 10, 1956

Ordained Deacon – 1954
Received on Trial – 1956
Ordained Elder – 1956
Received into Full Connection – 1958
Retired – 1975
Deceased – 1994

RUTH MARION ELLIS was born November 22, 1909. Ruth was a pioneer in the Northern New Jersey Conference, serving the Waterloo Church as a supply pastor even before her ordination, and then later as an elder. Port Morris was added to her circuit in 1957, and she served the Barryville and Eldred churches from 1963 until her disability leave in 1974. She retired in 1975 and lived her final years at Methodist Manor in Branchville, New Jersey. Ruth died April 15, 1994, at age eighty-four.[32]

Mary MacNicholl

Minnesota Conference (North Central Jurisdiction)
June 10, 1956

Ordained Deacon – 1950
Ordained Elder – 1952
Received on Trial – 1956
Received into Full Connection – 1958
Retired – 1972
Deceased – 1979

MARY MACNICHOLL was born April 21, 1915, in Merchantville, New Jersey. "Four of my father's uncles, all MacNicholls, were members of the New York East Conference of the Methodist Episcopal Church. I cannot tell the day when I decided to be a minister. I went into the first grade in 1921 determined to preach. I intentionally did nothing to hinder that dream and tried to do everything I thought would make me become one."[33]

After attending college to get a degree in education, Mary decided that it was time to pursue her dream of church work. She applied to the Woman's Home Missionary Society (WHMS) for service. After losing one job that was offered to her due to the resistance of her family, she finally accepted a job as a teacher of Intermediate Grades in the Navajo Methodist Mission School in Farmington, New Mexico–still waiting for an appointment from the WHMS. She was commissioned as a Home Missionary on June 16, 1943, and was sent to the Boylan Haven School in Jacksonville, Fla. After three years Mary applied for a sabbatical leave and enrolled in Drew Theological School in New Jersey. Following graduation in 1949, she applied to five annual conferences and accepted an appointment in southern Minnesota, where she served for the remainder of her ministry.

She was ordained as a deacon in 1950 and elder in 1952 and was finally received on trial in 1956 and into full connection in 1958. Mary served a number of years in cooperative ministry with other pastors and enjoyed that ministry. She was also active throughout her ministry, serving on many conference agencies and working with community organizations. She was the first woman to serve on the Minnesota Board of Ministry.[34]

"From 1949 to 1971, when she went on sabbatical leave, the Rev. Miss MacNicholl served rural charges in the Minnesota Conference out of a real dedication to rural ministry. Mary was an organizer and here in the Minnesota Conference her insight and abilities were well known and well thought of by her parishioners, the people in the communities she served, the districts and the conference.

"In 1971 she went on Sabbatical to care for her mother who had acted as Mary's housekeeper and home organizer.... Mary took her mother to Philadelphia, but even there used her organizational abilities."[35]

Mary completed her autobiography with these words: "Life has been good. God has been gracious and my lines have always fallen in pleasant places. Glory be to His name!"[36] Mary MacNicholl died February 14, 1979, at age sixty-three with these words for her partners in ministry, "Renew your ordination vows."[37]

Nancy J. Nichols

Iowa-Des Moines Conference (North Central Jurisdiction)
June 10, 1956

Ordained Deacon, Newark Methodist – 1954
Received on Trial – 1956
Received into Full Connection – 1958
Ordained Elder – 1958
Retired – 1993
Deceased – 1999

NANCY JOYCE NICHOLS was born February 26, 1931, in Oak Park, Illinois. Nancy begins her autobiography entitled *The Church Is Love* with these words: "I want…I need…to confess to a love affair that has been my life for 50 years now. It began when I was 17 years old, a freshman in college. That was when a Methodist pastor helped me to discover the Church. Since then, the Church–God and His people–have occupied my heart and mind and strength."

While an undergraduate at a teachers' college in central Wisconsin, Nancy went to live with the local Methodist minister and his wife, receiving room and board in exchange for child care. "This was the decision that changed my life, for Jans and Doris van der Graaf were unlike any church people I had ever known before." Jans led Nancy into the Methodist ministry. After graduating from Iowa Wesleyan College in 1953, she attended Drew University School of Theology as one of the few women in her class. She was ordained as a local deacon in the Newark Conference in 1954 and graduated from Drew University in 1956. That year Nancy was received into the Iowa-Des Moines Conference as the only woman.

> For quite a number of years–was it about twelve?–I was the only woman who was a full ministerial member of Conference. This led to a moment of great confusion for Bishop Corson in 1960, when he substituted for Bishop Ensley. The clergy had gathered for executive session, to vote on ministerial relationships, etc. Bishop Corson looked over the room, gavelled us to silence, and announced in a stern voice, "Anyone who is not a full ministerial member of this Conference is asked to leave, NOW." The brethren and I looked over the crowd, not able to glimpse anyone who didn't belong there. Bishop Corson: "Will one of the ushers please take care of this situation?" Dr. Shupe, who was serving as secretary, looked at the bishop questioningly; Bishop Corson pointed at the interloper: me! He was quickly set straight by Dr. Shupe. Gee, I was the cause of a bishop winding up with a red face!

Later she writes, "'Female preachers' are now commonplace. They have become district superintendents and even bishops…. How come I never ran into 'sexism'? Was it because I was the first and only one for a number of years–or was it because I genuinely loved and respected the brethren who accepted me? I like to think our mutual fellowship and dedication simply made any differences irrelevant."

When Nancy retired in 1993 her parishioners (current and former) gave her a rousing retirement party. "I've kept all the cards I received that day. Now I take them out every once in a while and remember the people who've been a part of my life. *For all these years we shared a faith in the love of God by sharing His love with each other.* I have no regrets, just a lot of thankfulness, that back in the late '40s God had led me to the van der Graafs."

Nancy Nichols died April 29, 1999, at age sixty-eight.[38]

Marion Kline

Detroit Conference (North Central Jurisdiction)
June 16, 1956

Deacon's Orders – 1948
Elder's Orders – 1950
Received on Trial – 1956
Received into Full Connection – 1958
Retired – 1986

MARION KLINE was born April 27, 1911, in Seattle, Washington.

"My 'call' was to general Christian Service just before I graduated from the University of Washington in 1933. After two years of Seminary (the Berkeley Baptist Theological Seminary in Berkeley, California), I worked at various jobs for about ten years. Then I became the Youth Worker in a Methodist church in Wisconsin. I became a Methodist, and after about two years there the pastor persuaded me and the Bishop that I should take a church on my own. After encouragement from the people of the church, and also from Dr. Georgia Harkness, and time of personal prayer, I agreed.

"During my second year I went to a summer session at Garrett Biblical Institute to take a course in Rural Church Administration, and one in preaching. Both professors persuaded me to transfer my credits and work toward a B.D. degree (now Master's). That was a new idea to me. I graduated (with Distinction) in 1950. I was the only woman in the class, although not the first to receive the degree from Garrett. I was ordained that year as a 'Local Elder,' having been ordained a 'Local Deacon' two years previously.

"My first church (January 1945) was in a town of about 400, but serving a farm community of about 1400. The people were shocked at having a woman come, but as I worked with the youth they almost forgave me. After three and a half years I was moved to another small church on the same District. I met up with lots of discrimination from other pastors, a minority in my own churches, and others. At the same time there were pastors who were very supportive, people in my own churches and people in the community who accepted me, sometimes even with a hint of affection.

"When an assistant to the new chairman of the Conference Board of Education was needed, I was asked to take that position. During my second year (1955) the Bishop was aware that at the General Conference in 1956 the question of women becoming full members of Conference was a major issue, and he told me that he would not have a woman member in his Conference. Thus, I took a similar position with the Detroit Conference, working in the Upper Peninsula of Michigan. This Bishop, Bishop Reed, was proud to be one of the first to admit women, and I was admitted as a probationary member (as they said a man would have been) in 1956 and in 1958 I was admitted into full connection. The difference in 'clout' was amazing."

After serving churches in Michigan's Upper Peninsula, Marion went to the Philippines for fifteen years, retiring to Olympia, Washington, where she eventually took a position on staff of the First United Methodist Church of Olympia, finally retiring at age seventy-five. "Through all of this I had no idea of being 'courageous,' I simply thought I was doing what God wanted me to do at that particular time. Nor did I think I was preparing the way for others, I was just concerned about serving God and the Church in the best way I could."

Marion currently lives in Des Moines, Washington, and, at age 94, continues to be active in her church and her community.

Frances W. Bigelow

Colorado Conference (Western Jurisdiction)
June 17, 1956

Received on Trial – 1956
Ordained Deacon – 1956
Received into Full Connection – 1958
Ordained Elder – 1958
Retired, Rocky Mountain Conference – 1979
Deceased – 1999

FRANCES W. BIGELOW was born March 15, 1913, in Denver, Colorado. She received a bachelor of arts degree from the University of Denver, a master of theology degree from Iliff School of Theology, and a master of arts degree from Columbia University.

Frances was admitted into probationary membership and ordained a deacon in the Colorado Conference in 1956, and admitted into full connection in 1958 as well as being ordained as an elder that same year. She served as assistant at First Methodist Church in Boulder; pastor of Calhan-Edison-Leader; Messiah MC at Pueblo, Rye Home MC; associate at Emmanuel in Denver; pastor of Faith in Cheyenne, Wyoming; associate at First United Methodist Church in Fort Collins, Colorado; and pastor of Pine Bluffs and Hillsdale, Wyoming. She retired in 1979. Though she could be both gruff and empathetic, she always presented herself as an authentic person. Frances died October 4, 1999, at age eighty-six.[39]

Margaret Scheve

Colorado Conference (Western Jurisdiction)
June 17, 1956

Ordained Deacon – 1950
Ordained Elder – 1952
Received on Trial – 1956
Received into Full Connection – 1958
Retired, Rocky Mountain Conference – 1981
Deceased – 2001

MARGARET SCHEVE was born February 27, 1907, in Palisade, Colorado. She graduated from West Denver High School in 1925 as the salutatorian. She then graduated from Colorado State Agricultural Mining College in 1929 with a degree in home economics and teaching. In 1934 Margaret graduated from Iliff School of Theology. She worked at First Methodist Church, Fort Collins, Colorado, as secretary and director of Religious Education and director of the Wesley Foundation at the college. She served at Warren UMC in Denver and then Grant Avenue Methodist Church in Denver for five years. She served as secretary to the bishop from 1951 to 1973. She was then appointed as pastor at Merritt Memorial UMC in Denver and retired in 1981.

Margaret stated that her strongest gifts for ministry were preaching, worship, and pastoral care. She said that she never felt discriminated against as minister, and did not like the term *clergyperson* because she believed that *clergyman* was a generic term. In an interview in 1983 she said that she believed that women would conquer sooner rather than later. Margaret died June 14, 2001, at age ninety-four.[40]

Jessie Orpha Todd

California-Nevada Conference (Western Jurisdiction)
June 17, 1956

Ordained Deacon – 1932
Ordained Elder – 1934
Received on Trial – 1956
Received into Full Connection – 1958
Retired – 1967
Deceased – 1975

JESSIE ORPHA TODD was born September 23, 1898, in Pontiac, Michigan. She was well known and greatly respected throughout the Methodist conference for her leadership in the area of children's work. After she graduated from the University of Oregon, she taught high school for several years. It was at that time that she felt the call to prepare for full-time Christian service and entered Boston University School of Theology with a major in religious education, graduating in 1930.[41]

Her first appointment was to the West Yolo Parish (Guinda) in 1933. From there she went to Fallon, Nevada, in 1936, serving until 1943. In 1944 California State law made it possible for children to be involved in "released time" Christian education and Jessie began to work as a weekday teacher for the Sacramento Council of Churches, and later for the San Mateo County Council. She became executive director for the San Mateo County Council of Churches in 1951. She left that position in 1953 to become director of Children's Work for the Conference Board of Education, a title later renamed (in 1959) to Conference Program Counselor. After retiring from that position in 1967, she then became director of Christian Education at Temple UMC in San Francisco. The onset of Parkinson's disease, however, finally forced her to give up her work and move to a retirement home.

"Jessie was a strong leader in the area of religious growth of children, conducting workshops and training conferences and providing resources for children's workers in local churches. She devoted a great deal of time to the Conference camping program for children and was lovingly known as 'Aunt Jessie' to numerous boys and girls. Children's work in the Conference reached its high point during her years of service."[42]

Jessie was exceedingly sensitive to the needs of others, supported progressive social movements, and energetically devoted herself to all conference causes. She had a hearty laugh, sang joyously, and always had a twinkle of awareness in her eye. Her Christian affirmations were amazingly simple and honest and at the same time they were intellectually disciplined, broadly social, and vibrantly alive.

Jessie Todd died March 8, 1975, at age seventy-eight.[43]

Mary Louise Long

California-Nevada Conference (Western Jurisdiction)
June 17, 1956

Ordained Deacon – 1951
Ordained Elder – 1953
Received on Trial – 1956
Received into Full Connection – 1958
Retired – 1977
Deceased – 1994

MARY LOUISE LONG (known as "Louise") was born February 14, 1908, in Selma, Alabama, in a Methodist parsonage. Of the first three women to be voted into conference membership, Louise Long was probably unique. Unlike the other two, she sought to fulfill her vocational call by the route of hospital chaplaincy. Her first church-related position was that of director of the Wesley Foundation at Oklahoma A & M University. From there she enrolled at Garrett Biblical Institute and majored in pastoral care and psychology. At Elgin State Hospital, in Illinois, she completed the course in clinical pastoral education and was "endorsed by the American Congress of Clinical Pastoral Education and was the first woman chaplain trained by the A.C.P.E. [Association of Clinical Pastoral Education]."[44]

After serving as the chaplain-supervisor at the state mental hospital in Little Rock, Arkansas, Louise went to California and, as a local pastor, served as chaplain at state hospitals in Modesto, Auburn (DeWitt State Hospital), and Atascadero. Nearing retirement age, she requested and received an appointment to the Mendocino Coast Parish, and served the churches at Elk, Fort Bragg, and Point Arena, before retiring in 1977.

Louise was hearty, outspoken, opinionated, and positive in her convictions. She was Freudian in her orientation and had little regard for other schools of psychology and counseling. Her ministry was effective, and she described it vividly in her book *Door of Hope*. She planned to write an autobiography to be entitled *Ten Cats and a Chicken* since Louise raised purebred Persian cats as a hobby and considered herself to be the "chicken." Unfortunately, Louise contracted Alzheimer's disease before the book could be written.

A positive testimony to her ministry was provided by one of the patients with whom she had worked as pastoral counselor and therapist at Modesto State Hospital. She had literally saved his life by helping him recover his mental and emotional health. He subsequently became the owner of a very successful business. During the last few years of Louise's life, when she needed around-the-clock care, he provided the finances to make this care possible for her. It was a small price to pay, he said, for all that Chaplain Long had done for him.

Mary Louise Long died April 24, 1994, at age eighty-six.[45]

Eva Banton Maxwell

California-Nevada Conference (Western Jurisdiction)
June 17, 1956

Received on Trial – 1956
Ordained Deacon – 1956
Received into Full Connection – 1958
Ordained Elder – 1958
Retired – 1964
Deceased – 1974

EVA BANTON MAXWELL was born July 26, 1896, in Canada. Like many other women who looked forward to a career in full-time Christian service, Eva Maxwell felt her calling to be that of a professional Christian educator.[46] After her husband, George, died, when Eva was fifty-one, she earned her theological degree at Pacific School of Religion. She worked primarily in Christian education, serving at the Church of the Crossroads in Honolulu; First Church, Sacramento; First Church, Palo Alto; and First Church, Oakland. It was her great joy to have worked collegially with two men who became bishops of the church, A. Raymond Grant and R. Marvin Stuart.

Eva like to see things grow–plants, churches, and people. Whatever she touched she nurtured with gentleness, love, and patience. She was strong, dignified, and courageous, daring to live *future* goods in difficult *presents*. Life brought to her a liberal share of burdens, but her faith in God enabled her to stand with a glad and gracious heart. "Oh," she would say, "life is good. God is very good!"[47]

Eva Banton Maxwell died November 7, 1974, at age seventy-eight.

 *Ellen Rose*

Montana Conference (Western Jurisdiction)
June 22, 1956

Ordained Deacon – 1943
Ordained Elder – 1947
Received on Trial – 1956
Received into Full Connection – 1958
Retired – 1971
Deceased – 1983

ELLEN HUNTINGTON ROSE was born in 1906 in Nehawka, Nebraska. In a state that highly values its pioneering heritage and spirit, Ellen Rose spent the years of her ministry breaking new trails in the attitudes of fellow Methodists toward women in ministry. That women not only had a right to the ordained ministry but also could be highly effective therein was proved in the churches she served across the conference.

Part of Ellen's success in ministry lay in her unswerving dedication to the ideals and standards she believed in. It was always more important for Ellen to "stand up and be counted" than to remain on the fence and be safe. A tireless fighter for social justice, Ellen believed that the validity of any program whether in church or government must be "what happens to people because of it."

As well as being serious about her ministry, Ellen had a dry and penetrating wit that often helped ease tensions during times of stress. At what was to be her last annual conference session (1983), Ellen was in the thick of things, as usual. During the debate on sexual preference as related to United Methodist clergy, Ellen stood to say that she "was and had always been a heterosexual…non practicing."

Beginning her ministry in 1936 soon after graduating from Nebraska Wesleyan College, Ellen was appointed to Winifred, Montana. These were the years of the Great Depression, and pastors were often paid in food items. Many a farm family paid its Sunday offering in chickens, since chickens could feed satisfactorily on the hordes of grasshoppers that infested the land at that time.

Later, soon after her return to Montana from three years at Boston University School of Theology, Ellen emerged as a real heroine in the town of Belt. A disastrous flood struck the community in 1954 and many residents were awakened in the middle of the night by Ellen in time to escape to higher ground.

In 1957, after being the first woman to be admitted on trial in the Montana Conference, she became the first woman admitted to the Order of Caleb, Montana's way of honoring ministers who have served twenty years or more in the conference.[48]

Jack Severns states,

> There is so much to say about this rich and unique person, it is hard to know where to stop. I will remember her for many things, especially during our three years of close professional relationship in Kalispell. But what stands out is her special touch with children, my own in particular. My daughters and son will remember their much loved "Aunt Rose" and I am grateful for her touch upon them during their growing years.
>
> Now Ellen herself has reached the higher ground far from the "flood of mortal ills prevailing." And we gently let her go to the One who knows and loves each of us better than we shall ever know ourselves.[49]

Ellen Rose died in 1983 at age seventy-seven.

Marie R. Tschappat

Ohio/East Ohio (North Central Jurisdiction)
June 23, 1956

Ordained Deacon – 1943
Ordained Elder – 1945
Received on Trial – 1956
Received into Full Connection – 1958
Retired – 1977
Deceased – 2000

MARIE R. TSCHAPPAT was born January 29, 1912, in Beallsville, Ohio, the heart of the original Swiss settlements of Ohio. When Marie was twelve years old, her family settled in Utica, Ohio.

"Soon after getting settled in Utica, I began to attend the Utica Methodist Church. In my early teens, I dedicated myself to God and the Church, and when I was seventeen, I felt the call to the Ministry. The 'Call' did not come as an 'explosive revelation,' but as a compelling conviction, and with it, a satisfying assurance that this is what God wanted me to do with my life. From that day to this, I have never had any reason to doubt it nor regret my decision to answer the call."[50]

Marie was given a license to preach in 1932, at age twenty, and was called to serve the South Vernon Community Church of Mt. Vernon, Ohio. "It was at this Church that I met Miss Iada Burris. She was a young lady with unusual musical ability and talent and so when I resigned the Pastorate, I asked her to accompany me in my Methodist work. Thus, a long relationship began. For over fifty years, she was my able and efficient co-worker for both Church and Parsonage life. Her capabilities and talents were an invaluable asset to my Ministry."

Marie then began to attend school—first at Marietta College and then at Oberlin Graduate School of Theology, while still serving churches full time.

> When I was working hard serving churches and doing College and Seminary work, I had no thought that some day I would be a full member of an Annual Conference, but when it happened, I was honored to be the *first* woman in the State of Ohio to be admitted into full membership of the Methodist Church–now the United Methodist Church....
>
> I loved the Preaching and the Worship Services. I am convinced that no one should be in the ministry unless they consider this function a very important part of the Ministry.... I liked calling on the Sick and conducting Funerals. It was not that I wanted people to be ill or to die, but I felt that much good could be done in a time of a person's physical stress, or at a time of sorrow.... I enjoyed the Administrative work of the Church and was always interested in the care and upkeep of the Church Property.... I loved the Congregations which had a lively sense of humor, who could laugh and have fun together....
>
> But, despite all the problems of Churches and Church people, I loved the ministry and the people of my Churches.... If I had my life to live over, I would want to be a Minister. I am grateful for the encouragement I received from the faithful Ministers of my home Church–Utica, and for the respect of my Colleagues and the "jury of my Peers." I hope the Story of "My Life in the Ministry" can be summed up in the words of Romans 10 (15-18)–"How beautiful are the feet of those that preach the good news"....As a Lady Minister, I would like to paraphrase [verse 18]: "*HER VOICE* has gone out to all the earth, and *HER WORDS* to the ends of the world!"

Marie R. Tschappat died November 24, 2000, at age eighty-eight.

Jane Ann Stoneburner Moore

Northeast Ohio/Ohio (North Central Jurisdiction)
June 23, 1956

Received on Trial – 1956
Ordained Deacon – 1956
Received into Full Connection – 1958
Ordained Elder – 1959
Retired – 2001 (from the United Church of Christ)

JANE ANN STONEBURNER MOORE was born in Zanesville, Ohio, on March 11, 1931.

"Growing up in an Ohio Methodist parsonage during the Depression and war, I heard my father, Charles William Stoneburner, preach; I played church with my brothers, Tony and John later ordained; I listened to my mother, Lois, talk about Bonhoeffer, Buber, Niebuhr, Tillich; I met missionaries, Japanese-American detainees, peace activists, black clergy, and, after studying at Ohio Wesleyan University, graduated from Yale Divinity School where I struggled with the big picture of evil–the most prominent Christian nation in Europe had allowed Nazism and the Holocaust to take place even as the USA winked at lynching and segregation. After the war, in the fifties, during that 'creative moment' when the mission of the church was expanding in all directions, I heard Reverend Harvey Cox urge young Ohio Methodists to become experts in all fields and use their 'know how' for the good of church and society. I began to explore African studies, sociology, politics, and history."[51]

Jane Ann has had a varied ministry over the past forty-nine years. She served as the director of Religious Education for the Lake Region Larger Parish in Barton, Vermont, and for Maple Grove Methodist Church in Columbus, Ohio. After receiving her MA and PhD degrees from the African Studies Program at Boston University, she taught as assistant professor in the African Studies program at Howard University. During the time she was studying at Boston University, she married William Moore, a pastor in the United Church of Christ and eventually transferred her membership to the United Church of Christ.

In 1971, she edited *Cry Sorrow, Cry Joy–Selections from Contemporary African Writers*. She served as a county council-woman for Montgomery County, Maryland, from 1974 through 1978 and established Martin Luther King Jr. Day (for the county). From 1979 until her retirement in 2001, Jane served as copastor with her husband at Irvine, California; Benton Harbor, Michigan; and DeKalb, Illinois.

Currently, Jane Ann and her husband, William, are codirectors of the Lovejoy Society and have recently (2004) edited *His Brother's Blood: Speeches and Writings, 1838–64 by Owen Lovejoy*, "about a powerful minister, antislavery leader, Underground Railroad conductor, Congressman, friend of Frederick Douglass and Abraham Lincoln, who proclaimed, 'Such a radical was Christ. He was a Negro equality man, for his divine precepts apply to all.'"

Of her ministry, Jane Ann said, "The connector that gives meaning to my life is applying theology and policy to enable greater equality among all God's people, with the hope of joining the ever-flowing stream bringing God's kingdom from heaven to earth."

Jane Ann Stoneburner Moore retired in 2001 from the United Church of Christ.

Sallie A. Crenshaw

East Tennessee Conference (Central Jurisdiction)
June 30, 1956

Ordained Deacon – 1932
Ordained Elder – 1936
Received on Trial – 1956
Received into Full Connection – 1958
Retired, Holston Conference – 1971
Deceased – 1986

SALLIE ALFORD CRENSHAW was born in 1900 in LaGrange, Georgia. She received her education in the Chattanooga public schools, Tennessee A&I State College, Tennessee Wesleyan College, and the University of Nebraska. Sallie joined the Wiley Methodist Church and began her pastoral ministry in 1931 as the lay pastor of the East Chattanooga and Tyner churches. She was ordained deacon in 1932 and elder in 1936, making her (along with Laura J. Lange) one of the first two women to be ordained as local elders in the Central Jurisdiction.[52]

In 1958, when she and Nora E. Young were received into full connection in the East Tennessee Conference, they became not only the first women to be received into full connection in the Central Jurisdiction but also the first two women received into full connection in the Holston Conference and the entire Southeastern Jurisdiction as well.

Sallie served as a missionary to the coalfields of Virginia and also served churches in Bakewell (Hamilton County, Tennessee); Elizabethtown, Tennessee; and Glade Spring and Wytheville, Virginia. She served as Church and Community Worker in the Bluefield District, and as Conference Director of Youth Work for three years.

Many of the events in the amazing life of the Reverend Sallie Crenshaw, in her own words, have been chronicled in *Trail of Mission: Falling Leaves*, by the Reverend Reid S. Wilson, published in 1985 by the Commission on Archives and History of the Holston Conference. Sallie Crenshaw is best known for her work in the St. Elmo Mission in south Chattanooga, which she served for thirty-four years. She returned there in 1947 at the request of the National Board of Missions and began with services held for sixty-five children and five adults in a beer joint. She established the Good Shepherd Fold in a house with a dirt floor. During all these years she preached and ministered in every way to all sorts of people, both black and white, but especially among black children. In 1983 the name of the center was changed to the Sallie Crenshaw Good Shepherd Fold, and in 1985 the governing board of the United Methodist Neighborhood Centers merged the programs of the Sallie Crenshaw Good Shepherd Fold and the Bethlehem Center, and renamed it the Sallie Crenshaw-Bethlehem Center.

Sallie retired in 1971 as a member of the Holston Conference and died December 12, 1986, at age eighty-six.

Nora E. Young

East Tennessee Conference (Central Jurisdiction)
June 30, 1956

Ordained Deacon – 1950
Ordained Elder – 1952
Received on Trial – 1956
Received into Full Connection – 1958
Discontinued – 1964

NORA E. YOUNG, like Sallie Crenshaw, served several years as a lay pastor in the East Tennessee Conference of the MC when women were not permitted to become full conference members. Her first appointment was in 1949, when she became the pastor of three churches in the West Virginia section of the conference. When she and Sallie Crenshaw were received into full connection in the East Tennessee Conference in 1958, they became the first women in the Central Jurisdiction, in the Holston Conference, and in all of the Southeastern Jurisdiction to be received into full connection.

All of Nora's pastoral appointments were in West Virginia–the last one at St. Luke Methodist Church in War, West Virginia, until 1961.[53] Little more is known of Nora Young as her ministry was discontinued in 1964.

Antonia Wladar

Hungary Conference/Central Conference of Central and Southern Europe
August 1956

Received on Trial – 1956
Ordained Deacon – 1956
Received into Full Connection – 1958
Ordained Elder – see narrative below
Deceased – 1992

ANTONIA WLADAR was born in Budapest, Hungary, on December 17, 1928, to a Calvinist mother and a Lutheran father. When her father became ill with tuberculosis, the family moved to the countryside and managed a poultry farm. After Antonia's father died in 1937 and her mother was taken to a sanatorium, the nine-year-old Antonia was left with responsibility for her younger sister and for managing and liquidating the farm by herself.

Antonia studied in a Calvinist school and then attended a German Lutheran boarding school. Her outstanding talent for languages appeared early and she was asked to work abroad as a radio announcer; however, Antonia chose to stay in Hungary. During World War II, when Antonia was only sixteen years old, there was a bomb attack on the office where she was working with two other people. One person was killed and the other one was left blind. Antonia was covered in the ruins of the building and lost her teeth and broke her jaw.

After the war, Antonia attended the youth group in the Central Lutheran Church in Budapest and there heard about an elderly pastor who preached the real gospel on the neighboring street in the Methodist chapel. With seven others, she attended the chapel and was converted. She rejected a promising career and started to serve God. In 1947 she started her ministry in the congregation and soon became the secretary in the office of the superintendent, representing the superintendent in negotiations with the new Communist regime. Her knowledge of languages was of great assistance in The Methodist Church, and during that time she began to study theology at the Reformed Theological Academy.

In 1956, the year that women were finally granted the right to conference membership, the World Council of Churches met in Hungary. It was the first time that a Methodist bishop had been allowed to travel to Hungary since the end of World War II. Antonia was received on trial and ordained a deacon that year, along with three men, becoming the first woman not only in Hungary but also in all of Europe to be ordained and received into conference membership. She was also the first woman in all of the Central Conferences to be received into conference membership. Records in the years following 1956 are sketchy and Methodist bishops were not allowed to travel to Hungary in their official capacity, only as private guests. It appears, however, that Antonia was received into full membership in 1958 but was never ordained as an elder due to the inability of the bishops to be present at annual conferences.

Antonia was the leader of several groups working with women in Hungary and participated in several international women's conferences. She was a member of the World Federation of Methodist Women, and was a member of the Executive Committee of Central Conferences for more than twenty years. In addition, she taught at the Theological Seminary of Free Churches in Hungary. "She was an intelligent, educated and active pastor…ready in every moment to serve the weak, the old, the men and women in need. She was ready to fight for justice in every moment. But she was a kind person full of humour. Her life was an example of faithful Christian life."

Antonia Wladar died March 1, 1992, at age sixty-three.[54]

Women in The Methodist Protestant Church Still Serving in 1956

As noted in chapter 1, a small number of Methodist Protestant women had been ordained as elders in full connection prior to the unification of The Methodist Protestant Church (MPC), The Methodist Episcopal Church (the MEC), and The Methodist Episcopal Church, South (MECS) in 1939 to form The Methodist Church (MC). Despite the fact that the MEC had granted women only limited rights as local deacons and elders and the MECS had never even granted women the right to have a license to preach, the agreement in the unification negotiations was that no one—male or female—would lose his or her clergy rights in the reunification. Therefore, the MC had no choice but to recognize and appoint these Methodist Protestant women. Three of these women have been identified as having full clergy rights and serving churches in 1956 and beyond, along with those women who came into conference membership in 1956 and 1958. Their stories deserve to be told here as well.

Louisiana Conference (Southeastern Jurisdiction)

Ordained Elder in Full Connection – 1939
Deceased – 1985

LEA JOYNER was born June 17, 1917, in Natchez, Mississippi, though she spent her life in Louisiana. From the time she was five years old, when she preached to her dolls and to the birds, Lea had wanted to preach. But it was after a conversion experience when she was fifteen years old that she became serious about her religion.[55]

"In 1938 [Lea] was a twenty-one-year-old college senior. Convinced that she had been called to preach, she had done what she could to prepare herself for the task. She had attended both a denominational junior college and senior college, taking as many Bible and religious courses as were consistent with her teacher-training major."[56] Lea was ordained an elder on New Year's day 1939, the year that the three branches of Methodist would merge.

> I'll never forget that day back in 1939 when I participated in the uniting conference. When the three branches of Methodism came together at that great conference, I was the only ordained woman among 600 men. It was awe inspiring, let me tell you. Some of them glared at me, many of them ignored me, and only a few welcomed me into the ranks of the ordained ministry. But I stood up to that challenge. I met it straight on and never flinched, no matter what people said or did. Somehow I believe that was a testing time, preparing me for this, the greatest challenge of my life.[57]

This challenge was her third appointment in the Louisiana Conference—"to found a mission church in the south side of Monroe or leave the ministry altogether."[58] The D.S. made the offer and showed her the site, but was not very encouraging.

"No church will have you, Lea," he had said, "and all my efforts to get you that position as assistant in New Orleans came to nothing. This is it. This vacant lot with no people, no building and almost no money is all there is to offer. If you want to try it, the bishop is willing to make the appointment and to authorize half of the usual $10,000.00 for your use in starting up. I couldn't get you any more than $5,000.00 because neither the bishop nor anybody else in the conference believes that you can make a success of starting this new church....

"Lea, you don't have any money, you don't have any leadership and you don't know what you're doing."[59]

Despite this amazingly negative proposal, after a great deal of prayer, Lea felt that God was calling her to accept this appointment. Not only did she succeed, she established a church named Southside and grew it to more than 2,250 members. For a time before her death, it was the largest Methodist church in the world to be pastored by a woman.[60]

For many years Lea was the only female member of the Louisiana Conference, but she would have one good friend and colleague, Fern Cook, who was the sole female member of the Arkansas Conference (see below). Lea and Fern met when they attended the Methodist Protestant school at Tehuacana, Texas. Fern says, "We became very close friends and often prayed together, shared together and sometimes cried together. That friendship continued across the years until eighteen months ago when she was murdered in her churchyard in Monroe, [Louisiana], by a young man she was trying to help with a problem. The inspiration will always be a blessing to me."[61]

Indeed, Lea came to be loved and respected not only in the churches she served but also throughout her conference and beyond. Her death, on March 12, 1985, at age sixty-seven, was a great tragedy and a loss to many people. Harry Hale has memorialized Lea and her ministry in the story of her life, *Standing in the Gap*.

Little Rock Conference (Southeastern Jurisdiction)

Probationary Membership, Louisiana Conference, Methodist Protestant Church – 1933
Ordained Elder, Louisiana Conference, Methodist Protestant Church – 1939
Retired – 1980
Deceased – 1994

FERN COOK was born March 27, 1910, in Emmet, Arkansas.

> I had known since I was a young child that God had something special for me to do.... My call to the ministry came soon after I finished high school but it wasn't as I expected. I expected to choose my own way that I would serve him.... One cold and rainy Sunday afternoon in October...I was sitting at a little table reading sermons by the late Dwight I. Moody, when God spoke to me very clearly and told me he wanted me to dedicate my life to spreading the Good News to everybody.... I stopped

reading and laid my head on the table and began to argue with God, "Now Lord, I plan to give my life in service for you but not by preaching." I had met a few lady preachers and heard them preach and they were wonderful in their preaching but I thought that men should do the preaching. I got up and went back to the bedroom and fell across the cold bed and asked God to take the call away from me. He didn't give up.[62]

One Sunday morning when she and her brother and sister were singing at a revival near Texarkana, the visiting minister approached Fern and asked her to preach at the morning service. "My heart leaped for joy and I gladly accepted the invitation.... Irene, Brady, and I spent most of the time in prayer until time for the service. I prayed like this, 'Lord if you really want me to preach let some one come to the altar and surrender his life to Christ or make a rededication of his/her life at the close of the service'.... Five young people came to the altar."[63] She continued to pursue her calling and was ordained in the Louisiana Conference of the MPC on May 10, 1939, the year that the MC was formed.

> This Uniting Conference changed my whole life. The state line became the conference boundary line which placed me in the Little Rock Conference. I was soon to learn that women had no place of leadership in the new church. I was [dis]inherited and not invited nor really wanted in this new church. I think that one of my district superintendents said it right well. We were talking about appointments one day and he said in a very harsh tone, "Why don't you get out, we don't like you anyway." He readily changed the statement, "We like you but we don't like what you are doing."
>
> Appointment time was always the most depressing time. There were young men who started in the ministry at the same time that I did. They went on to serve as District Superintendents or bishops while I was given the least appointments.[64]

Fern persisted, however, as the only woman in full connection until 1964 when Everne Hunter was received into full connection. She retired in 1980 after serving for forty years. "If [Fern] had one unfulfilled dream, it was to serve a station church (a single-church charge). 'I really wanted a station church,' she said. But her prayer was always, 'Lord, I'm in your hands. You can do what you want with me.'"[65]

She concluded, "In every church where I was appointed there were rewarding experiences, which gave me strength and hope which were always greater than the disappointments. I believe that God is in everything and he always lifts us up when we fall down."[66]

Fern Cook died May 26, 1994, at age eighty-four.

Harriette M. Gitterman

Central Illinois Conference (North Central Jurisdiction)

Received on Trial, Illinois Conference, MPC – 1933
Ordained Elder and Received into Full Connection
Illinois Conference, MPC – 1935
Retired – 1961
Deceased – 1982

HARRIETTE M. GITTERMAN was born November 1, 1895, in Illinois. "I had this call when I was young.... I would say in my early teens. I wanted to be a schoolteacher, but God spoke to me and said this, 'I've got something better for you'....'Well, Lord, what is it?' He said, 'I want to make a minister of you...preach the gospel.' I said, 'Lord, I will do whatever you want me to do'.... I went to Moody [Bible Institute] in 1923 and later graduated from there, I think in 1925."[67]

Harriette was received on probation in the Illinois Methodist Protestant Conference in 1933 and was sent to the Mt. Pleasant Church. "The conference had deserted the church but they sent me out there. They said, 'Build up the church.' Well, other sects had been out there and held some meetings and said, 'You leave this church and come into Canton.' But we[68] went out there and we said, 'You stick to your church.' So they did and that church is still going east of Canton."[69]

Harriette sometimes was offered a circuit that other pastors had refused. "Rev. Landers was out at South Park. They didn't want him any longer for some reason or other, so they offered him Canton Circuit, that's Banner, Breeds, and Monterey, and Maples Mills...Bryant...and Bethel.... They offered him that, and he said, 'You insult me by offering me that.' So they called me in and offered it to me. And I was so happy, I couldn't eat any supper." [Interviewer:] "You weren't insulted?" [Gitterman:] "No, I was happy. They paid $650 a year. Way back then, that meant a great deal of money."[70]

Harriette was serving the Canton Circuit at the time of the 1939 merger. "Well, you know at the merger somehow word got to the Methodist Protestants, because they would not take me in. Although I was ordained, they didn't believe in ordained women. But, my president, Frank Hanna said to me, 'Harriette, we are standing behind you. If they don't take you in, they won't get any of us.' At the merger, when we gathered around the altar, not a word was said."[71]

From there, Harriette went on to serve the Bryant Circuit, Smithfield Circuit, and Little York Circuit before she took a sabbatical leave in 1955. Then in 1956 she was sent to Norris, where she remained for more than twenty-five years, though she officially retired in 1961. "And when we went there, they were ready to close the church, and the bishop said to the district superintendent, 'Send her there if she will go.' I had taken a sabbatical year and I said, 'I will go anyplace.' So we went and we had three or four people the first Sunday, about that many the next Sunday. [A woman] came to me and [she] said, 'If you step on my toes, I won't be back.' I said, 'I preach the Word and if it hits your toes, I can't help it.' That woman is still coming, very prominent in the church. We have an average attendance of about 25 and that's about our membership."[72]

At the 1981 session of the Central Illinois Conference, a little more than a year before she died, Harriette was recognized for her many years of ministry as a clergywoman in the UMC.[73]

Harriette Gitterman died November 9, 1982, at age eighty-seven.

Notes

1. Jean Miller Schmidt, *Grace Sufficient: A History of Women in American Methodism 1760–1939* (Nashville: Abingdon, 1999), 346n10.
2. Georgia Harkness never did apply for conference membership, feeling that should be reserved for those in active parish ministry.
3. Information for this biography was taken from "Maud Keister Jensen Dies.... First Woman to Receive Full Clergy Rights in Methodist Church," *The Flyer* (General Commission on The Status and Role of Women) (Winter 1991): 3.
4. Grace E. Huck, *God's Amazing Grace: Stories from My Life* (Spearfish, South Dakota: Sand Creek Printing, 2005), 79.
5. Lewis H. Arends Jr., "'Pioneer' Woman Preacher Retires from Methodist Ministry," *Oregon Statesman Capital Journal* (Salem, OR), July 23, 1977.
6. The remaining information for this biography was taken from an interview by Alice Knotts, June 7, 1984, and an interview by Janice Barclay (n.d.). All information can be found in the Idaho Conference Archives at 5175 Howry Lane, Meridian, ID 83642-7043.
7. Information for this biography was taken from Emma Burrell's memoir, published in the 1989 Journal of the Baltimore Conference, UMC, 369, and from her service record and the service record of Florence Simms on file in the Baltimore-Washington Archives located at Lovely Lane Church, 2200 St. Paul St., Baltimore, MD 21218.
8. Information for this biography is taken from JoLorene Anderson's memoir, published in the 1997 Journal of the North Central New York Conference, UMC, 358, and from information taken from her pastoral profile (New York West Area) by the Reverend Gilbert Smith, chair of the North Central New York Conference Commission on Archives and History.
9. Information for this biography is taken from Gertrude Harris's memoir, published in the 1983 Journal of the Maine Annual Conference, UMC, 185.
10. Donna Ivery, "Interview with Rev. Alice T. Hart," n.d., 2.
11. Ibid., 3.
12. Ibid., 2, 4. The remainder of the information for this biography is taken from Alice Hart's memoir, written by Patricia J. Thompson, published in the 1992 Journal of the Maine Annual Conference, UMC, 236.
13. Information for this biography was taken from Esther Haskard's memoir, published in the 1986 Journal of the Maine Annual Conference, UMC, 191.
14. Margaret Henrichsen, *Seven Steeples* (Boston: Houghton Mifflin, 1953), 1.
15. Ibid., 3, 4.
16. Patricia A. Jewett [Thompson], *The History of Maine Methodism: Through the Women's Sphere* (Maine: Maine Annual Conference Commission on the Status and Role of Women, 1984), 38.
17. Paula Mojzes from Yugoslavia served as interim D.S. in Macedonia before she was even ordained as a deacon (see chapter 9, 192), and Gusta Robinette, an American woman serving in Sumatra, was appointed as a D.S. while she was serving as a missionary (see chapter 10, 208).
18. Margaret Henrichsen's memoir, written by Clarice Bowman, published in the 1976 Journal of the Maine Annual Conference, UMC, 139.
19. Feng-ming Chu, "The Ordination of the Reverend Miss Ellen Maria Studley," in *Chinese Student and Alumni Services-Midwest Area*, newsletter no. 19 (August 8, 1956): 5. A copy of this material may be found in the archives of the Indiana Conference, DePauw University Archives and Special Collections, Roy O. West Library, 400 S. College Ave., PO Box 37, Greencastle, IN 46135-0037.
20. Unless otherwise noted, information for this biography was taken from Ellen Studley's memoir, published in the 1990 Journal of the North Indiana Conference, UMC, 1756.
21. Roy Larson, "She's 'Cut Out to Be a Preacher,'" *Chicago Sun-Times*, January 11, 1975.
22. Ibid.
23. Myrtle Speer's memoir, published in the 1982 Journal of the Missouri West Annual Conference, UMC, 148.
24. Myrtle Saylor Speer's autobiography, *I Am a Pioneer Woman Minister*, 96, 103. A copy of this autobiography can be found in the Missouri Conference Archives, Central Methodist University, Fayette, MO 65248.
25. Ibid., 123. Since all of the other women received in 1956 were received on trial, it is likely that there was some agreement among the bishops that all women received into conference membership in 1956 would be received on trial.
26. Ibid., 124-25, 131-32.
27. Larson, "She's 'Cut Out to Be a Preacher.'"
28. Helena Champlin's memoir states that she was ordained a deacon in 1924 and an elder in 1926; according to research done by GCAH staff in the General Minutes of the MEC, however, Helena Champlin was not ordained a deacon until 1925 or an elder until 1927. Mabel Barker from Helena Champlin's conference was ordained a deacon in 1924 and an elder in 1926.
29. Duane W. Priset, *A History of The Western New York Conference: The United Methodist Church* (unabridged edition, n.d.), 10.
30. Unless otherwise noted, information for this biography is taken from Helena Champlin's memoir, written by Larry R. Baird, published in the 1989 Journal of the Western New York Conference, UMC, 340-41.
31. Priset, *A History of The Western New York Conference*, 10.
32. Information for this biography is taken from Ruth Ellis's memoir, published in the 1994 Journal of the Northern New Jersey Annual Conference, UMC, 255. The beginning of the memoir states that a more complete memoir will appear in the 1995 Journal, although none was published.
33. Autobiography of Mary MacNicholl in "The History and Ministerial Record of the Women Ministers of the Minnesota Annual Conference of The United Methodist Church 1856–1977," compiled and written by Elsie Hartman (Commission on Archives and History of the Minnesota Annual Conference, UMC, 1978), 55. A copy may be found in the Minnesota Conference Archives, Depository Room 400, 122 W. Franklin Ave., Minneapolis, MN 55404.
34. Ibid., 55-62.
35. Memoir for Mary MacNicholl, published in the 1979 Minnesota Annual Conference Journal, UMC, 266-67.
36. Autobiography of Mary MacNicholl, 65.
37. Memoir for Mary MacNicholl, 267.
38. Information for this biography is taken from Nancy J. Nichols's autobiography, *The Church Is Love* (unpublished manuscript, 1997), 1, 2, 16, 39, 41. A copy of this autobiography is available in the Iowa Conference Archives, Chadwick Library, Iowa Wesleyan University, 601 North Main Street, Mt. Pleasant, IA 52641.
39. Information for this biography was taken from Frances Bigelow's memoir, published in the 2000 Journal of the Rocky Mountain Conference, UMC, 323.
40. Information for this biography was taken from Margaret Scheve's memoir, published in the 2001 Journal of the Rocky Mountain Conference, UMC, 297.
41. Newell P. Knudson, *Adventure in Faith: The History of the California-*

Nevada Conference of The United Methodist Church 1948–1998 (West Sacramento: Commission on Archives and History, California-Nevada Annual Conference, UMC, 1999), 100.

42. Ibid., 101.

43. Unless otherwise noted, information for this biography was taken from Jessie Todd's memoir, written by Donald L. Kuhn, published in the 1975 Journal of the California-Nevada Conference, UMC, 257.

44. Dorothy Bartell, ed., *They Served for Love: The Story of 271 Women in Mission in the California-Nevada Conference of The United Methodist Church* (The Conference United Methodist Women and The Conference Commission on Archives and History, UMC, 1990), 102.

45. Unless otherwise noted, information for this biography is taken from Knudson, *Adventure in Faith*, 101-2.

46. Ibid., 101.

47. Unless otherwise noted, information for this biography is taken from Eva Maxwell's memoir, written by Donald J. Cunningham, published in the 1975 Journal of the California-Nevada Conference, UMC, 252.

48. George Harper, "Women Ministers in Montana Methodism" (two typewritten pages, 2002), 1.

49. Unless otherwise noted, the information for this biography is taken from Ellen Rose's memoir, written by Jack Severns, published in the 1984 Journal of the Yellowstone Annual Conference, UMC, 89.

50. The information for this biography was taken from Marie R. Tschappat's autobiographical statement, "My Life in the Ministry," written in 1995. A copy may be found in the Archives of Ohio Methodism, Beeghly Library, Ohio Wesleyan University, 43 Rowland Ave., Delaware, OH 43015.

51. Information for this biography is taken from a personal statement sent to Carol Hollinger, archivist at Ohio Wesleyan University and forwarded to the author.

52. Information for this biography is taken from Sallie Crenshaw's memoir, published in the 1987 Journal of the Holston Annual Conference, UMC, 228, and supplemented by research done by Roy Howard, president of the Holston United Methodist Historical Society. See also chapter 1, 26, for information on Laura J. Lange.

53. Information about this appointment is found in *The Women Came Early: A History of Women in the West Virginia Conference* (The Task Force on Women's History Project of the West Virginia Conference of The United Methodist Church, 1986), 153. The remainder of the information was provided by Roy Howard, president of the Holston United Methodist Historical Society.

54. Information for this biography was provided by the Reverend Patrick Streiff, e-mail to the author, October 22, 2004. Reverend Streiff is currently serving as Resident Bishop, Central Europe Episcopal Area.

55. Harry Hale Jr., *Standing in the Gap: The Life and Ministry of The Rev. Lea Joyner* (Lima, OH: Fairway, 1987), 33-34.

56. Ibid., 96.

57. Ibid., 139.

58. Ibid., 14.

59. Ibid., 15.

60. Ibid., 159, 109.

61. Fern Cook, "I Was Made a Minister," letter to Marcia Crossman, archivist, Arkansas Conference Archives (October 24, 1986), 2.

62. Ibid., 2.

63. Ibid.

64. Ibid., 3.

65. William Wilder, "A Call Answered," *Arkansas United Methodist* (March 6, 1992): 12.

66. Cook, "I Was Made a Minister," 3.

67. "Interview with Rev. Harriette M. Gitterman, September 1978, at her home, 335 South Fifth Street, Canton, Illinois, 1." No name is given for the interviewer; a copy may be found in the Central Illinois Conference Archives, Henry Pfeiffer Library–MacMurray College, 447 E. College Ave., Jacksonville, IL 62560.

68. Ibid., 15. In this interview, Harriette often refers to "we." She is referring to Hazel B. Irwin, whom she met when she attended Moody Bible Institute and who was a trained vocalist. Hazel and Harriette remained friends throughout the rest of their lives and served in the ministry together wherever Harriette was appointed.

69. Ibid., 2.

70. Ibid., 9.

71. Ibid., 16.

72. Ibid., 2.

73. *Central Illinois Reporter*, July 3, 1981.

Chapter 3

"Maintaining the Tradition": Women Elders and the Church of The Evangelical United Brethren in Christ[1]

WHEN THE FIFTIETH ANNIVERSARY TASK FORCE BEGAN MEETING to plan for the celebration of the 1956 decision to grant women in the United Methodist tradition full clergy rights, we were aware from the outset that one branch of the United Methodist tree–The Church of the United Brethren in Christ (UB Church)–had been ordaining women to full clergy rights since 1889. And there was agreement that these women needed to be acknowledged in some way as well.

Thus, in the early months of this project an attempt was made to collect the names of women who had been granted full clergy rights in the UB Church with the intention of including them in an appendix at the end of the book. As the project progressed, information was also submitted about Methodist Protestant women who had been granted full clergy rights. As noted earlier, a few of those women came into The Methodist church in 1939 and served with full clergy rights through 1956 and beyond. Again, the possibility of including a list of these women in an appendix was also considered.

Since the Methodist Protestant women serving through and beyond 1956 would have been the first to serve in their annual conferences with full clergy rights, however, it seemed only fair to include their stories in chapter 2, along with those who had been received on trial in 1956.

As more information was received and further research was undertaken, it also became clear that the customary understanding that the ordination of women ceased with the merger of The Evangelical Church (EC) and the UB Church in 1946 to form The Evangelical United Brethren Church (EUB Church) was, in fact, incorrect. As a result, there were women in the EUB Church serving with full clergy rights at the same time that women in the Methodist Church (MC) were claiming those rights for the first

time. Some of those women came into The United Methodist Church (UMC) in 1968 already having been granted full clergy rights, making them, in some conferences, also the first women to serve with full clergy rights. Thus, it seemed only appropriate to recognize those women and their history as well.

Since there is no attempt in this project to list all the women who have been received into full connection in the UMC, it was finally decided not to attempt such a listing for any predecessor denomination but instead to recognize those women who came into the various mergers with full clergy rights. Therefore, the stories of these EUB women will be told at the end of this chapter, following the history of the women receiving full clergy rights in the EUB Church.

Maintaining the Tradition

As recorded in chapter 1, women in the UB Church were the first in the United Methodist tradition to be granted full clergy rights by a General Conference when Ella Niswonger was ordained an elder at the 1889 General Conference. On the other hand, the EC never allowed women even the right to acquire a license to preach. Nevertheless, given the history of women in the United Methodist tradition who were called to preach, it seems appropriate to ask if there were not women from the EC who also experienced such a call.

Since that information was not requested as part of the research for this project, it is understandable that those stories–if, in fact, they were known–were not submitted. Yet, at least one annual conference did record the story of an Evangelical woman. Her name was Florence Yaggy Vandersall.

In her article on the contributions of women in the history of the Iowa Conference entitled *Between the Rivers: A*

History of Iowa United Methodism, Miriam Baker Nye reports: "Since neither the Evangelical Association nor the Evangelical Church ordained women, there were no women ministers to list in Deaver's *One Hundred Years with Evangelicals in Iowa*. However the reading of memoirs reveals the activity of women such as Florence Yaggy Vandersall (1878–1969), the well-educated wife of Charles Hammer Vandersall. Florence had 'long desired to preach the gospel as a missionary,' and she assisted her husband as a woman preacher during pastoral assignments in the Ohio Conference of the Evangelical Church. A district superintendent there 'appointed her to assist with the pastoral duties.'"[2]

The Vandersalls served several churches together throughout Iowa.

No doubt there were other Evangelical women as well who experienced a call to preach and lived out that call by marrying a preacher, as did many women in the UB Church and the various Methodist denominations. For the most part, however, it was understood that women preachers were not welcomed in the EC. This practice, then, created some problems when the EC united with the UB Church with its long history of ordaining women, resulting in "a clash of traditions."[3]

Apparently, not much research has been undertaken relating to the history of ordained women in the EUB Church. The primary sources for the information for this chapter come from the papers by Jonathan Cooney and James E. Will, cited in notes 1 and 3 respectively. Will states:

> As the merger negotiations proceeded, clergy rights for women were quietly abandoned. Prior to union there had been no indication that women would lose their right to be ordained. The official weekly papers of the two denominations were silent on the matter, and the respective General Conference minutes were, at best, vague. Remarks made at the 1941 General Conference of the Church of the United Brethren in Christ suggest that the issue was not being addressed openly. After Bishop G. D. Batdorf reported on the progress of the merger negotiations, he was asked whether or not women would be ordained. He responded that the matter was "sort of a sub rosa subject," but added that "the door is not closed completely."[4]

It seems, however, that a decision about the matter had been made previously. Will quotes a report read at the 1946 General Conference of the EUB Church by Bishop Edward Epp, who had served as secretary to the Joint Board of Bishops (for merger negotiations):

> The question as to whether there was record of any action regarding the status of women in and for the ministry in the Evangelical United Brethren Church was discussed at length. It was pointed out (a) we have committed ourselves to the position that church union as such would not change or take away the ministerial status of any man or woman in such ministry at the time of union, and (b) that at the Indianapolis meeting of the Joint Commissions on Church Union it was voted: "Another recommendation, to the effect that in the new Church there be no ordination as ministers granted to women, was likewise adopted." (Indianapolis, Nov. 11, 1939)[5]

Will goes on to report that the Board of Bishops of neither church made a record of this action and there are no existing files of the Joint Commissions on Church Union. It would also seem that this action was never actually voted on by a General Conference of the EUB Church, but was simply reported to the General Conference.

Will, then, concludes–incorrectly–that "the practice [of women's ordination] ceased with the creation of the Evangelical United Brethren Church in 1946. Thus several decades of ordained ministry by women faded into history as the women already ordained passed from active service."[6]

The fact is women did continue to be ordained into the traveling ministry of the EUB Church as ordained itinerant elders. Jonathan Cooney has done extensive research in this area. Even Bruce Behney and Paul Eller in their 1979 *History of the Evangelical United Brethren Church* do not fully explore the issue, though they do acknowledge that a few women were ordained. Cooney quotes Eller as saying, "Those isolated instances neither provoked any recorded objections nor inspired any generally accepted practice."[7]

Cooney did extensive research in EUB annual conference journals to identify women in ministry in the EUB Church from 1946 through 1968. (The EUB Church and the MC merged in 1968 to form the UMC.) Cooney lists over 150 women who were in ministry in the EUB Church in some capacity (though further research has identified at least three names on the list as males). Some of these women came into the EUB Church already ordained as active itinerant elders while others were ordained within the EUB Church. Many on the list served as local elders and never gained full clergy rights, while others started the process but never obtained officially recognized status.[8] Cooney states:

> At least 149 women held the order of elder in some form in the Evangelical United Brethren Church. The greatest numbers of these were in Ohio, Indiana, Pennsylvania and Nebraska.... Some sixty women served as active itinerant elders at some time during this period. Most of these served churches (some with their husbands) and only a few accepted appointments in a supply capacity. The annual conference with the greatest number of women elders was the Indiana South Conference (in every category it ranked highest or nearly so)....
>
> The EUB Church experienced a high incidence of clergy couples (a situation in which both marriage partners were ordained), probably because marriage to a minister was one of the few ways a woman could have a family and still participate in the ministry. There were fifty-two such clergy couples. The greatest numbers were in the Kansas, Indiana, and Allegheny Conferences. Twenty-four of the women in these relationships held the title of active itinerant elder at some time during their marriages. It was a UB trend that continued into the new church.[9]

Cooney also notes, "Despite the United Brethren tradition of ordaining women, some elders experienced a certain amount of discrimination and prejudice even though they served in annual conferences which were predominantly formerly United Brethren."[10] He quotes A. Glen O'Dell, who served as conference superintendent from 1954 through 1968 in South Indiana: "Their assignments were much more difficult to negotiate than for men due largely to the fact that this was a generation prior to the 'Woman's lib' movement. The ministry was not a fully accepted place for women." The sex barrier was no small issue. "The biggest problem was to get the congregation to accept a 'woman preacher.' We often had to say: 'Accept this assignment or none.' Also a woman's authority was much less acceptable than that of a man."[11]

Whatever the difficulties and the 1939 pre-union agreements by the Joint Board of Bishops not to ordain women, the EUB Church did continue to ordain women. There is also indication that knowledge of the pre-union agreement was not uniform across the denomination. Cooney points out that conference superintendent O'Dell was unaware of this agreement or any restrictions on the ordination of women. "If this was among the Council of Bishops," he wrote, "it did not become the law of the church."[12]

One of the first women with whom I had contact for this part of the project was Kathryn Bailey Moore, who was ordained an itinerant elder in the Susquehanna Conference of the EUB Church in 1967. I asked about her experience in being ordained in a denomination in which there was an agreement not to ordain any more women. Her first answer was one of surprise. "I got no sense of no more women. That's erroneous, I'm sure. The EUB's could no more hold back women in ministry than the earlier evangelicals could."[13]

I then sent Kathryn a copy of the article by James E. Will. She did some research on her own to test my contention that a prior agreement existed not to ordain women in the newly formed EUB Church. She contacted the woman with whom she was ordained, Norma Kinard. Kinard had never heard of the idea.[14] Neither had William Basom, who served a congregation in the Susquehanna Conference (now in the Virginia Conference) or Robert Close and William Woods, both district superintendents (DSs) in the Susquehanna Conference. Nor did Kathryn's own mother, a leading layperson originally from The Evangelical Church. She concedes that she has no way of denying the information I shared with her. She concludes, "It seems that *some* certain circles apparently *did* have such an understanding. I don't believe it was a generally held idea in the EUB Church at large. Other than normal cultural resistance, I did not experience a church mandate against women in my ministry as an EUB."[15]

At a recent meeting of the Northeastern Jurisdictional Commission on Archives and History, I attended a workshop given by the Reverend William Wolfe, former pastor and DS in the Eastern Conference of the EUB Church. I asked him about the agreement not to ordain women in the EUB Church. He too was unaware of it.[16] There do not seem, however, to have been any women from the Eastern Conference on the list that Jonathan Cooney compiled.

On the other hand, in response to the same question, Wil Bloy from the Wisconsin Conference wrote:

Yes, I recall here in Wisconsin that there was conversation and discussion that women were not to be ordained elder. Don't know where this came from or if it was ever written down. But that was the definite attitude, especially

on the Evangelical side when the Evangelical and United Brethren merged here in Wisconsin in 1952. I remember it because of two women who came from the UB side of the denomination when the EUB merger took place. They were faithful pastors, loved and highly regarded by the people in the congregations they served. Many churches scheduled them to speak at their women's meetings, mother-daughter banquets, etc., but I don't remember them getting invitations to speak at Sunday morn[ing] worship. There had been no women pastors on the Evangelical side. So there was a feeling of "what do we do with these two women pastors?" They always served as a team, both being appointed to the same church. Their names were…Sara Mouer…[and]…Mayte Richardson….

When I was ordained in 1956, the attitude towards women was more accepting, although not many women were studying for ordination. By the time the EUB-Methodist merger happened in 1969 here in Wisconsin there was a very cordial acceptance of women pastors.[17]

Thus, as noted earlier, knowledge of the pre-union agreement not to ordain women varied from conference to conference. And, as will be seen by the narratives provided by the clergywomen included in this chapter, understanding of the policies regarding ordination and appointment of women seems to differ, as well. Nevertheless, there is also indication that the issue was addressed at various times during the life of the denomination. Cooney reports that "in 1950 it was referred to the General Council of Administration for study. The Council passed the reference to the Board of Christian Education which in 1962 issued a murky conclusion: 'Whereas the *Discipline* (Par. 354) may be interpreted to include women, be it resolved that we continue to accept the intent of paragraph 354'"[18] Cooney notes that "Paragraph 354 simply outlined the educational and service prerequisites for advancement to elder. The language is curiously inclusive."[19]

Further, the 1955 *Discipline* of the EUB Church contained this paragraph:

Receiving Women Ministers:

"Question: Although through the use of the masculine article, paragraph 352 seems to imply that only male Ministers can be received from another denomination into the Evangelical United Brethren Church, is this paragraph to be interpreted that an ordained woman, coming from a denomination that ordains women as Ministers, cannot be received into our ministry?

Answer: While there was agreement in the Joint Commissions on Church Federation and Union 'That in the new Church there be no ordination as Ministers granted to women,' it was also agreed that 'Church union as such, will not change nor take away the ministerial status of any man or woman in such ministry at the time of union.' Whereas the Board of Bishops finds no specific paragraph in the Discipline that denies a woman to be licensed to preach or to become a Minister among us, therefore, be it resolved that the Annual Conference is competent to decide for itself with respect to the question raised above." (Paragraph 2455, page 602)[20]

Thus, it can be concluded that much like the MPC before it, the EUB Church left to the annual conferences the decision as to whether or not to ordain women, depending upon the inclinations of those with the authority to make such decisions. Consequently, some conferences ordained women; others did not. At the time of the union of the EUB Church with the MC to form the UMC in 1968, twelve women have been identified who had been ordained into full connection in either the UB Church or the EUB Church and carried their orders into the UMC and continued to serve in the UMC. Their stories are told below.

In addition, the 1968 union also marks the date that *all* women in the United Methodist tradition could finally claim the privilege of applying for full clergy rights.

United Brethren/Evangelical United Brethren Active Itinerant Elders Enter The United Methodist Church

Mary Hair Reisinger

Central Pennsylvania/Western Pennsylvania Conferences (Northeastern Jurisdiction)

Conference license to Preach in the Pennsylvania Conference, UB Church – 1924
Full Connection/Ordained Active Itinerant Elder – 1933
Retired – 1968, Erie Conference, EUB
Deceased – 2002

Although MARY REISINGER retired in 1968 at the time of the formation of the UMC, it seems appropriate to recognize Mary here for her longtime ministry in the UB and EUB churches and her exceptionally long life, which was recognized in the Western Pennsylvania Conference in 2000.

Mary Hair Reisinger was born September 17, 1900, in Perry County, Pennsylvania.

"I was born into a Christian home…and spent my childhood years in the town of New Bloomfield where my young parents joined the Trinity United Brethren Church. At the age of eleven, I accepted the Lord as my Savior and was baptized.…

"From that early age, I felt a sincere desire to serve the Lord and longed to become a missionary.…I enrolled in Lebanon Valley College in Annville, Pa., looking ahead to some mission field.…However, in my Senior year, the Mission Board rejected my application due to lack of funds, being in depression years."

Mary married Kenneth D. Reisinger and began the "Conference Course" of study; together they were ordained elders in the Pennsylvania Conference of the UB Church. "Thus I became the first ordained woman in Pennsylvania Conference. I was graciously accepted and always recognized by members of my Conference."

Mary served with her husband, Kenneth, both in local churches and then in interdenominational Christian education work until their retirement at the Erie Conference of the EUB in 1968, following thirty-five years of ministry. Kenneth died in 1977 but Mary remained active in weekly worship services, Sunday school, and Bible studies. She was honored in 2000 by Bishop Hae Jong Kim of the Western Pennsylvania Conference as the oldest living United Methodist clergy-

woman in the United States at age 100, and was presented with the James Mills Thoburn Memorial Cane, symbolic of that honor. Mary died October 22, 2002, at the age of 102.[21]

Dorothy Evelyn (Berger) Wright

East Ohio Conference (North Central Jurisdiction)

Associate Member, Ohio Sandusky Conference, UB Church – 1927
Full Connection/Ordained Active Itinerant Elder – 1929
Retired, East Ohio Conference, UMC – 1972
Deceased – 1988

DOROTHY EVELYN (BERGER) WRIGHT was born November 18, 1906, in Fremont, Ohio. In 1926, Dorothy married Clarence David Wright, whom she had met while attending Heidelberg College. Together they enrolled at Bonebrake Theological Seminary and were both ordained by the Ohio Sandusky Conference of the UB Church in 1929. The Wrights served churches together until the time of Clarence's death in 1960.

In 1962 Dorothy was appointed to the Sycamore Circuit, and participated in the merger of the Pleasant Home and Brokensword congregations. She then served Bucyrus, Olive Branch and finally Bucyrus, Mt. Zion (in the East Ohio Conference, UMC) until her retirement in 1972.

In 1985 the Commission on the Status and Role of Women of the East Ohio Conference published a tribute to Dorothy, written by Dorothy Cope Bailey, entitled *In Quietness and Confidence*, which described her life as a clergy wife, a clergy mother, and as a pastoral role model for women. Dorothy will be remembered for her great interest in the missionary work of the church, and especially for her years (1949–1954) as president of the Ohio Sandusky Branch of the Woman's Society of World Service during which the merger of The Evangelical Church with the United Brethren Church took place. Dorothy died April 20, 1988, at the age of eighty-one.[22]

Edna Beougher Hughes

West Ohio Conference (North Central Jurisdiction)

Full Connection/Received to the Itinerant Ministry, Michigan Conference, UB Church – 1937
Transferred in Full Connection to Ohio Southeast Conference, EUB Church – 1960
Retired, West Ohio Conference, UMC – 1971
Deceased – 1998

EDNA BEOUGHER HUGHES was born December 22, 1906, in Good Hope Township, Hocking County, Ohio. She married Freeman Hughes January 26, 1928. Freeman died on February 1, 1975.

Edna was involved in the ministry from the time of her early childhood. She was very active in church and evangelical services. In 1937, Edna was ordained as an elder in the Michigan Conference of the UB Church and appointed as an "evangelist-at-large." In 1960, she transferred her membership to the Ohio Southeast Conference of the EUB Church and continued her ministry as an evangelist until her retirement from the West Ohio Conference of the UMC in 1971.

Edna was a ventriloquist and often used her companion "Oscar" in her ministry with youth. In addition, she wrote and published several books of poetry and penned a number of hymns. Edna Beougher Hughes died July 19, 1998, at age ninety-two.[23]

Wilma Harner Allen

South Indiana Conference (North Central Jurisdiction)

Deaconess License, Indiana Conference UB Church – 1937
Probationer's License – 1945
Full Connection/Ordained to the Itinerant Ministry, Indiana Conference EUB Church – 1950
Retired – 1986

WILMA HARNER ALLEN was born January 31, 1924, in Washington, Indiana. She writes, "I began preaching at a little country church while I was still in high school. It was close to my home town (Washington, Indiana). I had a Deaconess license issued in 1937 and renewed in 1939 in the UB Church."

Wilma entered Indiana Central College in September 1941 and received a probationer's license in 1945, the year that she graduated from Indiana Central.[24]

"I served a church for 3 years while I was in college, and then pastored churches in the Indiana Conference of the EUB and the South Indiana Conference of the UMC. My work in ministry was under the guidance and help of J. W. McMartry, who was my pastor and guide from a child until I went away to college. He encouraged me to believe that in the years ahead lady ministers would be pastoring many churches. My biggest regret is that I did not attend a seminary. In the former UB Church that was not a requirement for ordination but I am sure it would have been most helpful."

Although she officially retired in 1986, she pastored the Morristown UMC from 1986 to 1995 and served as pastor of visitation at University Heights UMC from 1995 to 2002. In 2000 she wrote *The Life of a Lady Minister* so that her family and friends could have a record of her experiences during her sixty-plus years in the ministry.[25] She says, "This has been an exciting journey." Wilma retired in 1986.

C. Maxine Krisher

West Ohio Conference (North Central Jurisdiction)

Probationer's License, Ohio Southeast Conference, EUB Church – 1952
Full Connection/Ordained to the Itinerancy – 1957
Retired, West Ohio Conference, UMC – 1977
Deceased – 2002

CRYSTAL MAXINE KRISHER was born September 26, 1911. She began serving her first church in 1944 while she was still

in school. She received probationary status in 1952 and was ordained to full connection in 1957. During her active ministry she served appointments in the Laurelville Circuit, Mt. Zion, Fairview, Black Oak, and the Gibsonville Charge Circuit, retiring in the West Ohio Conference of the UMC in 1977. Maxine died August 10, 2002, at the age of ninety.[26]

Esther E. Edwards

South Indiana Conference (North Central Jurisdiction)

Ordained in the Salvation Army – 1942
Transferred in Full Connection to Indiana Conference, EUB Church – 1959
Retired, South Indiana Conference, UMC – 1985

ESTHER E. EDWARDS was born September 7, 1922.

"I guess that I just always wanted to be a minister; from the age of 7 or 8, I knew that was what I wanted to do. I was originally ordained in the Salvation Army in Chicago and served with them for seventeen years. Though the people in the Salvation Army were very dedicated individuals, it was set up along military lines and I had difficulty with that. And even though there were as many women as there were men in the Salvation Army, from my earliest days, I was aware that women were not given very many opportunities to advance. I transferred to the EUB in 1959. They accepted me without question, though they also made it clear that they did not want women in droves. Though I never ran into any outright objections, I was always aware that as a woman I had to prove myself. I had to excel at whatever I was doing. Being 'good' was just not enough."

Besides serving in local churches, Esther worked at the General Board of Christian Education (EUB Church), then as assistant general secretary for Student Loans and Scholarships, Board of Higher Education and Ministry (UMC).

"It has been a very winding path, sometimes a very troublesome path, but always a good path and I wouldn't change any of it. I can't regret any of it. It was all worthwhile because I was so convinced of my call that I didn't let anything deter me." Esther retired in 1985.

M. Lucile Esbenshade

South Indiana Conference (North Central Jurisdiction)

Probationer's License, Indiana South, EUB Church – 1964
Full Connection/Ordained to Itinerant Ministry, Indiana South, EUB Church – 1968
Retired, South Indiana Conference, UMC – 1982
Deceased – 2003

MARY LUCILE ESBENSHADE was born in Bird-in-Hand, Pennsylvania, in 1916. She graduated from Lebanon Valley College with a bachelor's degree and then earned a master's degree in religious education from Hartford School of Religious Education.

Prior to entering the ordained ministry, Lucile taught religious education in Indiana and Pennsylvania. She then served as a missionary for the EUB Church in the Philippines and in Africa. In 1964, Lucile was granted a probationer's license in the Indiana South Conference of the EUB Church and served as the director of religious education at Terre Haute First Church of the EUB. She was ordained into full connection in 1968. Lucile served churches in Medora, Cates, Newport, Guilford, Hope, and Morgantown. From 1974 to 1978 she was program consultant for the South Spencer Group Ministry, retiring in 1982.

At the time of her death, Lucile was a member of St. John's UMC in Paradise and participated in the annual Walk to Emmaus seminars.[27] She died December 26, 2003, at the age of eighty-seven.

Nellwyn Brookhart Trujillo

West Ohio Conference (North Central Jurisdiction)

Probationer's License, Ohio Sandusky, EUB Church – 1946
Full Connection/Ordained to the Itinerancy – 1950
Retired, West Ohio Conference, UMC – 1988

NELLWYN BROOKHART TRUJILLO began her ministry in the Ohio Sandusky Conference of the EUB Church in 1945 when she was under a special appointment to the Vallecitos Mission School in New Mexico. She received her probationer's license in 1946 and was appointed to attend school. In 1948 she was appointed to the Velarde Mission School. She was ordained an elder in 1950 and appointed to the Vallecitos Mission School in 1951. After serving there for eleven years, she was appointed to the McCurdy School in Santa Cruz, New Mexico. In 1966 she was again appointed to the Vallecitos Mission School. In 1970, after the formation of the UMC, she received a special appointment from the West Ohio Conference to the Vallecitos Mission School as manager and caretaker, retiring in 1988. She currently resides in Santa Cruz, New Mexico.[28]

Kathryn Louise Bailey Moore

Baltimore-Washington Annual Conference (Northeastern Jurisdiction)

Probationer's License, Susquehanna Conference, EUB Church – 1964
Full Connection/Ordained to the Itinerancy – 1967
First European American woman to serve in full connection in the Baltimore Conference, UMC – 1970
Retired, Baltimore-Washington Conference – 2003

KATHRYN LOUISE BAILEY MOORE was born November 8, 1940, in Sayre, Pennsylvania, to parents who came out of an Evangelical Church background.

"I never knew a time when I was not called to be doing ministry. I taught and preached for the first time around the 8th grade. By 10th grade I knew my career course would relate specifically to the church. I went to seminary intending to teach philosophy of religion in college. But the only EUB job I could find at Oberlin Graduate School of Theology in Ohio as educational assistant and supply pastor to an Inner City Group Ministry in Cleveland, Ohio.

"Sitting on a window seat in my room at Henry Street Settlement House in New York City, I watched life on Henry Street: its ethnicity, its terror, its beauty, the church across the street. I fell in love with the inner city and spent my entire ministry in appointments within or near Washington, DC. There was one exception: the year I earned my doctorate in urban ministry, I was appointed to a rural dairy parish. I learned to love cows and still receive gifts of them from friends. In all, I served 12 churches or group ministries, ten in the United Methodist tradition, one in the UCC and one ecumenical. This included two churches in the RMN–Reconciling Ministries Network of the UMC–churches open to persons of all sexual orientations. It has been my proud and cherished privilege to serve forty-one years as an ordained pastor in The United Methodist Church and its antecedent communions. Thanks be to God for this indescribable gift of ministry."

Kathryn retired in 2003.

Norma Jean Kinard

Central Pennsylvania Conference (Northeastern Jurisdiction)

Probationer's License – 1966
Full Connection/Ordained to Itinerant Ministry, Susquehanna Conference, EUB Church – 1967
Retired – 2005

NORMA JEAN KINARD was born September 8, 1942, in Dallastown, Pennsylvania.

"It is hard to say exactly when I experienced my call. Instead of playing with dolls, I would line then up on my bed and preach to them. I was born with cerebral palsy and I had a number of surgeries during my young years, was paralyzed and couldn't walk. I grew up with my grandparents who were not a church-going family. But the local EUB minister came to pray for my grandfather, who was an amputee, and the other folks from the church would bring copies of their Sunday school quarterlies to me. They would strap me to a door and bring me to church and lay me on the front pew. I was nurtured by those old Sunday school quarterlies, and I had a growing desire for the ministry.

"My doctor, Dr. Cushman, said that I would never walk again. But during one of my visits, he kept looking at me and decided to measure me for braces. They were huge braces, but he told me to take them home, try to get into them, and then come back in two weeks. I did get into the braces, but when I had only three days left, I said to the Lord, 'Lord, I have to be a preacher. Lord, I want to be a minister but no man can make me walk.' I woke up in the middle of that night and I could walk perfectly! But I was afraid that if I walked, it would go away. After my grandparents went to work, I got the braces on and I walked with the crutches. The second day, I walked without the crutches. The third day I went to the doctor and I walked in and he saw me and sent me down to x-ray. He said, 'Something happened to you, you're not telling me.' I used the braces for awhile to build up my strength, but I could walk.

"I wanted to go to college and seminary, but I knew that I didn't have any money. When I was young, a man from the Pennsylvania State Rehabilitation Department had met me when he came to see my grandfather. When I was in the 8th grade, he visited me at school and asked where I wanted to go to college. The State Rehabilitation Department paid my entire way through college and seminary–something that they had never done before and never did again.

"I attended United Theological Seminary, and they wanted me to enroll in the MRE program. But I kept telling them that I wanted to be in the BD program and finally they let me in. But they were not going to ordain me when I graduated because they had to guarantee me an appointment. All my male classmates said that they would refuse to be ordained if I wasn't ordained, too. When the District Superintendents came to interview the guys, they were called one by one. Then finally one of my classmates came running up to my room and said, 'They want to see you.' And I was given two churches up in the middle of nowhere. But all the guys were so excited that they picked me up on their shoulders and we all got ordained together.

"Many years later I was visiting York Hospital and I heard a nurse speak Dr. Cushman's name. I told her that I used to be a patient of his. She took me into his room and he was there dying of cancer. By then I was using just one Canadian crutch. He said to me, 'Something happened to you that you never told me about.' I told him then what had happened those many years ago and that I had become a minister. He asked me if I would give him communion and I happened to have my Communion set with me and gave him communion. He died later that night.

"There have been a lot miracles–a lot of miracles. That's the way my life has been from beginning to end."

Norma Kinard retired from active ministry in 2005.

Susan Wolfe Hassinger

Eastern Pennsylvania Conference (Northeastern Jurisdiction)
Full Connection/Ordained Elder, Susquehanna EUB Church – 1968
First European American woman to serve in full connection in the Eastern Pennsylvania Conference, UMC – 1968
Retired from the episcopacy – 2004; bishop in residence and adjunct professor in practical theology at Boston University School of Theology; designated liaison between Council of Bishops and deans and presidents of the Association of United Methodist Theological Schools

SUSAN WOLFE HASSINGER was born in Hanover, Pennsylvania, November 29, 1942. Susan's call to the ministry developed while she was in college. During the summer after her sophomore year, she attended a summer work camp in Ecuador. "This trip was a revolutionary experience for me. That's where I began to raise questions about the Church, believe it or not.... As my understanding of the gospel grew, I began to see...paternalism and racism as antithetical to the gospel."

The following summer Susan attended three EUB Church summer camps to interpret the work camp experiences and to invite others to participate. "I have no idea why, but in that New York camp...I had this sense of being called to pastoral ministry. And I knew–it was so clear–that my calling was not to be a Christian educator, not to be a missionary, but to be a pastor.... According to the United Brethren rules, ordination of women was okay. But the people I was with were not UB. Bishop Kaebnick was from the Evangelical tradition."

Susan attended seminary at United Theological Seminary in Ohio where she met and married her husband in 1966. Her husband graduated and was appointed to a church in Pennsylvania, so Susan transferred to Lancaster Theological Seminary and completed her master of divinity degree. "When I began the process of ordination and membership, the questions I remember them asking me were not about theology, but about my plans for a family: What happens if you get married? Or the bigger question: What happens if you get pregnant? if you have a baby? 'I'll have a baby!' was my answer. And I wasn't trying to be disrespectful. But if you become pregnant, then you have a baby!"

Susan and her husband were both ordained elders in 1968 in the Susquehanna Conference of the EUB Church. "But," she says, "under the EUB rules, I didn't have to have an appointment. So, I was ordained but without an appointment for several years." Susan became the first ordained elder in full connection in the Eastern Pennsylvania Conference and she received her first appointment in 1970. After that her ministerial career soared. After serving local churches for thirteen years, she became the first woman in the Eastern Pennsylvania Conference to be appointed as a D.S. Following that, she served on the annual conference staff as local church consultant and in other roles, concluding as head of the Office of Resourcing. In 1996 Susan was elected bishop and served in the New England Conference until her retirement in 2004–the first and only woman from an Evangelical United Brethren background to be elected to the episcopacy.

Bishop Judith Craig says of Susan: "It is a gift of God to the church that God's vision reached further than Susan's vision.... Though she is soft spoken, her wisdom and understanding of life's twists and turns and how people and institutions interact make her a powerful woman in the midst of trouble and conflict. Though she may not think of herself as a pioneer, her leadership helps people move into the new understandings and ways of being. Deeply rooted spirit, quiet leader, and wise counselor are all appropriate phrases to describe this woman of God."[29]

 *Betty Jane Clem*

Virginia Conference (Southeastern Jurisdiction)

Probationer's License, Shenandoah Conference, EUB Church –
1969
Full Connection/Ordained into the Itinerant Ministry – 1969
First European American Woman to Serve in Full Connection
in the Virginia Conference, UMC – 1969
Leave of Absence – 1982
Honorable Location – 1988
Withdrew – 1990

BETTY JANE CLEM, known as B. J., was ordained in the Virginia Conference of the EUB Church in 1969, the last year that separate ordinations were observed. Conference that year was at Shenandoah College in Winchester, Virginia. In the EUB tradition there was no ordination as a deacon. B. J. received both probationary membership and full conference membership in 1969, the year of her ordination as an elder. It appears from existing research that B. J. was also the only woman ordained elder outside of the Northeastern and North Central Jurisdictions, and was the last woman to be ordained an elder in the EUB Church. In fact, she does not appear on Jonathan Cooney's list of women ordained in the EUB Church. With the full unification in 1970, the new UMC officially recognized all elders with full conference membership from any of the predecessor denominations. Thus B. J. became an elder in full connection in the Virginia Conference in 1970, the first woman to serve in the Virginia Annual Conference.

In 1969 B. J. received her first appointment. She was appointed as the associate minister at Collingwood UMC in Toledo, Ohio, where she had worked while a seminary student at United Theological Seminary. Because of this, when she began serving churches in Virginia some people mistakenly thought she was a transfer from the Ohio Conference. In 1970, following full unification, B. J. began to serve churches in the newly formed Virginia Conference of The United Methodist Church. She served continuously until 1982. Her last appointment was to Dulin UMC, Falls Church, Virginia, as the associate pastor. B. J. is currently working for the Red Cross in northern Virginia.[30]

Notes

1. The title of this chapter is taken from a paper written by Jonathan Cooney for a church history seminar for United Theological Seminary (Dayton, OH, Fall 1986). See his "Maintaining the Tradition: Women Elders and the Ordination of Women in the Evangelical United Brethren Church," in *Methodist History* 27, no. 1 (October 1988).
2. Miriam Baker Nye, "Women's Contributions," in John A. Nye, *Between the Rivers: A History of Iowa United Methodism* (Iowa: Commission on Archives and History, Iowa Conference UMC, 1986), 153.
3. James E. Will, "Ordination of Women," in *Women in New Worlds: Historical Perspectives on the Wesleyan Tradition*, ed. Rosemary Skinner Keller, Louise L. Queen, and Hilah F. Thomas (Nashville: Abingdon, 1981-82), 2:296.
4. Ibid.

5. Ibid.
6. Ibid., 296-97.
7. Cooney, "Maintaining the Tradition," (1986), 4.
8. Ibid., 18-28.
9. Jonathan Cooney, "Maintaining the Tradition" *Methodist History* 27, no. 1 (October 1988): 26-29.
10. Ibid., 29.
11. Ibid.
12. Ibid., 31.
13. Kathryn Bailey Moore, e-mail message to author, February, 2005.
14. Note, however, in her biography on pages 69-70 that she did receive resistance at United Theological Seminary when she applied for ordination.
15. Kathryn Bailey Moore, follow-up e-mail to author, March 1, 2005.
16. William Wolfe, personal communication to author, May 10, 2005, in Esopus, NY.
17. Wil Bloy, e-mail message to author, March, 2005.
18. Cooney, "Maintaining the Tradition," 13-14.
19. Ibid., 14n21.
20. The Reverend Clair Troutman, "Clergywomen in the Evangelical United Brethren Church," in *The Licensing and Ordination of Women in the Central Pennsylvania Conference, The United Methodist Church* (Central Pennsylvania Conference: Commission on Archives and History, 1980), 5.
21. Material that is quoted directly is taken from the autobiography of Mary Hair Reisinger in *The Licensing and Ordination of Women in the Central Pennsylvania Conference*, 46. Material that is not quoted directly is taken from Mary Reisinger's memoir, published in the 2003 Journal of the Western Pennsylvania Conference, UMC, 326-27.
22. Information for this biography is taken from Dorothy Wright's memoir published in the 1989 Journal of the East Ohio Conference, UMC, 123.
23. Information for this biography was taken from Cooney, "Maintaining the Tradition," 22; Edna Hughes' memoir which was published in the 1999 Journal of the West Ohio Conference, UMC, 371; an obituary found at http://www.obitcentral.com/obitsearch/obits/oh/oh-hocking43.htm; and an e-mail from Carol Hollinger, archivist of the West Ohio Conference, dated December 16, 2005.
24. "'A Lady Minister': The Story of the Reverend Wilma Harner Allen '45," in *Women in Ministry Associated with Indiana Central and the University of Indianapolis: Chapters from a Neglected Story of "Education for Service,"* Crossings Project Booklet No. 2 (Indianapolis: University of Indianapolis, n.d.), 13, 14.
25. Ibid.
26. Material for this biography is taken from Maxine Krisher's memoir, published in the 2003 West Ohio Conference Journal, vol. 2, 375, and the Ministerial Roll from the 1969 Journal of the Ohio Southeast Conference, UMC, 23.
27. Material for this biography is taken from Lucile Esbenshade's obituary, which appeared in the *Lancaster* (Pennsylvania) *New Era* (December 26, 2003), and is used here with permission; and from her service record from the 2004 Journal of the South Indiana Conference, UMC, 418.
28. Information for this biography comes from Nellwyn Brookhart Trujillo's service record from the West Ohio Conference, UMC.
29. Material that is quoted in this biography is taken from Judith Craig, comp., *The Leading Women: Stories of the First Women Bishops of The United Methodist Church* (Nashville: Abingdon, 2004), 79-80, 81-82, 83, 87. © 2004 Abingdon Press. Used by permission.
30. Information provided by the Reverend Margie Turbyfill, clergywoman in the Virginia Annual Conference of the UMC.

Chapter 4

First Women of the Northeastern Jurisdiction to Receive Full Clergy Rights

CHAPTERS 4 THROUGH 9 WILL IDENTIFY AND PROVIDE A SHORT BIOGRAPHICAL STATEMENT on the first women in each annual conference, in every ethnic group represented in that conference, either to "serve" in full connection or "to be received" into full connection. That is, in some instances women may have been received into full connection in one conference and then transferred to another conference where they were the first women in full connection to serve in that conference. If these women were the first to be received in the conference from which they transferred, their biography will be included in the conference in which they were first received into full connection and then cross-referenced in the conference in which they are serving. If they were not the first in their original conference, their biography will be included in the annual conference where they were the first to serve in full connection. This pattern of transferring from one conference to another is an important aspect of the journeys of these "first" women and an important part of the overall story as well.

One chapter has been allowed for each jurisdiction and one for the central conferences. I have allowed a half page for each biography and, in doing that, I recognize that it is difficult to describe a lifetime journey in a half page. Thus, the emphasis has been placed on how each clergywoman received her call and how she experienced her journey in the ministry. Unless otherwise noted in the notes, material for these biographies is taken from personal communication with the author, either by e-mail, letter, fax, or telephone. The stories are as varied as the clergywomen themselves. Some stories are very short; others were hard to condense to a half page. And some women have chosen not to respond. In those cases, I have used whatever information I was able to glean about those clergywomen. Where the information was available, I have attempted to include personal reflections on call and how the journey has been for the clergywoman whose biography is being presented. Where that information is not available, I focused more on where the clergywoman attended school and the particular churches she served. Thus, there will be a great variety among the biographical sketches. To the extent possible, I chose to leave the autobiographical accounts as they were sent to me (with the exception of deleting some material due to space constraints) in order to allow each woman to convey her story in her own words and style. Though a few stories may be disturbing to some readers, the decision was to honor the candor and depth of the experiences of each woman. Appointments were current as of the time the autobiographical statements were submitted. It is quite possible that some may have changed.

As noted in the foreword, however, The United Methodist Church (UMC) has been blessed by the ministry of amazing and diverse clergywomen whose presence has enriched and continues to enrich the UMC and the many congregations and appointments beyond the local church that have been served by these women. As the stories are told, it will become clear that many of these women have served at great personal pain and sacrifice and yet, always with joy, for the opportunity to live out their call from a God who has sustained them through it all.

There are currently thirteen annual conferences in the Northeastern Jurisdiction. I have included Puerto Rico since it was a part of the jurisdiction until it became independent in 1992. This jurisdiction reported sixty-six "first" women–more than any jurisdiction, continuing the trend established in 1956 when one-third of the first women to be received on probation came from the Northeastern Jurisdiction. One woman has served in two conferences, although she was only counted once. Twenty-one of the sixty-six women, or 32 percent, are now deceased. Eleven of the women–including Bishop Hassinger–or 17 percent, are currently retired. There are twenty-two women, or 33 percent, who are currently in ministry at the local church level. This is also the highest percentage of women serving the local church. Seven women, or 12 percent, are appointed to extension ministries, including two district superintendents (D.S.) and one working at the general church level. The remaining 6 percent include one woman appointed to attend school, one on leave of absence, one on Honorable Location, and one who has withdrawn.

In terms of ethnic background, twenty-seven, or 40 percent, of the women are European American. In addition there were seventeen African Americans, seven Korean women, six Hispanic/Latina women, three Indian women, two Japanese women, two African women, one Chinese and one Native American woman. The Northeastern Jurisdiction has the first Hispanic/Latina woman to be received into full connection in the UMC (Puerto Rico) and in the United States.

BALTIMORE-WASHINGTON ANNUAL CONFERENCE

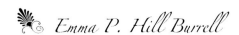

(AFRICAN AMERICAN)
First Woman to Be Received into Full Connection in the Former Washington Conference in 1959

(See chapter 2, 36)

First European American Woman to Serve in Full Connection
Received into Full Connection in the Susquehanna Conference, EUB Church, in 1967

(See chapter 3, 69)

First European American Woman to Be Received into Full Connection

Received on Trial – 1970
Ordained Deacon – 1970
Received into Full Connection – 1973
Ordained Elder – 1973
Current Appointment – Rockville, Maryland UMC

REBECCA KAY BARGER, better known as Kay, was born August 26, 1947, in Hagerstown, Maryland.

"God's call upon my life to enter the ordained ministry came at the age of twelve (1959) when I was attending a weeklong Junior High conference event held at Western Maryland College. There was no blinding light nor were there voices speaking to me, but by the end of the last outdoor service, there was no doubt in my mind and my heart that this was what God wanted me to do with my life. The idea at the time was pretty laughable, since I was very shy and hated to get up in front of people! But a counselor at that event told me to trust God to provide me with the gifts to do what God was calling me to do, but in God's time. And was she ever right!

"Since that day in my life when I knew God was calling me to ordination in the Methodist Church, I have never doubted that call upon my life nor regretted responding to it. I have been so blessed with opportunities to serve as the pastor of six different congregations in this conference since graduating from seminary in 1972. While there have been struggles for acceptance, in each setting we grew to love each other and love being in ministry together! Although I am aware that others in the conference call me a 'pioneer' (and I guess that's true), all I know is, I have been so wonderfully blessed by God's faithfulness to God's call to me of forty-six years ago. As each year goes by, I continue to pray that I have been and will continue to be faithful to God's call upon my life."

First Korean Woman to Be Received into Full Connection

Received on Trial – 1983
Ordained Deacon – 1983
Received into Full Connection – 1985
Ordained Elder – 1985
Current Appointment – Consultant for Korean American United Methodist Women, Women's Division of General Board of Global Ministries

HEA SUN KIM was born March 1, 1954, in Seoul, South Korea.

"I first heard the call to ministry when I was fifteen, in the jungles of Borneo Island. As a daughter of missionaries who were working there, I was deeply involved in ministry myself. But when I shared my call, everyone around me wanted me to be a pastor's wife. Something didn't feel right about that guidance, but for the next fifteen years that was the only door open to me. Only when I met with other clergywomen in the Baltimore-Washington Conference, and with their encouragement, did I seek ordination.

"Remembering where I have been as a woman in Korean churches, I chose to focus on empowering Korean Christian women to their full potential. The Women's Division has been most generous and mission-minded in the empowerment of Korean women. For the last thirteen years, I have done national leadership trainings, conducted seminars and retreats, translated numerous books for spiritual growth studies, published story books on the lives of Korean immigrant women, written bilingual devotional books, and led mission trips to raise awareness of the connectional mission of The United Methodist Church. Today, the Korean United Methodist women have grown to hold key leadership positions in the organization, including the president of the Women's Division."

Yolanda Pupo-Ortiz

First Hispanic/Latina Woman to Serve in Full Connection
Received into Full Connection in 1985 in the Southern New England Conference

(See below, 83)

Saroj Sabitha Sangha

First Indian Woman to Be Received into Full Connection

Received on Trial – 1993
Ordained Deacon – 1993
Received into Full Connection – 1996
Ordained Elder – 1996
Current Appointment – Maryland City Community UMC, Laurel, Maryland

SAROJ SABITHA SANGHA was born July 7, 1949, in India. She graduated with a bachelor of divinity degree (the equivalent of a master of divinity) from Leonard Theological College in 1971 and a master of theology degree from United Theological College in Bangalore, India, in 1977. "It was a challenging experience to study as the only woman student in these courses."

Saroj served churches in India before moving to the United States and has served churches in the Baltimore-Washington Conference since 1993. Saroj served as associate pastor at the Colesville UMC in Silver Spring, Maryland, in 1993, and has served as pastor of the Maryland City Community UMC in Laurel, Maryland, since 1994. She says, "I enjoyed my ministry in India and I am enjoying my ministry here in the United States."

Her husband, Moses, is also a United Methodist pastor.

Cristian de la Rosa

First Hispanic/Latina Woman to Be Received into Full Connection

Received on Trial – 1988
Ordained Deacon – 1988
Received into Full Connection – 1991
Ordained Elder – 1991
Transferred to Nebraska Conference – 1997
Transferred to Rio Grande Conference – 2001
Current Appointment – Agape Memorial UMC, Dallas, Texas, Rio Grande Conference

CRISTIAN DE LA ROSA was born December 14, 1961, in Ciudad Diaz Ordaz, Tamaulipas, Mexico.

"I experienced my call to ordained ministry as a youth in my local church when I was in high school as a volunteer with Acampo Community Church in Lodi, California. I wanted to serve in the church and was going to be a nun, but the pastor did tell me that we did not have nuns in the UMC. I decided to continue my journey into youth ministry but I then met Anglo clergywomen and did find out that women were able to serve as pastors and be ordained.

"My journey as a Hispanic clergywoman in the UMC has been challenging yet balanced by tangible signs of God's grace. My response to Spanish speakers when they ask about how I am doing is *aqui siempre en la lucha* ("as always, in the struggle"). This expression encompasses and communicates my experience in ministry–always aware that it has been and that it will continue to be a struggle in the context of the institutional church of the United States. However, I am convinced that in my participation as a Hispanic ordained clergywoman I am part of the grace of God within the institution. At difficult times I remind myself that I am God's grace to the church and that I am called, in the spirit of the Old Testament prophets, to serve God and God's people. As I remember and review Micah 6:8–"What does the Lord require of you but to do justice, and to love kindness, and to walk humbly with your God?"– I remain within the church and seek creative ways to continue in the journey. I find courage in the experience of those that came before me and hope in those that are preparing for a very exciting future."

CENTRAL PENNSYLVANIA ANNUAL CONFERENCE

 *Maud Keister Jensen*

(EUROPEAN AMERICAN)

First Woman to Be Received into Full Connection in 1958

(See chapter 2, 33)

 *Mercy Mwazviwanza Mujati Kasambira*

First African Woman to Be Received into Full Connection

Received on Trial – 1979
Ordained Deacon – 1979
Received into Full Connection – 1981
Ordained Elder – 1981
Deceased – 1994

MERCY MWAZVIWANZA MUJATI KASAMBIRA was born September 6, 1933, at Mutambara, Zimbabwe, Africa.

> My first inspiration to want to be a minister was caused by my father's faith. He was not educated, but he became a local preacher.... In my father's religion, some women were recognized as preachers and faith healers as well.... My next inspiration was caused by my first class meeting teacher in the United Methodist Church...Mrs. Katherine Kanogoiwa...who used to encourage us...to give testimonies about what God meant to us.... After many years of searching, the many doors were eventually opened and I was able to obtain seminary training.[1]

As Mercy's husband of forty-one years, I found her to be a deeply religious and committed Christian. Borrowing from her former District Superintendent and a soul sister, "She was a gallant woman, a person of intense spirit. Mercy served on the Chambersburg District from 1989 to 1993. In those four years, she strove to receive, integrate and heal with her own unique spirit, the racism of this district, the indifference to the poor and disenfranchised, and the scorn toward another's culture whose accent marks her as a stranger. No road was too long for Mercy to travel, no resistance was too steep for her to forgive, and no effort was too great if the church would be served."[2]

Mercy Kasambira died unexpectedly February 11, 1995, at age sixty-one, as the result of an automobile accident.

 *Bernice D. Stevens*

First African American Woman to Be Received into Full Connection

Received on Trial – 1986
Ordained Deacon – 1988
Received into Full Connection – 1989
Ordained Elder – 1992
Retired – 1994

BERNICE D. STEVENS was born April 9, 1932, in Broad Run, Virginia.

"Significant to my call to ministry is the fact that I am a third-generation United Methodist clergy from the Davis family. I had my first spiritual experience when I was about eight years old." Bernice nearly drowned one day while swimming at the beach. She was rescued by an unknown man, who put her on his shoulders and brought her to shallow water.

"When I reached the shore, I wanted to look back, but it was as if a voice was saying, 'Don't look back.' Many years later, I was awakened during the night and sensed that there was a presence in my room. There was no one there. I tried to get out of bed and after struggling to do so, I gave up. Remembering the biblical story of Samuel, I asked if God were present. Just then there was a mist that began to circle the room. It moved toward the window and passed out of the room. After that I was able to get out of bed. After at least seven years of struggling to determine God's will for me, I recognized God's call to ordained ministry.

"The process to obtain the recommendation for elder's orders from the Board of Ordained Ministry was very painful for me. Many of the members of the board had probably never seen an African American woman like me 'up close and personal' though there were many of us around. I was required to have counseling, which delayed my ordination by one year. I still believe the board was unjust in dealing with me, and that the basis for their behavior was racism on the part of some members of the board. However, when this was all over, I reaped the usual benefits, and more, of being a pastor. Last fall I found myself back in the classroom as a substitute teacher. I went into the ministry kicking and screaming, but as I walked into the classroom in 2004, it was as if I heard God saying, 'See Bernice, I told you I would take care of all things.' Praise the Lord!"

EASTERN PENNSYLVANIA ANNUAL CONFERENCE

 *Susan Wolfe Hassinger*

(EUROPEAN AMERICAN)

First Woman in Full Connection to Serve in the Conference
Received into Full Connection in the Susquehanna Conference,
EUB Church, in 1968

(See chapter 3, 70)

 *Elaine B. Barnes*

(EUROPEAN AMERICAN)

First Woman to Be Received into Full Connection
Received on Trial, Northern Philippines Conference, MC – 1965

Ordained Deacon, Northern Philippines Conference, MC – 1965
Received into Full Connection – 1974
Ordained Elder – 1974
Retired – Elder in residence, Johnson Memorial UMC

ELAINE B. BARNES was born May 12, 1941, in Camden, New Jersey.

"I heard the call gradually starting in high school, in the late 1950s. I started toward Christian education. In college I began to move more toward ordained ministry. At the beginning of my seminary years I was beginning to think of teaching at the college or seminary level in the area of Old Testament studies. After involvement in the civil rights push in Durham and Chapel Hill, I needed to rethink my involvement in the church. With the help of a mission professor at Duke Divinity School, I went to the Philippines as a missionary. While there, my commitment to ordained ministry grew and I was ordained deacon.

"My ministry has been a journey of joy and of pain. I have been the 'first woman minister we ever met' in most of my congregations. The joy has come as I have seen the congregations move from opposition to acceptance as they came to know me as their pastor. In all, I gained a deep appreciation of our connectional structure and of the local church as a center of ministry. The pain has been an ongoing lover's fight with the annual conference over issues

of clergywomen's salaries, having served at or below minimum salary most of my appointment career. I have seen opposition grow as the number of women clergy grows. I believe that it is harder now for women than it was when I first began. The joys outweigh the pain. The ministry has been a Spirit-guided journey that continues to be joy for me."

 *Milca Celeste Alvarez-Plaud*

First Hispanic/Latina Woman to Be Received into Full Connection

Received on Trial – 1977
Ordained Deacon – 1977
Received into Full Connection – 1980
Ordained Elder – 1980
Current Appointment – Co-op City UMC, Bronx – New York Conference

MILCA CELESTE ALVAREZ-PLAUD was born June 5, 1953, in Puerto Rico.

"I always wanted to be a missionary…. My father was a United Methodist minister in Puerto Rico, and I grew up in the church. I was always involved in the life of the church. I became a teacher at the age of twenty and taught Christian education for five years at a Christian school in Puerto Rico. But my job became more than teaching; it was ministry among students and parents. Through the study of scripture, feeling fulfilled in my work, and through personal experiences with the Lord, I understood that God was calling me for the ordained ministry.

"A few months after my first pastoral appointment in Puerto Rico, I was invited to come to Lancaster, Pennsylvania, as a student pastor. Suddenly, I was part of two minority groups–I was Hispanic and I was a clergywoman. Most of the time I was the only Hispanic female pastor present in church activities. In a very short time I was representing the Hispanics in different events at the conference and national level of the UMC. After five years I accepted a special appointment as editor of Spanish Resources for the General Board of Global Ministries. In 1984 the Lord opened a new door that I entered with joy– as the pastor of the Co-op City UMC in the Bronx. My twenty-one years as the pastor of this congregation have been a challenging and fulfilling experience. I have experienced rejection and lots of pain at times, but I have also received much love and support from many members–sufficient to overwhelm all negativity. The church has grown spiritually, numerically, financially, and programmatically and in May of 2005 consecrated a 3.5 million dollar church building [their very first in thirty years]. Together we are successfully performing the ministry that the Lord has called us to carry out."

Jacqueline Ann Sanders-Hines

First African American Woman to Be Received into Full Connection

Received on Trial – 1985
Ordained Deacon – 1985
Received into Full Connection – 1987
Ordained Elder – 1987
Currently on leave of absence and living in Maryland

JACQUELINE ANN SANDERS-HINES was born August 18, 1956, in Derby, Connecticut.

"On my knees in prayer, I experienced God's call to ministry. I was attending Eastern (Baptist) College at the time.

"Early in ministry I relied upon my experience and training as a guide. Presently, as I minister 'outside the box,' while waiting to be appointed to the Baltimore-Washington Conference, I find myself thrust into a ministry to the incarcerated, the homeless, and those yearning for a closer walk with Jesus. Many are unchurched. I am, at times, clueless as to how to respond with integrity. This ministry drives me as never before to 'wait upon the Lord' who knows our deepest needs and is ever ready."

Sukja Bang

First Korean Woman to Be Received into Full Connection

Received on Trial, Northern New Jersey – 1997
Ordained Deacon, Northern New Jersey – 1997
Received into Full Connection – 2000
Ordained Elder – 2000
Current Appointment – Calvary UMC, Ambler, Pennsylvania

SUKJA BANG was born March 12, 1953, in South Korea. After graduating from Methodist Theological School in Seoul, South Korea, with both a bachelor's degree and a master's degree, "I worked for the Korean Church Women United as a full-time staff person for three years. I felt I needed to study more about women's issues and enrolled in The Theological School at Drew University in Madison, New Jersey, in 1992. I thought about pursuing ordained ministry in Korea, but my journey of ordination actually began while I was studying at Drew. In faith, I was able to overcome many obstacles in my life and to learn to love myself as a daughter of God. So through the ordained ministry, I want to dedicate my life to the Lord to share the good news of the gospel with those who need to know God's unfailing love and grace.

"Presently, I am serving Calvary UMC, an English-speaking congregation. I received this cross-cultural appointment at the end of June 2003. I have been enjoying my ministry. Our love and understanding here at Calvary are mutual and we work in harmony for the Kingdom. I am blessed and privileged to be able to minister to this loving and caring congregation. As a woman, a person who contracted polio, and an ethnic minority pastor, I certainly have not had an easy journey to this point. But looking back at my footprints, there has always been another set of footprints beside mine–the Lord's. Through positive and negative experiences, God helps me to grow and mature. I don't know what's in store in my future, but I do know that God will continue to walk beside me in my journey toward home."

Felicia Ethel Dorcas Kumar

First Indian Woman to Be Received into Full Connection

Commissioned as Probationary Member – 2001
Received into Full Connection – 2005
Ordained Elder – 2005
Current Appointment – Associate Pastor, Jarrettown UMC, Dresher, Pennsylvania

FELICIA ETHEL DORCAS KUMAR was born February 22 in Cheenai, India.

"My call to ministry began when I was in India working as the Correspondence Analyst in the Sponsor Relations Department with World Vision of India, a Christian humanitarian relief organization. I had been in ministry with World Vision for thirteen years. That was the foundation to my call to ministry.

"I came to the United States in 1988 and I began my seminary studies in the fall of 1989. After I finished my seminary education, I was offered the position as the director of Christian education at the Narberth United Methodist Church in 1993. It was there that my call to ordained ministry became very clear when I became the pastoral assistant–preaching, teaching, counseling, visiting, and ministering to people of all ages. It was then that I began my candidacy process, was approved as a candidate, and was given my first appointment in July 1999.

"The journey toward ordination has been quite long but very meaningful and memorable indeed! As the journey continues, I joyfully proclaim the good news of Christ and his love to people of all ages, races, and cultures, and particularly to a hurting and broken world. The God who has called me is faithful and will never leave me nor forsake me and will *always* be with me even until the end of this age. Thanks be to God!"

GREATER NEW JERSEY ANNUAL CONFERENCE

 *Ruth Marion Ellis*

(EUROPEAN AMERICAN)
First Woman to Be Received into Full Connection in the Former Newark Conference in 1958

(See chapter 2, 45)

 *Florence Ridley*

First African American Woman to Be Received into Full Connection in the Former Northern New Jersey Conference

Received on Trial – 1977
Ordained Deacon – 1977
Received into Full Connection – 1979
Ordained Elder – 1979
Current Appointment – Extension Ministries, Prison Chaplain/Supervisor of Chaplain Services, Edna Mahan Correctional Facility For Women, Clinton, New Jersey

FLORENCE RIDLEY was born June 15, 1944, in Philadelphia, Pennsylvania.

"I experienced the call to ministry at age ten, age fourteen, age twenty-two, and age thirty as God revealed it to me through the Holy Spirit, but I did not respond to the call to ordained ministry until age thirty because I believed God was not calling me directly into the ministry but as a minister's wife. I entertained the thought of entering the Peace Corps to work as an evangelist but, upon serious reflection on God's call on my life, I opted instead to respond and I began to prayerfully pass through a patriarchal protocol when I began Princeton Theological Seminary in 1975.

"Once I accepted the call to ordained ministry, my journey has been focused. I pastored a church for three years, but it was during the seminary field education time that I realized my special calling to outreach ministry in a prison setting. Additional clinical pastoral education refined my skills for this specialized extension ministry. Appointments of clergywomen were plentiful in our conference in 1978; however, being the first ethnic clergywoman and Afro-American presented the problem of not being well received by a congregation. An attempt to place me at a church was so drastically opposed that one trustee rumored the parsonage would be burned down if I were placed there. The second church I interviewed with was impressed with my résumé, but when I met face to face with the pastor-parish relations committee, they wanted to change their minds. However, the district superintendent and cabinet forced them to take me. We had a difficult three years as pastor and congregation. Then an opening at the prison occurred in 1981 [which is] when I began prison ministry, and I moved to the supervisor's position in 1988, and I will retire from the position in 2006 after twenty-five years of prison ministry. My ministry after retirement will continue with a focus on paroled women through the Sister Aftercare Ministry–a mentoring and ministry assessment collaborative which I founded in 1999."

 *Rebeca M. Radillo*

First Hispanic/Latina Woman to Be Received into Full Connection in the Former Northern New Jersey Conference

Received on Trial, Florida Conference – 1980
Ordained Deacon, Florida Conference – 1980
Received into Full Connection – 1986
Ordained Elder – 1986
Current Appointment – Extension Ministries, Professor of Pastoral Care and Director of the Supervised Ministry Program, New York Theological Seminary

REBECA M. RADILLO was born in Havana, Cuba, to very active Methodist parents.

"Their lives, faith, and emotional support laid a solid moral, ethical, and spiritual foundation for both of their daughters' life journeys. Education was indeed a nonnegotiable at home, and when the time came to attend school, the Central Methodist School became the home away from home. Home and school became the formation context for my ministry, which I understand as the outcome of a developmental expression of my vocation. In the merging of my pastoral formation and emerging identity, the process of immigration, working with refugees and migrants as well as my seminary education and CPE [Clinical Pastoral Education] (Candler School of Theology and Grady Memorial Hospital) had direct and profound bearing upon what I understand my calling to be–'an incarnational expression of my beliefs and a tangible expression of how I believe God has called me to be and to do.'

"I have been privileged in that I have served multicultural congregations as well as English-speaking churches. I am the founder and executive director of the Latino Pastoral Care Institute (ILCP) in the South Bronx. Prior to the present appointment, I taught at Drew University School of Theology in the MDiv and DMin programs. I believe every area of ministry in which God has allowed me to participate has been indeed within the *kairos* of God. As a pastor, an endorsed chaplain, and now a professor, I have experienced grace and the challenges of ministry. Therefore, I move into the future with a great deal of anticipation and trust the words of God to Joshua in the opening nine verses of the book."

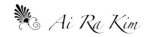 *Ai Ra Kim*

First Korean Woman to Be Received into Full Connection in the Former Northern New Jersey Conference

Received on Trial – 1986
Ordained Deacon – 1986
Received into Full Connection – 1989
Ordained Elder – 1989
Retired – 2004 – Professor Emerita – United Theological Seminary
Current Appointment – Professor at Hoseo University, United Graduate School of Theology, South Korea

AI RA KIM was born August 1, 1938, in Seoul, Korea.

"The time for my decision to pursue ordination came while I was studying for the MDiv degree at Drew University School of Theology from 1982 to 1986. Since 1986, as pastor, I have served Denville Community Church and Flanders United Methodist Church in New Jersey, and First United Methodist Church in Stony Point, New York. After obtaining a PhD degree from Drew University in 1991, I have taught at Pacific School of Religion, New York Theological Seminary, Drew University Graduate School of Theology, Garrett-Evangelical Theological Seminary, and United Theological Seminary from which I retired as professor emerita in June 2004. Also, as Fulbright Scholar, I taught at Ewha Woman's University in Seoul, [South] Korea. Since my retirement, I have been teaching at Hoseo University, United Graduate School of Theology, in Korea.

"Reflecting upon my life/ministerial journey, I am so grateful to my two daughters and my loved ones, who have shared my journey, as well as to the Northern New Jersey Annual Conference. Above all, I give my utmost thanks to my God."

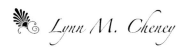 *Lynn M. Cheney*

(EUROPEAN AMERICAN)
One of the First Three Women to Be Received into Full Connection in the Former Southern New Jersey Conference

Received on Trial – 1975
Ordained Deacon – 1975
Received into Full Connection – 1977
Ordained Elder – 1977
Voluntary Location – 1985

LYNN M. CHENEY was born November 21, 1950, at Point Pleasant Beach, New Jersey. "I experienced my call while I was a student at Drew University. After graduating from Drew in 1975 I obtained an MDiv degree from Candler School of Theology in Atlanta. I returned to New Jersey, where I served churches in the [now] Greater New Jersey Annual Conference, including Glendale, Magnolia, and Westville. For the past fifteen years, I have been serving as the director of social services at Ocean View Center, formerly a Lutheran Home."

 *Carolyn J. Montgomery*

(EUROPEAN AMERICAN)
One of the First Three Women to Be Received into Full Connection in the Former Southern New Jersey Conference

Received on Trial – 1975
Ordained Deacon – 1975
Received into Full Connection – 1977
Ordained Elder – 1977
Current Appointment – Extension Ministries Appointment to Doylestown Hospital, Doylestown, Pennsylvania

CAROLYN J. MONTGOMERY was born October 11, 1944, in Sellersville, Pennsylvania.

"On Christmas Eve 1972, while walking my dog in the fog, the idea that I could be a minister in the parish came to me in a gentle and beautiful way. This was in the context of volunteering and spending a great deal of time in the church over the previous six years. I had also developed a deep friendship with my pastor who became my mentor. I probably would not have gone further had he not been so excited and encouraging and gotten me into a seminary the following January.

"I had never met a woman who was a minister. My entry into conference was a little more difficult. I was the first woman interviewed by the Southern New Jersey Conference Board of Ordained Ministry. I was turned down. It was hard to tell if that had to do with my call or readiness or their concern that as a single person I might get married, have a family, and not be able to itinerate. In any case, the next year I was approved, and I had such support from my mentor and friends that the process was affirming.

"I have been happy being a chaplain and have had a meaningful ministry. However, I was headed for the parish in the beginning and had no significant knowledge of other types of ministry. My preparation for chaplaincy was through CPE and really confirmed for me my direction. In 1985 I was led to Doylestown Hospital were I still find myself. It is with satisfaction that I see the changes over twenty years. We started with a department with one chaplain and five volunteers. Now, not counting myself, we now have a chaplain for hospice, a chaplain for our retirement community, and over forty volunteers. However, the very touching and meaningful moments come with the stories of our patients and the sacred but often painful times spent here at a time of crisis and change."

Margaret Abrams Parker

(EUROPEAN AMERICAN)
One of the First Three Women to Be Received into Full Connection in the Former Southern New Jersey Conference

Received on Trial – 1975
Ordained Deacon – 1975
Received into Full Connection – 1977
Ordained Elder – 1977
Withdrew – 1986

MARGARET ABRAMS PARKER was appointed to attend school in 1975. In 1976, she was appointed to Wesley in Pleasantville and Bethel in Somers Point. In 1977 she was appointed to Billingsport and Repcupo in Paulsboro. From 1980 to 1983 she served Hannonton and Batsto. In 1984 she was appointed to Batsto, and in 1985 she served Gloucester First. In 1986, Margaret withdrew from the ministry.[3]

Marion Alberta Jackson

One of the First Two African American Women to Be Received into Full Connection in the Former Southern New Jersey Conference

Received on Trial – 1986
Ordained Deacon – 1986
Received into Full Connection – 1988
Ordained Elder – 1988
Current Appointment – Senior Minister, First UMC, Montclair, New Jersey

MARION ALBERTA JACKSON was born June 21, 1944, at Glen Ridge, New Jersey.

"I was baptized and confirmed at St. Mark's Methodist Church in Montclair, New Jersey. I began my prayer life at age two (according to my baby book) and I knew by the age of nine that I was 'consecrated' to God in some way. I was unsure of how that 'consecration' translated to a vocation, as I did not know of any women preachers or Protestant nuns. Those seemed to be the only two options I could think of, and I saw no evidence of either in my world. I assumed that something unknown would be revealed, or that I would be the first of one or the other. Throughout my youth at St. Mark's, I held several leadership positions.

"My young adult life, however, was troubled and took many unfortunate turns. I temporarily left the church and began a journey that led down many roads exploring various faith traditions, including Eastern religions. Eventually, one of those roads led first to a renewed relationship with Christ on February 3, 1980, followed by a reaffirmation of my call and then to a return to The United Methodist Church. I served several churches and was a district superintendent in the former Southern New Jersey Conference (the second woman and first black woman to do so)."

In her appointment as director of Continuing Education, Clergywomen's Concerns and Spiritual Formation at the General Board of Higher Education and Ministry, Marion was the shepherd for the Fiftieth Anniversary Task Force for the Celebration of Full Clergy Rights for Women and will be greatly missed as she returns to New Jersey.

Mildred Lee Stanford

One of the First Two African American Women to Be Received into Full Connection in the Former Southern New Jersey Conference

Received on Trial – 1986
Ordained Deacon – 1986
Received into Full Connection – 1988
Ordained Elder – 1988
Retired – 1993
Deceased – 2003

MILDRED LEE STANFORD was born July 26, 1926, and grew up in Rock Hall, Maryland. Her parents made God and church a central part of her life and laid the roots that became the foundation from which she built her life and religious focus. After retiring from thirty-one years in the teaching profession, Mildred recognized that there was a deeper, more spiritual need that she had not met. Through assessments and prayer she heeded God's calling and entered Eastern Baptist Theological Seminary in Philadelphia where she earned a master of divinity degree.

Mildred's first pastoral assignment was to Rhoads Temple UMC in Sadlertown, New Jersey, as a student pastor. In June 1985, she became the first female pastor at the historic Mt. Zion UMC in Lawnside, New Jersey, and served this congregation until her retirement in 1993. After she retired, however, Mildred continued her ministry, working as assistant pastor at St. Paul UMC in Willingboro, New Jersey, and then in July 1998, starting as senior pastor at John Wesley UMC in Bridgeton, New Jersey, "retiring again" in 2002.

Mildred placed particular emphasis on youth-related programs and was instrumental in ensuring that young people played a key role in all aspects of the services provided by the church. She was an outstanding pastor and caregiver. Mildred served God while sharing herself, her experiences, talents, and God-given gift of loving all people and working solely for the Almighty Savior. Mildred Stanford died January 23, 2003, at age seventy-six.[4]

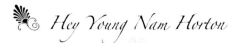
Hey Young Nam Horton

First Korean Woman to Be Received into Full Connection in the Former Southern New Jersey Conference

Received on Trial – 1997
Ordained Deacon – 1997
Received into Full Connection – 1999
Ordained Elder – 1999
Current Appointment – Associate Pastor, First UMC, Moorestown, New Jersey

HEY YOUNG NAM HORTON was born January 28, 1964, in Seoul, South Korea.

"I was a full-time lay missionary for eight years before I decided to enroll in seminary. During those years I developed a strong passion to learn more about God and the theology I was professing, so that I could become a more effective missionary. It was in my second year of seminary that I became convinced that God was calling me to become a full-time ordained minister.

"I have encountered some hardships because of being a Korean woman pastor. Some members found it difficult to accept me because of my race and gender. I have also been blessed to meet many members who supported me in my ministry. I truly feel my journey has been blessed with some minor struggles that have made me even stronger. I am very happy with my current appointment. I feel nurtured and supported by the congregation's prayers and words of encouragement."

NEW ENGLAND ANNUAL CONFERENCE

 *The 4-Hs*

Gertrude Genevra Harris, Alice Townsend Hart, Esther A. Haskard, and Margaret Kimball Henrichsen (EUROPEAN AMERICAN)

First Four Women to Be Received into Full Connection in the Former Maine Annual Conference in 1958

(See chapter 2, 38, 39, 40, 41)

 *Inez Yvonne James*

First African American Woman to Be Received into Full Connection in the Former Maine Annual Conference

Received on Trial – 1983
Ordained Deacon – 1983
Received into Full Connection – 1985
Ordained Elder – 1985
Transferred to New York Conference – 1985
Deceased – 1993

INEZ YVONNE JAMES was born September 7, 1955, in Philadelphia, Pennsylvania. Her family was active in the African Methodist Episcopal Church (AME Church), and when Inez was ten years old she understood that God was calling her to preach. "Her pastor, the Reverend Gabriel Hardaman Sr., recognized God's call upon the precocious young lady, and under his leadership she was licensed to preach at the age of eleven. Inez felt very keenly about the sacred trust of preaching, and as a result preached barefoot in the pulpit, reminding herself that the sacred desk was 'holy ground.'"

"Even in her early years of preaching," Inez "showed a gift for biblical interpretation and took the text with great seriousness." After graduating from the Theological School at Drew University, Inez affiliated with the Maine Annual Conference of The United Methodist Church and served for two years at the Fairfield and Fairfield Center United Methodist churches.

Although she was received into full membership and

ordained an elder in 1985, after her transfer to the New York Conference, she continued to serve for two additional years as a probationary member before her full membership was recognized. In the New York Conference, Inez served at Valley Stream and then as pastor of John Wesley parish in Brooklyn. There "she realized a culmination of her dream to bring together her deep appreciation for the proclamation of the Word with her training in social work to bring about real transformation in the community. She was committed both to personal piety and discipline, as well as social holiness and witness." Inez James died April 18, 1993, after a sudden, brief illness, at age thirty-seven.[5]

 *Faith Adams Chandler*

(EUROPEAN AMERICAN)

First Woman to Be Received into Full Connection in the Former New Hampshire Conference

Received on Trial – 1957
Ordained Deacon – 1957
Received into Full Connection – 1959
Ordained Elder – 1959
Retired – 1982
Deceased – 1983

FAITH ADAMS CHANDLER was born November 26, 1921, in New Hampshire. Prior to entering the ministry, she worked as an engineer's assistant at the Raytheon Company in Waltham, Massachusetts. After completing her theological studies, Faith served churches in the New Hampshire Conference, including Canaan and Canaan Street, Colebrook (where she was director of the Parish of The Headwaters), Sundown and West Hempstead (where she facilitated the merger of the two churches), and, finally, the Franklin and Tilton-Northfield Charge. She retired on disability leave in 1982.

Faith's call to ministry brought her joy and pain, success and frustration, but in all this she continually found strength to serve her God through Christ. Faith took time to smell the flowers and to help others enjoy beauty in life. She found that beauty so vividly that evangelism became her joy, which she shared both in the local church and the larger church.... Faith will stand as a pioneer in ministry in the New Hampshire Conference as she dared tread where women had not ventured before. She met the challenge and [stood] proud among women in ministry.

She left a rich heritage among Christ's servants. Faith Chandler died February 19, 1983, at the age of sixty-one.[6]

Gwen Jones-Lurvey

(EUROPEAN AMERICAN)
First Woman to Serve in Full Connection in the Former Southern New England Conference
Received into Full Connection in the Missouri West Conference in 1970
Transferred to Southern California-Arizona in 1975

(See chapter 6, 133)

Julieanne Sotzing Hallman

(EUROPEAN AMERICAN)
First Woman to Be Received into Full Connection in the Former Southern New England Conference

Received on Trial – 1970
Ordained Deacon – 1970
Received into Full Connection – 1973
Ordained Elder – 1973
Retired – 2005

JULIEANNE SOTZING HALLMAN was born August 30, 1943, in Troy, Ohio. Julieanne grew up in the Evangelical Lutheran Church.

"My mother gave me a diary on my twelfth birthday. There I discovered I could write down all my secret thoughts. I began reflecting on my first experience with God at age nine. One summer day I lay on the grass in my backyard. I looked up into the heavens and tried to imagine where the sky and all the rest came from. I felt swept to the edges of the heavens and saw new horizons. A voice said, 'This is God, you see–God.' I concluded that I indeed knew God and felt loved by God. In retrospect that experience sealed my faith. I had an unwavering inward assurance of God's presence and power to heal. I felt a growing desire to help people, especially those who are suffering, to know the holy love of their Creator.

"The day I was ordained deacon and received as a probationary member of the conference, I remember looking in the mirror and realizing suddenly that I was one of only two ordained women in ministry I knew. I looked forward to meeting the other woman."

Since 1980 Julieanne has served in extension ministry as professor of Supervised Ministry and director of Field Education at Andover Newton Theological School, from which she retired in September 2005. "Thanks to God's amazing grace, a community of wonderful colleagues, and excellent mentors, I have been blessed to meet the challenges

of ministry and of theological education as pastor, supervisor, teacher, and field educator. I am grateful beyond words for the rich relationships and rewarding work of these years. Abundant indeed is God's grace in my life!"

Yolanda Pupo-Ortiz

First Hispanic/Latina Woman to Be Received into Full Connection in the Former Southern New England Conference

Received on Trial – 1983
Ordained Deacon – 1983
Received into Full Connection – 1985
Ordained Elder – 1985
Transferred to Baltimore-Washington Conference – 1989
Retired – 2005

YOLANDA E. PUPO-ORTIZ was born September 14, 1937, in Holguín, Oriente, Cuba.

"I discerned my call to serve God at age twelve. At that time I decided that the best way to serve God was through the law. I announced to my parents that I wanted to become a lawyer so I could be a judge and work for justice. This first call evolved so that by the time I was fifteen I was clear that I was being called into the ministry. I was blessed to have a family and a church that, in spite of my young years, encouraged and empowered me to live out my call, even when there were not many women in the ordained ministry.

"And what a journey I have had in that ministry! A small congregation that embraced and respected me even when I was very young (twenty-two); a larger congregation that struggled with us through very difficult and critical years in my country; a bishop who enabled us to make what became the major decision of our lives: leaving our country and becoming first exiles and then permanent residents (later citizens) of the United States. In the United States, I faced changes, adaptation, clash of cultures, divorce, and more changes and challenges, especially of language, ethnicity, and culture. And in the midst of all, the new appointments, the barriers to bring down, the good and the bad, the constant presence of the God who called me and never abandoned me; the support and love of my blood family and the sisters and brothers of the larger family that is the church. Indeed, that family has been there for me in Florida, in Connecticut, in Massachusetts, in Maryland, and in Washington, DC."

Young Kim

First Korean Woman to Be Received into Full Connection in the Former Southern New England Conference

Received on Trial – 1984
Ordained Deacon – 1984
Received into Full Connection – 1986
Ordained Elder – 1986
Current Appointment – Danielson UMC, Danielson, Connecticut

YOUNG KIM was born September 17, 1941, in Korea.

"Even before I knew what ministry was all about, I kept praying for my vocation that was more than a job. My desire was not to separate my job from my life. Then I began to sense that God was pulling me into something called 'ordained ministry.' Now, here am I in a pastoral position. I cannot separate my life from church life. I got what I prayed for.

"My journey in ministry has been a covenant, starting with Jesus' question, 'Do you love me more than others?' When I responded with a yes, Jesus told me to feed his people. The journey in ministry has been like parenting–a modern concept not unlike shepherding in ancient times. It requires continuously watching over the children of God. They are in need of growing in every aspect. Sometimes they fight, hurt, envy, and hate one another. Other times they love and care for one another. I need to be there with understanding of human nature. My experience as a grandparent has deepened my love for the people. Of course, by presenting prophetic sermons, I trust they will grow in conscience of peace and justice. There are many other images in my ministry as in yours."

Julia Adelaide Mendes Thomas Doutaz

First African American Woman to Be Received into Full Connection in the Former Southern New England Conference

Received on Trial – 1984
Ordained Deacon – 1984
Received into Full Connection – 1992
Ordained Elder – 1992
Current Appointment – Somerset UMC, Somerset, Massachusetts

JULIA ADELAIDE MENDEZ THOMAS DOUTAZ was born June 26, 1945, in Providence, Rhode Island.

"The call to the ministry came when I was about eight or nine years old. We received many missionaries in our church. I was attentive to the needs of the sick and the shut-in. I also studied the history of The United Methodist Church. I was extremely active in the church with fellowship and all worship services.

"I have served five churches and served as a hospital chaplain (Temple, Texas). Through the years, pastoral care has stood out as a special gift. Some people struggled with my height, color, gender, and quiet manner. All of these things added to my gifts in the ministry. No female in my family had ever entered religious life and I had to prove the seriousness of my call because I married at a young age. By the time I was twenty-one years old I had four children. Those children were supportive of my ministry. This has been a journey of faith. God has opened the doors that I needed [opened] at the time of my need."

Dorothy Yaa Ofobi Adomakoh Asare

First African Woman to Be Received into Full Connection

Received on Trial – 1992
Ordained Deacon – 1992
Received into Full Connection – 1998
Ordained Elder – 1998
Current Appointment – First UMC, Milford, Massachusetts

DOROTHY YAA OFOBI ADOMAKOH ASARE was born August 11, 1947, in Kumasi, Ghana, West Africa.

"When I asked Jesus into my life in my early teens, I was so excited about it that I told everybody and anybody who was willing to listen. I learned very quickly to sharpen the skills needed to facilitate that communication. I studied the Bible, took advantage of all spiritual formation opportunities, and loved sharing my faith. I was given numerous opportunities for leadership training for the next five years by Scripture Union (a group that nurtures young people in Bible study and devotional practices) in Ghana. I was speaking to groups on a regular basis but never considered a 'call to ministry' because that was the exclusive domain for the male species. When I was an undergraduate at the University of Ghana, Legon, I preached regularly at the university chapel. I received a lot of affirmation each time I preached but never considered a 'call to ministry' for the reason stated above.

"My family emigrated to the United States in 1984. On our arrival, we got involved in the Emmaus Renewal movement where I served as a speaker on numerous retreats. There was always that constant affirmation, and, at this point, gentle nudges to consider 'specialized ministry.' Finally, in 1990 I enrolled at Boston University School of Theology in the Master of Divinity program and never looked back.

"Being in a local church for the past ten years has been both rewarding and challenging. I have had to deal with the challenge of being an African woman in New England. Talking with other female colleagues, the issues are similar for African American and white women. But As Paul says in 2 Cor. 4:7 (KJV), 'We have this treasure in earthen vessels,' and it is such a pleasure and joy to see God at work in the ministry in spite of all those struggles. I give thanks to the faithful God who called me to be a servant in ministry with others."

Hikari Kokai Chang

First Japanese Woman to Be Received into Full Connection

Ordained Deacon, United Church of Christ, Japan – 1986
Transferred to UMC – 1999
Received into Full Connection – 2003
Ordained Elder – 2003
Current Appointment – Armonk UMC, New York Conference

HIKARI KOKAI CHANG was born May 16, 1961, in Saitama, Japan.

"As a child who was raised up in the minister's family, a question about the relationship between faith and culture was an essential part of my spiritual formation: How can I be a Christian and, at the same time, a Japanese? To seek an answer to this question, I enrolled in seminary in 1980. During my seminary years, my heart was opened to see God's affirmation of who I am and his blessing on faith expressed through different cultures. I felt God's calling in my life to be an ordained pastor, and I was ordained by the United Church of Christ in Japan in 1986.

"After my ordination, I came to the United States for further study and married Hak-Soon Chang, a native Korean and an elder in the UMC. We started to build a family of two cultures in America. I had been seeking the direction of God's calling in my life. Then, the experience of love expressed by the church family at the time of our daughter's sickness and healing of leukemia helped open my heart to the broader parish of Christ's church, and I decided to serve in ministry in the UMC. Now I have an assurance of God's calling in my life to serve wherever and to whomever I am sent and to share my gifts as a Japanese woman in ministry to all people. My ministry is to bring the Word and the sacraments of salvation and forgiveness through Jesus Christ to all people in teaching and caring and to work on peace and justice in the world as the sign of God's reign. I pray that I may become salt and light of the world as a disciple of Jesus Christ through my whole being with words, deeds, and presence as a Japanese minister in American culture."

NEW YORK ANNUAL CONFERENCE

 *Barbara B. Troxell*

 *Noemi Amanda Vasconcelos Diaz*

(EUROPEAN AMERICAN)

First Woman to Be Received into Full Connection in the Former New York East Conference

Received on Trial – 1958
Ordained Deacon – 1958
Received into Full Connection – 1961
Ordained Elder – 1961
Retired – 2001 (continuing part-time teaching, offering spiritual direction, and leading retreats in retirement)

BARBARA B. TROXELL was born August 31, 1935, in Brooklyn, New York.

"I began to sense a call when I was a teenager in my wonderfully responsive home church, King's Highway Methodist Church, Brooklyn. But the 'Church Vocations' films shown in MYF [Methodist Youth Fellowship] always had clean-cut white, young men as the recipients of calls, so I felt ordained ministry was not open to me. However, in college, when I served a couple of summers in rural Vermont doing vacation church school, teaching and living in homes of families, I sensed a real call and felt led to go for it.

"My ministry has been a wondrous journey of increasing mutuality in ministry, claiming integrated authority, and deepening my trust in the creative spirit of God. Though I served as solo pastor in my first charge and, later, in positions of executive authority (e.g., in the superintendency and in positions in theological seminaries), I am most grateful, in all the settings, for having been part of collaborative ministry teams with both laity and clergy. My calling throughout has included the linkages between spiritual formation and justice for all persons (loving God with all our being and our neighbors as ourselves), for these are central to the gospel message of Jesus."

First Hispanic/Latina Woman to Be Received into Full Connection in the New York Conference and in the United States

Ordained Deacon, New York East, MC – 1959
Ordained Elder, New York East, MC – 1961
Received on Trial – 1965
Received into Full Connection – 1967
Retired – 1982
Deceased – 1996

NOEMI AMANDA VASCONCELOS DIAZ was born June 18, 1912, in Nueva Paz, Cuba. It was there that she did her primary school studies. She was called to preach at age eleven and accompanied her pastor to do evangelistic visitation. By the age of fourteen, Noemi was teaching Sunday school.

In June 1955, Noemi moved to New York and joined the staff of the Church of All Nations in Lower Manhattan as an assistant pastor. There, she began a Hispanic church and worked with them for nineteen years. Under her leadership, attendance reached one hundred twenty, quite a feat in New York City back then. Three hundred young people responded to her ministry there, as well.

In 1974 Noemi was appointed to Knickerbocker UMC where she worked with enthusiasm and determination until her retirement in 1982. When the church building was destroyed by fire in 1977, she oversaw the construction of a new building, which was dedicated in 1981. After her retirement, she was appointed part-time to the Far Rockaway Mission.

Noemi was a pioneer in the New York Conference–a woman of deep faith, a visionary, and a seeker of excellence. She walked among us as one who served her God and the church, and was loved by all. Noemi graced us with her presence and we thank God for her life and example. Noemi Diaz died September 16, 1996, at age eighty-four.[7]

 *Ruthenia Helen Finley*

One of the First Two African American Women to Be Received into Full Connection

Received on Trial – 1980
Ordained Deacon – 1980
Received into Full Connection – 1983
Ordained Elder – 1983
Retired – 2002
Deceased – 2003

RUTHENIA HELEN FINLEY was born in Georgetown, South Carolina, in 1933. Ruthenia was a member of Metropolitan Community UMC from childhood until the family relocated to the Bronx, when she transferred her membership to Butler Memorial UMC. Under the guidance of the Reverend William P. Johnson and the Reverend Granville A. Forde, Ruthenia honed her skills as a church leader. After working for the New York Public Library for twenty-seven years, she answered the call to ministry at Butler and was given many opportunities to develop her preaching. Ruthenia was involved in the church throughout her entire life and the call to ministry was the natural culmination of a life dedicated to service in the church.

Prior to being appointed as associate program director of the New York Conference in the areas of evangelism, church growth, and revitalization, Ruthenia served John Wesley UMC and St. Mark's UMC, both in Brooklyn. She then went on to serve at St. Mark's UMC in Manhattan and Union UMC in Brooklyn prior to her retirement in 2002.

After a short illness, Ruthenia died August 28, 2003, at age seventy. At the service of celebration for her life, Ruthenia's wit and humor were mentioned many times, as well as her insistence on good work and diligence. Ruthenia Helen Finley served the church and humanity with strength, grace, humility, and love for all.[8]

 *Linda Elaine Thomas*

One of the First Two African American Women to Be Received into Full Connection

Received on Trial, Baltimore Conference – 1981
Ordained Deacon, Baltimore Conference – 1981
Received into Full Connection – 1983
Ordained Elder – 1983
Current Appointment – Extension Ministries, Professor of Theology and Anthropology at the Lutheran School of Theology at Chicago, Chicago, Illinois

LINDA ELAINE THOMAS was born in Baltimore, Maryland.

"My call to ministry came when I was twelve years old. The Reverend Leslie A. Dyson was my spiritual father, and his wife, Antoinette Dyson (I would now call her copastor), was my spiritual mother. While I was in church one Sunday at the age of twelve listening to Rev. Dyson (a very fiery preacher) preach, I became aware that even with all his charisma, I was at that moment in tune with another source of meaning and power. It

had my total attention. I call it my primordial experience of God's presence. I went home from church and prayed. I asked God if God wanted me to be a minister. Before I finished asking the question, I knew the answer from God was 'yes.'

"I have had a significant ministry preparing women and men to be spiritual leaders in a very complex and changing world. My commitment to understanding culture, religious beliefs (Christian and other), and issues of race, gender, class, and sexual orientation led me to do PhD work in anthropology. I believe that Christians need cultural literacy in order to be effective rather than offensive. My commitment also includes working with people trapped by systematic poverty in black African townships in South Africa. My first book, entitled *Under the Canopy: Ritual Process and Spiritual Resilience in South Africa*, presents my research. I also write on womanist theology."

 *Youngsook Han-Kim*

First Korean Woman to Be Received into Full Connection

Received on Trial – 1983
Ordained Deacon – 1983
Received into Full Connection – 1985
Ordained Elder – 1985
Current Appointment – Metropolitan-Koryo UMC, Manhattan, New York

YOUNGSOOK HAN-KIM was born September 27, 1948, in a small town in South Korea.

"I entered Ewha Women's University to study Christianity and graduated from the University in 1971 and graduate school in 1974. After graduation I taught Christianity at the University until 1979. One day in early spring 1978, I committed myself to be a pastor in order to proclaim that gospel that made me free. Then I came to the United States to study at Union Theological Seminary in 1979, and finished my master of divinity program in 1982.

"Since 1982, I have been the pastor of Metropolitan-Koryo UMC, a Korean congregation in Manhattan. I started this church from the bottom. Since this church is located in Manhattan, I have experienced a 20 percent shift in membership every year. My biggest frustration has been sharing the church building. Yet, I am thankful to have lived my life to study the Bible and preach the gospel."

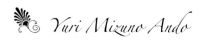 *Yuri Mizuno Ando*

First Japanese Woman to Be Received into Full Connection

Received on Trial – 1985
Ordained Deacon – 1985
Received into Full Connection – 1987
Ordained Elder – 1987
Current Appointment – Appointed to School to Study Gestalt Pastoral Care

YURI MIZUNO ANDO was born March 9, 1954, in Tajimi City, Japan.

"I received my call to ordained ministry in 1983, when I was enrolled in the Christian education program at Union Theological Seminary.

"My training is in Gestalt Pastoral Care, which includes spiritual companioning, Gestalt growth work, and prayer for healing. This is a ministry to heal our brokenness in our body, mind, emotions, and spirit. I also work at Parish Resource Center part-time as a consultant to help the ministries of local churches. I work with laity and clergy on various programs in their own churches and offer occasional workshops.

"My journey has been great knowing that God has been leading me all along. It has not been a smooth road and has been rocky from time to time, but it's all part of my journey and I give thanks to God for that!"

Snehlata Kunjravia-Patel

First Indian Woman to Be Received into Full Connection

Received on Trial – 1990
Ordained Deacon – 1990
Received into Full Connection – 1992
Ordained Elder – 1992
Current Appointment – Woodrow UMC, Staten Island, New York

SNEHLATA KUNJRAVIA-PATEL was born June 9, 1942, in Thamna, Gujarat, India.

"My father was a pastor, so I spent almost my whole life in the parsonage. Then I married a pastor! The only time I have not lived in the parsonage was from 1983 through 1990, which was when my family and I arrived in the United States. When God called me to ministry in the United States, I was not prepared. English is a second language and I was in my forties. However, God saw me through it all. I received my MDiv from Union Theological Seminary in 1989 and my DMin from Hartford Seminary in 1997.

"I was appointed to a two-point charge in 1990– Higganum UMC and South Middletown UMC, located in Connecticut. I served at these churches for ten years when, in 2000, I was appointed to Woodrow UMC in Staten Island, New York. God has blessed me tremendously during the journey. I am particularly happy that my daughter, Iwy Patel-Yatri, is a candidate for ordained ministry. We are the first Indian mother and daughter team in the New York Annual Conference. Interestingly enough, we serve 'mother and daughter churches' in Staten Island. She serves at St. Mark UMC, which is an offshoot from Woodrow UMC (also known as the 'mother' church of Staten Island), where I have been serving for the past four-and-a-half years.

"God called me when I was nine years old and has used me as a teacher, evangelist, church leader, and a deaconess (which is parallel to ordained ministry in India). God has used me to make a difference in many lives. I am grateful to God for the many blessings that God has bestowed upon me and to others through me."

First Chinese Woman to Be Received into Full Connection

Received on Trial, North Georgia Conference – 1998
Ordained Deacon, North Georgia Conference – 1998
Received into Full Connection – 2003
Ordained Elder – 2003
Current Appointment – First UMC, Port Jefferson, New York

HUIBING HE was born June 19, 1955, in Guangzhou, China.

"I am from Mainland China and grew up during the Communist revolutionary years. When the church was reopened in China after being closed for twenty years, I was baptized and became a Christian in the summer of 1980. As I look back, I realize God had called me even before I was aware of his call. People in my generation in China who grew up in an atheistic society and a Confucian culture knew very little about Christianity and were skeptical about religion. They do, however, thirst for truth. They sought for the meaning of life and wondered if there was divine power or a creator of the universe and what our relationship is with this creator. When the Nanjing Theological Seminary in China reopened, I strongly felt the need to be trained and to learn about theology so that I could be equipped to share and articulate my experience of God's grace and salvation to people of my generation. I graduated from Nanjing Theological Seminary in 1986 and became a teacher there. In 1992, I emigrated to the United States and joined St. James UMC in Atlanta, which eventually recommended me for the ordination process. When I was ordained deacon, Bishop Lindsey Davis announced at the ordination ceremony that I was the first Chinese woman to be received into conference membership in the Southeast Jurisdiction.

"I am currently serving an Anglo American congregation with 360 members. As an ethnic woman, serving in this church, I find it both a great challenge and a great blessing. In my ministry to the congregation, I have learned enormously about American culture and tradition and it has increased my appreciation and respect for American culture. As a result of having an Asian clergywoman as their pastor, along with the sharing of my Chinese culture, my congregation now sees things from a different perspective and has come to appreciate the diversity of God's gifts and grace. It is a joy for me to see the grace and love of God touching people's hearts and changing their lives through my ministry. As I give myself in ministry, I, too, experience, every day of my life, renewal and transformation."

NORTH CENTRAL NEW YORK ANNUAL CONFERENCE

JoLorene Miller Parker Anderson

(EUROPEAN AMERICAN)
First Woman to Be Received into Full Connection in the Former Central New York Conference in 1958

(See chapter 2, 37)

Elizabeth Suydam Foster Mowry

(EUROPEAN AMERICAN)
First Woman to Be Received into Full Connection in the Former Northern New York Conference

Received on Trial – 1972
Ordained Deacon – 1972
Received into Full Connection – 1974
Ordained Elder – 1974
Current Appointment – Oneida First UMC, Oneida, New York

ELIZABETH SUYDAM FOSTER MOWRY was born August 5, 1944, in Jamaica, Long Island, New York.

"I experienced my call in August 1957 and answered yes in August 1961. I began my study for a license to preach in the New York East Conference in September 1961 and was granted the license by the Brooklyn South District, New York East Conference, in April 1962.

"I was married in 1964. While attending seminary, first at Drew [Theological School] and then two years at Iliff School of Theology, I gave birth each year! It was difficult to find a conference that was willing to take the 'uncharted course of a married woman with children in ministry.' God swung open the door of Northern New York Conference. I am completing thirty-three years of full-time ministry as a pastor in our conference. I am active in district, conference, and community activities. I have attended each one of the church's clergywomen's convocations. I didn't know the journey would be so hard but God has allowed no turning back."

Inell R. Claypool

First African American Woman to Serve in Full Connection

Received on Trial, Southern New England – 1988
Ordained Deacon, Southern New England – 1988
Received into Full Connection, Southern New England – 1996
Ordained Elder, Southern New England – 1996
Transferred to North Central New York – 2000
Current Appointment – Delta UMC, Rome, New York

INELL RICHARDSON CLAYPOOL was born August 21, 1958, in Auburn, New York.

"I experienced my call to ministry when I was an undergraduate at Cornell University. I was involved in a campus Bible study group, started by a local Sunday school teacher. I grew tremendously in my faith and as a result led many students to Christ and began to disciple and nurture the younger Christians. Gradually, I began to feel a call. I can remember sitting at my kitchen table and having an overwhelming sense that God was calling me to the ministry and arguing with God (out of my Baptist background), 'God, you don't call women to the ministry.' Finally, I told the teacher of the Bible study group of my experience. She responded, 'Well, we've been wondering when you would finally realize this.'

"The journey has been both fulfilling and challenging. The exciting part is seeing people who finally 'get it,' discipling people and seeing them blossom and grow in their faith. The challenges have come mostly from opposition from men. My appointments have been cross-racial/cross-cultural. It is not always easy to determine whether the opposition is because I am a woman or because of my race–or both. The church treasurer in my first appointment refused to send in the apportionments because the conference had sent me to the church. But when I confronted him with scripture and how we operate as Christians, he broke down in tears. Shortly after the confrontation, the treasurer left the church. I worked well with the rest of the congregation, and we grew and developed many ministries. Unfortunately, after I left, things did not go very well and the church merged with another congregation. What I really learned in that situation was to trust God and not to be intimidated by powerful white men."

PENINSULA-DELAWARE ANNUAL CONFERENCE

 *Dorothy Evelyn White*

 *Charlotte Ann Nichols*

(EUROPEAN AMERICAN)

First Woman to Be Received into Full Connection in the Former Peninsula Conference

Received on Trial – 1972
Ordained Deacon – 1972
Received into Full Connection – 1977
Ordained Elder – 1977
Leave of Absence – 1979–80
Retired – 1981
Deceased – 1992

DOROTHY EVELYN WHITE was born in Big Island, Virginia, in 1941. Prior to entering the ministry, Dorothy graduated from the University of Georgia with a bachelor's degree in chemistry. She later worked as a research chemist at the University of Delaware. From 1972 to 1975 Dorothy attended Emory University and graduated with a master of divinity degree.

From 1976 through 1977 Dorothy served the churches at Mt. Lebanon and Mt. Salem, and in 1978 she was appointed to community ministries, after which she took a leave of absence. She retired in 1981.

Dorothy was active in environmental issues in Sussex County, was vice president of the Delaware Audubon Society, and served on the Audubon Society board. She was instrumental in starting the downstate Sussex chapter of the Audubon Society. She was a member of the Nanticoke Watershed Preservation Committee, and worked heavily on legislation pertaining to the watershed area. She was also a member of the Sierra Club and the Sussex County Chapter of the Daughters of the American Revolution. Dorothy White died June 17, 1992, at age fifty-one.[9]

First African American Woman to Be Received into Full Connection

Received on Trial – 1979
Ordained Deacon – 1979
Received into Full Connection – 1981
Ordained Elder – 1981
Current Appointment – District Superintendent, Salisbury District

CHARLOTTE ANN NICHOLS was born in Hurlock, Maryland, November 3, 1950.

"I began to experience my call in 1977. I was ordained deacon in 1979 and became an elder with full clergy rights in 1981. I started as a Christian education assistant at Jones Memorial United Methodist Church in Washington, DC, while working on my master of religious education [degree] at Wesley Theological Seminary. After completing my MRE, I continued at Wesley and earned a master of divinity [degree]. It was in seminary that I received my call to ordained ministry.

"After graduation, I was the pastor for two charges–Girdletree charge and Easton-Miles River charge. In December of 1989, Bishop Joseph Yeakel appointed me as district superintendent for the Easton District, to start in July 1990."

For Charlotte, this prayer describes her journey: "Lord, humble me and let me do your will."

PUERTO RICO PROVISIONAL CONFERENCE

 *Julia Torres Fernandez*

(HISPANIC/LATINA)

First Woman to Be Received into Full Connection in the Former Puerto Rico Provisional Conference (Now Iglesia Metodista Autonóma Afiliada de Puerto Rico)

First Hispanic/Latina Woman to Be Received into Full Connection in the UMC

Ordained Deacon – No date available
Received on Trial – 1959
Ordained Elder – 1960
Received into Full Connection – 1961
Retired – 1971
Deceased – 1988

JULIA TORRES FERNANDEZ was born in Ponce, Puerto Rico, in 1904. Julia was the first clergywoman (among all denominations) on the whole island of Puerto Rico and became one of the most famous pastors in Puerto Rico. She was active in United Methodist women's organizations and was involved with the Women's Division. She used to teach at the School of Missions and was one of the writers for the Women's Division Program Book. She also wrote articles for *El Interprete*, the Spanish version of *Interpreter* magazine.

Julia was recognized by the Catholic Church as she shared ministries with Sister Ferre, a well-known nun. Julia had been a schoolteacher for many years, and later established and directed a school for underprivileged children in her hometown of Ponce, which now bears her name.

Julia was a historian, a poet, and a writer. She used to write the *semblanzas* (biographical sketches) for all the ministers who made the *bodas de plata ministeriales* (ministerial silver weddings, twenty-five years of service in the ministry, an occasion for a big celebration in Puerto Rico) as well as biographical sketches for those who were retiring. She used the pen name "Azucena de los Valles" for her poems.

She was a great preacher, energetic, with a good sense of humor, and was loved and respected by all. Julia Torres Fernandez died April 6, 1988, at the age of eighty-four.[10]

TROY ANNUAL CONFERENCE

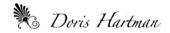 *Doris Hartman*

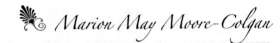 *Marion May Moore-Colgan*

(EUROPEAN AMERICAN)
First Woman to Be Received into Full Connection

Ordained Deacon – 1944
Ordained Elder – 1946
Received on Trial – 1959
Received into Full Connection – 1963
Retired – 1981

DORIS HARTMAN was born November 2, 1913, in Cedarville, Ohio. "I guess the date when I began my journey toward ministry was 1939 when I entered Hartford Seminary Foundation after teaching school in Ohio for five years. I felt the call to be in Christian work but not at that time to seek ordination. Actually I had never known a woman minister and I thought the role of women should be in Christian education."

After graduating with an MA degree in Christian education, Doris went to work for the Vermont Council of Churches, setting up weekend clinics in various small churches to train teachers and to speak on Sundays about the importance of Christian education. When that job came to an end, the council secretary wanted to keep Doris in Vermont. She was offered the small church in Waterville where she not only pastored the church but also taught Bible in some of the area rural schools. It was during this time that Doris gradually began to feel the call to the ministry. After serving six years in Barton as associate pastor, Doris "applied to become a J-3 which was a special program for young people to teach English and Bible in a Christian school in Japan during the early postwar years." She spent the remainder of her ministry in Japan and assisted in starting a new church in an outlying area where there was no Protestant church. "Three years before my retirement, the lay people were able to build a small sanctuary near where our 'house church' had been, and they called a Japanese woman pastor. I found the work very fulfilling and even though I sort of fell into becoming a pastor, I did feel a real call to the ministry during my years as a pastor."[11]

First Native American Woman to Be Received into Full Connection

Received on Trial – 1985
Ordained Deacon – 1985
Received into Full Connection – 1991
Ordained Elder – 1991
Current Appointment – Poultney and Fair Haven UMC, Vermont

MARION MAY MOORE-COLGAN was born March 13, 1951, at Mooers Forks, New York. "Looking back, I would describe my ministry as a healing ministry. From my first charge (three churches on a forty-eight-mile circuit), through the next three (two-point charges), each charge needed a special healing from some form of brokenness. Each time I went to the cross, felt their pain and sorrow, and sought God's grace in bringing healing, new hope, and new ministries. In each church, I have also worked in various capacities in service to my Native American brothers and sisters (e.g., Native American International Caucus, National United Methodist Native American Center, General Commission on Religion and Race)."

WEST VIRGINIA ANNUAL CONFERENCE

 *Margaret Ann Marshall*

(EUROPEAN AMERICAN)
First Woman to Be Received into Full Connection

Commissioned as a Deaconess – 1927
Ordained Deacon – 1956
Received on Trial – 1960
Received into Full Connection – 1962
Ordained Elder – 1962
Retired – 1968
Deceased – 1992

MARGARET ANN MARSHALL was born May 21, 1902, in Whalton, England.

The place I need to start is when I became a local minister.... I was working in Arkansas. And I went before the committee to get my local preacher's license. I had been working down there for ten years or so. I didn't know what to expect from the committee. But when I got there the chairman of the group said, "I just want to ask you one question," and this was it: "Why did you do it?" And my answer was "Because I couldn't keep from it any longer." So there's where I got into the ministry...

When I went before the committee, Dr. Shaffer [the district superintendent] told me all the reasons why I shouldn't become a minister–that women were…hard to work with. They didn't retire when they should. They crossed their legs to act like men. They did all kinds of interesting things. And…I said, "Dr. Shaffer, you don't have to have me in your district. There are two or three of the men who said they'd accept me." Then he said, "But, I want you Margaret."[12]

Margaret ends with these words: "Don't be afraid. And be sure of your calling. You've got to be sure of your calling. And then risk your life. You've got to put it on the line. And you will have to take risks. There's just nothing like it. I've said that I've suffered, maybe not all the same kind of things that Paul suffered, but I'm black and blue in spots. But I wouldn't give up what I have done, work as a minister in a local church–it's the highest calling anybody can have."[13]
Margaret Marshall died August 4, 1992, at age ninety.[14]

 *Elizabeth Allen-Villinger*

First African American Woman to Be Received into Full Connection

Associate Membership – 1982
Ordained Deacon – 1982
Received into Full Connection – 2000
Ordained Elder – 2000
Retired – 2004

ELIZABETH ALLEN-VILLINGER was born March 21, 1945, in Pulaski, Virginia.

"I experienced my call one day after I had attended a West Virginia conference meeting for small churches. On the way home I received an invitation from God to become a minister to these small, rural churches in small communities. I called my district superintendent to explain what I had been feeling. He called back and said, 'How would you like to become a pastor?' In June 1975, I was appointed to four small African American churches in southern West Virginia. I served those churches for five years and I finished local pastor's school at Duke Divinity School. At the time, I did not feel a need to work toward an MDiv degree. God eventually led me to Pittsburgh Theological Seminary. In 2000, I finally was received into full connection and ordained elder.

"The journey has been exciting and a challenge because I am both a woman and an African American. There were disappointments along the way, but God's grace and love continues to strengthen me. Finally, one winter day in 2003, after serving twenty-eight years in pastoral ministry, I was standing in my living room near the phone when I heard God say, 'It is time.' I felt a great joy and knew it was time to take an early retirement in 2004.

"I am now working on my doctorate in bereavement. I know that God has given me a special gift in communication, helping people who are grieving death of a loved one. I have had a long and wonderful walk with the Lord, and my journey continues to be God-inspired, as I meet people with whom I share this special gift."

WESTERN NEW YORK ANNUAL CONFERENCE

Helena L. Champlin

(EUROPEAN AMERICAN)
First Woman to Be Received into Full Connection in the Former Genesee Conference – 1958

(See chapter 2, 44)

Melba Varner Chaney

First African American Woman to Serve in Full Connection

Received on Trial, Baltimore Conference – 1982
Ordained Deacon, Baltimore Conference – 1982
Received into Full Connection, Baltimore Conference – 1985
Ordained Elder, Baltimore Conference – 1985
Transferred to Western New York Conference – 1986
Current Appointment – Hilton UMC, Hilton, New York

MELBA VARNER CHANEY was born in Summerville, South Carolina.

"My journey toward ordained ministry began in the late 1970s when I became aware that God was calling me to servant leadership in the church. One passage of scripture describes my journey of life and ministry: 'You will know the truth, and the truth will make you free' (John 8:32). While sitting in worship one Sunday, I heard these words in a more profound way. I knew God was drawing me toward a new search for truth. From that moment I began making the transition from administration and public policy to ordained ministry.

"Although I expected to serve churches in the Baltimore Annual Conference, I was recruited in 1986 by the bishop of the Western New York Annual Conference to serve as a 'local church vitalization' pastor at Lincoln Memorial UMC, a predominantly African American congregation in the city of Buffalo. Nine years at Lincoln were followed by seven years as pastor of a rural, Caucasian congregation near Lake Ontario. After having served three very different congregations in this region–central city, rural, and suburban–in nineteen years, I have learned to trust this profound statement made by Jesus Christ so long ago. Truth–often illusive, sometimes hidden–may be expressed in a still, small voice, but it always points to reality. However it presents itself, it moves beyond parochialism and prejudice to freedom in the spirit of Christ. The journey is sometimes a struggle, at other times a search; yet always with the goal of eternal verity."

Gwendolyn Toomer Wilson

First African American Woman to Be Received into Full Connection

Received on Trial – 1988
Ordained Deacon – 1988
Received into Full Connection – 1991
Ordained Elder – 1991
Current Appointment – Union Hill, New York, and Henrietta, New York; 7.5 hours per week at the Lighthouse (a residential drug treatment program for women) in Buffalo, New York

GWENDOLYN TOOMER WILSON was born June 21, 1941, in Buffalo, New York.

"I began my journey toward ministry shortly after I recommitted my life to the Lord on August 3, 1980. By the following year, I began earning a BS degree in Bible at Houghton College. During my second year I was accepted at Asbury Theological Seminary in Wilmore, Kentucky. In the fall of 1982, as I struggled with Greek, I prayed, 'Lord, I hear what you are saying and if I pass this Greek course, I will do everything in my power to find out what I need to do to become a pastor. But Lord, since I don't know what to do, you will have to show me.' I am not sure when the call began, but it must have happened while I was at Houghton College because people kept saying, 'You will make a wonderful pastor,' while I kept saying, 'No, I won't.'

"I was the first African American woman to graduate from Asbury. I was also the first African American woman to be a part of the clinical pastoral education program at the Baptist Hospital in Lexington, Kentucky.

"I am currently in my fifth appointment. All my appointments have been in cross-racial settings. I also hold a part-time position at the Lighthouse, a residential drug treatment program for women. The church I serve in Henrietta is selling the facility and grounds, creating a new role for me as a transition person, assisting them in the sale and termination process."

WESTERN PENNSYLVANIA ANNUAL CONFERENCE

 *Madge Black Floyd*

(EUROPEAN AMERICAN)

One of the First Three Women to Be Received into Full Connection

Received on Trial – 1968
Ordained Deacon – 1968
Received into Full Connection – 1970
Ordained Elder – 1970
Retired – 1999
Deceased – 2005

MADGE BLACK FLOYD was born September 23, 1935, in Atlanta, Georgia. Madge attended Emory University where she received a bachelor of arts degree in Bible and religion. She then graduated from Pittsburgh Theological Seminary with a master of divinity degree, and Boston University School of Theology where she earned a doctor of ministry degree in preaching and worship. Madge was an accomplished musician in her youth and one of her mentors was Ethel Byers of Atlanta, who taught that music is the vehicle that carries the message in worship and that "we sing ourselves into the grace of believing."

In addition to serving local churches, Madge was the executive director for five years of the "Together" program, a $6 million fund-raiser and stewardship program for the Western Pennsylvania Conference. She also served as a stewardship associate for the General Board of Discipleship, leading workshops all around the country. She served for eight years on the General Board of Pensions of the UMC. In 1984, she was appointed as the first female district superintendent to serve in the Western Pennsylvania Conference. When she was appointed to the Clarion First UMC, she became the first pastor to serve as senior pastor of a multi-staff church. At the time, Clarion was the fourteenth-largest in the conference, with more than 1,000 members.[15]

Madge Floyd died March 10, 2005, at age sixty-nine.

 *Harriette Elizabeth Dalbey*

(EUROPEAN AMERICAN)

One of the First Three Women to Be Received into Full Connection

Ordained Deacon – 1956
Ordained Elder – 1958
Received on Trial – 1968
Received into Full Connection – 1970
Retired – 1970
Deceased – 1990

HARRIETTE ELIZABETH DALBEY, better known as Betty, was born February 9, 1903.

> She would engage you in conversation on a variety of subjects; she would challenge your preconceptions, your comfort, your knowledge or lack thereof; she would enlist your faith and seek your response to the call of God upon your life and in answer to human needs; she would add the punch line and laugh with her whole being; she could be feisty, compassionate, persuasive, persistent, and so much more. She was Betty Dalbey, public school teacher, home missionary, foreign missionary, deaconess, pastor, executive director of inner city work and women's advocate.... She was a steady friend and constantly in the employ of sharing–until her health broke and curtailed the activity she loved.

In a letter to a colleague preparing for a missionary weekend, she wrote: "Besides giving general information about my life and a challenge for God-filled lives to give themselves in Christian service–I would try to urge everyone to be in mission for Jesus Christ. Thus I hope to come prepared to do whatever is needed, to present my life as a challenge for Christian living."

"Thus she was and thus she will be, for all who knew Betty Dalbey. God blesses us through her life and work. Thanks be to God for His grace in Christ and for his faithful daughter Betty."[16]

Betty Dalbey died January 4, 1990, at the age of eighty-six.

Enid V. Pierce

(EUROPEAN AMERICAN)

One of the First Three Women to Be Received into Full Connection

Ordained Deacon, Pittsburgh Conference – 1942
Ordained Elder, Pittsburgh Conference – 1946
Received on Trial – 1968
Received into Full Connection – 1970
Retired – 1978

ENID V. PIERCE was born July 18, 1909, in West Finley, Pennsylvania. She married the Reverend Homer Pierce and eventually received a license to preach in 1938. "At the time of my husband's death, I was called soon after as a lay pastor at the church where he was serving in Masontown until the following Western Pennsylvania Annual Conference. I was at the time enrolled in the Pittsburgh Conference Course of Study. I was reappointed to the Masontown Church for the next twenty years." During the time that she was serving at Masontown, Enid graduated from West Virginia University with an AB degree in psychology and philosophy.

Enid later served as the associate pastor at Laketon Heights from 1964 through 1967, and as pastor at Sheraden Terrace from 1967 through 1973. After completing a course in clinical pastoral education at Western Pennsylvania College in Pittsburgh, and a supervised counseling experience at the Pittsburgh Pastoral Institute, Enid served as the chaplain of the Methodist Home in Mount Lebanon until her retirement in 1978.

Enid currently resides in New Port Richey, Florida, where she has written and published two books: *Drift by Design* and *How Much Farther?*

Martha Marie Orphe

First African American Woman to Be Received into Full Connection

Received on Trial – 1984
Ordained Deacon – 1984
Received into Full Connection – 1987
Ordained Elder – 1987
Current Appointment – District Superintendent Pittsburgh District

MARTHA MARIE ORPHE was born September 3, 1959, in Lafayette, Louisiana.

"In 1974, when I was fourteen years old and a freshman in high school, I gave my life to Jesus. I remember how some of the older teens and young adults at Mallalieu United Methodist Church in St. Martinville, Louisiana, had this joy and constantly spoke about Jesus. I remember saying I wanted what they had. One day I fell on my knees in the front bedroom of my parents' home. I can remember the peace. When I was sixteen years old, I said yes to God to be God's servant. Growing up in southern French Catholic Louisiana, the only way I knew God used girls was as nuns. My parents agreed that I could convert from United Methodist to Catholic in order that I could become a nun. The summer I was to enter the convent, however, my mother sent me to Denver, Colorado, instead.

"One Sunday, I met a woman minister for the first time in my life. Her name was Carolyn Knight. I have told her several times since that I do not remember anything she said during that first meeting. It was like I was in a trance. She spent time with me in prayer and counseling throughout the summer. By the time I returned home, I had told God, 'Yes, I will go into the ministry.'

"My journey has not always been easy especially since I am a single, divorced, black, forty-five-year-old woman. For some people, if it is not my race, then it is my gender; if not my gender, then my age–or all of the above. In the midst of it all, I count it a joy to live for Jesus Christ in all of life's circumstances. I have had the same joy I saw in the lives of my friends in Mallalieu Church over thirty years ago. It has been because of God that I have been able to make it through my journey. I would not change my journey of joy and struggle. I thank God for the strength and prayers of others who have gone before me in the past, those who stand in the prayer gap for me currently and for those in the future who will come to know Jesus because of what God is doing in our lives. I live with joyful, passionate anticipation for the future years of my life journey in Jesus Christ."

Ha-Kyung Cho-Kim

First Korean Woman to Be Received into Full Connection

Received on Trial – 1986
Ordained Deacon – 1986
Received into Full Connection – 1988
Ordained Elder – 1988
Current Appointment – Leominster UMC, Leominster, Massachusetts, New England Conference

HA-KYUNG CHO-KIM was born September 22, 1938, in Pyung-Yang, Korea.

"I felt God's call a few years before I began my seminary education at Pittsburgh Theological Seminary in Pittsburgh, Pennsylvania, in 1983. However, I was discouraged and blocked by Korean clergymen. In 1977 my mother and I started a Korean congregation for the women married to the American servicemen while [stationed] in Korea.

"I answered God's call into the ordained ministry at age forty-five, leaving my vocation in drug research as a PhD. Because I have been involved in the ministry of Christ as both a layperson and an ordained minister, I have been an advocate for lay empowerment. Because I have served both Anglo churches and Korean churches, I have taught the need of understanding different cultures. Because I have served as pastor of large membership churches and of small membership churches, I have helped churches to identify their own unique visions and become vital congregations. Because I have served on the staff of three different annual conferences, I have been a bridge maker between the judicatories and local churches. I am the first Asian American woman to run for the episcopacy at the Northeastern Jurisdictional Conference, which I did in July 2004."

WYOMING ANNUAL CONFERENCE

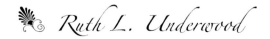 *Ruth L. Underwood*

 *Cordella J. Brown*

(EUROPEAN AMERICAN)
First Woman to Be Received into Full Connection

Ordained Deacon – 1944
Ordained Elder – 1946
Received on Trial – 1957
Received into Full Connection – 1959
Retired – 1971
Deceased – 1977

RUTH L. UNDERWOOD was born December 1, 1900, in Westford, New York, the daughter of a Methodist clergyman. When Ruth was growing up, she often accompanied her father when he went calling from house to house, "assisting him in whatever ways he deemed needful, caring for the records and such."[17] She attended East Stroudsburg State Teacher's College and earned a bachelor of religious education degree at Hartford Seminary.

"Feeling a strong urge to serve in the pastoral ministry, she embarked on this holy enterprise in 1943, being assigned to the McClure charge on the Oneonta District, where she remained until 1949."[18] While there she proposed to the Conference Board of Education, of which she was secretary, the purchase of the famous Kilmer Estate to be used as a youth center, today known as Sky Lake. During the time she served the Duryea Church, she oversaw the building of a much-needed $60,000 educational wing for the church.

> When appointed to a charge, oftimes the congregation wondered how a woman would fit into the situation; but they soon found out. Sound preacher, indefatigable pastoral visitor, leader of youths, staunch friend of the aged and infirm; keen thinker, possessed of an undeniable sense of humor, she quickly endeared herself to every congregation, as her long pastorates attest.[19]

Ruth Underwood died June 11, 1977, at age seventy-six.

First African American Woman to Be Received into Full Connection

Received on Trial, AME – 1968
Ordained Deacon, AME – 1968
Ordained Elder, AME – 1970
Transferred to Peninsula Conference, UMC – 1977
Received on Trial, Central Pennsylvania Conference, UMC – June 9, 1989
Recognition of Elder's Orders, Central Pennsylvania Conference, UMC – June 9, 1989
Received on Trial, Wyoming Conference – June 14, 1989
Received into Full Connection – 1992
Current Appointment – Wesley UMC, Springfield, Massachusetts, New England Conference

CORDELLA J. BROWN was born October 16, 1944, in Harrisburg, Pennsylvania.

"In 1947, our church (Monumental AME Church, Steelton, Pennsylvania) received a clergy couple as pastor and spouse. He was appointed and she was an evangelist. After that, all I talked about was becoming a preacher, and I used to stand in the stairwell of our house and preach to the dining room chairs. As I grew older, the calling became clearer. We moved to Harrisburg and I started attending the AME church around the corner from our house. The pastor, the Reverend Hezekiah Benjamin Barkley, believed in my call, but said if it was real, it would hold until I finished high school, then we would work on it. That led to the 1962 preaching of a trial sermon and becoming a local licentiate at Bethel AME, as I left for college in Ohio.

"My ministry spans over forty years, in two Methodist judicatories, six conferences, eleven churches (including two multiple-point charges) in rural, small-town areas–black and white congregations–as well as urban centers. I have been the first female pastor in all but my current congregation and the first black pastor in one (Wilkes-Barre, Pennsylvania). I have participated in the establishment of both a rural and urban cooperative ministry in two separate conferences, and led the renovation/restoration of an urban church for nearly $500,000. In all small membership churches, approximately one hundred twenty-five people have been confirmed and forty have been baptized. And, I have served on several conference committees. My journey has been unique and varied, conflicting and clear, but always with a profound sense of love for Christ and his church."

Notes

1. Information in this paragraph is from the autobiographical statement by Mercy Kasambira in *The Licensing and Ordination of Women in the Central Pennsylvania Conference*, 37-38.

2. Information in this paragraph is from Mercy Kasambira's memoir, written by her husband, Daniel P. Kasambira, published in the 1995 Journal of the Central Pennsylvania Conference, UMC, 446.

3. Margaret Parker's service record was gathered by research done in the General Minutes by staff at the General Commission on Archives and History.

4. Information for this biography is taken from Mildred Stanford's memoir, written by her daughter, Myra S. Bryant, published in the 2003 Journal of the Greater New Jersey Conference, UMC, 423.

5. Information for this biography is from Inez James's memoir, written by Harold Dean Trulear, published in the 1993 Journal of the New York Conference, B-13, and from her service list published by the General Board of Pension and Health Benefits, UMC.

6. Information for this biography is from Faith Chandler's memoir, published in the 1983 Journal of the New Hampshire Conference, UMC, 169-70.

7. Information for this biography was taken from Noemi Diaz's memoir, written by the Reverend Dr. Alicia Fils-Aime Wentler and prepared for publication in the 2005 Journal of the New York Conference, UMC.

8. Information for this biography is taken from Ruthenia Finley's memoir, written by her sister, Joan E. Neal, and published in the 2004 Journal of the New York Annual Conference, 292-94.

9. Information for this biography is taken from Dorothy White's obituary, which appeared in the *Delaware State News* (June 19, 1992), and from her service record provided by the Peninsula-Delaware Conference, published in the 1982 Journal of the Peninsula Conference, UMC, 457.

10. Information for this biography came from Liana Peréz-Félix (e-mail message to author, May 18, 2005) and Milca C. Plaud-Alvarez (e-mail message to author, June 2, 2005), both of whom knew Julia Fernandez personally, and from information gathered by the General Commission on Archives and History.

11. Information for this biography came from a personal letter from Doris Hartman to Lee Flanders, chairperson of the Troy Annual Conference Commission on Archives and History, May 10, 2004, and forwarded to the author.

12. Lois K. Almond, "Risk Your Life: A Conversation with Margaret Marshall," in *The Women Came Early: A History of Women in the West Virginia Conference* (Task Force on Women's History Project of the West Virginia Conference, United Methodist Church, 1986), 154-55.

13. Ibid., 159.

14. Margaret Marshall's memoir, published in the 1993 Journal of the West Virginia Annual Conference, UMC, 328.

15. Information for this memoir was taken from Madge Floyd's obituary, which appeared on the Western Pennsylvania Conference Web site following her death.

16. Information for this biography was taken from Betty Dalbey's memoir, published in the 1990 Journal of the Western Pennsylvania Conference, UMC, 290-91.

17. Gladys Fortuna-Blake and Judith Present (in collaboration with Frank Underwood), "Ruth Underwood," a play about the life of Ruth L. Underwood, n.d., 4.

18. Ruth L. Underwood's memoir, written by Harry Everett Brooks, published in the 1978 Journal of the Wyoming Conference, UMC, 238.

19. Ibid.

Chapter 5

First Women of the Southeastern Jurisdiction to Receive Full Clergy Rights

THERE ARE FOURTEEN ANNUAL CONFERENCES IN THE SOUTHEASTERN JURISDICTION AND fifty-one "first" women were reported. Again, one woman served in two conferences, but was only counted once. Only eight, or 16 percent, of the fifty-one women are deceased. Only thirteen of the women from this jurisdiction were received into full connection prior to 1970. This a reflection of the fact that, on the whole, women entered the ordination process relatively late in the South, probably due to the reluctance of the region to accept women in the pulpit. Twelve women, including Bishop Leontine Kelly, or 24 percent, are retired. There are only thirteen women, or 21 percent, currently serving in the local church, however. Another sixteen, or 32 percent, including two district superintendents, two bishops and one person serving at the General Church level are currently serving in extension ministries. Of the remaining two women, one is a missionary and one has withdrawn.

Nineteen women, or 37 percent, are European American women. There were sixteen African American women, six Hispanic/Latina women, three Koreans, three Native Americans, one Japanese, two Chinese, and one Indian woman. The Southeastern Jurisdiction has the first woman to be received into full connection in Mexico and the first two African American women to be received into full connection after the 1956 decision.[1]

ALABAMA-WEST FLORIDA ANNUAL CONFERENCE

 *Lucy Campbell Hathaway*

 *Elizabeth J. Walker*

(EUROPEAN AMERICAN)
First Woman to Be Received into Full Connection

Received on Trial – 1963
Ordained Deacon – 1963
Received into Full Connection – 1965
Ordained Elder – 1965
Retired – 1981

LUCY CAMPBELL HATHAWAY was born July 14, 1913, in Dale County, Alabama.

"I was saved at age eighteen at a revival at my church just before Easter. I had taught Sunday school and other classes since then. My husband, Reuben Hathaway, and I answered the call to the ministry in 1959. We served churches and charges together until his sudden death in 1976. We received our first appointment in Montgomery in 1960.

"After my husband died, I continued to serve by myself until 1981. I retired that year and began serving in our local church, Mt. Hebron UMC, in Pinckard, Alabama. I continued lay work, teaching Sunday school and various other work. We organized a Wednesday morning prayer breakfast in the mid-1980s and it has grown from five or six around the breakfast table to thirty members. Since then, it has since been named 'The Lucy Hathaway Cornerstones.' Our group sends support to a young lady who is going into the ministry at Asbury College. We also send support to our local hospice and Samaritan's Purse.

"I am still on my journey and have never looked back even though I am almost blind and deaf and I am immobile. The benefits and blessings are too numerous for me to ever tell and I thank God for him using me through these years."

First African American Woman to Be Received into Full Connection

Received on Trial – 1986
Ordained Deacon – 1986
Received into Full Connection – 1989
Ordained Elder – 1989
Current Appointment – Extension Ministries, Professional Pastoral Counselor, Georgia Association for Pastoral Care, Decatur, Georgia; Associate Professor, Pastoral Care/ Psychology of Religion, the Interdenominational Theological Center, Atlanta, Georgia

ELIZABETH J. WALKER was born in 1955 in Oxford, North Carolina.

"I spent most summers and holidays in Oxford with my grandparents. We were members of St. Cyprian's Episcopal Church. I received my call to ministry at St. Cyprian's when I was eight years old, and again at twelve years old after my confirmation experience. The Episcopal Church did not ordain women at that time and Father Stanley, my rector, guided me in my thoughtful, intelligent, spiritual pilgrimage of self-discovery before God. The question became, 'How may I embrace myself and my particular religious experience and vocation as a woman of color? Moreover, how may I bring my experience to bear upon my environment in a way that is helpful and healing for me and for God's community?'

"In 1981 the call was so great and clear that I found the courage to leave the Episcopal Church and join The United Methodist Church where I began my formal journey toward ordained ministry. I was called to be a prophet/priest with the particular work to prepare for ministry leadership, teach and minister to ministers, counsel ministers, and write. I also understood that I would be the first in many instances and that being the first was a part of my call. I am the first and only African American woman to be admitted into full connection in my conference."

 *Aida Lea Barrera-Segura*

First Woman to Be Ordained Elder in the Mexico Methodist Church

First Hispanic/Latina Woman to Serve in Full Connection

Consecrated Deaconess, Mexico Methodist Church – 1968
Received into Full Connection, Mexico Methodist Church – 1978
Ordained Elder, Mexico Methodist Church – 1978
Transferred to Alabama-West Florida Conference – 1983
Current Appointment – On Loan, La Casa del Pueblo de Dios, Decatur, Alabama

AIDA LEA BARRERA-SEGURA was born April 24, 1946, in Mexico.

"When I finished *preparatoria* (nine grades in Mexico), I really wanted to get away from my home and I talked with my father about what I should do. My father had always wanted to have a minister in the family. When I told him that I was thinking about attending seminary, I thought he would say no, but instead he wanted me to attend.

"It was during my second year that I really began asking, 'Why am I here, God? Please tell me what you want me to do.' While I was home on vacation, I attended a revival and I asked God again, 'You must tell me if you really want me to be a minister.' That is when I got the confirmation of my call. At that time, however, women in Mexico could only be consecrated as deaconesses. Then in 1974 the decision was made to allow women to be ordained. I completed a four-year Course of Study school and in 1978, I was the first woman in Mexico to be ordained as an elder. Only two persons were ordained that year. One was a man; I was the other one. The man was appointed to a nice church quite near his home, while I was appointed to a very small church many hours away from where I lived. My home was broken into, and I was robbed. These are the kinds of appointments that women are often given in Mexico.

"When I met and married a man from Mobile, Alabama, I came to the United States with my husband and, with the support of Bishop Lloyd Knox, I was eventually given an appointment in the Alabama-West Florida Conference. I am now serving on loan to the North Alabama Conference in an appointment to a Hispanic mission church, supported in part with funds from the General Board of Global Ministries [GBGM].

"Many people said it [would be] difficult to be a Hispanic woman pastor in the South because people would refuse to come to church. But they come to know the Lord through me; so the fact that I am a Hispanic woman doesn't matter. Both men and women attend."

FLORIDA ANNUAL CONFERENCE

 *Charlene Payne Kammerer*

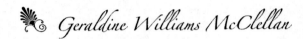 *Geraldine Williams McClellan*

(EUROPEAN AMERICAN)
First Woman to Be Received into Full Connection

Received on Trial – 1975
Ordained Deacon – 1975
Received into Full Connection – 1977
Ordained Elder – 1977
Current Appointment – Resident Bishop Richmond Area

CHARLENE PAYNE KAMMERER was born January 5, 1948, in Orlando, Florida.

"For a long time, [Charlene] pursued her ambitions with no role model. It was in high school when she first felt her calling, though she identified it as a desire to work in the church. 'I had never thought about being a minister. I didn't know it was possible…I had never heard of a woman clergy or seen one preach.'"[2]

"I began my journey to ordained ministry upon completion of my MCE [Master of Christian Education] degree from Garrett-Evangelical Theological Seminary in 1972. I enrolled in the MDiv degree [program] as a response to my unfolding call to pastoral and ordained ministry. Once I declared that decision publicly, I never looked back. The call has never changed.

"The journey has been fraught with many ups and downs, as the church has resisted my call. The United Methodist Church has, at the same time, embraced my call and given me opportunities for service that I would never have dreamed about. As a pioneer pastor in Florida and the Southeast Jurisdiction, part of my calling was a series of 'firsts'–first woman to serve as D.S. in Florida and first woman to be elected bishop from the Southeastern Jurisdiction. God's grace has sustained me and given me fulfillment in this calling. I am now entering my thirtieth year and it seems some days I just got started, and at other times that I have lived fifty years' of experience."

First African American Woman to Be Received into Full Connection

Received on Trial – 1980
Ordained Deacon – 1980
Received into Full Connection – 1982
Ordained Elder – 1982
Current Appointment – District Superintendent Gainesville District

GERALDINE WILLIAMS MCCLELLAN was born September 12, 1948, in Palatka, Florida.

"My journey into ministry started early in life even before 1969, as I marveled at the passion and the compassion that both my parents shared as they ministered to the physical, spiritual, and emotional needs of people from all walks of life. That experience was etched deep in my heart. As I became involved in Methodist Youth Fellowship (MYF), mission projects, and other areas of the church, I yearned for the day that God would prepare me as he had prepared them to serve.

"Twenty-five years in the ministry and a lot of pruning have prepared me to continue the journey in spite of the pitfalls. God has truly smiled on me as he has walked with me through dangers seen and unseen, as I have allowed myself to be used by God to bear fruit that has served to meet the needs of others. My ministry focus has been centered in John 15. It provides me with the discipline, ongoing instruction, and training that is so critical to being in ministry. The joy of being in ministry has been a great reward."

Lia Icaza-Willetts

First Hispanic/Latina Woman to Be Received into Full Connection

Received on Trial – 1988
Ordained Deacon – 1988
Received into Full Connection – 1990
Ordained Elder – 1990
Current Appointment – Senior Pastor, First UMC, Tampa, Florida

LIA ICAZA-WILLETTS was born March 10, 1954, in Santurce, Puerto Rico.

"God called me to ministry at age seventeen when I felt that God wanted me to help people and I dreamed of being a medical missionary in Africa. After college I didn't know where to look for help in following my call. I became a successful business manager, but I felt empty inside because my life was not making a difference or helping people. In 1983, I joined Coral Way Hispanic United Methodist Church. It was there one night in a prayer group that I accepted God's call to the ministry. I didn't know how to become a minister and someone told me to go to Scarritt Graduate School for Christian Workers in Nashville, Tennessee. There I discovered that to be a minister I needed to go to seminary. I enrolled at Candler School of Theology, Emory University.

"Since my first day as a pastor, I focused on building a bridge between two cultures and being a witness of Christ's love to help open doors for Hispanic ministries and other minorities. No matter how successful my ministry is in a congregation, I have found that racism and sexism are present and active in the UMC. I have been faithful in preaching the gospel, sharing the love of God, and having compassion for people who discriminate. I have felt God's blessing in every ministry I served.

"My hope is that one day The United Methodist Church will really become part of the reign of God, accepting people of all ages, nations, and races with love, justice, and mercy for all."

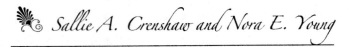
Sallie A. Crenshaw and Nora E. Young

(AFRICAN AMERICAN)
First Two Women to Be Received into Full Connection in the Former East Tennessee Conference in 1958

(See chapter 2, 57, 58)

Brenda Diane Fogelman Carroll

One of the First Two European American Women to Be Received into Full Connection

Received on Trial – 1972
Ordained Deacon – 1972
Received into Full Connection – 1976
Ordained Elder – 1976
Current Appointment – Copastor (with husband) of First UMC, Maryville, Tennessee

BRENDA DIANE FOGELMAN CARROLL was born April 15, 1949, in Lebanon, Virginia.

"My earliest memory of expressing my call is as a five-year-old. 'Mother, I want to be a preacher like Preacher Jordan.' My precious mother had never heard of a woman being a minister. So she counseled me, 'Girls can't be preachers. But girls can be missionaries.' It was enough to keep the doors of my mind and heart open. This would have been around 1954, two years before General Conference made their historic decision. God's timing was a gift to me even then.

"It has been a journey of complete grace, for I should have been a factory worker in Russell County. But God called me in a direction that was impossible–except with God. When I graduated from Candler School of Theology, women weren't such good news and certainly clergy couples weren't, except that God meant it to be good news. After thirty-two years, including being a district superintendent, I am still humbled by God's call, excited about being a pastor, and eager to see what God through Christ will do next through incarnational/spiritual presence in this world and in this parish. My challenge now, as always, is to be in ministry to a community and not just to a church; to focus the church on the footsteps and heart of Jesus, and not just on its own

maintenance and comfort; and to listen prayerfully enough to hear the particulars of my call this day."

Mary Virginia Kilgore Taylor

One of the First Two European American Women to Be Received into Full Connection

Received on Trial – 1974
Ordained Deacon – 1974
Received into Full Connection – 1976
Ordained Elder – 1976
Current Appointment – Resident Bishop Columbia Area

MARY VIRGINIA KILGORE TAYLOR was born March 3, 1950, in Washington, DC.

"My call is very much intertwined with my spiritual formation. As I reflect about my faith journey, I can see God's hand at work upon my life. I went to college and majored in psychology with the desire to prepare myself to work with people. In the fall of my senior year in college, I felt a deepening of that call to pursue pastoral counseling. The seminary experience broadened my horizons. I discovered that pastoral ministry was something I really enjoyed and that I wanted to expend my life in service to others. Even though my call was gradual, many times I questioned if this really was what God wanted of me. With each new step forward in faith, I have a deep inner sense of peace and reassurance from God.

"The one word that best describes my ministry is 'joy.' It has all been such a gift. I am grateful for every opportunity to serve in ministry. Of course, along the way there have been struggles when hearts and doors were closed to women pastors. Even with the barriers, there have also been incredible opportunities and support from folks along the way. My election to the episcopacy in July 2004 was a wonderful surprise. Now each new day is filled with more surprises. I am finding that my various experiences in the church through the years are helping me to understand and enjoy this new role. I feel my complete dependence upon God in a greater way than ever before."

KENTUCKY ANNUAL CONFERENCE

 *Marietta Mansfield*

(EUROPEAN AMERICAN)

First Woman to Be Received into Full Connection in the Former Louisville Conference

Received on Trial – 1959
Ordained Deacon – 1959
Received into Full Connection – 1961
Ordained Elder – 1961
Deceased – 2003

MARIETTA MANSFIELD was born January 4, 1917, in Warren County, Kentucky. She served as a missionary to India from 1944 through 1958 and contracted polio while there. She returned to America in 1958 and began to explore the possibility of training in communication skills in ministry. She enrolled in a chaplaincy internship program and later graduated from Vanderbilt Divinity School in Nashville.

> After my graduation…I was appointed pastor of a church in Brooks, Kentucky…. No woman had ever been appointed pastor of a Louisville Conference Methodist Church. There was no model to give me pointers in my pastoring. Understandably I had many questions. As I thought of the congregation entrusted to my care, I wondered how the men of the church would perceive me. That concern was to be answered during the first Sunday morning worship service. An elderly man sat near the front of the church…. He never took his eyes off me during the entire service. Following the Benediction I stood at the door to greet the people…. When he took my hand in his work-hardened gnarled hands and looked at me with an angelic smile, he said, "You look just like my mother." Right then I knew everything was going to be all right. And it has been, all these years.

> Despite my post polio weakness, my ministry has been rewarding. I have been called upon not only to give pastoral care to the churches I served, but also to Catholics and other Protestants as well. My pastoral care has included ministering to the alcoholic, the lonely, the troubled, the young and the old alike. My caring for people included a medical referral service, and aid to the unemployed in finding suitable employment.

> As a woman in ministry I experienced no difficulty, either in my preaching or in the administration of the churches I pastored.[3]

Marietta Mansfield died December 22, 2003, at age eighty-six.

 *Mildred S. Ashby Watson*

First African American Woman to Be Received into Full Connection in the Former Louisville Conference

Received on Trial, Tennessee-Kentucky Conference, Central Jurisdiction – 1966
Ordained Deacon, Tennessee-Kentucky Conference, Central Jurisdiction – 1966
Received into Full Connection – 1968
Ordained Elder – 1968
Retired – 1985

MILDRED S. ASHBY WATSON was born April 27, 1921, in Jefferson County, Kentucky, the granddaughter of Laura J. Lange, the first African American woman to be ordained deacon and one of the first two to be ordained elder in the Central Jurisdiction.[4] At age twenty-three, Mildred was converted and baptized in the Pilgrim Baptist Church, Anchorage, Kentucky. She gained valuable training and experience at Pilgrim and studied voice for three years, preparing herself to be a religious singer. From this background Mildred was "drafted" into the ministry.

"Realizing there was a deeper need in her life, she severed her ties with Pilgrim Baptist Church and united with Hobbs Chapel (United) Methodist Church in 1958. She was granted a local preacher's license at the District Conference in 1959 and began building her ministry at Hobbs Chapel." She served first in the Lexington Conference and then the Tennessee-Kentucky Conference prior to its merger into the Louisville Annual Conference in 1968. She served churches in Parkland, Irvington-Hardinsburg-Hawesville Circuit, Beaver Dam, Anchorage-Jeffersontown Circuit, and Calvary East in Louisville. She also served as a community minister at R. E. Jones UMC.[5]

Mildred retired from full-time service in 1985.

(EUROPEAN AMERICAN)
First Woman to Be Received into Full Connection

Received on Trial – 1976
Ordained Deacon – 1976
Received into Full Connection – 1979
Ordained Elder – 1979
Retired – 2005

BARBARA LONGYEAR FRANKS was born November 21, 1944, in Evergreen Park, Illinois.

"At five years of age I stopped coloring and listened to the pastor's message. I knew I would be working in the church. It wasn't until my teen years that I defined my calling. The call became clear after talking and praying with one of my high school teachers. It was a driving force from within leading me toward ordained pastoral ministry. Nothing would quench the thirst from within.

"At the beginning of my twenty-nine years of serving, it was a hard struggle, painful, lonely, and joyful. About two-fifths of the clergymen were not receptive to having a woman serving as an ordained pastor. On the other hand, the laity were quite supportive, both men and women. The youth thought it was neat. The joy came from bringing men and women and children to Christ, baptisms, and marrying couples who later joined the church. Sometimes it was seeing a smile from one who had suffered a great loss. Much of my ministry has centered on crises and on bringing healing to the wounded individual and/or congregation. Children always knew they were welcome in church and had a friend in me. Throughout my ministry I never forgot the words of the Rev. Pauline Carr, an associate member of the Kentucky Conference. 'Don't lose yourself while serving.' I spent seventeen years of ministry serving on the Board of Ministry seeking to guide incoming pastors to be themselves while fulfilling their call. In summary, I am a clergywoman called by God, who brought the healing love of God into the midst of chaos and hurt within the lives of individuals and congregations."

Barbara Franks retired from full-time ministry in 2005.

First Korean Woman to Be Received into Full Connection

Received on Trial – 1992
Ordained Deacon – 1992
Received into Full Connection – 1994
Ordained Elder – 1994
Current Appointment – Holy Spirit Korean UMC, Woodbridge, Virginia (Extension Ministries Appointment by GBGM)

SUZY HAM-SON was born January 19, 1943, in Busan, Korea.

"When I first came to Chicago in the mid-1970s to work as a nurse, my husband, Paul, and I were struggling to make enough money to live comfortably and live the American dream. Besides the struggle to make ends meet, I also began feeling tired. So I decided to see a doctor, who was also Korean. He invited Paul and me to go to meet God at church. We weren't too interested at that time. All of that changed when I learned that I had tuberculosis. Still the doctor spoke to me about God and I decided to listen. That led to me going to a revival where I heard the scripture from Matt. 11:28, 'Come to me, all you that are weary and are carrying heavy burdens, and I will give you rest.' It was then I accepted Jesus Christ into my heart and began a new life—not to serve my own interests, but God's mission.

"I can truly say that it has taken a tremendous amount of courage to serve God ever since I began my first ministry in Louisville at a mission church. At that time women in the clergy were few and far between and I was a first as a Korean woman in the Kentucky Conference. Only by the grace of God have I been able to continue in times of joy and times of hardship serving to glorify his kingdom.

"My current ministry is made up of the challenges of all of my past ministries combined. God has granted me courage in the past to find different successes in each ministry. Now I believe he is working to build an even greater success in this current ministry, laying the groundwork for a bold future, to glorify his kingdom in northern Virginia and around the world."

MEMPHIS ANNUAL CONFERENCE

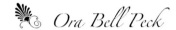 *Ora Bell Peck*

 *Lenn Harris Milam*

(EUROPEAN AMERICAN)
First Woman to Be Received into Full Connection

Received on Trial – 1966
Ordained Deacon – 1968
Received into Full Connection – 1968
Ordained Elder – 1970
Retired – 1994

ORA BELL KING PECK was born March 16, 1932, in Obion County, Tennessee, near Union City. It was not until 1954, however, when she heard God speaking clearly to her, calling her to be a preacher. "I received my license in May 1955. The district superintendent who issued my license moved in June. The new D.S. didn't believe in women ministers and vowed that I would never preach as long as he was D.S. He refused to renew my license yearly though it was required by the *Discipline*. In 1960 District Superintendent Dr. Wayne Lamb reviewed my service to the church and issued me a new license to preach."

Although Ora Bell was granted a scholarship to attend Vanderbilt Theological School, her bishop refused to appoint her to attend school. After attending the course of study at Candler School of Theology in Atlanta, she was asked to enroll as a regular student. "This required an interview with the bishop and cabinet of the North Georgia Conference for an appointment to seminary. I shall never forget how they laughed and ridiculed the very idea. I continued to pastor full time and my D.S. advised me to move about every three years to hopefully reach appointments above the lowest level at a quicker pace. In 1975 the Annual Conference broke new ground by appointing my husband Paul and me to the Fulton Area Team Ministry. This was the first team model of its kind and proved to be very successful."

Since Ora was the only female clergyperson for some time, she was given the opportunity to serve on nearly every board and committee in the annual conference, including the Board of Ordained Ministry, Council on Finance and Administration, General Commission on the Status and Role of Women (COS-ROW), and the General Board of Church and Society. She was a delegate to General Conference once and to Jurisdictional Conference three times. Ora and her husband retired in June 1994.

First African American Woman to Be Received into Full Connection

Received on Trial – 1977
Ordained Deacon – 1977
Received into Full Connection – 1979
Ordained Elder – 1979
Current Appointment – Extension Ministries, The Samaritan Counseling Centers of the Mid-South

LENN HARRIS MILAM was born August 13, 1953, in Memphis, Tennessee.

"My preparation for pastoral care, counseling, and ministry began in early childhood and was formed and impacted by three distinct systems: my family, my community, and my church. The local congregation (Centenary United Methodist) where I was christened, baptized, confirmed, and affirmed in the call to the ordained ministry was influential in my journey. The idea of a woman entering the ordained ministry was still a novelty in 1975. Yet this church community embraced me and supported me on this phase of my life's journey. My teen years in Memphis were during turbulent racial unrest and social upheaval. I was in a faith community that was not only preaching social justice and liberation theology from the pulpit, but was living out this gospel message.

"In addition to the three systems that have formed me, my pastoral role in counseling ministry has also been influenced by the ebb and flow of life. Through my parish ministry and CPE experiences, my own therapy, my married life, and the life experiences of the people I have encountered in and outside the counseling room, I have learned about loss and grief, suffering and redemption, hope and hopelessness, fragmentation, integration, and, finally, healing. Ministry in the pastoral counseling arena allows me to be with people who have become derailed on their life's journey. And, while each person's life experience is unique to them, there are points of connection between their journeys and mine. It is in the sanctuary of the therapy room where the commonality of the human experience is played out, and I am reminded of the power of community and its impact on the healing process."

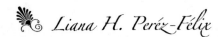
Liana H. Peréz-Félix

First Hispanic/Latina Woman to Serve in Full Connection

Received on Trial, Puerto Rico – 1986
Ordained Deacon, Puerto Rico – 1986
Received into Full Connection, Puerto Rico – 1991
Ordained Elder, Puerto Rico – 1991
Current Appointment – Extension Ministries, Program
Ministries Associate Director and Coordinator of Hispanic and
Inclusive Ministries

LIANA H. PERÉZ-FÉLIX was born August 8, 1941, in Vieques, Puerto Rico. "In 1962, while in college, I received God's call for the ordained ministry. I was then engaged to a ministerial candidate. We went to ask our district superintendent for advice. He said that to be a pastor and be married to one would not be good since we would be appointed to different cities, and that would not help in raising a family. With sadness, and being so young, I decided to postpone that call. I became a teacher and we were married for thirteen years."

During that time Liana moved with her family to Boston and was eventually divorced.

"In 1980 we went back to Puerto Rico, and church leaders and close friends were insisting that I finally answer God's call into ministry. I became a ministerial candidate, was certified, and began to take evening courses at the Evangelical Seminary of Puerto Rico. In 1991 I was ordained elder in the UMC. That same year two other pastors and I were appointed acting district superintendents because, at the time, the church in Puerto Rico was still part of The United Methodist Church. It became an affiliated autonomous church–*Iglesia Metodista Autonoma Afiliada de Puerto Rico*–at the General Conference in 1992. In June 1992 we elected our first Puerto Rican bishop, and the three acting district superintendents became district superintendents, making me the first woman district superintendent in the new denomination.

"In 1997 I was appointed missionary to *Iglesia de la Nueva Comunidad* (Church of the New Community) in St. Louis, Missouri, where I took care of an English-speaking and a Hispanic congregation, as well as helping at the church's health clinic for Hispanics/Latinos. In 1998 I was appointed missionary to the Memphis Conference, working as Program Ministries Associate Director and Coordinator of Hispanic and Inclusive Ministries."

In 2004 Liana became the first female Hispanic/Latina candidate for the episcopacy from the Southeast Jurisdiction. "During peaceful times and times with strong winds and turbulent waters, I have known one thing for sure: the Lord has been with me all the way, has strengthened me, and, even with broken wings, I have been able to fly high with an assurance that I am here to serve him and help those in need."

MISSISSIPPI ANNUAL CONFERENCE

 *Ruth Wood*

(EUROPEAN AMERICAN)

First Woman to Be Received into Full Connection in the Former North Mississippi Conference

Ordained Deacon – 1961
Ordained Elder – 1962
Received on Trial – 1965
Received into Full Connection – 1967
Retired – 1989

RUTH WOOD was born August 10, 1925. Ruth began her ministerial journey in 1959 when she was appointed to the Booneville Circuit where she served until 1961, when she was then appointed to the West Prentiss Parish. At a special session of the Annual Conference in 1962, Ruth was ordained deacon. She served the West Prentiss Parish until she came into full connection in 1967. From 1967 to 1972 she served at Golden. Then Ruth served Box Chapel at Corinth until 1980 when she was appointed to Lake Cormorant. She served there until 1984 when she went to Byhalia, where she stayed until 1987. Ruth retired in 1989 and is still living today in Olive Branch, Mississippi.[6]

realities and a search for a personal relationship with God. Having a deeply personal religious conversion at an early age, I was drawn to serve others in their soul journeys, particularly around issues of justice and freedom when persons' souls are oppressed. This religious value and conviction gave me the courage to pursue an unconventional path for women in the 1970s–which was a path leading to ordained ministry. This journey was extremely difficult given the cultural and societal values that were predominant in Mississippi in those years. Sexism and racism were deeply entrenched in the cultural patterns in those days, and women were not allowed full participation in leadership positions in The United Methodist Church in Mississippi. With the encouragement and support of professors at Candler School of Theology and others in Georgia, I was able to complete the journey toward ordination in 1980.

"For twenty-two years, my ministry has been marked by serving others in their soul journeys and 'soul's work.' Theologically, this type of ministry is modeled after Jesus' healing ministry in which the soul of the person with whom one ministers is of utmost importance and value. It has been a privilege and honor to have supervised almost five hundred seminarians and clergy in preparation for ministry, as well as to minister to countless patients and families over the years."

 *Dorothy Dale Yarborough Owen*

(EUROPEAN AMERICAN)

First Woman to Be Received into Full Connection in the Mississippi Conference

Received on Trial – 1974
Ordained Deacon – 1974
Received into Full Connection – 1980
Ordained Elder – 1980
Current Appointment – Extension Ministries, Codirector and ACPE, CPE Supervisor of the North Atlanta Tri-Hospital Clinical Pastoral Education Center at Saint Joseph's Hospital of Atlanta

DOROTHY DALE YARBOROUGH OWEN was born October 6, 1946, in Tylertown, Mississippi.

"My call evolved over a lifetime and has had many layers to it. Having had exposure to the Christian faith from an early age, my spirit seemed particularly attuned to religious

 *Emma Louise McNair*

First African American Woman to Be Received into Full Connection in the Mississippi Conference

Received on Trial – 1981
Ordained Deacon – 1983
Received into Full Connection – 1985
Ordained Elder – 1985
Retired – 2000

EMMA LOUISE MCNAIR was born March 11, 1935, in Mississippi.

"I experienced my call to the ordained ministry at the age of eleven in the backyard on my mother's wash bench. In my early years, I defined it as the call to the mission field. I used to hear my mother praying during the day and at nighttime. I would peep in wherever she was to see whom she was talking to. One day, I heard the name 'Jesus' and I asked my mother who Jesus was. She said, 'I could tell you who and what he is to me, but you need to get to know him for yourself.'

"When I became a widow with six children after my husband was killed in Vietnam, I made a decision never to remarry. After my children were old enough to help themselves and others, I started back to school. For over twenty years of stop-and-go studies, I finished college. I entered seminary, but after a year and a half, I was faced with the choice of having to drop out of seminary if I were unable to get my four younger children to live with me. I am grateful for a small rural church that adopted my children and me, enabling me to finish my studies.

"I did not know I was the first African American woman to be received into full connection in Mississippi, as all I was doing was answering the call. I stayed in the local church for nine years, and then I entered a two-and-a-half-year training program for chaplains. Again, I did not know that I was the first black person to be certified by a national board. As I said earlier, all I did was to answer the call. I have truly been blessed by people from all over the world who I will never meet again."

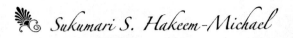

Sukumari S. Hakeem-Michael

First Indian Woman to Serve in Full Connection
Received into Full Connection in the Former South Dakota Conference in 1997
On loan to Mississippi Conference since 1998

(See chapter 7, 152)

NORTH ALABAMA ANNUAL CONFERENCE

 *Estelle Jones Pinegar*

(EUROPEAN AMERICAN)
First Woman to Be Received into Full Connection

Received on Trial – 1960
Ordained Deacon – 1962
Received into Full Connection – 1963
Ordained Elder – 1964
Retired – 1980
Deceased – 1999

ESTELLE JONES PINEGAR was born October 31, 1915, in Jefferson County, Alabama.

Dr. Estelle J. Pinegar was a pioneer lady, lover of God, her family, her church and all the people she made contact with no matter where in the world they were found.

I first came to know [Estelle] twenty-two years ago at my first appointment, which was also her first appointment. Many people referred to her as "that woman." I met her at my first District meeting. She introduced herself to me and told me how things were and offered her support to me and my ministry in any way she could be of help. And that she did! This is the way she was with all the young people coming into pastoral ministry, no matter how old they might be. She had a deep love for each and every one of us. [She] prayed for each one of us and for our ministry. Her prayer was that God would bless the work, keep us strong in the faith, and that we would never falter from the work we were called to and had begun…

[Estelle's] greatest love was for the small membership congregation, cause and needs. Although [she] was retired from active service as pastor-in-charge for eighteen years, she never stopped serving her Lord in any way she could, proclaiming the good news of God's love, singing the songs of victory, and praying for the lost and for the faithful.

Dr. Estelle Pinegar was a lady I am grateful crossed my path, gave her hand as an example, as a teacher, a preacher, a mother, and a friend to all.[7]

Estelle Pinegar died March 28, 1999, at age eighty-three.

 *Julia McClain Walker*

First African American Woman to Be Received into Full Connection in the Former Central Alabama Conference Methodist Church, Central Jurisdiction

Received on Trial – 1959
Ordained Deacon – 1959
Received into Full Connection – 1960
Ordained Elder – 1960
Deceased – 1999

JULIA MCCLAIN WALKER was born June 11, 1935, in Philadelphia, Pennsylvania.

Julia…was a highly educated being, because God was her scholar. She had a passion for teaching the gospel according to Christ.… Her first major appointment was as Chaplain at the historically black Rust College, where she led the march of students from Rust to the steps of the University of Mississippi to support James Meredith as he became the first black student accepted in 1962. Julia Walker and the Rust students rallied around James Meredith along with U.S. Marshals to protect him from Mississippi State Troopers who wanted to keep him from entering the all-white institution.…

The fact that she lived love, gave love, is love and loved…to love, made her life absolute. Her love was so great, she loved me off of crack cocaine. Every time she saw me "strung out" she loved…ME! Nothing else to be said! Even in her last breath she spoke words representing the true essence of her life. "We love because God is love." The Lord was expedient in showing His pleasure, thunderously applauding, "Well done my good and faithful servant, well done. You have been faithful over a few things. Now I will make you ruler over many!"[8]

Julia Walker died January 12, 1999, at age sixty-three.

 *Aida Lea Barrera-Segura*

First Hispanic/Latina Woman to Serve in Full Connection

(See above, 101)

Gladys R. Williford

(EUROPEAN AMERICAN)

First Woman to Be Received into Full Connection

Received on Trial – 1971
Ordained Deacon – 1972
Received into Full Connection – 1975
Ordained Elder – 1975
Retired – 1993

GLADYS RUTH RUNION WILLIFORD was born December 24, 1930, in Englewood, New Jersey, and grew up on a farm in central New York.

"In the fourth year of elementary school teaching, I married Raymond M. Williford and moved to North Carolina. Fourteen years later, the sudden death of my husband left me as the widowed mother of four young children. Dealing with this abrupt change in life and responsibility brought me to renewed spiritual commitment. God's answer was an unmistakable call to pastoral ministry.

"I entered divinity school at Duke University in the fall of 1971. After ordination as a deacon in June 1972, I was appointed to a student pastorate. I graduated from divinity school in 1974 and was ordained elder in 1975.

"Acceptance by conference hierarchy was very gracious, but local congregations had much more difficulty with the notion of a 'petticoat preacher'! Nevertheless, twenty-nine years in pastorates has given me many dear Christian friends.

"As a 'retired clergy' since 1993, I have had many opportunities for ministry, first in the Florida Conference and, now, in the North Georgia Conference. What a joy to live and work with our Lord and his other people!"

Edith Lee Gleaves

First African American Woman to Be Received into Full Connection

Received on Trial – 1984
Ordained Deacon – 1984
Received into Full Connection – 1988
Ordained Elder – 1988
Current Appointment – Extension Ministries, Deputy General Secretary for the Mission Personnel Program Area, General Board of Global Ministries (first African American female clergyperson to hold a position at this level in the history of GBGM)

EDITH LEE GLEAVES was born February 17, 1960, in Laurinburg, North Carolina.

"I first became aware of my call as such in 1976 at the age of sixteen, though I think I was born called. My pastor was preaching from Isaiah 6 and I heard the voice of God speak to me saying, 'Whom shall I send, and who will go for us?' I immediately answered, 'Here am I–send somebody else!' I had never heard or seen a woman pastor and had no intention of being the first. God took my objection seriously, and within a year sent the Rev. Emma Ruth McLean (at the time, one of the few female local pastors if not the only African American female local pastor in the North Carolina Annual Conference) to the three-point charge of which my local church was a part. She was a great encourager and role model to me. I eventually decided to pursue the pastorate as a beginning point, but have never believed or sensed that venue to be the only one through which I would serve out my calling.

"Since the time I first received my call into full-time ministry at age sixteen, ministry has been a proving ground. Through the years, I have had to prove my gifts and graces as a pastor and leader over and over again due to a mixture of racism, sexism, and sometimes ageism. Over time I have seen the number of these encounters diminish, and the resistance to me as a person and to my ministry dissipate or turn into acceptance, respect, and support. There have also always been those who offered me support, love, affirmation, and encouragement along the journey. Through it all, God has proved to be present, loving, and faithful, enabling and empowering me with courage and boldness to keep on keeping on into the future."

Carolyn Mae Cummings-Woriax

First Native American Woman to Be Received into Full Connection

Received on Trial – 1995
Ordained Deacon – 1995
Received into Full Connection – 1999
Ordained Elder – 1999
Current Status – Bolton Charge, Wilmington District; Working as a Part-Time Nephrology Social Worker, Goldsboro, North Carolina

CAROLYN MAE CUMMINGS-WORIAX was born April 18, 1941, in Robeson County, Pembroke, North Carolina.

"I was about eight to ten years of age when I knew within my heart that God had called me into the ministry. I felt the conviction very strongly that I was to go to others to share with them about Jesus Christ. My ministry has been one of resistance and affirmation. Most of the resistance came during the years 1991 to 1995 when I did not receive an appointment in the North Carolina Conference, due to the culture and teachings of this area. I had two strikes against me–being a female and an American Indian.

"Affirmations have been many. I am involved in missions and health ministry. These two areas have been challenging and rewarding. I have worked to establish opportunities of growth and discipleship in each congregation. I have worked in establishing an outreach program for children in a poor neighborhood. Also, I was able to develop a 'soup bag' ministry to the homeless and street persons in a local downtown. And I have witnessed those receiving Jesus Christ as their Lord and Savior as God's affirmation of my ministry. Since 1995, I have traveled to Bolivia with a mission work team and, recently, with a Native American relief work team to the Houma Indians in Dulac, Louisiana.

"My call to ministry has been a very real part of my life. It is ever before me. God's words–that I would be sent to 'another people'–continue to be fresh in my mind. The experiences and rewards are overwhelming. I know and believe that I would not have had this opportunity had I not had the privilege to serve as a United Methodist clergyperson. I thank the UMC for affirming my call. Most of all, I thank God for calling me into ministry."

Lily Ker Tong Chou

First Chinese Woman to Be Received into Full Connection

Received on Trial – 2000
Ordained Deacon – 2000
Received into Full Connection – 2002
Ordained Elder – 2002
Current Appointment – Brownings-Smith Chapel UMC, Mount Olive, North Carolina

LILY KER TONG CHOU was born October 6, 1941, in Shanghai, China.

"My call came to me as early as ten years of age after God healed me from tuberculosis. But I postponed full-time ministry for half a lifetime. I told the bishop that I was a city girl, having been born in the largest city of the world, Shanghai, and having lived in New York, Los Angeles, and Hong Kong for many years. But I truly thank God for the privilege of ministering to two rural churches consisting mostly of farmers. I am in the tiny village of Dobbersville, which does not even boast of one stoplight! Grocery shopping has to be done either in Mount Olive, eleven miles to the east, or Newton Grove, eight miles to the west. Black bears crossed the street twice at the same spot and same time right in front of our car! But I love the peace and the quiet and especially the people. Fresh produce from the fields mysteriously appears at the parsonage door from loving members. Cotton fields surround me on three sides. When it is ripe, it looks like snow. I am so grateful to be with people who live close to the earth. I do not miss city life, cultural events, or shopping, at all.

"I offer the children and even a few adults in the church free piano lessons. Smith Chapel has just purchased a baby grand piano. One Sunday in September will forever go down in history as 'the day of the baby grand and the grand baby.' I baptized someone's grandbaby on the same Sunday the baby grand piano arrived. My ministry consists of hospitality–cooking Chinese meals for my church members, taking care of the elderly, giving massages with my 'snake oil,' marrying, burying, and baptizing–and loving them."

NORTH GEORGIA ANNUAL CONFERENCE

 *Ruth Elizabeth Rogers*

(EUROPEAN AMERICAN)
First Woman to Be Received into Full Connection

Ordained Deacon – 1952
Ordained Elder – 1956
Received on Trial – 1957
Received into Full Connection – 1959
Retired – 1974
Deceased – 1994

RUTH ELIZABETH ROGERS was born May 21, 1905, in Gainesville, Georgia. Ruth was a lifelong Methodist. The Eakeses, her mother's family, were a family of Methodist ministers. Ruth experienced her call to preach after the death of a nephew, Billy (whom she adopted), at age fourteen, followed by her mother two years later. Among Billy's last words to her were, "Aunt Ruth, you are going to have to do my preaching." Her beloved mother died in her arms, saying, "Don't you see Christ? I can see Christ.... He's right on the edge of the crowd. He's opening the eyes of the blind."

After Billy's death, Ruth did a great deal of thinking "and praying about it." But she was not willing "to take on the enmity of the preachers in the conference" by answering the call to preach. After the glorious experience of Christ at her mother's deathbed, "I felt I had to tell the story whether I wanted to or not."

Ruth was licensed to preach in The Methodist Church in February 1949. For many years she was the only woman minister in the North Georgia Conference. Being a pioneer was not easy. With a few happy exceptions, she was ignored at best; and being insulted or maligned was not unusual.

After she preached at a district conference, the vote was unanimous to accept her call and she pastored for nearly twenty years until her retirement in 1974. Ruth Rogers died September 18, 1994, in Atlanta, Georgia, at age eighty-nine.[9]

 *Sayde Wylena Westbrooks*

First African American Woman to Be Received into Full Connection in the Former Georgia Conference, Methodist Church, Central Jurisdiction

Ordained Deacon – 1946
Received into Full Connection – 1960
Ordained Elder – 1960
Received on Trial – 1958
Deceased – 1972

SAYDE WYLENA WESTBROOKS was born December 29, 1905, in Atlanta, Georgia.

Her extensive education was arduous and ambitious. She achieved much, and gave herself without stint to mentally handicapped and exceptional children in the Georgia cities of College Park, Atlanta, Grantville, Richmond Hills, Savannah, and Fairburn; and in Greenville, S.C. and in Detroit, Michigan. With this rich and varied experience she was well qualified and disciplined to serve as minister of the Asbury Mission in the Thomasville area of Fulton County; and later as minister of Lamar-Johnson United Methodist Church (1961–1971) in Forest Park, Georgia. She piloted this church through its days as a mission into a full charge. She made extensive additions to its plant and program....

The J. F. Beavers' School honored her as Teacher of the Year in 1964. She was named Bronze Woman of Religion (1963) by the Delta Chapter of Iota Phi Lambda Sorority. The 1966 Edition of *Who's Who in American Women* lists her achievements in the ministry, in the field of teacher education, as an author of articles on religion and special education....

The Reverend Sadye Wylena Westbrooks' life motto, "It is no secret what God can do," was on her lips moments before her death. With her sister's challenge of "He's got the whole, wide world in His hands" she met her God with the faith and courage of the Methodist minister she was.... She now rests from her labors, and leaves the example of an intrepid spirit, and prodigious industry to guide those whose lives have been touched and enriched by hers.[10]

Sayde Westbrooks died February 12, 1972, at age sixty-six.

 *Aida Luz Beltran-Gaetan*

 *Millie L. Kim*

First Hispanic/Latina Woman to Be Received into Full Connection

Received on Trial – 1993
Ordained Deacon – 1993
Received into Full Connection – 1995
Ordained Elder – 1995
Current Appointment – Lagrange District to Start a Hispanic Congregation

AIDA LUZ BELTRAN-GAETAN was born January 6, 1944, in Fajardo, Puerto Rico.

"I have had multiple experiences of receiving God's call to ordained ministry since I was a five-year-old child. At age seventeen, and being a Roman Catholic, I believed God wanted me to be a teaching nun among the poor. So I began that process. In 1962 I had a 'conversion experience' in a Pentecostal church and was sure I was to serve God in ministry. But I fell in love and got married. So I put my calling aside. In 1978 I received a call through prophetic messages, and I heard God's voice directing me to study the Bible. I enrolled in a Bible college, where I discovered my desire and passion for preaching. In 1980 I moved to Atlanta to answer that call. When I saw the situation of the Hispanic people in this nation, I was captured by a vision to be in ministry to serve them, helping them through services that met their needs and spiritual nurture. While at Candler School of Theology, I saw a female clergyperson for the first time—an Episcopal priest celebrating the Sacrament of Holy Communion. I began to long to be able to do so myself. I also discovered my pastoral heart and desire to be a healing instrument of God.

"The journey toward ordination was full of great expectations, hopes, and dreams. I was sustained by clergywomen's gatherings and fellowship during the process. I came from the Church of God, where there is no hope of being ordained as a woman. So coming to the UMC was a very hopeful time. After ordination, the journey has been full of joy for the great privilege of being ordained to serve God and God's people and full of the hope for the seeds planted and the lay missioners I have trained. Yet the special nature of my ministry–Hispanic ministries among the non-Hispanic United Methodist churches–has seen its share of frustrations, brought on by poor timing, misunderstandings, and disappointments. Nonetheless, I look forward with hope to the future of Hispanic ministries in our denomination. I thank God and many clergywomen who have supported me in this journey."

First Korean Woman to Be Received into Full Connection

Received on Trial – 2000[11]
Ordained Elder – 2003
Received into Full Connection – 2003
Current Appointment – Missionary to Mongolia; Pastor of The United Methodist Mission Center in Mongolia

MILLIE L. KIM was born October 14, 1970, in Daegu, South Korea.

"I was active in church (UMC) during my college years and, by chance, entered theology school. I was a classics major in college; and a classics professor, who also taught in theology school, really pushed me and recommended the master of theological studies program. This is how I began my theological journey. In the second year I was privileged to study abroad in Germany on full a scholarship. There, I had a powerful conversion experience in which God talked to me directly to abide in God's house. I dedicated myself to God, changed my degree from MTS to MDiv, and began my journey of ministry. It is remarkable that God called me to Mongolia because I never thought I would become a missionary. It was not in my plan at all! I love parish ministry and preaching so much. Moreover, I felt that I did not fit the traditional image of 'missionary.' Nevertheless, I responded to God's call and now I am serving the people of Mongolia with heartfelt joy and gratitude everyday.

"I feel very fortunate and grateful for all the clergywomen who have gone before me. Due to their suffering and sacrifice, I had it easy. Many clergy (both male and female) have constantly encouraged me to go into ministry. In many respects, I was not mature enough to go into ministry, which delayed the process by almost ten years. My difficulty in the ordination process had to do more with my political stand rather than my gender or race. My generation of clergywomen in North Georgia, for the first time in the history of the conference, had plenty of excellent role models (clergywomen) and mentors. I give God the glory and extend my sincere gratitude to all the clergywomen who have gone before me."

 *Karen Miyoshi Kagiyama*

First Japanese Woman to Serve in Full Connection
Transferred from Western North Carolina Conference

(See below, 124)

RED BIRD MISSIONARY CONFERENCE

(The Annual Conference does receive members, but to date has not received a woman into full connection.)

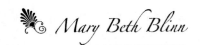 *Mary Beth Blinn*

(EUROPEAN AMERICAN)

First Woman in Full Connection to Serve While a Member of the Virginia Conference

Received on Trial – 1983
Ordained Deacon – 1983
Received into Full Connection – 1985
Ordained Elder – 1985
Current Appointment – District Superintendent Danville District

MARY BETH BLINN was born January 17, 1955, in Lexington, Kentucky.

"I experienced a call to ministry while in college at Emory and Henry College. I entered seminary, pursuing an interest in pastoral counseling, and taking along with me my husband and one-year-old son. During my seminary years, and through an internship, I began to understand that I had gifts for pastoring and that God could use me in the local church. This has been confirmed time and time again, beginning with my first student appointment.

"I have been blessed in pastoring three churches as my first full-time appointment in Virginia (which was actually a six-point parish I copastored with my husband, Bob); copastoring three churches in Harlan County, Kentucky (Red Bird Missionary Conference), pastoring a medium-size church in the Shenandoah Valley of Virginia, and now serving as district superintendent. I have been welcomed in each situation and given the freedom to use my gifts by the grace of God. I am thankful for a church that has affirmed my call and given me diverse places to serve."

SOUTH CAROLINA ANNUAL CONFERENCE

 *Vivian Patricia McFadden*

(AFRICAN AMERICAN)
First Woman to Be Received into Full Connection

Received on Trial – 1972
Ordained Deacon – 1972
Received into Full Connection – 1974
Ordained Elder – 1974
Retired – 2000

VIVIAN PATRICIA MCFADDEN was born March 30 in Kingstree, South Carolina. She received the AB degree from Claflin College in 1969 and her MDiv from Gammon Theological Seminary in 1973. She was licensed to preach in April 1971 in the Florence District on recommendation of Zion Church, Kingstree Charge. Her appointments were as follows: She spent 1972 in school; was associate at Johns Island UMC in 1973; and served as a chaplain in the U.S. Navy in 1974. She continued in this appointment until she took the retired relationship to the annual conference in 2000.[12]

 *Susan Thurston Henry-Crowe*

First European American Woman to Be Received into Full Connection

Received on Trial – 1974
Ordained Deacon – 1974
Received into Full Connection – 1977
Ordained Elder – 1977
Current Appointment – Extension Ministries, Dean of the Chapel and Religious Life, Emory University, Atlanta, Georgia

SUSAN THURSTON HENRY-CROWE was born January 1, 1951, in Asheville, North Carolina.

"My journey in ministry probably began around the time of confirmation and my involvement in United Methodist Youth Fellowship (UMYF) and church school at Central UMC in Asheville, North Carolina, and later at Buncombe Street UMC in Greenville, South Carolina. The stirrings were an intellectual interest in religion and theology. My senior-high director of education, Olene Civils (deaconess and director of Christian education at Buncombe St.), engaged in wonderful pedagogy by creating an environment that encouraged study and learning along with healthy and open social interaction. In college I was interested in the study of philosophy and religion and was active in the Wesley Foundation, being nurtured and mentored by outstanding campus ministers. In 1973 when applying to graduate schools I was interested in pursuing anthropology and/or law. When a program at Hartford Seminary was discontinued, I applied to Candler School of Theology with no idea of what I would do with a degree. I was very unclear about ordination in those days, but upon graduation I pursued ordination.

"I serve as the dean of Cannon Chapel and Religious Life at a research university with twelve thousand students. The religious demography of Emory University is Christian, strongly Jewish, Hindu, Muslim, Baha'i, and Buddhist. In addition to overseeing services in the chapel, and religious activities and services, I oversee and help coordinate the work of thirty religious groups on campus for faculty, staff, and graduate and undergraduate students. I have been at Emory for fourteen years."

Susan is also the only clergywoman to serve on the Judicial Council.

 *Miyoung Paik*

First Korean Woman to Be Received into Full Connection

Received on Trial – 1990
Ordained Deacon – 1990
Received into Full Connection – 1992
Ordained Elder – 1992
Current Appointment – Associate Pastor, Lexington UMC, Lexington, South Carolina

MIYOUNG PAIK was born September 7, 1958, in Seoul, South Korea. Miyoung began her journey toward the ordained ministry during her junior year in college in New York at a Korean church revival service.

"After graduating from high school in Korea, I came to the United States at the age of nineteen. I attended Parsons School of Design in New York City and The Theological School at Drew University in New Jersey. After finishing my education in 1990, I moved to South Carolina. I found the experience harder than the experience of moving to the United States years before.

"Being a pastor and living in South Carolina was a long wilderness experience. After eight years of ministry, I was totally worn out and had no energy to go on. By the grace of God, I took a sabbatical year in 1998 through 1999. It was the best gift God gave me. I was refreshed and renewed, and ready to be sent anywhere by the bishop. Through fourteen years of ministry, I have experienced that in the wilderness, all of a sudden the flowers bloom."

 *Sandra Hardin Hatchell*

First Native American Woman to Be Received into Full Connection

Received on Trial – 1996
Ordained Deacon – 1996
Received into Full Connection – 1999
Ordained Elder – 1999
Current Appointment – Cottageville Charge, Cottageville, South Carolina

SANDRA HARDIN HATCHELL was born February 29, 1956.

"In reexamining my call to write this brief autobiography, I discovered that I actually experienced two distinct and separate calls. I believe Wesley when he talked about prevenient grace–the grace that gently pulls us toward Christ. My first call was to a personal relationship and the journey to Christ as my personal Savior. The second call was to servant ministry. My husband and I were attending a Methodist church while I was in school working toward my master's degree in counseling. However, a change in our financial circumstances made school unaffordable. I checked with the college that I was attending to see if I could drop out and pick up my studies again the next year. The college agreed on the condition that I write sermons. I agreed. I arranged to preach for my Sunday school class. However, being a minister had never crossed my mind.

"The prearranged Sunday morning arrived. I could not breathe. I stood up and began my sermon and something strange happened. I felt for the first time that I fit. When I had finished preaching and sat down, I couldn't look at anyone. 'Can they sense what I felt?' I wondered. God's words to Jesus at his baptism truly spoke to me. God had touched me and said, 'You are my child and I am well pleased.' At lunch, my husband and I discussed ministry. The next morning I 'declared' my intentions to the D.S. I have never looked back or slowed on my journey with Christ or my journey in ministry. I can only say that God can bring glory when we accept grace."

SOUTH GEORGIA ANNUAL CONFERENCE

(EUROPEAN AMERICAN)
One of the First Two Women to Be Received into Full Connection

Received on Trial – 1975
Ordained Deacon – 1975
Received into Full Connection – 1978
Ordained Elder – 1978
Current Appointment – Senior Pastor, First UMC, Waycross, Georgia

MARCIA JANE COCHRAN was born June 8, 1942, in Bainbridge, Georgia.

"In high school and the first year of college, I felt 'called'–really more a sense of 'oughtness.' Since I didn't know any clergywomen or if any existed, I wasn't clear on the path I could follow.

"The journey has been a difficult, interesting, rewarding, and treacherous one at times. I have many scars from those first years of trailblazing and at times I have wanted to quit. Other times I have been so blessed by the support and encouragement of the laity that I can't imagine not serving in the ministry. Throughout the controversy that surrounds the ordination and ministry of women, I find myself amused that any woman would go through all of this if she didn't believe she was called by God!"

(EUROPEAN AMERICAN)
One of the First Two Women to Be Received into Full Connection

Received on Trial – 1975
Ordained Deacon – 1975
Received into Full Connection – 1978
Ordained Elder – 1978
Current Appointment – Extension Ministries, Pastoral Counseling Center, Savannah, Georgia

After attending Candler School of Theology in Atlanta, ALLISON RHODES MORGAN was appointed as assistant to the staff at Wynnton UMC in 1966. From 1977 to March 1980, she served the Geneva UMC. In March 1980, Allison took maternity leave until 1982, when she was appointed to attend school at Auburn University. From 1985 until 1988, she was a counselor at the Pastoral Institute in Columbus, Georgia, a Christian counseling center founded by United Methodists. Since 1989 Allison has served as a counselor at the Pastoral Counseling Center in Savannah, Georgia.[13]

First African American Woman to Be Received into Full Connection

Ordained Deacon – 1975
Associate Membership – 1985
Received on Trial – 1987
Received into Full Connection – 1993
Ordained Elder – 1993
Retired – 2000

ESSIE C. SIMMONS was born June 2, 1926, in Glynn County, Brunswick, Georgia.

"Early in life I began to enjoy going to church with my parents. My father, a man committed to his calling, was a Methodist minister. My interest in the ministry started with my upbringing, which was, perhaps, a bit atypical for the times. We children were expected to complete high school, and most of us went on to college.

"As time passed, I tried to evade the call to ministry but couldn't. God called me and I had to answer. I saw no peace until I said yes to the Lord. Actually, I believe I received the call in high school. Then again God worked on me, again and again in college, but I was most reluctant then to enter the ministry because I was a woman. In later years when I became sure, I found I could not evade the issue any longer. God kept working on me; and the moment I answered the call I felt relief. Only a person who has received the call can appreciate, understand, and enjoy what I'm saying because there is a mystery about this type of thing. This includes living out our relationship to God and our relationship to others.

"I enjoyed my ministry. This was my first priority, and I truly tried, with God's help, to do my very best. I was very happy with my work. I like working with people–I always have and I feel this is what my ministry was all about. I thank God that I have never had any problems as a woman in the ministry. I have been well accepted by both the men and women in the local churches. If God is for you, who can be against you?"

Essie retired from full-time ministry in 2000.

TENNESSEE ANNUAL CONFERENCE

 *Faith Cornwall*

 *Karen Young Collier*

(EUROPEAN AMERICAN)

First Woman to Be Received into Full Connection

Received on Trial – 1971
Ordained Deacon – 1971
Received into Full Connection – 1973
Ordained Elder – 1973
Retired – 1985

FAITH CORNWALL was born December 13, 1917, in Rupert, Indiana.

"When I was twelve years old I attended a series of evangelistic meetings with my mother. They were nondenominational and emphasized the importance of dedicating one's life to Christ. They were fiery in nature, and I must confess, they frightened me. Nevertheless, my dedication was sincere, and before long I felt called to be an evangelist. The opportunity never opened up, but as the years passed, and through the understanding of our Methodist minister, I was given places of service in the church while my call persisted. There seemed to be no place for a woman minister there, but I continued to nurture the call to preach. In time, I attended seminary and was accepted into the ministry in the Methodist denomination.

"Along with my call to the ministry, I have had a special interest in and concern for the mentally ill since my teen years. I determined, while in seminary, to become trained to minister to them. While attending seminary at Vanderbilt University I had many opportunities to gain training in group work, counseling, and psychology. Upon graduation, I applied for a position as chaplain at Middle Tennessee Mental Institute. I was first a half-time assistant chaplain, and then head chaplain, then director of pastoral services in an institution very open to the part religion can play in therapy.

"It pleases me to think that I may have opened up a path for other women. I have now been retired twenty years. In a gathering of ministers, women rarely have to say, 'I was the only woman there.'"

First African American Woman to Be Received into Full Connection

Received on Trial – 1972
Ordained Deacon – 1972
Received into Full Connection – 1978
Ordained Elder – 1978
Current Appointment – Extension Ministries, Chairperson of the Religious and Philosophical Studies Department, Fisk University, Nashville, Tennessee

KAREN YOUNG COLLIER was born July 2, 1949, in Nashville, Tennessee. "I received my call to teach as I was growing up. I knew two things. First, I would always be working in the church, and, second, I wanted to teach. The two did not come together until I actually went to get my PhD. Now, I have a teaching ministry."

Karen describes herself as an educator, clergywomen, and church leader. She has pastored two United Methodist churches–Patterson Memorial and Seay-Hubbard–and served on several committees in the Tennessee conference. Karen's "life and work represent her commitment to global justice, and her special sensitivities to the issues facing people of color, particularly in religious circles." To that end, she is currently a member of the American Academy of Religion; Black Methodists for Church Renewal; coordinator and mentor for the UNCF/Mellon Undergraduate; mentor for a McNair Scholar; convener and mentor for The United Methodist Women of Color Doctoral Programs; and member of the Society for the Study of Black Religion. She has traveled and worked in Kenya, Liberia, Sierra Leone, Brazil, the Bahamas, Belize, Trinidad, Italy, Switzerland, and France. She was an observer at the organizing meeting of Black Methodists in England. Karen has served on the Board of Global Ministries (Women's Division and World Division), the Executive Committee of the World Methodist Council, and the General Council on Finance and Administration. She has also been a workshop leader for several conferences, a teacher in The United Methodist Women Schools of Christian Mission, and speaker and participant at several meetings and consultations, including the International Clergywomen's Consultation (member of the steering committee in St. Charles, Illinois).

VIRGINIA ANNUAL CONFERENCE

Betty Jane Clem

(EUROPEAN AMERICAN)
First Woman to Serve in Full Connection
Ordained in the Virginia Conference, EUB Church, in 1969

(See chapter 3, 71)

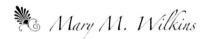
Mary M. Wilkins

(EUROPEAN AMERICAN)
First Woman to Be Received into Full Connection

Received on Trial – 1968
Ordained Deacon – 1968
Received into Full Connection – 1971
Ordained Elder – 1971
Retired – 2002

MARY M. WILKINS was born October 4, 1939, in Quicksburg, Shenandoah County, Virginia.

"From early adolescence, I knew I wanted to be a minister. But never having seen or heard of a woman minister, I kept this to myself. In the meantime, I practiced preaching sermons in front of the mirror. In my sophomore year of college my faculty adviser heard me speak in the college chapel and asked if I had considered ordained ministry. I acknowledged that I had. He invited me to join with other preministerial students on campus in going out to small rural churches without full-time pastors to lead worship and preach on Sundays. This experience confirmed my earlier sense of call.

"In 1969 I received my first appointment to a two-point charge. I invited open discussion and sharing of opinions about having a woman minister. There were strong feelings on all sides of the issue but a good base of support as well. I later learned that my district superintendent had promised the congregation that if they would take a woman for a year and they then wanted me moved he would do so without question.

"In 1971 I requested an appointment to pursue clinical pastoral education in Chicago. In my work as a CPE supervisor I have had the privilege of walking alongside hundreds of students and dozens of supervisors-in-training as they explored who they are in ministry, learned the art of pastoral care, and integrated knowledge, experience, and personhood in their practice of ministry. As I begin with each new group of students I always remember the feeling in the pit of my stomach as I drove up to my first appointment and suddenly realized, 'Wow, I'm their pastor.' I retired in 2002 but have continued to do some CPE supervision on a part-time basis."

Leontine Turpeau Current Kelly

First African American Woman to Be Received into Full Connection
First African American Woman to Be Elected to the Episcopacy in 1984 in the Western Jurisdiction

Ordained Deacon – 1972
Received into Full Connection – 1977
Ordained Elder – 1977
Received on Trial – 1974
Retired from the Episcopacy – 1989

LEONTINE TURPEAU CURRENT KELLY was born in Georgetown, Washington, DC, in 1920.

From an early age she knew she would be in a job where she served others. "When I was a teenager the YWCA executive secretary was my hero. Oh, I just loved her. I wanted to be a YWCA secretary.... Then there was Mrs. Bethune. I remember her, oh, so clearly. I could see her figure through the window of our front door. I opened the door. I'd just come down the steps at the Calvary parsonage, and she stood there and said, 'Young lady, what do you plan to be?' I didn't answer her. And she said, 'You must plan to be somebody.' And then she said, 'I'm Dr. Mary McCloud Bethune of Bethune Cookman College....' I just knew she was somebody. She became my hero because she was an amazing woman."[14]

When Leontine's husband, Rev. David Kelly, died, her district superintendent came to the house and told her that the officers of his church asked for her to be their pastor. She replied that she had been called to the classroom, not the pulpit. Rev. Carson persisted saying that both he and Bishop Goodson believed she had the gifts for ordained ministry. She responded, "Well, you and the bishop can appoint but only

God can call me to ministry, and he hasn't called. I believe in a called ministry." Little did she know that in just a few months God would call. It occurred at the Virginia Conference School of Christian Missions. She was teaching *The Inner Life*, by Harvey Potthoff. "In teaching that class, she experienced God's call in a powerful way."[15] Bishop Kelly says she has been "blessed beyond my wildest imagining in all of the gifts and opportunities God has given to me."

Janice Maria Rivero

First Hispanic/Latina Woman to Be Received into Full Connection

Received on Trial – 1979
Ordained Deacon – 1979
Received into Full Connection – 1981
Ordained Elder – 1981
Current Appointment – Extension Ministries, Campus Minister/ Director of Wesley Foundation at UNC, Chapel Hill, North Carolina

JANICE MARIA RIVERO was born September 24, 1953, in New York City, New York.

"I first began to experience the call in the late 1960s when I first heard a sermon preached by a woman in ministry. Over the twenty-five years that I have served under United Methodist appointment, I have served small, rural congregations, medium size churches, and megachurches, as well as three college campuses.

"It has been a journey of both blessing and challenge. The blessings have come in the moments when grace has abounded and love has prevailed: in baptisms and at Eucharist, in weddings and at funerals, in hospital rooms and at board meetings. Most of the challenges have come at the annual conference level, where my voice was not heard or was discounted, where my gifts for ministry have been ignored or dishonored. Through it all I have learned that God is our ever-present strength and help; and that for every moment of pain there is a moment of beauty or grace to give balance and maintain hope. That is enough to sustain my journey."

Ann On-lin Tang

First Chinese Woman to Be Received into Full Connection

Received on Trial – 1996
Ordained Deacon – 1996
Received into Full Connection – 1998
Ordained Elder – 1998
Current Appointment – Associate Pastor, Immanuel UMC, Annandale, Virginia

ANN ON-LIN TANG was born December 16, 1956, in Hong Kong.

"I began my journey toward ordained ministry when I was in England visiting relatives in the summer of 1981. The Lord showed me the need of pastoral ministry. Then, in 1984, God gave me a personal sign through my late aunt. She told me that I was probably a twin and the other did not survive. In 1985, I returned to England for theological training and, after graduating in 1989, I went back to Hong Kong as a local pastor. I came to the United States in 1992 and entered Wesley Theological Seminary in Washington, DC.

"I am the first (only) Chinese female chaplain in the U.S. Army. On February 10, 2003, I was called up for deployment to Iraq and ministered to soldiers in combat. I experienced the hardship of military life with limited resources, separation, and a life-threatening environment. Yet I had opportunities to minister to Christian contractors from different countries, led a few Iraqi interpreters to Christ, and conducted worship services, through interpretation, to Iraqi Chaldean Christians, even in the prison camp. In February 2006, I received the National Reserve Officers Association's Chaplain of the Year award.

"Over the years ministering in churches, I have had to face a lot of odds–the first ethnic minority person, the first woman clergyperson, being single. Even my body structure and voice became issues in some churches where I served. I have to face difficulties of gender, language barriers, ethnic background, morality, and even authority issues. As I reflect on these odds, I recognize that it was, above all, the grace of God and my call that have kept me focused. Also, I am a person of purpose and determination; so whatever comes, I put it in prayer and set my goals to accomplish it. I do that because I know if it is pleasing to God, God will give me strength and endurance to overcome all the odds. Furthermore, networking with other clergywomen has given me the support I needed in ministry (both in church and in military settings). Though I have experienced the odds in my ministry as the first Asian clergywoman in my annual conference, I am not alone. God will call other Chinese and ethnic Christian sisters to join me in this journey."

WESTERN NORTH CAROLINA ANNUAL CONFERENCE

 *Maloie Bogle Lee McCrary*

(EUROPEAN AMERICAN)

First Woman to Be Received into Full Connection

Ordained Deacon – 1948
Ordained Elder – 1952
Received on Trial – 1957
Received into Full Connection – 1959
Deceased – 1994

MALOIE BOGLE LEE McCRARY was born March 21, 1907, in Hiddenite, North Carolina.

By 1944, while living in Elkin, "M.B." (as she was known) began to respond to God's call upon her heart to full-time Christian ministry and was licensed to preach. In 1946 she was first listed as a local preacher. At annual conference the following year, 1947, she became (along with Isabelle Hull) the second woman (after Mamie Dennis Newell) to receive a pastoral appointment in the Western North Carolina Conference when she was appointed to Hazelwood, where she served until 1952.

As a minister, M.B. was always known as an outstanding pastor. Of special interest and concern to her were the children and youth, and she especially sought to share Christ's love with them and to help them to grow in the faith. She also paid careful attention to details, always doing things "by the book," so that no one would have any questions.

Her love for music was always an important part of M.B.'s life. Prior to her entering the ministry, and again in her retirement, she taught music lessons to children and youth, showing them that same love and concern, and demanding from them precision and accuracy. M.B. was never one to bring attention to herself, only to the Lord whom she loved and served. And yet, she was one who did not hesitate to enter into previously uncharted areas–becoming the first woman to be received into full connection in the Conference.[16]

M.B. McCrary died June 6, 1994, at age eighty-seven.

 *Sadye Joiner Milton*

First African American Woman to Be Received into Full Connection

Received on Trial – 1975
Ordained Deacon – 1975
Received into Full Connection – 1977
Ordained Elder – 1977
Current Appointment – Extension Ministries, UMC Campus Minister at North Carolina State University Wesley Foundation, Greensboro, North Carolina

SADYE JOINER MILTON was born August 12, 1948, in rural Rockingham County, North Carolina. Her journey toward ordained ministry began in the early 1970s. Sadye graduated with a bachelor of arts degree from Bennett College in 1971, and received an MDiv degree from Duke in 1976.

"I am currently serving the only full-time appointment I have ever had. I am the United Methodist campus minister at the North Carolina State University Wesley Foundation, Greensboro, North Carolina. To describe my journey to now is difficult. It began with the allure of social justice. The Social Gospel, with its liberating, inclusive message, took me to seminary. I have always loved worship, personal devotion, and fellowship within the body, having come from the type of community where the church was our flagship. But it was God's profound message of liberation cumulating in the person Jesus Christ that seemed to define and identify me. Drinking from this cup is extremely hard and painful. Sometimes my prayer is that I don't lose my soul through my orders and ordination. I have had everything done to me that the psalm says. But I can't imagine doing anything else. After all, 'Whither shall I go but to the Lord?'"

 *Diana Julia Wingeier-Rayo*

First Hispanic/Latina Woman to Be Received into Full Connection

Ordained Deacon, Cuba – 1996
Received on Trial, Northern Illinois Conference – 1998
Received into Full Connection, Mexico Methodist Church – 2001
Ordained Elder, Western North Carolina – 2004
Current Appointment – Director of Hispanic Ministries, Albemarle District

DIANA WINGEIER-RAYO was born June 19, 1965, in Matagalpa, Nicaragua.

"I began my journey toward ministry in 1992. I was a missionary with the General Board of Global Ministries in Cuba, serving The Methodist Church. At first, my intentions were to study for a master's degree in pediatric nursing. I experienced my call when I saw the third generation of Cuban kids who knew nothing about our Lord. They had no hope, only misconceptions about life and personal healing. I started to believe that I needed to share my faith with them. But my knowledge was limited. I enrolled in the *Seminario Evangelico de Matanzas* in Cuba to prepare myself for ministry. Three years later, in 1996, I was ordained a deacon in Cuba.

"In 1997 I returned to the United States to serve in The United Methodist Church. In 2000 I was invited by the General Board of Global Ministries to go to Mexico for three years to serve in The Methodist Church there. Later, upon an invitation by the Western North Carolina Conference, I once more returned to the United States to serve in Monroe, North Carolina, where I work with Hispanic ministries in the Albemarle District.

"I am organizing the first Hispanic church in this district, called *Centro Cristiano Hosanna* UMC (Hosanna Christian Center). Serving in this area has been a challenge. The Hispanic population is the fastest-growing minority group in the county. Therefore, racism, discrimination, and poverty are facts that our people need to know how to address. It is powerful to be part of the daily struggle Hispanic immigrants have to go through. In our center, we encourage single mothers to learn the language and we also train them with job skills."

 *Karen Miyoshi Kagiyama*

First Japanese Woman to Be Received into Full Connection

Received on Trial – 1991
Ordained Deacon – 1991
Received into Full Connection – 1994
Ordained Elder – 1994
Current Appointment – St. Andrew UMC, Carrollton, Georgia, North Georgia Conference

KAREN MIYOSHI KAGIYAMA was born December 15, 1964, in Misawa, Japan.

"I was raised in a home where we attended church regularly until sometime in my teenage years. The end of my family's active church participation coincided with a move from one part of the country to another. We experienced tremendous cultural adjustment. I became active in The United Methodist Church in high school on my own. I came to college seeking a deeper spiritual life in a community where I could learn and grow as a disciple. I found what I was looking for in two campus ministry groups–the Wesley Fellowship, and the Intervarsity Group. After several mentors and a complete stranger suggested I attend seminary, I sensed that God was calling me toward some kind of ministry. At the time, the only female clergy I had ever known was the associate campus minister, an Episcopal priest. I had never heard a United Methodist female pastor preach.

"For me, the journey has been a twisting, winding, uphill, downhill, through, and all-around path of interesting, challenging, heartbreaking, celebratory, wondrous moments and people whose gracious acceptance and willingness to try something new have opened doors of ministry and grace for all of us. Despite some early obstacles and closed doors, God has faithfully shown up to open a new window, and the people on the other side have been amazing and more loving than I could possibly imagine. Those of us who have stayed the course and still love what we do know that all good things come from God and that the servants of God must stay focused on the call to love God and our neighbors.

"Alongside my ministry, my family has been the other call of my life, and I am learning how to better integrate the two calls into a seamless whole that is pleasing to God. I remain open to the unfolding call upon my life and gifts and keep my trust fully in God's goodness and love for me."

 *Donna Lynn Strickland Smith*

First Native American Woman to Be Received into Full Connection

Received on Trial – 1999
Ordained Deacon – 1999
Received into Full Connection – 2002
Ordained Elder – 2002
Current Appointment – Grace UMC, Salisbury, North Carolina

DONNA LYNN STRICKLAND SMITH was born September 22, 1962, in Lumberton, North Carolina.

"My journey toward ordained ministry was preceded by exploring diaconal ministry. Then, one-and-a-half years into seminary, I switched to the ordained ministry track. I have been in music ministry since a child. I officially worked as a music director at Immanuel Baptist Church in Greensboro after graduating from college in 1980.

"I was called to lead the music program at the new Triad Native American UMC starting in Greensboro. While there, the minister asked me to preach one Sunday. I said, 'You are kidding,' and he said, 'No, I am not.' I preached the first sermon, and I was amazed that God could use me to preach. I gave an altar call and, to my amazement, several people responded. Somehow the Holy Spirit had used me to touch them. Each time I preached, something happened that affirmed me. I finally went to seminary, spending 1996 through 1999 at Duke University Divinity School.

"I had thought about going into the ministry, but having growing up Baptist, I did not even think of being an ordained minister—maybe a music director or a youth director, but never a pastor. People expect men to be pastors. More than once, I heard comments to the effect that women did not need to be in ministry, nor were they supposed to be. That held me back a long time. When I got into the UMC I learned things were looked at differently. It was great. I have loved going into the ministry. My gifts are in compassion and healing due to lots of the hurts I have dealt with in my life—some abuse, identity issues, and otherwise."

Notes

1. The first African American woman to be received into full connection in the United Methodist tradition was Minnie Jackson Goins from The Church of the United Brethren in Christ in 1904. See chapter 1, 17.

2. Patricia Merritt, "Bishop Nominee," *Lakeland (FL) Ledger*, June 1, 1996.

3. Marietta Mansfield, "Epilogue," in *Fortitude on the Mountain: A Story of Courage and Hope* (Spring 2003) as yet unpublished. Used with permission from Cathy Morton Ward, executor of the Mansfield estate.

4. See chapter 1, 26.

5. Information for this biography was taken from an article about Mildred Watson sent by her in response to a request for information. The source was not identified.

6. Information for this biography was provided by the General Commission on Archives and History of the UMC.

7. Information for this biography is taken from Estelle Pinegar's Memoir Statement, written by the Reverend Ben Hogan, published in the 1999 Journal of the North Alabama Conference, UMC, 520.

8. Information for this biography was taken from Julia Walker's Memoir Statement, written by Machion Garrison, published in the 1999 Journal of the North Alabama Conference, UMC, 532.

9. Material for this biography was taken from an interview with Ruth Rogers, conducted by Ruth Baird Shaw, a clergywoman in the North Georgia Conference.

10. Information for this biography is taken from Sadye Westbrooks's memoir, written by Ruth Elizabeth Rogers, published in the 1972 Journal of the North Georgia Conference, UMC, 178.

11. Millie Kim was received into full connection under the Order of Elder in Full Connection and was, therefore, not ordained as a deacon.

12. Material for this biography was taken from Vivian McFadden's Service Record, provided by the South Carolina Conference, UMC.

13. Information for the biography was taken from the 2002 Journal of the South Georgia Conference, UMC, provided by Christopher Shoemaker, member of the South Georgia Conference.

14. Judith Craig, comp., *The Leading Women: Stories of the First Women Bishops of The United Methodist Church* (Nashville: Abingdon, 2004), 143-44. © 2004 Abingdon Press. Used by permission.

15. Bishop Leontine Kelly, telephone interview with Margie Turbyfill, member of the North Carolina Conference, September 2004.

16. Information for this biography was taken from Maloie McCrary's memoir, written by James Pyatt, member of the Western North Carolina Conference,and e-mailed to Patricia J. Thompson.

Chapter 6

First Women of the South Central Jurisdiction to Receive Full Clergy Rights

THE SOUTH CENTRAL JURISDICTION CURRENTLY HAS FOURTEEN ANNUAL CONFERENCES AND forty-two "first" women. Ten of the forty-two women, or 24 percent, are deceased and nine, or 21 percent, are retired. Thirteen, or 31 percent, are currently serving in the local church, and only eight, or 19 percent, are serving in extension ministries. These figures include Bishop Minerva G. Carcaño, who is actually serving in the Western Jurisdiction. In addition, there is one woman on incapacity leave and one who is on voluntary location.

Twenty, or 48 percent, of the women are European American. There are thirteen African Americans, eight Hispanic/Latina women and one Native American woman from the Oklahoma Missionary Conference. There were no Asian women reported as serving in the South Central Jurisdiction, but this jurisdiction had the highest number of Hispanic/Latina women. The first Hispanic/Latina woman to be elected to the episcopacy came from this jurisdiction.

ARKANSAS ANNUAL CONFERENCE

 *Fern Cook*

(EUROPEAN AMERICAN)
First Woman to Serve in Full Connection in the Arkansas Conference
Received into Full Connection in the Louisiana Conference, Methodist Protestant Church, in 1939

(See chapter 2, 60)

 *Everne Hunter*

(EUROPEAN AMERICAN)
First Woman to Be Received into Full Connection

Ordained Deacon – 1957
Ordained Elder – 1959
Received on Trial – 1962
Received into Full Connection – 1964
Retired – 1982
Deceased – 2003

EVERNE HUNTER was born April 28, 1910, in Desha, Arkansas.

[Everne] felt a call to the ministry when she was just a child, but she was forced to drop out of school because of family responsibilities. She returned to school and graduated from the Valley Springs Methodist High School, a sort of mountain mission school, when she was thirty-five years old. After taking some correspondence courses and classes at Arkansas College in Batesville as she could afford them, she began speaking in churches around Independence County. In 1956, her name first appears in the North Arkansas Conference appointments as a "part-time supply, without authority to administer the sacraments." The next year she applied for ordination.

It has been said that when [Everne] first appeared before the board of ordination, the men in the room turned their chairs around so that none of them were facing her. In spite of other hurtful attempts to dissuade her, she persevered toward full ordination. Always soft-spoken and smiling, she finally became a deacon in 1957, an elder in 1959, was admitted on trial in 1962,

and recognized as a full member of the conference in 1964.

Even then, [Everne] could not avoid criticism from those who opposed women in the ministry. A man doing maintenance work at one church she pastored once asked her, "When you get to hell with all the people you've led there, how will you feel?" She later stated in an interview that her personal philosophy and her faith helped her turn away such remarks. "If you know what you want," she stated, "and what the Lord wants for you, He will give you the strength."[1]

Everne died April 20, 2003, at the age of ninety-two.

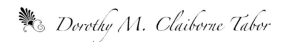 *Dorothy M. Claiborne Tabor*

(EUROPEAN AMERICAN)
First Woman to Be Received into Full Connection in the Former Little Rock Conference

Ordained Deacon – 1968
Received on Trial – 1968
Received into Full Connection – 1970
Ordained Elder – 1970
Retired – 1981
Deceased – 2001

DOROTHY M. CLAIBORNE TABOR was born June 14, 1917, in Little Rock, Arkansas.

From her youth until she was admitted on trial into the Little Rock Conference, [Dorothy] was active in the life of Winfield Methodist Church, participating in Sunday School, the Epworth League, women's circles, and, for almost fifteen years, teaching fifth and sixth grade Sunday School classes....

When her son and daughter were well into their college careers, she decided to go to college herself. It was during this period that she understood clearly that the Lord was calling her to the ordained ministry. In the Fall of 1966, just after graduating from Little Rock University with a Bachelor of Arts degree in Fine Arts, [Dorothy] and her husband locked the door of their Little Rock home, and left for Dallas, where she enrolled in Southern Methodist University's Perkins School of Theology....

On May 20, 1970, [Dorothy] became the first woman

in the 117-year history of the Little Rock Annual Conference to be ordained an elder. With humble gratitude, she always remembered that she could not have fulfilled her call to ministry without the blessings and support of many persons. She was particularly thankful for her husband, her most ardent champion, whose love and selfless devotion was critical to her answering God's call.[2]

Dorothy M. Claiborne Tabor died November 3, 2001, at age eighty-four.

Maxine Yvonne Allen

First African American Woman to Be Received into the Former Little Rock Conference

Received on Trial – 1995
Ordained Deacon – 1995
Received into Full Connection – 1999
Ordained Elder – 1999
Current Appointment – Trinity UMC, North Little Rock, and Arkansas Conference Minister for Ethnic and Multicultural Ministries

MAXINE YVONNE ALLEN was born May 4, 1950, in Dallas, Texas.

"I received the call to ministry at age fourteen during a Thanksgiving weekend youth retreat. At the time, I was told that I must be mistaken, because God did not call women to preach. I was told that maybe I misunderstood and should consider being a missionary in Africa. I was thirty-five years old when I could no longer deny what God was really calling me to do. By that time, also, there were some other women who could serve as role models for ministry.

"I am the first black woman to be ordained *and* appointed in Arkansas. I began my ministry as a part-time local pastor serving a small church in Lonoke, Arkansas. I worked full-time as a manager at Southwestern Bell. I went to seminary in January 1993 and graduated in May 1997. My initial appointment out of seminary was as the chaplain at Philander Smith College in 1997. I served the college in several positions: chaplain, dean of the chapel, interim dean of students, interim business office manager, interim title III director, associate chief operating officer, and finally, dean of the Kendall Center–all while serving as adjunct faculty member in the department of philosophy and religion."

CENTRAL TEXAS ANNUAL CONFERENCE

 *Karen Ann Greenwaldt*

(EUROPEAN AMERICAN)
First Woman to Be Received into Full Connection

Received on Trial – 1975
Ordained Deacon – 1975
Received into Full Connection – 1978
Ordained Elder – 1978
Current Appointment – Extension Ministries, General
Secretary, General Board of Discipleship

KAREN ANN GREENWALDT was born October 31, 1950, in Waco, Texas.

"I began my journey toward ordained ministry in the spring of 1973, and I enrolled in Perkins School of Theology, Southern Methodist University, in the fall of 1973.

"Across my ministry, I have worked to blend my love of the gospel and the church and my love of Christian spiritual formation and education into my work. I believe that effective ministry is led by those who are growing in their faith and who know how to lead others to faith and growth in faith. There are disciple-making systems that can be strengthened and nurtured in local church and annual conference life, and the work of those ordained is to order the ministry of the church in ways that support the disciple-making processes of people from birth to death within the context of the communities of faith. Most of my ministry has been spent at the general church level even though I am active in local church and community life. In addition to my work as an ordained elder, I also am a fabric and bead artist and am married to a studio potter. Part of our common ministry is to build relationships within artistic communities and to find ways that art and the work of making art can find a gracious home in the life of the church."

 *Georgia Mae Ellis Allen*

First African American Woman to Be Received into Full Connection

Received on Trial – 1977
Ordained Deacon – 1977
Received into Full Connection – 1980
Ordained Elder – 1980
Current Appointment – Polytechnic UMC, Fort Worth, Texas

GEORGIA MAE ELLIS ALLEN was born May 15, 1941, in Crockett, Texas. "In 1975 after experiencing my call to ministry, I entered seminary at Brite Divinity School at Texas Christian University in Fort Worth, Texas.

"I've been very blessed in my ministry. I have had the opportunity to minister in several churches in the Central Texas Conference and in the North Texas Conference where I served from June 1982 to June 1988, pastoring the Trinity UMC in Grand Prairie for two years and the Lambert UMC in Dallas for five years."

KANSAS EAST ANNUAL CONFERENCE

 *Laura Emma Bradbury*

(EUROPEAN AMERICAN)

First Woman to Be Received into Full Connection in the Former Kansas Conference

Ordained Deacon – 1949
Ordained Elder – 1953
Received on Trial – 1957
Received into Full Connection – 1959
Retired, Kansas West – 1968
Deceased – 1999

LAURA EMMA BRADBURY was born December 12, 1900, on a farm in Sioux County, Iowa. Laura was always active in her church. In 1920, just after finishing high school, she was granted an exhorter's license.

"I was thinking of entering the Methodist ministry," she said. "But after graduating from college, I taught a year before I married E. Leo Bradbury, an ordained Methodist minister, in 1925. After my marriage, I began substituting in the pulpit for my husband when he couldn't be there. I took part-time seminary work when my husband studied full-time. I never graduated from seminary, but at that time you only had to be one-fourth through seminary to be admitted to the conference.

"My admission to the Kansas Conference (now the Kansas East Conference) threw the pension board into a dither, I was told. My husband and I were the first case where two ministers were married to each other in the United Methodist Church in the whole United States and they didn't know how to handle it....

"I found some prejudice against women ministers, but taken as a whole, the congregations were receptive.... I found most parishioners didn't care if I was a woman, just as long as I gave good sermons, visited the sick and served the people. I kind of broke ground for women....Through the years I learned not to be bothered too much by unfair criticism. If you do, you let other people control your life."[3]

 *Elma Joyce Harris-Scott*

First African American Woman to Be Received into Full Connection

Received on Trial, Arkansas – 1980
Ordained Deacon, Arkansas – 1980
Received into Full Connection – 1981
Ordained Elder – 1981
Current Appointment – Monticello UMC, Shawnee Mission, Kansas

ELMA JOYCE HARRIS-SCOTT was born July 24, 1950, in Little Rock, Arkansas.

"I was called to the ministry at age sixteen. When I was called to the ministry, I did not realize that I would be a pioneer. I have always had a passion to serve. I was thrust into justice ministry, primarily because of the injustice that has always seemed to be present in my ministry. I have had mixed feelings about recognizing injustice to myself and others and how to respond to it. I stay in trouble with the status quo, because it does not really know how to include my gifts and graces.

"I have not been apologetic for how God made me. Then, I thank God for putting my spirit into a black woman's skin, so that I know what it is like to be unappreciated by some, yet made in the image of God. Perhaps if I would not have been a black woman, I would never have known what it is like to be a black woman in this society, a society constantly dealing with how to be just. I now realize that I do not have to know what God wants for me. I just attempt to remain faithful to the covenant of ministry in The United Methodist Church and to be available to God through the abundance of God's grace."

KANSAS WEST ANNUAL CONFERENCE

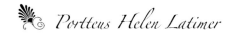 *Portteus Helen Latimer*

 *Cheryl Lynn Jefferson Bell*

(EUROPEAN AMERICAN)

First Woman to Be Received into Full Connection

Ordained Deacon – 1953
Ordained Elder – 1956
Received on Trial – 1957
Received into Full Connection – 1959
Retired – 1973
Deceased – 2005

PORTTEUS HELEN LATIMER was born in November 1907 in Kansas.

Portteus grew up in a family of two sisters and one brother. Her father was a preacher and a teacher who moved from "pillar to post." Portteus felt a strong call to ministry and seminary. Instead, the family needed her at home. Money was very scarce so Portteus learned to be frugal and "make do." She cared for both parents until their death as she raised a garden, canned nearly everything they had to eat and gave piano lessons to help them survive. After her parents died, Portteus answered the call to ministry and seminary.

She began the challenge of serving churches as the first woman pastor to step through their doors–doors she had to open herself. Gentlemen would always open and hold a door for a lady. They let the door slam in the face of Reverend Portteus Helen. That did not discourage Portteus. She demanded respect and won respect with her brilliant mind, professional leadership and grace-filled skills. She conducted herself as one who was worthy of respect and received respect, eventually. In her last and longest appointment to Alden UMC where she retired, she was and is still fondly called "Preach."

From 1977 to 1985 Portteus served as mayor of Alden, having been elected initially on a write-in ballot. Her long-time neighbor in Alden, Margaret Lipp, recalls how Portteus returned to college to brush up on advanced algebra and other subjects when she was 87 years old. Tours of the Holy Land and world travels added depth to her strong academic skills and gifted preaching. Portteus Latimer died July 12, 2005, at age 97.[4]

First African American Woman to Be Received into Full Connection

Received on Trial – 1993
Ordained Deacon – 1993
Received into Full Connection – 1995
Ordained Elder – 1995
Current Appointment – District Superintendent Wichita East District

CHERYL LYNN JEFFERSON BELL was born April 30, 1956, in Detroit, Michigan.

"Prior to accepting my call to full-time ministry I had been an electrical engineer for ten years. Although I had been successful in my profession, I was not fulfilled with my work. Having worked in virtually every area in the church, it wasn't until my pastor asked 'Have you considered working for the church?' that I considered the ministry. My first reaction was 'I'm making too much money. God surely isn't calling me to work in the church full-time!' Thus was the seed planted, and in December 1989, I acknowledged my call to ministry. I haven't looked back since!

"The journey to full-time ministry as an elder in The United Methodist Church has been one full of grace and mercy. Born in 1956 (destiny?) in Detroit, Michigan, raised in a single-parent household with my father, and going through a troubled childhood, church and school have been my saving grace. School led me to pursue electrical engineering as a career and consequently helped me to obtain a master of divinity degree. The church–Methodist and then United Methodist–has been my spiritual home. My family was part of those 'who stayed' with The Methodist Church. My loyalty to God has been nurtured, sustained, and strengthened through my relationship with The United Methodist Church. I can't imagine myself living out my faith anywhere else but The United Methodist Church! Where God leads me, I will follow!"

LOUISIANA ANNUAL CONFERENCE

 *Lea Joyner*

(EUROPEAN AMERICAN)

First Woman to Serve in Full Connection in the Louisiana Conference

Received into Full Connection in the Louisiana Conference, Methodist Protestant Church, in 1939

(See chapter 2, 60)

 *Carole Cotton Winn*

(EUROPEAN AMERICAN)

First Woman to Be Received into Full Connection

Received on Trial – 1970
Ordained Deacon – 1970
Received into Full Connection – 1972
Ordained Elder – 1972
Current Appointment – Extension Ministries, Director, The Academy for Spiritual Leadership

CAROLE COTTON WINN was born July 13, 1943, in Lebanon, Pennsylvania.

"I served as a US-2 in the Mississippi Conference as a church and community worker. That was the experience in which I confirmed my hunch and call to ministry. It was at Perkins School of Theology that I felt the call to become ordained and enter the itinerant ministry. I graduated with a BD degree in 1970.

"Following an eight-year term as district superintendent (the first female district superintendent in Louisiana), I was appointed to begin a new ministry for our annual conference–The Academy for Spiritual Leadership. For me, this has been a 'fullness-of-time' season in which my strengths and passion for ministry have found a home. The academy has welcomed hundreds of laity and clergy who bring their longings and emptiness to our retreats and find their joy, their call, and their path. It has served to rekindle the flame in persons as well as local churches. The journey from seminary to this point, thirty-five years later, has unfolded in ways I could have never imagined, and gives me hope that the best is yet to be."

 *Carolyn Stokes Lambert*

First African American Woman to Be Received into Full Connection

Ordained Deacon – 1986
Received on Trial – 1987
Received into Full Connection – 1990
Ordained Elder – 1990
Transferred to Northern Illinois Conference, UMC – 2003
Current Appointment – Maple Park UMC, Chicago, Illinois

CAROLYN STOKES LAMBERT was born March 3, 1954, in New Orleans, Louisiana.

"I grew up and was nurtured in the Methodist/United Methodist Church. Peck UMC, New Orleans, gave me the biblical and spiritual foundation I needed to prepare me for a life of servanthood and good stewardship. I participated on all levels of the church. My pastor, Reverend Julius Jefferson, supported my decision to follow the Spirit's lead to seminary. Others felt I was having a meltdown.

"My ministry and tenure in the Louisiana Conference were a mixed blessing. On one hand, I celebrate the hundreds of lives I touched through my ministry and the wonderful people who loved and affirmed my ministry until this day. On the other hand, I had to deal with the disparities that people of color and clergywomen face. My zeal and passion for ministry and for addressing social inequities and other punitive issues were met by some with mixed cries, songs of praise, and 'hallelujahs,' while others responded, 'Crucify her.'

"Only by God's grace and intervention, I married Alvin and relocated to Chicago (1996). While on leave, I took another CPE residency. My life was transformed. I was able to face my pain and regain my self-worth. I feel like I have been liberated and am free to do what I love best–*serve*. I am healthier and even more passionate about ministry. I serve on conference and district committees, the opportunity for which was never afforded to me before. I am still very much involved in civic and community affairs. Twenty years later, life is good!"

MISSOURI ANNUAL CONFERENCE

Myrtle Saylor Speer

(EUROPEAN AMERICAN)

First Woman to Be Received on Trial in the Missouri Conference in 1956

(See chapter 2, 43)

Gwen Jones-Lurvey

(EUROPEAN AMERICAN)

First Woman to Be Received into Full Connection in the Former Missouri West Conference

Received on Trial – 1968
Ordained Deacon – 1968
Received into Full Connection – 1970
Ordained Elder – 1970
Transferred to Southern New England – 1971
Transferred to Southern California-Arizona – 1975
Retired, California-Pacific – 2002

GWEN JONES-LURVEY was born January 4, 1939, at home on a farm in Woodbine, Kansas.

"'Have you considered church work?' the vocational counselor asked. I responded, 'Who wants to be a missionary?' God's nudge toward ministry came in the fall of 1958. Academic probation brought an unhappy, architectural engineering student to seek help. God expanded my vision. The Wesley Foundation pastor told me about seminaries and MRE programs. A friend said, 'Get a BD degree rather than an MRE.' Then I met women doing campus ministry. At St. Paul School of Theology, Dr. Cecil Murray focused my call as I heard him say, 'Gwen, you can preach.' God confirmed it again and again. A young female teen said, 'Are you really a pastor?' Then, 'I've been feeling God was calling me to be a pastor, but I didn't think women were allowed to do that. I haven't told anyone because I thought they would think I was crazy.'

"Being the 'first woman' brought great blessing and a great burden. A parishioner said, 'I used to feel sorry for a church with a woman pastor. Now I know they are the lucky ones.' I received the COSROW Cal-Pac 'Barrier Breaker'

award. A district superintendent said, 'I can't try to talk them into taking a woman.' A chair of the staff-parish relations committee observed, 'I don't think our church is ready for a woman pastor.' Twenty years of challenges drove me to a month's leave. I wept saying, 'I can't do this any longer.' Then God said, 'If you'll quit doing it alone and let me do it, you'll have the strength to keep going.' And I did.

"People find hope in the midst of despair, experience healing, are touched by the Spirit, grow in their faith, hear God's call to serve in new ways, and witness to the wonder of God's grace through my ministry. Gratitude overflows as I guide interns and ordination candidates, see more ordained women, am blessed by a husband who is a life partner in ministry and know that whatever happens, God works in it. That's the bottom line. God did the ministry and I went along for the ride!"

Michele Sue Shumake-Keller

First African American Woman to Be Received into Full Connection in the Former Missouri West Conference

Received on Trial – 1987
Ordained Deacon – 1987
Received into Full Connection – 1984
Ordained Elder – 1984
Current Appointment – St. Luke's UMC, Raytown, Missouri

MICHELE SUE SHUMAKE-KELLER was born February 19, 1943, in Kansas City, Kansas.

"I was an elementary school vocal music teacher in Kansas City, Missouri. I remember having become uncomfortable with only being able to say to my students that 'some people believe that Jesus was the Son of God' when I would introduce new Christmas songs to them in class. I was also involved in my local UM church but had started to say no to requests for more leadership involvement there. After a while I felt so guilty about saying no that I promised God I would say yes the next time someone asked. I said yes to becoming the music leader at a black church celebration held at Saint Paul School of Theology. At the event, a minister invited me to do the same thing in Dallas at a national convocation on the black church. I accepted the invitation. It was at the convocation that people began to ask me if I would consider becoming a minister. I said no, but later received an invitation to an orientation on ministry at Gammon Theological Seminary in Atlanta. It was there that the vocation of ministry opened to me in a wonderfully amazing way. I said yes and never looked back.

"Following seminary, I served as a part-time assistant pastor at Ben Hill UMC in Atlanta. I was unable to obtain a full-time appointment in Georgia. I returned to Missouri despite being told by a representative of the Missouri West ordained ministry team that it would be difficult to place me in Missouri. Though the conference was reticent at first to itinerate an African American woman elder, by the 1990s open itinerancy had come a long way under Bishop Ann Sherer's leadership. Now we are doing well. I served for eight years as district superintendent for the Heartland South district. In 2003 I was endorsed as an episcopal candidate."

Mary Ellen Meyer

(EUROPEAN AMERICAN)

First Woman to Be Received into Full Connection in the Former Missouri East Conference

Received on Trial – 1974
Ordained Deacon – 1974
Received into Full Connection – 1976
Ordained Elder – 1976
Retired – 1998

MARY ELLEN MEYER was born June 21, 1933, in Pittsburg, Kansas.

"In 1970, our pastor asked me to come on staff to work with the Christian education program. Prior to that time I had been active in the lay work of the church. I began taking seminary courses part-time for a year while working on the church staff with the goal of becoming the minister of Christian education. The first clergywoman I knew was a United Church of Christ minister who taught ministry with children. By my senior year in seminary I experienced the call to pastoral ministry and was encouraged by our seminary registrar to pursue ordination, although Missouri East had no women elders in full connection.

"In 1970, as the wife of an accounting manager with Southwestern Bell Telephone, and the thirty-six-year-old mother of three elementary age children, I was not a typical seminary student. In 1973, having nearly completed seminary and seeking a license to preach, the district superintendent asked me, 'Why would you want to be ordained when you have a husband who can support you comfortably?' In my interview with the full board, one member remarked, 'The church has come a long way. We are now ordaining housewives.' However, they recommended me to the conference and the vote proved to be unanimous.

"Being elected as chair of the Board of Ordained Ministry was of immense help in bringing a woman's perspective to the process. My goal through the years has been to be faithful to God's call, to be as effective as possible in order to help pave the way for other women, giving encouragement to others who were exploring the call to ministry and engaged in the journey."

NEBRASKA ANNUAL CONFERENCE

 *Vivian Joyce Hand*

 *Charlotte Abram*

(EUROPEAN AMERICAN)

First Woman to Be Received into Full Connection

Received on Trial – 1965
Ordained Deacon – 1965
Received into Full Connection – 1967
Ordained Elder – 1967
Retired – 1986

VIVIAN JOYCE HAND was born December 20, 1920, in New York State. In a 1998 interview, Joyce was asked about her call to the ministry.

> Well, it's been part of my whole life, probably. But I was working. I was in the service in World War II, and then I was in the business world for 20 years. I was involved in the church; I just felt this was what I wanted to do. And the minister there supported me, and we looked into what could be done and I had to get some hours of college work, before I could go to seminary because I didn't have all the prerequisites. I went to seminary at Drew University in 1964 and got my Master of Divinity degree. I don't know *how* I landed in Nebraska. It is one of those things. I had three or four options.
>
> I was the very first clergywoman in the Nebraska Conference. They did *not* know what to ask, they *did not* know how to handle me.... At the district committee it was very interesting.... Some didn't want me at all, although they didn't exactly *say* it, I knew they didn't. And some were welcoming.[5]

Asked about how she was received in churches, Vivian answered, "Some liked me, some disliked me; some rejected a woman completely, and others accepted me.... If there was an objection, they moved [me]. *Men* they would let stay, but they had to move me."

Vivian served by herself as the only ordained woman in the Nebraska Conference for six years and served for a total of twenty years before she retired in 1986.

First African American Woman to Be Received into Full Connection

Received on Trial – 1988
Ordained Deacon – 1988
Received into Full Connection – 1991
Ordained Elder – 1991
Current Appointment – Pearl, Trinity, and Asbury UMC, Omaha, Nebraska

CHARLOTTE ABRAM was born January 17, 1948, in Omaha, Nebraska.

"I tried not to answer the call because of all the baggage involved: women had not been pastoring that long, and certainly African American women hadn't been in the ministry for long. Yet I still felt as if all roads were leading to a point where I was working in the church using all the gifts God had given me—I just felt like I needed to be there.... I have a clear memory of looking at the pulpit [in 1998] and hearing a voice—either external or internal, I couldn't tell—which said, 'If you were a man, you would be a minister by now.'[6]

"Ministry for me has been an opportunity to experience God's grace and strength, in the midst of my humanity. I experience both great acceptance and public rejection. Let's talk about the rejection first. I am an African American woman in a position that had been reserved for men. Consequently, I have been publicly fanned away from the pulpit and directed to the lectern on occasions when asked to speak in congregations that do not accept women in that role. The authenticity of my call has been challenged by women as much as men. Yet each time I engage in those discussions (fewer and fewer, thank God) I feel a glimmer of hope... as some persons conceded that God uses whomever God wishes to use.

"Now, let's talk about the acceptance. As an African American woman in a multicultural denomination, I have had great opportunities to share my gifts and exercise leadership. I have also been accepted and affirmed by men and women who experience a woman's leadership for the first time and realize the uniqueness it can bring in pastoral care and preaching. Next to seeing persons come alive in the faith, I suppose what thrilled me most was the look in little African

American girls' eyes…when they realized that God calls women to preach and pastor too."

Cristian de la Rosa

First Hispanic/Latina Woman to Serve in Full Connection
Received into the Baltimore-Washington Conference – 1991
Transferred to Nebraska Conference – 1997
Transferred to Rio Grande Conference – 2001

(See chapter 4, 74)

Alicia A. Ring

First Hispanic/Latina Woman to Be Received into Full Connection

Received on Trial – 1996
Ordained Deacon – 1996
Received into Full Connection – 1998
Ordained Elder – 1998
Disability Leave – 1999
Deceased – 2000

ALICIA A. RING was born October 23, 1942, in Dallas, Texas. Alicia attended Perkins School of Theology at Southern Methodist University, graduating with a master of divinity degree in 1994. She served Bayard UMC, Fremont Calvary UMC, and Grand Island Trinity UMC before going on disability leave in 1999.

Bishop Minerva G. Carcaño says,

> I was serving at Perkins School of Theology when someone informed me that a clergy sister from Nebraska was gravely ill in a hospital in Dallas. I did not know her but went to see her. I visited her every day at the hospital until she died. She was a kind, thoughtful person with a clear commitment to ministry. Her son was present and it was clear that they had a very close relationship–one of mutual respect and admiration not only for the typical mother-son reasons but also because of the kinds of decisions that particularly Alicia had made about how she would live her life. She was in the ministry as a second career.
>
> She spoke about all the theological and biblical books she had and how much she loved her books. Her son was working hard at caring for her books in a manner that would honor her after death. Alicia was a loving sister in the faith who died a peaceful death.[7]

Alicia Ring died February 6, 2000, at the age of fifty-eight.

NEW MEXICO ANNUAL CONFERENCE

 Elizabeth Ann Lopez

 Helen R. Neinast

(HISPANIC/LATINA)
First Woman to Be Received into Full Connection

Received on Trial – 1971
Ordained Deacon – 1971
Received into Full Connection – 1977
Ordained Elder – 1977
Transferred to Minnesota Conference – 1996
Current Appointment – District Superintendent Metro West District, Minnesota Conference

ELIZABETH ANN LOPEZ, known as "Liz," was born September 28, 1946, in San Antonio, Texas.

"My journey of ministry has been with me all of my life. My family was very active in La Trinidad UMC in San Antonio, Texas, in the Rio Grande Conference. My godparents, Rev. Dr. Alfredo and Clotilde Náñez, were instrumental in my life and my faith formation. My family has a history of early circuit riders, and so the connection has always been with me. When I was twelve years old, my family moved to Jefferson UMC in San Antonio in the Southwest Texas Conference, where I became very active. The pastors in that church were instrumental in encouraging me in a church career.

"My call to ordained ministry happened over the course of several years while I was in seminary. Dr. Náñez was teaching at Perkins School of Theology and creating the Mexican American program there. He invited me to visit. The visit became permanent, and through my seminary years my call was formed. I have been blessed in my ministry, serving five churches. I also served in many arenas at the general church level, where I have experienced the goodness of our United Methodist Church."

Just prior to her current appointment, Liz was serving the Rochester UMC and was the Hispanic/Latina woman serving the largest membership church in the UMC.

First European American Woman to Be Received into Full Connection

Received on Trial – 1977
Ordained Deacon – 1977
Received into Full Connection – 1979
Ordained Elder – 1979
Current Appointment – Extension Ministries, UM Publishing House

HELEN R. NEINAST was born September 14, 1953, in Slaton, Texas.

"I grew up in the Missouri Synod Lutheran Church, and from an early age I yearned to be an acolyte, to be part of the morning services. This denomination does not ordain women (to this day); so I was refused–at age nine! I didn't have much direction after finishing college; so graduate school looked like a good option. I was still interested in theology and still active in the church. So when I entered Duke Divinity School and took my first biblical studies course, I knew I wanted to go into the ministry. I became a United Methodist (the United Methodist campus minister at my undergraduate school was the best) and started the ordination process.

"I started out in campus ministry at a state university in New Mexico. I also served local churches there, first as an associate and then as a copastor. During this time, when I began to meet opposition to my ministry, I decided to look at other ways to live out my calling. I worked part-time at a law firm, studied Spanish in Mexico, considered law school, and worked on staff at a local women's center. After a few years I realized that higher education ministry was my best calling, and I went to Nashville to work at the General Board of Higher Education and Ministry. The work was great. Ten years of travel, though, left me ready to live in one place for a while. I took a break to write full-time, and enjoyed the solitude and discipline of writing. After two years, my husband (a clergy member of the Florida Conference) and I got the chance to share the United Methodist campus ministry position at Emory University in Atlanta. We were there for eight rich and full years. I have now returned to writing full-time, working in large part for the United

Methodist Publishing House. Through it all–during the tough appointments as well as during the rich times–God has been faithful. Despite the early obstacles (and these were mostly from the institutional church, rarely from the laity), I have loved my work as a United Methodist minister. I am grateful."

 *Felicia Pringle Hopkins*

First African American Woman to Be Received into Full Connection
Received on Trial, Southwest Texas – 1996
Ordained Deacon, Southwest Texas – 1996
Received into Full Connection – 1998
Ordained Elder – 1998
Current Appointment – Associate, St. Mark's UMC, El Paso, Texas

FELICIA PRINGLE HOPKINS was born November 14, 1960, in San Francisco, California.

"My call story really began in April 1979 when I was in college, and I remember God telling me I would preach the gospel, as I was walking down a sidewalk. I laughed and ignored it, because I was raised Baptist and women *never* got to preach or pastor, just speak from the floor. I experienced my call through a series of events that began while singing at a concert in Kansas City. For the first time, I felt the power of God in a very personal way and knew for myself that God was indeed real. But having grown up poor and thinking that black preachers by and large were poor and had to work two jobs to survive, I chose to turn away from the pastorate as a full-time viable option. I was truly rooted in the middle class and did not want to be poor ever again. But, on an Easter Sunday morning while singing again, I could hear God tell me audibly 'there is room at the cross for you.' I knew he meant 'room to preach.'

"I guess the most courageous thing I have done has been to lead this congregation. I am an African American woman pastoring a large, primarily Caucasian congregation. (Ten percent of the congregation is black and another 10 percent is Hispanic.) I didn't inherit this group; God grew it this way. I think my experience as a member of a minority group has helped me to survive. I learned a long time ago to do what I could and to allow God to do the rest. Sure, I have experienced discrimination. I've been on the receiving end of racist remarks in the conference and in the local church. I truly believe the fruit of my ministry speaks for me and for what God has called me to. So I do not engage in discussions of gender about the pulpit or leadership roles in the pastorate. I just continue the struggle."

NORTH TEXAS ANNUAL CONFERENCE

 *Velma Hart Franklin*

(EUROPEAN AMERICAN)

First Woman to Be Received into Full Connection

Ordained Deacon – 1946
Ordained Elder – 1948
Received on Trial – 1960
Received into Full Connection – 1963
Retired – 1966
Deceased – 1996

VELMA HART FRANKLIN was born April 15, 1910. "Velma Hart Franklin was one of the earliest female clergy in the North Texas Conference, serving churches in the early nineteen sixties and taking retirement in 1966."[8] Two of the early appointments she served were in Denton County, Texas: Spanish Fort (1957–1959) and Era-Spring Creek (1960).[9] In 1961 and 1962, she was appointed to Sonset-Park Springs. In 1963 she served the Paradise Circuit and in 1964 the Sunset Circuit. She did not have an appointment in 1965.[10] Velma died May 24, 1996, and was buried in El Reno, Oklahoma. Her husband, W. L. Franklin, preceded her in death in 1983.

 *Sheron C. Patterson*

First African American to Be Received into Full Connection

Received on Trial – 1989
Ordained Deacon – 1989
Received into Full Connection – 1992
Ordained Elder – 1992
Current Appointment – St. Paul UMC, Dallas, Texas

SHERON C. PATTERSON was born June 6, 1959, in Charlotte, North Carolina.

"My call to ministry came in spring 1981, during the second semester of my senior year at Spelman College in Atlanta, Georgia. I was an English/Mass Communications major, with every intention of heading on to graduate school to study film. I had a classmate over at Morehouse College who was also into film; and we had plans of greatness together as moviemakers. His name is Spike Lee, and he has indeed done great things! I was sitting in my dorm room planning out all the money I would make as a cinematographer when I heard the Lord speak to my heart, 'Use your gifts to glorify me instead of self.' I instantly knew this was the Lord's voice because for several months I had been consumed by a desire to make my life a sacrifice to the community. Suddenly, it all made sense.

"My journey as the first African American woman ordained in the North Texas Annual Conference has been both rocky and smooth. Being the first is no picnic. I longed for 'sheroes' who had gone ahead of me to blaze the trail, but there were none. So I had to blaze it alone. Seminary was challenging because I did not see a reflection of me and I experienced tremendous isolation. Sexism and racism were always around; and I had to toughen up and realize that just because someone calls himself or herself a Christian does not mean he or she is one!

"Sometimes, I was my own obstacle. Fear, anxiety, and worry were ever present. With God's help and the support of many people, I was ordained and given a relatively plum assignment–Crest-Moore King, an inner-city congregation of two hundred members. I was there for five years, after which I was assigned to Jubilee, a new-church start of 250 people. I spent six years at Jubilee before being moved to St. Paul United Methodist Church, the oldest African American congregation in Dallas, with over seven hundred people."

 *Norma Saenz Salinas*

First Hispanic/Latina Woman to Serve in Full Connection

Received on Trial, California-Nevada – 1984
Ordained Deacon, California-Nevada – 1984
Received into Full Connection, California-Nevada – 1987
Ordained Elder, California-Nevada – 1987
Transferred to North Texas – 1994
Current Appointment – Extension Ministries, Behavioral Health Care, Dallas, Texas

NORMA SAENZ SALINAS was born in 1945 in Alamo, Texas.

"I began my journey toward the ordained ministry in 1977 while I was assistant professor of social welfare at the University of Wisconsin-Whitewater. My call was the result of a five-year process of inner struggle, including the death of a dream, the search for clarity in life purpose, and the longing for healing. God converted me and called me to preach that God is love. With the conversion I first found peace, joy, and clarity about my life's purpose and direction. In the 'frozen desert' of Wisconsin, this Methodist, baptized as an infant in Alamo, Texas, and raised in Texas Methodist Wesley Foundation and Methodist summer youth camps, was a long distance from church roots and family. I found my way into United Methodist ministry by joining an African American UM church pastored by the first clergywoman I had known. I also joined a team, teaching a large confirmation class in the Anglo UM church located in the town where I resided. Within six months I was appointed to two Wisconsin country churches and served them on weekends until my move to California, where I entered the MDiv program at the Pacific School of Religion.

"A personal health crisis caused me to reevaluate my life and ministry. In 1993 I moved to Dallas to be available to my aging parents and pursue postgraduate education as a pastoral counselor. Currently I am appointed to extension ministry, where I conduct psychological assessments, psychotherapy, and psychoeducation in Spanish and English to Anglo, African American, Mexican, and Mexican American men and women in chronic pain. This is an illness rooted in our physical, mental, and spiritual lives. Chronic pain forces the choice to faith or despair. Individual and group prayer and Bible study sustain and deepen my faith."

NORTHWEST TEXAS ANNUAL CONFERENCE

 *Hazel Jane Arnold House*

 *Sammie Ellis Rainey*

(EUROPEAN AMERICAN)

One of First Two Women to Be Received into Full Connection

Received on Trial – 1974
Ordained Deacon – 1974
Received into Full Connection – 1978
Ordained Elder – 1978
Deceased – 1991

HAZEL JANE ARNOLD HOUSE was born October 18, 1920, in Truce, Jack County, Texas, the daughter of a Methodist Episcopal minister.

Hazel was a beauty operator in Jacksboro, [Texas], for several years prior to marrying Jay House. The Houses moved to Newburgh, Indiana, in 1950 to purchase and operate a weekly newspaper and in 1959 returned to Sudan, Texas, as co-owners of the weekly newspaper there....

[Hazel] studied for the ministry at South Plains College, Wayland Baptist College, and Perkins School of Theology. As one of the first fully accredited woman ministers, she was fully aware of the reluctance of some members of West Texas churches to accept a woman as pastor. She met this challenge with love and determination to serve the people and her Lord the best way she could, winning over most of those who were opposed to having a woman pastor. After her death, several members of the churches she had served wrote to her family and told how much they loved her as their pastor. Some echoed the sentiments of one former member at Bula Methodist who wrote, "We were mostly unhappy at first with the appointment of a woman pastor, but we all cried when she left a few years later because she was just what we needed, and we had learned to love her and Jay so much."[11]

Hazel House died March 7, 1991, at age seventy.

(EUROPEAN AMERICAN)

One of First Two Women to Be Received into Full Connection

Received on Trial – 1976
Ordained Deacon – 1976
Received into Full Connection – 1978
Ordained Elder – 1978
Incapacity Leave – 2000

SAMMIE ELLIS RAINEY was born in Fort Worth, Texas.

"I received the call to ministry in eleventh grade in 1968 while a member of the youth group at Kirkwood UMC in Irving, Texas. During my senior year, I went with the church youth choir on a mission trip to Mexico, where I felt my calling confirmed. Following graduation from college, I was invited to lead the children's program at the Texas Christian Ashram held at Lakeview Methodist Assembly near Palestine, Texas, where E. Stanley Jones was one of the speakers. Again, I felt my call affirmed. At the same time, my own pastor advised me against becoming a preacher. What I really wanted to be, he thought, was a missionary. But this was not what I had heard God calling me to do; so I put things on the back burner for a year. Over and over, I heard God calling me to reach out to people who were hurting. My office was across the hall from the morgue and next door to the emergency entrance. I decided perhaps God wanted me to be a hospital chaplain. So in July of that year I applied to Perkins School of Theology.

"When it came time to do my yearlong internship, I figured that I would do CPE. However, the intern committee would not allow me to do that since I had had no previous church experience. I ended up going to Pineville, Louisiana, in an associate position. That is where I fell in love with ministry! I loved working with senior citizens, doing hospital and home visits, and I grew to love preaching.

"There were difficult times in ministry, but there were also great times. Some members from the first little church I served recently told me I was their pastor for twenty-nine years. It seems that I have had opportunities to pastor their family in many areas of the country."

Clara Mae Reed

First African American Woman to Be Received into Full Connection

Ordained, Church of God Militant Pillar and Ground of the Truth, Pentecostal – 1977
Received on Trial, Northwest Texas – 1987
Received into Full Connection – 1993
Ordained Elder – 1993
Transferred to North Texas – 1998
Current Appointment – All Nations UMC, Dallas, Texas

CLARA MAE REED was born March 4, 1953, in McRoberts, Kentucky.

"I was always very active in the church. I experienced my call as an older youth but did not want to become a preacher. Having had both male and female pastors in my home church, The Church of God Militant Pillar and Ground of the Truth, and because my mother was an ordained evangelist, I was very familiar with the life of persons in ministry. Basically, I felt that they did not have a life because they were devoted to serving others. I loved the Lord and attempted to satisfy the call through other means of service in the church. Finally, I accepted the call and was ordained in the Pentecostal Church in 1977.

"In June 1987 I transferred into the UMC in the Northwest Texas Conference. When I entered into probationary membership, I became the first African American female to become part of the ordained ministry in this conference. The ironic part of my journey was that because of the racism and sexism present at the time, I was both accepted into probationary membership and placed on leave of absence in the same meeting. No appointment was found for me, so I was placed on leave of absence.

"I accepted a position as pastor of St. Paul CME in Midland, Texas, and then served for five years as a hospice chaplain/bereavement coordinator with Vitas Hospice Care in Dallas. It was at the end of that appointment that I was given the opportunity to serve as the church planter for a new congregation. Thus, All Nations United Methodist fellowship was planted in 1998, as a multicultural, multiethnic church that is 'Christian by Faith, Diverse by Design.'

"I think the struggle is part of the process of preparation. God has blessed my journey and allowed me to serve as both adjunct professor of homiletics at Perkins School of Theology and also as chair of the Board of Ordained Ministry for the North Texas Conference. In each of these settings, my goal is to embrace our diversity, and equip and empower others to usher in the kingdom of God so that God's will is done on earth as it is in heaven."

Hilda Cavazos

First Hispanic/Latina Woman to Be Received into Full Connection

Received on Trial – 1998
Ordained Deacon – 1998
Received into Full Connection – 2000
Ordained Elder – 2000
Current Appointment – Wesley Borger UMC, Borger, Texas

HILDA CAVAZOS was born in Reynosa, Tamaulipas (across the Hildalgo/Texas border), Mexico.

"I experienced the call to ministry in the summer of 1988, when I saw the need to bring Christ to the Hispanics/Latinos by means of word and action. The road to the ministry in the Methodist church began in the summer of 1990.

"The journey has been a growing experience. I have grown spiritually and personally through the different kinds of ministries God has given me. I am currently serving an Anglo church in Borger, Texas, within the Pampa District. I am still active in the Hispanic/Latino Ministry Task Force of the Northwest Texas Conference.

"All in all the ministries in the different churches have been the same, though in different languages. The love of God through Christ is universal. That love is equal in all languages if it is offered in action."

OKLAHOMA ANNUAL CONFERENCE

 *Mary Lou Branscum*

(EUROPEAN AMERICAN)

First Woman to Be Received into Full Connection

Received on Trial – 1966
Ordained Deacon – 1966
Received into Full Connection – 1969
Ordained Elder – 1969
Voluntary Location – 1975

MARY LOU BRANSCUM attended seminary at Perkins School of Theology at Southern Methodist University in Dallas, Texas. During her ministry, Mary Lou served at Fletcher Methodist Church during 1967 through 1968. She served as associate pastor at Trinity UMC in Tulsa in 1969. From 1970 through 1972, she served as associate at First UMC, Bartlesville, and from 1973 through 1974, she pastored Okmulgee and Butler-Council Hill. Mary Lou went on voluntary location in 1975.[12]

became a member of the AME Church and through that denomination was appointed to a United Methodist congregation to pastor for a year. I loved it and at the end of that year I didn't want to leave. That is how I came to be a United Methodist clergywoman.

"My journey has not always been difficult, although I could testify to difficulties! I was always able both to sing and to preach a message. So I have had numerous opportunities to minister in various ways and to a variety of groups. I was a teacher before I went to seminary, and I would preach to my eighth-graders as well as to my high-school students. Most important, I have been embraced by both black and white laity and clergy. Being open to God's people, anywhere, though there have been some difficulties, my ministerial journey has not been a rough and rocky one.

"In my current extension appointment, I am the minister of music at a black Baptist church. I get to teach, and to preach as well! It is the best of both worlds, and I love it. God has always been with me and I have found favor in the United Methodist denomination."

 *Janette Kotey*

First African American Woman to Be Received into Full Connection

Received on Trial – 1985
Ordained Deacon – 1985
Received into Full Connection – 1987
Ordained Elder – 1987
Transferred to North Texas – 1996
Current Appointment – Extension Ministries, Minister of Music, First Missionary Baptist Church, Huntsville, Alabama

JANETTE KOTEY was born August 28, 1952, in Joliet, Illinois, and raised in St. Louis, Missouri.

"I received my call to preach in a dream when I was twelve years old. I always sang, but in the dream I was standing up in front of a group of people in a long white dress preaching. I graduated from Harris Teacher's College and eventually attended Oral Roberts University School of Theology and Mission. As part of our graduation process, we were supposed to have a meeting with our pastor and adviser. My pastor did not come for the interview. So I

 *Laura Eileen Brewster*

First Hispanic/Latina Woman to Be Received into Full Connection

Received on Trial – 1995
Ordained Deacon – 1995
Received into Full Connection – 1998
Ordained Elder – 1998
Transferred to Southwest Texas – 2000
Current Appointment – Associate, St. Mark UMC, McAllen, Texas

LAURA EILEEN BREWSTER was born February 1, 1961, in McAllen, Texas.

"My 'call' unfolded during an extended period of time. Early on, I didn't recognize it as a call. I was working in the field of television news and living in Tucson, Arizona, when I began to feel a yearning to leave that profession and seek a new direction. I spoke with my wonderful pastor, Rev. Stan Brown, and he encouraged me to explore the possibility of becoming a diaconal minister and working in the field of Christian communications. As a result, I did some freelance work with the program 'Catch the Spirit' and also worked with a community affairs program, but finally decided not to pursue that path. However, my other pastor, Rev. Gary Harber, told me I had the gifts and graces for ordained ministry. The possibility began to take root in my heart and yet I couldn't quite believe that God could use me in that capacity. I didn't feel capable and I certainly didn't feel worthy. I struggled as I prayerfully considered the idea. I finally saw how God had been at work providing me with a myriad of experiences that had helped form and prepare me to eventually serve as an ordained pastor.

"Serving in Oklahoma was a blessed experience. The bishops and my fellow clergy afforded me ample opportunities to serve on district and conference committees that dealt with communications and minority issues. I was even invited to serve on *La Junta Consultiva de Comunicaciones*. Through those committees, I was able to help support the growth of Hispanic ministries and I feel good about that. Within a few years though, I felt the tug to come 'home' to Texas. Unlike other clergywomen I know, I do not feel particularly courageous or bold. However, I continue to seek to do God's will to the best of my ability where I serve. I trust that God can somehow use my meager efforts on behalf of his kingdom."

OKLAHOMA INDIAN MISSIONARY CONFERENCE

 *Lois V. Glory-Neal*

(NATIVE AMERICAN)

First Woman to Be Received into Full Connection

Received on Trial – 1984
Ordained Deacon – 1984
Received into Full Connection – 1989
Ordained Elder – 1989
Retired - 2001

LOIS V. GLORY-NEAL was born July 22, 1931, in Tahlequah, Oklahoma, capital of the Cherokee Nation.

"In 1979, I received this most 'sacred, intimate call' to the ordained ministry. I realized that fulfilling this call included four years of college and then seminary. The ordained ministry was a goal fulfilled, led by God's Spirit to greater heights than any woman could have achieved. I was bold enough to enter Oklahoma City University, a private United Methodist college, at age fifty. After raising seven children and serving with my late husband, Reverend Oliver Neal, in the Oklahoma Indian Missionary Conference for thirty years, I graduated from OCU with a BA degree in May 1984. That fall, I entered Saint Paul School of Theology–I was fifty-seven when I graduated. Seven long years were spent in preparation. God's Spirit has led this 'ole Cherokee woman' all the way."

After serving on the reservation in Horton, Kansas, while attending seminary and then serving four years on the Kickapoo/Potowatomi reservation, Lois became the first Native American woman to serve as a district superintendent. "The journey of ordained ministry within the Oklahoma Indian Missionary Conference has been a most gratifying, challenging, and spiritual growth for Lois Glory-Neal. To be a part of one of the greatest conferences in The United Methodist Church is to bask in the beauty and wonder of one's heritage, which includes the beginning of Methodism in Oklahoma. The Oklahoma Indian Missionary Conference, having celebrated 150 years of spirituality in 1994, continues the journey with a new vision for the future."

RIO GRANDE ANNUAL CONFERENCE

 *Minerva G. Carcaño*
 *Ronda Jean Wagner*

(HISPANIC/LATINA)
First Woman to Be Received into Full Connection
First Hispanic/Latina Woman to Be Elected to the Episcopacy

Received on Trial – 1976
Ordained Deacon – 1976
Received into Full Connection – 1980
Ordained Elder – 1980
Current Appointment – Resident Bishop Phoenix Area

MINERVA G. CARCAÑO was born January 20, 1954, in Edinburg, Texas.

"As a five-year-old helping my father replace the vinyl flooring in my church's kindergarten classroom (my and one of my sister's classroom), my father asked me to wait for him in the room as he fetched something he needed. Sitting between the old and the new roll of vinyl I felt the presence of God. It was the experience of being enveloped in God's love. I felt a sense of homecoming. From that moment forth I believed that I was meant to live in God's house. At that age I did not know what it all meant. I could not even articulate the experience, but in the years that followed, the experience never left me. I knew then that I belonged to God and would serve God.

"When I started in ministry, congregations protested my appointment to them because I was a woman, but we grew to love each other in spite of the initial resistance. I knew that I was there to be their pastor and not to prove to them that I was called to ordained ministry. It was not always easy, but the support of other women and men, both clergy and lay, and that of my family, strengthened me. Above all, God has been faithful, loving, and gracious.

"I have received the gift of being able to preach and teach throughout the United Methodist connection at annual conference sessions, schools of Christian mission, and numerous general church events. God has been amazingly gracious in allowing me to serve as a clergyperson in Christ's church. It has been a blessed journey."

First European American Woman to Be Received into Full Connection

Received on Trial – 1977
Ordained Deacon – 1977
Received into Full Connection – 1981
Ordained Elder – 1981
Transferred to Northwest Texas – 1981
Disability Leave – 1987
Retired – 1994

RONDA JEAN WAGNER was born June 24, 1952. "I was attending an American Baptist church, but the only thing that I was allowed to do in the service was the children's story. I wanted to do more. So, eventually I became a United Methodist."

Ronda graduated from Perkins School of Theology and then served El Getsemane in Artesia, Texas (Rio Grande Conference), for two years before being appointed to the Methodist Hospital CPE Program in Lubbock, Texas. She then transferred into the Northwest Texas Conference in 1981 and was appointed to attend school at Miami Valley Hospital, Pastoral Services Program in Dayton, Ohio. In 1984 Ronda was appointed as an army chaplain and she served in that capacity until she was diagnosed with multiple sclerosis.

"Although I enjoyed the work as an army chaplain very much, I had to work very long hours. Eventually it led to a diagnosis of MS. I took disability leave in 1987 and retired in 1994."

SOUTHWEST TEXAS ANNUAL CONFERENCE

 *Carolyn Louise Stapleton*

(EUROPEAN AMERICAN)

First Woman to Be Received into Full Connection

Received on Trial – 1971
Ordained Deacon – 1971
Received into Full Connection – 1973
Ordained Elder – 1973
Current Appointment – Cross-racial, cross-conference appointment as associate pastor of Chinese UMC (Chinatown), Manhattan, New York

CAROLYN LOUISE STAPLETON was born July 19, 1947, at West Point, New York.

"I began to experience my call to ordained ministry at Michigan State University where I was very active in the Wesley Foundation and the University Christian Movement. Both my pastor and campus minister (who were male) encouraged me to go to seminary and wrote references for me. Also, while I was at MSU, we got an associate director of the Wesley Foundation who was a woman. She was not ordained but was ordainable–she had a seminary degree. Because I saw a woman functioning in campus ministry (and she was the only woman I had ever seen in any form of professional ministry), I applied to seminary with the express purpose of becoming a campus minister. Interestingly, I was in the middle of my second year of seminary before I witnessed an ordained woman preaching and presiding at worship.

"I have seldom experienced direct discrimination as a result of being a clergywoman (it's usually been more subtle than that). However, I'll never forget the experience of attending the initial national clergywomen's consultation in Nashville in 1975. That was the first time I'd ever been in the presence of so many clergy sisters, and I felt like I'd died and gone to heaven! It was both affirming and inspiring to participate in the worship, workshops, and other events, and to feel fully included–for the very first time in my ministry."

 *J. Brendonly Cunningham*

First African American Woman to Be Received into Full Connection

Ordained Deacon – 1977
Received on Trial – 1979
Received into Full Connection – 1980
Ordained Elder – 1980
Retired – Serving as Staff Pastor (Senior Associate) at St. Paul UMC, San Antonio, Texas

J. BRENDONLY CUNNINGHAM was born April 8, 1933, in Hallettsville, Dewitt County, Texas.

"I received and accepted my call as a preacher at age five. I immediately organized a 'rock' congregation. I met daily with my parishioners under our house, which set on posts high enough for the cat, the dog, and me to comfortably take sanctuary. I told my parents and, of course, they didn't take me seriously. After all, I was only five. But I made a prophecy to my mother of what I was going to do for her. At age twenty-five, while enjoying the bright lights of the big city, I came home to attend to my ailing mother. She walked me through our humble home and pointed out that I had done everything I promised I would do for her. She said God had enabled me to fulfill my promise to her and that whatever I promised God, I should do it. I buried my mother within a month, but her words stayed with me. It was some seventeen years later, when my daughter, age thirteen, heard me preach into a tape recorder in our bathroom and encouraged me to honor that call.

"My impenetrable faith allowed me to have an awesomely courageous past. I truly believed I could do all things through the grace of God. I believed God spoke through me and I lived what I believed. My passion was always for the historic black church, where I served as senior pastor in several different congregations for nineteen years. My past experiences were challenging but good. I hope, with boldness, for an even better future for my sisters who are tenaciously blazing the trails and living in and out of the trenches. I am still bold in my faith, through my preaching, teaching, and writing. I am self-published and presently working on my fifth book of inspirational devotionals."

Lydia Salazar Martinez

First Hispanic/Latina Woman to Serve in Full Connection

Received on Trial, Rio Grande – 1980
Ordained Deacon, Rio Grande – 1980
Received into Full Connection, Rio Grande – 1985
Ordained Elder, Rio Grande – 1985
Transferred to California-Pacific – 1992
Transferred to Southwest Texas – 1995
Retired – 1999

LYDIA SALAZAR MARTINEZ was born in Alvin, Texas. She shares this poem to express her struggle to go into the ordained ministry.

> God, me a minister?
> It can't be –
> I'm a woman –
> You must mean something else.
>
> I have a husband
> and five children.
> I'm a woman –
> You must mean something else.
>
> I'll be glad to work in the church
> to sing, type or teach
> But–Lord, not preach–
> You must mean something else.
>
> Lord, I'm trying to really listen
> Have gone through so much in my life–
> So much toil, so much strife–
> You must mean something else.
>
> My husband is good and kind.
> The kids are great, they're really fine.
> But to go to school for such a long time?
> You must mean something else.
>
> There are so many with so much need
> I must listen to your heed.
> Because I am a woman–
> Must you mean something else?[13]

"My ministry has consisted of serving several churches in Texas. I was at Wilshire in Los Angeles during the civil unrest. Serving on both the General Commission on the Status and Role of Women and the General Board of Church and Society, as well as on many conference boards and agencies, has allowed me to travel in the United States and abroad and has given me a real appreciation for Wesley's claim that the world is our parish.

"In my ministry I have always prayed for God's wisdom and the guidance of the Holy Spirit. I have always relied on God's word found in scripture. I have fought for justice and the inclusion of all people at all levels of the church and the community. I am a preacher, a poet, an artist, and a lover of people; and I have a passion for life. *La lucha sigue! Adelenate Pueblo! Viva Raza!*" ("The struggle continues! Forward my people! Long live our race!")

TEXAS ANNUAL CONFERENCE

Perrie Joy Jackson

(AFRICAN AMERICAN)

First Woman to Be Received into Full Connection in the Former Texas Conference, Central Jurisdiction

Received on Trial – 1962
Ordained Deacon – 1960
Received into Full Connection – 1967
Ordained Elder – 1967
Retired – 2005

PERRIE JOY JACKSON was born January 2, 1936, in Galveston, Texas. She was nineteen when she gave her first message, and twenty-one when she got her local preacher's license. She was accepted into probationary membership in the Texas Conference in 1960 and was ordained a deacon in 1962. She was received into full membership and ordained elder in 1967. The Texas Conference [in the Central Jurisdiction], which was the African American conference, became the Gulf Coast Conference at the time of merger in 1968.

Perrie Joy says her ministry has been enjoyable and fulfilling. "It was a journey that started at birth and has been especially real since I was eleven years old. I sought God and I found God."

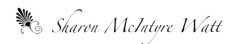

Sharon McIntyre Watt

First European American Woman to Be Received into Full Connection

Ordained Deacon, Central Texas – 1964
Received on Trial – 1966
Received into Full Connection – 1968
Ordained Elder – 1968
Retired – 2000

SHARON MCINTYRE WATT was born July 29, 1940, in Houston, Texas.

"The church is where I first experienced acceptance and inclusion. I was barely six years old. Seeing me pushed aside and all but stepped on by those around me, the Reverend Emmett O. Dubberly took me into his arms, walked down to the nursery, and showed me what was causing all the excite-ment. It was my new baby sister. Brother Dubberly showed God's love for me and for others in this simple caring act. Early in 1956, I heard a radio announcement concerning 'full clergy rights' being granted to women in the Methodist Church—my church! And ringing in the back of my ears and heart was the echo, 'That means you!' Such was my call to ministry.

"Some would have had me listen more closely. Did God mean being an educational worker or missionary teacher? All the while, the women of our local Wesleyan Service Guild/Women's Society of Christian Service seemed to understand and embrace my call. They began to open doors for me to the whole church. I was a part of their study and work. I was 'sponsored' (sent) on a mission tour to the Midwest to see the vastness of God's work in the church. They let me preach, inspire, and lead them. I kept moving forward by their strength and encouragement. In college, Dr. Alice Wonder took me under her wings. She introduced me to the congregations in Fort Worth, as a student pastor. 'I have a young woman studying for the ministry, a clergy-woman. Let her teach you. She can fill your pulpit.'

"Such encouragement and faith in the church prepared me to expect the 'opposition' that would surely come, not as stumbling blocks, but as stepping-stones. We (the church and I) would grow together, and so we have."

Notes

1. Nancy Britton, "'Firsts' among Arkansas Methodist Clergywomen" (unpublished paper, n.d.), 2. See chapter 1n211.
2. Information for this biography is taken from Dorothy Claiborne Tabor's memoir, published in the 2002 Journal of the Little Rock Conference, UMC, 255-56.
3. Information for this biography is taken from an interview by Dolores Challender, "Pioneer minister," in *The Newtonian* (July 17, 1992).
4. Material for this biography was provided by the Reverend Nancy Goddard, with assistance from Margaret Lipp.
5. Information for this biography is taken from an interview with Vivian Hand, by Charlotte Reed, on May 8, 1998, and available in the archives of the Nebraska Annual Conference, Cochrane-Woods Library, Nebraska Wesleyan University, Lincoln, NE 68504-0533.
6. Material is quoted from an interview with Charlotte Abram, which appears in *Today's Omaha Woman* (March/April 1991), 20, and provided by Maureen Vetter, archivist for the Nebraska Conference Archives of the UMC.

7. Information for this biography is provided by the Nebraska Conference Archives and from an e-mail from Bishop Minerva Carcaño to the author, June 20, 2005.

8. Unless otherwise noted, information for this biography is taken from Velma Franklin's memoir, written by Wm. T. Stephenson, published in the 1996 Journal of the North Texas Conference, UMC, 240.

9. Information provided by Frances Long, Archivist/Researcher at Bridwell Library, Southern Methodist University.

10. Information provided by the General Commission on Archives and History, UMC.

11. Information for this biography is taken from Hazel House's memoir, written by her son, Dalton Wood, published in the 1991 Journal of the Northwest Texas Conference, UMC, 307-8.

12. Information for this biography was provided by Christina Wolf, archivist for the Oklahoma Conference Archives located at the Dulaney-Browne Library, Oklahoma City University, 2501 N. Blackwelder, Oklahoma City, OK 73106.

13. This poem was published under the name Lydia Saenz in *Images: Women in Transition*, comp. Janice Grana (Nashville: The Upper Room, 1976), 126.

Chapter 7

First Women of the North Central Jurisdiction to Receive Full Clergy Rights

THE NORTH CENTRAL JURISDICTION CURRENTLY HAS TWELVE ANNUAL CONFERENCES AND fifty-one "first" women–including the first woman to be elected to the episcopacy. Eleven of the women, including one bishop, or 21 percent, are deceased and nine, or 18 percent, are retired. Seventeen of the women, or 33 percent, are serving in the local church. Eleven others, or 21 percent, including four district superintendents, are serving in extension ministries. One is a missionary and two others are on incapacity leave. Two of these women have become pastors in the United Church of Christ.

Fifteen of the women are European American, fifteen of the women are African American, eight are Korean, six are Hispanic/Latina, two are Native Americans, and there is one Indian, one East Indian, two Filipina women and one Vietnamese woman. This Jurisdiction has the first Filipina woman to serve in full connection in the United States and the first Indian, East Indian, and Vietnamese woman to be received into full connection.

DAKOTAS ANNUAL CONFERENCE

Grace E. Huck

(EUROPEAN AMERICAN)
First Woman to Be Received in Full Connection in the Former North Dakota Conference in 1958
First Woman to Serve in Full Connection in the Former South Dakota Conference in 1972

(See chapter 2, 34)

Barbara Louise Miller Bullock

First European American Woman to Be Received into Full Connection in the Former South Dakota Conference

Received on Trial – 1972
Ordained Deacon – 1972
Received into Full Connection – 1975
Ordained Elder – 1975
Transferred to United Church of Christ – 1983
Current Appointment – Salem UCC, Alleman, Iowa

BARBARA LOUISE MILLER BULLOCK was born August 2, 1949, in Colton, South Dakota.

"Sometime in 1970, I met with the Board of Ordained Ministry of the South Dakota Conference at Dakota Wesleyan University, where I was a student. When I went in to meet with them, shortly after my husband, Keith, met with them, I was told that I could not be a minister. Shortly before, another student told me that women could indeed be ministers, although personally I did not know any. When I asked the board about their decision, they told me it was because my husband was going to be a minister. Whatever would they do with both of us in the system? I didn't have any answers. My husband was talking to Bishop James Armstrong when I finished. When I walked in, I was in tears. After the bishop learned what happened, he said, 'You wait right here.' He returned and told me to go back for another visit with the board. I wasn't too anxious to go, because I know he'd read them the riot act. They apologized, and we went on with the interview."

Two years after Barbara and Keith were both ordained elders in full connection, Keith began to have health issues and decided to leave parish ministry to pursue a degree in speech pathology. After graduation, he took a job in Minnesota, and

Barbara continued serving UMC churches in North Dakota. Unable to obtain a transfer into the Minnesota Conference without being away from her children five days a week, Barbara eventually began serving churches in the United Church of Christ. In 1983, she left the UMC to become a pastor in the UCC. She is currently serving Salem UCC in Alleman, Iowa, where she says, "I was hurt so badly in my last parish, I have found it hard to trust that these people won't do the same thing. I had come to the point of questioning my ministry and whether or not I was fit. I worked with the Committee on Ministry and I was in counseling and still am." Despite the pain, however, Barbara persists in her ministry.

Sukumari S. Hakeem-Michael

First Indian Woman to Be Received into Full Connection in the Former South Dakota Conference and in the UMC

Received on Trial – 1985
Ordained Deacon – 1985
Received into Full Connection – 1987
Ordained Elder – 1987
On Loan to Mississippi – 1998
Current Appointment – Abbeville Circuit, Oxford, Mississippi

SUKUMARI S. HAKEEM-MICHAEL was born February 25, 1939, in Bidar, Karnataka State, India, in a parsonage.

"My father was a Methodist minister. During the 1980s I felt the call to preaching ministry. I was always involved in the church as a Christian education director, teaching church school and active in the United Methodist Women. UMW friends had encouraged and affirmed my call. In September 1982 I left with my two children for seminary. It was a trying time for my children to change schools and leave their father behind. I finished seminary in two years and a summer. I drove sixty-five miles one way to preach every Sunday and worked in the library during the week. Life was a constant struggle.

"It was not easy for me because I am an ethnic woman. Eventually, my husband and I were divorced, on the thirtieth anniversary of our wedding day, leaving me to struggle as both a single woman and an ethnic woman.

"I moved to Mississippi in 1998 and have been serving churches in Oxford. Life seems to be getting better after all these years of struggle. I would not trade my place for any other job. Now I am happy and content and enjoy my preaching ministry."

DETROIT ANNUAL CONFERENCE

 *Marion Kline*

(EUROPEAN AMERICAN)

First Woman to Be Received into Full Connection in 1958

(See chapter 2, 48)

 *Janet Gaston Petty*

First African American Woman to Be Received into Full Connection

Received on Trial – 1979
Ordained Deacon – 1979
Received into Full Connection – 1982
Ordained Elder – 1982
Current Appointment – Hope UMC, Associate Pastor of Counseling and Pastoral Care, Southfield, Michigan

JANET GASTON PETTY was born January 5, 1956, in Detroit, Michigan.

"My journey began during the summer of my sophomore year of college. I was a student at Adrian College, home for summer break, when my pastor, Rev. Donald A. Scavella, set up an appointment to talk with me. During our meeting he asked if I had ever considered full-time ministry. I promptly broke out into a laugh that was rather disrespectful. After I gathered my composure, I assured Rev. Scavella that ministry was not what I had in mind for my life. He encouraged me to transfer to Scarritt College in Nashville, Tennessee, where I could continue my studies in the social sciences and pick up a course or two in religion. I agreed to transfer. My first semester was business as usual but then something happened. I was visiting Eastern Michigan University when I had an encounter with the Holy Spirit like none other. I returned to Scarritt where every free hour was spent reading and studying the Word of God.

"I have had the privilege of serving in two annual conferences in a variety of appointments. The first nine years of my ministry were spent in the Detroit Annual Conference. On July 1, 1989, I became a member of the California-Pacific Annual Conference where I served until June 30, 2002. I returned to Detroit July 1, 2002, after the death of my mother.

"Ministry has been both exciting and draining. It has provided my greatest joy and my greatest challenges, and through it all I praise God for the journey. When mentoring those who are exploring their call to ministry I often remark, 'You cannot do this job without a calling because some days your calling is what keeps you.' I don't know what the future holds, but with God new mercies are revealed every day so I press on. God's peace be with you!"

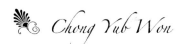 *Chong Yub Won*

First Korean Woman to Be Received into Full Connection

Received on Trial – 1991
Ordained Deacon – 1991
Received into Full Connection – 1995
Ordained Elder – 1995
Current Appointment – Oak Grove UMC, Howell, Michigan

CHONG YUB WON was born February 16, 1948, in Taejon, South Korea.

"In the late 1960s sometime after I received the gift of the Holy Spirit (April 1967), I knew that the path I was about to take would be different from the 'normal' path most Korean women would choose to follow. This call was reaffirmed in December 1987 when the leadership of my home church, then in Birmingham, Michigan (Central Korean United Methodist Church), encouraged me to consider becoming an ordained clergyperson in the UMC. That same afternoon, in a soul-searching struggle in prayer, I sensed that my ministry would not be smooth sailing. However, I answered the call that evening with an assurance and peace from the Lord. 'God is the one who began this good work in you, and I am certain that he won't stop before it is complete on the day that Christ Jesus returns' (Phil. 1:6, CEV).

"Looking back on my ministry, the challenges that I had to deal with were mostly due to lack of openness and set expectations on the part of those in leadership in the churches. Also, in some cases, cultural misunderstandings from both sides probably also contributed. Nevertheless, I have come to realize that 'God is always at work for the good of everyone who loves him' (Rom. 8:28, CEV). I celebrate the fact that those years of good and not so good times were God's molding agent to make me and those I served more useful vessels. I am very grateful for the presence of those in the denomination and in the churches who held uncompromisingly to faith in the Lord and showed their support and love toward me and my ministry."

 *Karen Vo-To*

First Vietnamese Woman to Be Received into Full Connection in the Conference and the UMC

Received on Trial – 1995
Ordained Deacon – 1995
Received into Full Connection – 1998
Ordained Elder – 1998
Current Appointment – Missionary, GBGM, Assigned to Southeast Asia for Pastoral Training

KAREN VO-TO was born January 16. "Reflecting on her experiences, [Karen] recalls a visit to the region with a team exploring the establishment of United Methodist congregations. On her return, she says her husband, who was also on the team, told her he felt God calling him to go to Southeast Asia as a missionary. He asked her about her calling. 'The thought of becoming a missionary at one time put fear in me,' she says of that moment, 'until the Lord began to free me from this.' She says that since that time, she too has felt the call 'to be a part of God's ministry in Southeast Asia.'"[1]

Karen earned a BRE degree in pastoral studies at Emmanuel Bible College in Kitchener, Ontario, Canada, and an MDiv degree from Methodist Theological School in Ohio, in Delaware, Ohio. Prior to her commissioning as a GBGM missionary, she served for four years as an associate pastor in Detroit. During that time, she also served on the Commission on the Status and Role of Women and the Ethnic Local Church Concerns Committee. For four years, she was president of Vietnamese United Methodist Women on the national level. She was also pastor of a local church in Dearborn Heights, Michigan, for a year. Karen is the only Vietnamese woman reported for this project.

She says, "I had a call to be an ordained pastor when I was a little girl. Now I am so glad to see my dream come true."

EAST OHIO ANNUAL CONFERENCE

Marie R. Tschappat

(EUROPEAN AMERICAN)
First Woman to Be Received into Full Connection in 1958

(See chapter 2, 55)

Mae Charlotte Morrow

First African American Woman to Be Received into Full Connection

Received on Trial – 1980
Ordained Deacon – 1980
Received into Full Connection – 1983
Ordained Elder – 1983
Retired – 2002

MAE CHARLOTTE MORROW was born October 25, 1947, in Heidelberg, Mississippi.

"My actual call, I discovered over a period of time, was just there. Over the years, I had begun to work more and more hours in my home church of St. Matthew. I was involved in ministry. All doors were opening in that direction for me, while doors in other directions were closing. I met Dr. Major J. Jones, dean at Gammon Theological Seminary, and we discussed my entering seminary. A full scholarship was offered, as well as student employment and housing. So I answered my call and started seminary in 1978.

"My journey has been tumultuous. As the first black woman in the East Ohio Conference, I lacked support from my comrades. Since then, I have made an effort to support others as they came along. The conference seemed reluctant to accept me, not seeming to know what to do with me. One of the many rewarding experiences in my ministry was at a church in the northwestern part of the state. I enjoyed being in ministry with a group of people (with some exceptions) who accepted my leadership and me as a person. Unfortunately, one of my most frustrating experiences was also at this church, as my leadership as pastor was undermined from various other sources/levels of the church. Another good experience in my ministry was as president of the Black

Pastors' Fellowship of the conference. Providing organization and structure as a planner, I was able to assist this organization to become more focused and directed during my tenure. Not everyone necessarily appreciated this. But as Rom. 8:37 says, "In all these things we are more than conquerors through him who loved us."

Edna Isabel Stahl

First Hispanic/Latina Woman to Be Received into Full Connection

Received on Trial – 1993
Ordained Deacon – 1993
Received into Full Connection – 1995
Ordained Elder – 1995
Current Appointment – Norwalk UMC, Norwalk, Ohio

EDNA ISABEL STAHL was born in Baja Vera Paz, Guatemala.

"I began my journey into ministry after graduating from Baker University, Baldwin City, Kansas, in 1986. Afterward, I found myself with no direction. Finding no satisfaction in my secular job, I spent time fasting and praying. I then enrolled at Methodist Theological School in Ohio and graduated with the master of divinity degree in 1991.

"It has been both a challenge and a blessing to serve God and The United Methodist Church. My current appointment as associate pastor at Norwalk UMC is awesome. It allows me to serve God and be available to my family as they grow. God has blessed my husband and me with five children, ages three (twins) to eleven. I am a third-generation clergyperson. My grandfather and father are both United Methodist pastors. God has blessed me for serving him. I am pleased to say it has been fourteen years since my first appointment."

 *Gina Moon Kim*

First Korean Woman to Be Received into Full Connection

Received on Trial – 1988
Ordained Deacon – 1988
Received into Full Connection – 2000
Ordained Elder – 2000
Current Appointment – Amboy UMC, Conneaut, Ohio

GINA MOON KIM was born November 28, 1954, in Seoul, South Korea.

"In 1990, I went on a short-term mission trip to Paraguay. Inviting, teaching, preaching, and sharing the love of Jesus was so invigorating and exciting that I felt like a fish put back into the pond after being caught. Upon returning from the mission trip, I could not concentrate on my job as a computer systems analyst. All I wanted to do was preach and teach. I wanted to be in ministry full time. I had passion for the souls of people and a burning desire to preach the Word of God. I spent many days and nights in intensive prayers and fasting. The Lord confirmed through his Word that he wanted me to feed his lambs and take care of his sheep.

"When I clearly heard God's calling, my first reaction was that God couldn't possibly be calling me into the ordained ministry, because I believed a woman should not be a senior pastor. As a result, I assumed that God was calling me into youth ministry. I enrolled in seminary and studied Christian education. Soon my home church hired me as a youth pastor.

"During the prime time of my ministry, the Lord forced me to move to Ohio by the way of a job transfer for my husband. In Ohio, I had more time to reflect, search my soul, and revisit the scripture references that had hindered me from going into ordained ministry. Through the prayers and encouragement of my husband and mentors, I was able to shed my own prejudice against women that was formed in my culture and upbringing. I have served two cross-cultural appointments since 1997. My initial fear of being the only Korean in the midst of an all-Caucasian community dissipated quickly. People received me warmly as their pastor. I will continue to love the people Jesus loved and died for, challenge them to have a personal relationship with Jesus, teach and preach the Word of God, disciple them, and send them out into the world to reach out. I love being a pastor. If I were to die and come back to life, I would still want to be a pastor."

ILLINOIS GREAT RIVERS ANNUAL CONFERENCE

Katherine A. Shindel

(EUROPEAN AMERICAN)
First Woman to Be Received into the Former Southern Illinois Conference

Received on Trial – 1971
Ordained Deacon – 1971
Received into Full Connection – 1975
Ordained Elder – 1975
Retired – 2004

KATHERINE A. SHINDEL was born March 30, 1945, in Alton, Illinois.

"I've always struggled to hear God's call. I worked in every job in the church, including being a missionary, until I was forced to preach while studying religious education in seminary. When I accepted my call, I discovered that others had a hard time hearing also. I can't believe that it was thirty-three years ago that I stood on the stage at the old Southern Conference as their first woman seminarian to receive deacon's orders. The presiding bishop lectured us on the importance of the married ministry. Looking down the line at us, he stared me straight in the eyes as he told us, 'I want all of you men to get wives.' That night, I processed into my ordination service to the hymn 'God Send Us Men.' The following winter, a district superintendent visited me at seminary and told me there was no need to discuss an appointment because he was sure that some young man would come riding in on his white charger and sweep me off my feet. Despite such an awkward start, I want to thank everyone who believed in me and supported me in my ministry.

"I remember the joy of my congregations and then the struggle with God's call to enter the Air Force. There I found a ministry beyond my wildest dreams as I served our brave young men and women and their families. The highlight of all my ministry was the Christmas Day worship services I led in the ancient cave church in Antioch–which might be the very one where Barnabas and the congregation nurtured Paul and sent him out on his first missionary journey.

"As I retire, I remember that young woman of thirty-three years ago and I think of the young men and women who will stand before you in the future. Listen to people who tell you they have been called. Take the time to observe their gifts and graces. Encourage and mentor them. Who knows what lives you will touch and how God will use them."

Lisa Michelle Scott Joiner

First African American Woman to Be Received into Full Connection in the Former Southern Illinois Conference

Received on Trial, Wisconsin – 1984
Ordained Deacon, Wisconsin – 1984
Received into Full Connection – 1987
Ordained Elder – 1987
Transferred to Missouri – 2000
Current Appointment – North Park UMC, St. Louis, Missouri

LISA MICHELLE SCOTT JOINER was born January 31, 1962, in Milwaukee, Wisconsin.

"I received my call to ordained ministry at age eighteen. God revealed to me in a vision that I would be a minister/pastor to many. At the time, I was a student at Clark College in Atlanta, Georgia. Upon receiving the call, I entered the ordained ministry track and by age twenty had finished the candidacy program. After graduating from college, I enrolled at Garrett-Evangelical Theological Seminary in Evanston, Illinois.

"I would simply describe my ministry as that of 'sister in the wilderness.' As an African American woman of God in ministry, I often found my ministry to be less than a 'crystal stair.' I was and am the reluctant pioneer: the first black woman ordained deacon in the Wisconsin Conference and the first black woman pastor in East St. Louis. My first appointment out of seminary was to a small, new church. It was a privilege to serve there, but it was also very unstable and isolating. Other opportunities to serve as a pastor in Southern Illinois were remote. This experience sent me further into the wilderness.

"Then God led me to serve a number of years in hospital chaplaincy in which I was a board-certified and endorsed chaplain at three hospitals. Here too I was a pioneer–the first black female chaplain. Out of the wilderness experience, God made provisions: first to further my education and training in ministry and, second, to return me to the parish ministry, as an associate pastor to a large, black urban church in St. Louis, and senior pastor in my current appointment. In both instances I was the first black female clergyperson. I realize that through my ministry experiences, God was reshaping and reforming me spiritually to fulfill my call. By coming through the wilderness, I have experienced tremendous spiritual depth and growth as well as Spirit-filled joy and wisdom to do ministry with holy boldness."

In-Sook Hwang

First Korean Woman to Be Received into Full Connection in the Former Southern Illinois Conference

Received on Trial – 1988
Ordained Deacon – 1989
Received into Full Connection – 1993
Ordained Elder – 1993
Current Appointment – Pana First UMC, Pana, Illinois

IN-SOOK HWANG was born May 18, 1953, in Pusan, South Korea.

"My calling has been coming to me gradually since my teen years. I always knew that God had a very special purpose for my life, without knowing what it was specifically. When I came to seminary in the United States, it was eye opening to see so many female students in a classroom. It was a joy to discover that a woman could be a pastor. With enthusiasm, I responded to God's call to be an ordained pastor.

"Since I left my home country and family, churches have been my home and congregations my family–partners in God's mission and companions on my spiritual journey. I have been growing as God's servant through ministering to his people and being ministered to by them. I continue to learn more about servanthood and feel privileged to serve God's people who are living in so much pain, spiritual hunger, and rapid changes."

Harriette M. Gitterman

(EUROPEAN AMERICAN)
First Woman to Serve in Full Connection in the Former Central Illinois Conference
Received into Full Connection in the Illinois Conference, Methodist Protestant Church, in 1935

(See chapter 2, 61-62)

Sondra Sue Newman

(EUROPEAN AMERICAN)
First Woman to Be Received into the Former Central Illinois Conference

Received on Trial – 1966
Ordained Deacon – 1966
Received into Full Connection – 1970
Ordained Elder – 1970
Incapacity Leave – 2005

SONDRA SUE NEWMAN was born July 10, 1943, in Danville, Illinois.

"On January 1, 1962, at the East Bay Camp at Lake Bloomington, Illinois, at a statewide college retreat of Wesley Foundations over Christmas break, I was involved in a midnight Communion service, followed by a night of silence. The question was asked, 'So, what are you doing in your life for Christ?' I was the last to come forward for Communion. After receiving the bread, I looked up at the large white cross. The Christ was dying on it in front of my very eyes. I will never forget the pain and the love I saw. When I drank the juice that night, it had turned into blood! This is the only time it has ever happened. I left, crying, and ran to my room hoping to escape into sleep. When I picked up my Bible, I knew God wasn't finished with me. I returned to a vacant room I had found earlier. I turned on the light, shut the door, and threw my Bible across the room shouting, 'What do you want?' God responded, 'You will be a minister.' 'It's unfair,' I argued. 'I'm female. That's a man's job!' An hour later, I said, 'Okay. I can't fight you.' A peace filled me that lasted about a month–a truly precious time. I have based the past forty years of my life on that peace.

"The journey has been a joy and delight, for which I thank God. However, it has also had its difficulties. I was accused of being a 'bra-burning woman's libber' or 'looking for a husband.' Personally, I find bras comfortable and I have remained single–out of love for Jesus my Lord, I gave my life to God. The greatest pain has been in being rejected because I am female or being criticized about something that wouldn't even have raised an eyebrow if I were a man. Finally, I came to accept this as sharing in Jesus' suffering. But as we move forward to the bold future needed to make us all one in Christ, it must be done with joy–joy and love."

Margaret Misal

First East Indian Woman to Be Received into Full Connection in the Former Central Illinois Conference and the UMC

Received on Trial – 1979
Ordained Deacon – 1979
Received into Full Connection – 1981
Ordained Elder – 1981
Retired – 2004 (Supply Pastor at First UMC, Grant Park, Illinois)

MARGARET MISAL was born November 28, 1938, in Miraj, India.

"Before I accepted God's call to become a pastor, I was a high-school teacher in India. I was very content in my job. I had no ambition or any plans to be a pastor. However, as I look back, I know that the Lord had planned my life in a baffling way. I did not have a vision nor did I see any bright light, but somehow traumatic incidents began to take place around me. Finally, I realized that God was calling me into ministry. After strong resistance, I surrendered to God's will in 1971. In 1972 I enrolled in Princeton Theological Seminary for a master of Christian education degree, because I was still unclear about the call. I had to leave my husband and two precious young children, ages three and four, and for two years live eight thousand miles away. Leaving family, home, friends, and country behind made for a very lonesome journey. I continued further studies in the MDiv program at the Theological School at Drew University."

In 1979 Margaret was given an appointment in the Central Illinois Conference. "It was a long journey. We had no family, no home, no friends–nothing. We had only our strong faith and God's promise to always be with us. To our delight the church welcomed us graciously. Soon I found out that I was the only ethnic woman in the conference at that time. I had more advantages of being ethnic clergy than disadvantages. People were very receptive of me and my family. However, I realized that I had to work harder than any other pastors due to the language barriers and to prove that I was very capable to be a church leader.

"My journey will continue as long as God leads me and wants me. I am eternally thankful to the Lord for being my friend and guide on this long journey."

Carol Sue Lakota Eastin

First Native American Woman to Be Received into Full Connection in the Former Central Illinois Conference

Received on Trial – 1982
Ordained Deacon – 1982
Received into Full Connection – 1985
Ordained Elder – 1985
Current Appointment – Pastor, Native American Fellowship-Dayspring Church

CAROL SUE LAKOTA EASTIN was born February 19, 1956, in Peoria, Illinois.

"I felt a strong call to ministry at the age of fourteen during a lay witness mission at my home church. I entered college with the intent of entering some church vocation. At age nineteen I was asked by the superintendent in Jacksonville, Illinois, Dr. Joseph Mason, to pastor some rural churches while going to college. God's call was clear and certain; I knew I wanted to serve in the church. But when he asked me to pastor churches, I felt uncertain. After all, I had never heard of a woman pastor. 'Oh yes,' he said, 'there is another one in our conference, preaching up north. It would be nice if you could meet her sometime.' So after three days of prayer and on the word that there was such a thing as a woman minister, I said boldly, 'I'll give it a tentative try.'

"My first churches were amazingly supportive of this teenage girl, but by the time I was twenty-eight years old, I was weary of the battle. Some clergy from other denominations refused to include me in local ecumenical efforts (at least not preaching). One pastor told me that I should stop preaching lest I end up in hell for it. My worldview and theology were out of place in these rural areas. I had grown up in a city environment, with a strong upbringing in Native American values as well as Christian teachings.

"Through my involvement in a local history project in Peoria, I helped develop a powwow in my hometown. I found a sense of joy and home working with the Native community, creating healing opportunities for our people. Gradually, a ministry evolved. Starting with a gathering in my living room, and later becoming a worshiping fellowship, this group of full- and mixed-blood Natives, as well as Caucasians and Mexicans, has grown into a church. Bringing together our Native ways and our Christian faith is the joy of our fellowship. It was critical for me to venture outside of the church to find my parish, and my true calling. My advice: follow your passion; it is your call. Do what you are meant to do. Then, maybe, you can convince someone to pay you for it."

Beverly Loray Wilkes

First African American Woman to Be Received into Full Connection in the Former Central Illinois Conference

Received on Trial, Missouri East – 1988
Ordained Deacon, Missouri East – 1988
Received into Full Connection – 1992
Ordained Elder – 1992
Current Appointment – Superintendent, Mississippi River District

BEVERLY LORAY CARTER BELL YANCEY HILL WILKES was born July 23, 1959, in Hopkins County, Kentucky.

"My birth name is Beverly Loray Wilkes; however, upon working to redeem the legacy of my family and to ensure that the women of my family were not lost to the generations who will follow me, I have included the names of those who came before. I began experiencing my call when I was approximately three years old. I grew up in a Baptist home and remained Baptist until I was introduced to the UMC in 1981 at age twenty-two. Being a preacher or a pastor in the Baptist Church was not an option that I could even consider. It was not until 1982 that I was able to acknowledge my call formally at Saint Luke UMC in Hayti, Missouri.

"From 1962 until now, as I write these words, I have never once doubted that God has called, claimed, and named me to be a preacher, a pastor, and a prophet. Though my call has always been clear, the demons of racism and sexism have often sought to destroy my very being. If it had not been for God working through the saints of the church, I would be mentally insane and institutionalized because of the systemic terror of discrimination in The United Methodist Church heaped on the backs of African American clergywomen. I am still here and reasonably sane and spiritually healthy because of the saints. The keepers of my soul have been African American, Native American, Hispanic/Latino, and Caucasian men and women. Racism and sexism have only encouraged me to be intentional about embracing God's kaleidoscopic view of the human family. I thank these living saints: Bishop Leontine T. C. Kelly, Rev. Dr. Susan S. Vogel, Bishop Woodie W. White, Bishop Sharon Ann Brown Christopher, Bishop Linda Lee, Rev. Dr. Kenneth L. Franklin, Rev. Donald Jarvis, Rev. Clyde Snyder, Rev. Cynthia and Rev. E. Michael Jones, Rev. Dr. Cynthia Belts, Rev. Dr. Sherry Daniels, Rev. Rose Booker Jones, Rev. Lois Neal, Rev. Charlotte Abram, Rev. Donna Dudley, laywomen Brenda Barton, Betty Story, Roslynn Sikes, and Diane Johnson. I honor the deceased saints: my supervising elder Reverend Benjamin Anderson, laywoman and clergy spouse Dianne Bass, and supply pastor Vince Ramirez. I know that I have been blessed to sit at the feet of some of God's most gentle, wise, strong, gracious, faithful, and diligent saints of all colors, male and female."

Nancy J. Nichols

(EUROPEAN AMERICAN)
First Woman to Be Received into Full Connection in 1958

(See chapter 2, 47)

Dora Dalli Campbell

First Hispanic/Latina Woman to Be Received into Full Connection

Received on Trial – 1973
Ordained Deacon – 1973
Received into Full Connection – 1975
Ordained Elder – 1975
Retired – 1991 (Still Assisting with Hispanic Ministry in the Mason City District)

DORA DALLI CAMPBELL was born in Guadalajara, Jalisco, Mexico.

"I came to the United States with a full scholarship to attend Vennard College in University Park, Iowa. It was there that I accepted Christ as my Lord and Savior and decided to go into full-time Christian service. After finishing four years of Bible College, I went back to Mexico to teach in the Methodist Deaconess School in Mexico City. After teaching there for one year, I enrolled in Asbury Theological Seminary in Wilmore, Kentucky. There I met a lady who offered to pay for my seminary training. Also, I met Don Campbell, and we were married during our final year at Asbury.

"We planned to go to Mexico as missionaries, but the Lord had other plans for us. While serving our first pastoral charge, a missionary from Puerto Rico visited our district and told us we were the perfect match for the need for a missionary couple in Puerto Rico. We accepted the challenge to organize and build a new Methodist church in Ponce, Puerto Rico. After serving there for twelve years, we came back to minister in Iowa. While serving our first charge back in Iowa, I decided to become ordained.

"My ministry has been very rewarding among the Spanish-speaking people in Puerto Rico and here in Iowa. I give thanks to God for the privilege of being able to introduce them to the saving grace of Jesus Christ. In the 1970s when I started, there was only a small number of clergywomen; and we were treated with great respect. Now they tell me there are nearly as many women studying for the ministry as men. I give thanks to God for the blessings I have received in serving my Lord as a woman in ministry."

Thelma Colorado Subramanian

First Filipina Woman to Serve in Full Connection
First Woman to Be Received into Full Connection in the Philippines Annual Conference

(See chapter 9, 203)

Hee-Soon Kwon

First Korean Woman to Be Received into Full Connection

Received on Trial – 1991
Ordained Deacon – 1991
Received into Full Connection – 1993
Ordained Elder – 1993
Current Appointment – Extension Ministries, Teaching Faculty, Methodist Theological Seminary, Seoul, South Korea

HEE-SOON KWON was born in Yesan, Chung-Nam, South Korea.

"I began my journey toward ordained ministry when I was a junior in high school. However, back then, married women were restricted from ordination in the Korean Methodist Church. Therefore, I finally got ordained at the age of forty in the Iowa Annual Conference of The United Methodist Church, not in the Korean Methodist Church.

"My ministry is to teach at a Methodist seminary in Seoul, helping those who are preparing for ministry. I feel great to be able to go on the journey with women seminarians who are courageously dreaming of their ministry–which, in my experience, is still not easy."

Debra Manning Burks

One of the First Three African American Women to Be Received into Full Connection

Received on Trial, North Georgia – 1998
Ordained Deacon, North Georgia – 1998
Received into Full Connection – 2000
Ordained Elder – 2000
Incapacity Leave – 2003

DEBRA MANNING BURKS was born February 27, 1956, in Jackson, Hinds County, Mississippi.

"I attended the 1985 Texas Annual Conference as a lay delegate from my church, located in Spring, Texas. During the Communion services I awaited my turn in the balcony. As I looked below, I heard a quiet, still voice tell me, 'You should be there,' as I watched the celebrants. Puzzled by this tug at my heart, I told my then spouse but did nothing much to further explore the matter. Three years later, while living in New Orleans, I openly confessed this situation to my pastor, Dr. Alonzo Campbell. He responded, 'You've been waiting all this time?' After that, God opened doors and Reverend Campbell assisted with my entry to seminary.

"I attended Gammon Theological Seminary in Atlanta from 1990 through 1993 and graduated with an MDiv degree. My fifteen years have been marked with both highs and lows. I see my current medical challenge as God's way of pulling me aside to refresh, restore, and rejuvenate me for future ministry challenges."

Celestyne C. DeVance

One of the First Three African American Women to Be Received into Full Connection

Received on Trial – 1997
Ordained Deacon – 1997
Received into Full Connection – 2000
Ordained Elder – 2000
Current Appointment – St. John's UMC, Des Moines, Iowa

CELESTYNE C. DEVANCE was born June 13, 1944, in Baltimore, Maryland.

"I began hearing God's call at age twelve. I answered the call in 1986 only after experiencing women pastors for the first time. Their boldness gave me courage to leave a secular career to enter seminary and follow the call of God.

"The call of God on my life is to make radical disciples for Jesus Christ in cross-racial settings. While it has not been easy to serve in Iowa (with a minority population in the state of only 3 percent), God's favor has been afforded me to be welcomed in all-white congregations in my last two appointments and to be successful in leading both those congregations in numerical and spiritual growth."

Abena Safiyah Fosua

One of First Three African American Women to Be Received into Full Connection

Received on Trial – 1990
Ordained Deacon – 1990
Received into Full Connection – 2000
Ordained Elder – 2000
Transferred to Greater New Jersey – 2002
Current Appointment – Extension Ministries, Director of Invitational Preaching Ministries, General Board of Discipleship, Nashville, Tennessee

ABENA SAFIYAH FOSUA was born September 12, 1951, in Kansas City, Kansas.

"I received a call to ministry in 1982 and enrolled in seminary in 1985. From 1996 through 2000, I served as a missionary in Ghana, West Africa, for the General Board of Global Ministries. I completed the requirements for ordination from overseas, which takes a lot longer. The process was slowed down further by my being appointed (along with my husband, who was also seeking ordination) to start a new congregation that worshiped in the African American tradition. Iowa requires CPE training for ordination, and I always seemed to have received appointments that made it difficult to commute to a CPE site while fulfilling the demands of the appointment. I do not think this was intentional, just insensitive to my needs to finish fulfilling requirements for full connection.

"The early years of my journey were very difficult for me and for my family. To their credit, my congregations adjusted better than some others that were receiving their first woman pastor. Yet, the double-minority combination of being both woman pastor and African American in a cross-cultural appointment made it difficult to truly belong anywhere. In the early years, I longed to be more than the newest religious oddity in the community. Subsequent appointments in another annual conference have been quite different. After a few weeks in my most recent (cross-cultural) pastoral appointment, I was embraced, included, and received as a pastor. Overall it has been a worthwhile journey."

MINNESOTA ANNUAL CONFERENCE

Mary MacNicholl

(EUROPEAN AMERICAN)
First Woman to Be Received into Full Connection in 1958

(See chapter 2, 46)

Gloria Roach Thomas

First African American Woman to Be Received into Full Connection

Received on Trial –1995
Ordained Deacon – 1995
Received into Full Connection – 2000
Ordained Elder – 2000
Current Appointment – Lead Pastor, Camphor Memorial UMC, St. Paul, Minnesota (Formerly in the Central Jurisdiction)

GLORIA ROACH THOMAS was born January 25, 1951, at Fort Knox, Kentucky, a fifth-generation Methodist.

She grew up in Camden, South Carolina, where she was a member of Shiloh UMC. Shiloh church is the church that her eighty-eight-year-old father was born into and the church that his great aunt and uncle founded in 1877. She grew up in rural, segregated South Carolina where life was tough for blacks. Even when the world said to her that "she was nobody," it was her black elders and the "church" who told her that "she was somebody." It was her hard-working and God-fearing parents and the church that helped to give her a "vision of God's love for her" that has sustained her over the years through the good times and the hard times of life. She discerned her call in May 1989 and attended seminary from September 1989 to December 1997.

Gloria is currently the lead pastor of Camphor Memorial UMC (formerly in the Central Jurisdictional Conference) in St. Paul, Minnesota. Prior to her appointment to Camphor church she was associate pastor at Brooklyn UMC (a cross-racial appointment) in Brooklyn Center, Minnesota. In addition to her pastorate, Gloria is appointed as professor at the University of Minnesota in the mortuary science department. She teaches [classes in] death, dying, and bereavement across cultures to mortuary students.

As she looks back over her life and sees where she has come from, she lifts her voice, and cries out, "Thank God for how I got over!!!!!" Gloria says of her ministry, "God has sustained me and has brought me from a mighty long way."[2]

Elizabeth Ann Lopez

First Hispanic/Latina Woman to Serve in Full Connection

(See chapter 6, 137)

NORTHERN ILLINOIS ANNUAL CONFERENCE

Constance Hasentab Elmes

Barbara C. McEwing

(EUROPEAN AMERICAN)

First Woman to Be Received into Full Connection in the Former Rock River Conference

Ordained Deacon – 1926
Ordained Elder – 1930
Received on Trial – 1957
Received into Full Connection – 1959
Deceased – 1969

CONSTANCE HASENTAB ELMES was born March 22, 1902.

In the early 1920's [Constance] began work with the deaf as an assistant to her father, the Rev. Philip Hasentab. He was the first Methodist missionary to the deaf in America, founding this work in the Midwest in 1893, with a five-state circuit [Indiana, Ohio, Kentucky, Missouri, and Illinois]. At first on horseback, later by day coach, he became a nationally known deaf preacher, and–having no sons to assist and carry on his work–he accepted the help of his daughter, Constance. She had begun pre-medical studies at the University of Chicago, intending to become a medical missionary to China. As a result of studies in sociology, she became aware of a vocation to the deaf as a culturally and linguistically isolated group in real need of missionary outreach. Having complete command of the sign language, as a child of deaf parents, she decided that the deaf were "*her* people" and began studies at the University of Chicago theological school, qualifying for full ordination in 1930. [After the death of her father] she assumed complete charge of the Chicago congregation, as well as editorship of the newspaper for the Methodist Deaf, *The Silent Herald*."[3]

Constance reflected on her ministry with the deaf on the occasion of the centennial celebration of the Rock River Conference. Her love for the people is abundantly evident. She writes: "They were singing with their hands with rhythmic gestures as their hands moved in unison. Here was rhythm without tones. Emotion and beauty without sound. Spirituality expressed in gestures. Pointing upward with reverence they sang of God and Heaven. Marking the nailprints in His Hands they sang of Jesus."[4]

Constance served the Chicago Mission for the Deaf until her death on July 12, 1969, at age sixty-seven.

(AFRICAN AMERICAN)

First Woman to Be Received into Full Connection in the Former Lexington Conference, Methodist Church, Central Jurisdiction
First to Serve in the Former Rock River Conference

Received on Trial – 1961
Ordained Deacon – 1961
Received into Full Connection – 1963
Ordained Elder – 1963
Transferred to Rock River – 1964
Deceased – 1981

BARBARA C. MCEWING was born August 3. "Her call to the ministry was influenced by her mother who is a devout Christian.... During her teen years, Barbara was a member of Youth for Christ. She did extensive mission work, visiting those confined in various institutions."

She was a graduate of DePaul University and Northern Baptist Theological Seminary and obtained several degrees, including a teaching degree and many honorary degrees. Barbara labored tirelessly to extend God's teachings and never allowed her gifts to falter.

Barbara served churches in Indianapolis, Indiana; Springfield, Ohio; and St. Paul in Robbins in the Lexington Conference. In 1964, she transferred to the Rock River Conference and served Sherman in Evanston. Her final appointment was to Washington Heights in Chicago, where she served until her death.[5] The Washington Heights church dedicated a stained-glass window in Barbara's memory.[6] Barbara McEwing died April 4, 1981.

America Tapia-Ruano

First Hispanic/Latina Woman to Be Received into Full Connection

Received on Trial – 1977
Ordained Deacon – 1977
Received into Full Connection – 1980
Ordained Elder – 1980
Retired – 1988
Deceased – 1990

AMERICA TAPIA-RUANO was born December 19, 1917, in Cuba.

In 1961 America fled Cuba with her husband, Carlos, and their three daughters (America Pawlik, Carlin Tapia-Ruano, and Esther). The Reverend Carlos Tapia-Ruano was also under appointment in the Northern Illinois Conference from 1970 to 1988. Their presence as a Hispanic clergy couple in The United Methodist Church set them apart in both the Cuban community of Chicago and The United Methodist Church. They were outstanding immigrant-rights activists in the Greater Chicago area. Carlos, a onetime attorney in Cuba, served as president of the Cuban Bar Association and chairperson of the Spanish-speaking United Methodist clergy community in Chicago. America was an active member of the Northern Illinois Conference Board of Ordained Ministry in the 1980s, serving as the chairperson of the scholarships and loans committee.[7]

America served the Northlake UMC during the twelve years of her ministry in the NIC. America Tapia-Ruano died December 12, 1990, seven days short of her seventy-third birthday.

Adele Gonzales

First Filipina Woman to Serve in Full Connection in the Northern Illinois Conference and in the United States

Received into Full Connection – 1982 (On Transfer from the United Church of the Philippines)
Retired – 1993

ADELE GONZALES was born in the Philippines.

[Adele] is a graduate of the Divinity School of Silliman University in the Philippines.... She was ordained in the Philippines in the United Church of Christ. In 1970 she came to the United States and five years later completed her Clinical Pastoral Education under the auspices of the Chicago Temple....

[Adele] was presented to the Northern Illinois Conference (NIC) at the 1982 Annual Conference held in June at Northern Illinois University. "I am very thrilled and happy to have the privileges of a fully ordained minister of the Methodist Church," [she] said. "I would like to devote as much time and energy as possible to help in any way I can."

At the time she joined the NIC she was Chaplain of Bethany Methodist Terrace in Morton Grove, Illinois, a division of the Bethany Methodist Corporation, which encompasses the 206-bed Bethany Methodist Hospital, and the 265-resident Bethany Home for the Elderly. "I consider all the wonderful Terrace residents as part of one big family, [she] says. "Each person is a unique and beautiful individual whatever their age."[8]

Adele was appointed to Norwood Park United Methodist Church in Chicago in 1987 and served there until her retirement in 1993.

SungJa Lee Moon

First Korean Woman to Be Received into Full Connection

Received on Trial – 1988
Ordained Deacon – 1988
Received into Full Connection – 1990
Ordained Elder – 1990
Current Appointment – First UMC, Des Plaines, Illinois

SUNGJA LEE MOON was born October 16, 1949, in South Korea.

"I was born in Korea to a devoted Methodist family. My mother was the first woman to influence me about ministry; she taught me about the joy of serving the Lord. When I was working at my alma mater, Seoul Women's University, I happened to be appointed to serve as a supervisor for the Student Religious Organization in the University. I was responsible for planning the worship services, leading the Bible studies, and delivering the sermon to the college students. It was an exciting and rewarding experience and it gave me confidence that God was calling me to be in ministry. As I answered God's calling, my goal for my life changed from teaching in the university to serving the Lord in any way the Lord wanted me to do.

"In 1980, my husband and I came to the United States and both of us enrolled in seminary. While there, I was encouraged by many pastors to consider ordination–something I had never dreamed of. Up to then, I had never seen a woman pastor. I was fully recommended for ordination by the Board of Ordained Ministry in 1985. But due to the lack of available churches for ordained clergy in Northern Illinois Conference, the candidates who were fully recommended could not be ordained at the annual conference. The following year was exactly the same situation. I was deeply disappointed and frustrated about the process. I decided to take time off from the process to revisit my calling.

"My district superintendent, Rev. Donna Atkinson, visited me one day and asked me to return to the process. Without hesitation I said no. But she didn't give up on me. Her caring heart and encouraging words persuaded me to return to the process. It was an honor to be the first but I was also aware of my wonderful privilege to open the door for others, especially women, who are coming into ministry after me."

NORTH INDIANA ANNUAL CONFERENCE

Ellen Maria Studley

(EUROPEAN AMERICAN)
First Woman to Be Received into Full Connection in 1958

(See chapter 2, 42)

Michelle A. Cobb

First African American Woman to Be Received into Full Connection

Received on Trial – 1993
Orders Recognized – 1993
Received into Full Connection – 1995
Ordained Elder – 1995
Current Appointment – District Superintendent Lafayette District

MICHELLE A. COBB was born in Chicago, Illinois, in the 1950s.

"My journey into ordained ministry began when I was a young adult. I resigned from a teaching career in order to enroll in seminary as a lay professional. On the first day of classes I came in contact with a laywoman who talked about the ministry of the laity. I was convinced that I had found my niche in life–serving our Lord Jesus Christ as a lay religious professional. What I did not know then but have come to understand now is that my call has evolved, from lay worker in the local church to religious lay professional on staff at a local church to, finally, an ordained clergyperson. Overall, my ministry has been affirmed.

"I began a relationship with The United Methodist Church as a pastor from another denomination. My reason for uniting with The United Methodist Church was simple: as a single African American woman, I wanted to be free to pursue my call to the ordained ministry without the entanglement that a called or congregational system would possibly create. (I have since discovered that The United Methodist Church is not perfect.)

"The quote that best describes my ministry journey comes from a sign that was on the lawn of a United Methodist church in Evanston, Illinois. I passed the church returning home from my first day of seminary classes. It read: 'A sure sign of God's leading is that you end up where you didn't plan to go.'"

Juanita Arrieta Ramos

First Hispanic/Latina Woman to Be Received into Full Connection

Received on Trial – 1995
Ordained Deacon – 1995
Received into Full Connection – 1997
Ordained Elder – 1997
Current Appointment – Hyde Park UMC, Hammond, Indiana

JUANITA ARRIETA RAMOS was born August 19, 1960, in Monterey, Nuevo León, Mexico.

"When I began to attend John Wesley Seminary, my first goal was to study theology. In my second year I was assigned as assistant to a pastor and I began to feel called to the entire ministry. But ministry in Mexico is always difficult for women; they are always assigned to be an assistant to the pastor.

"I met my husband, Oscar, and we got married while we were still students and in 1990 we were invited to come to the United States as missionary workers for eight weeks during the summer. The next summer we were invited back and at the end of the summer we were asked if we would like to come to the United States to study. The district supported us both through seminary. It was like a miracle. After we finished seminary, we decided to stay in the United States.

"During the early years of ministry, when I was serving as copastor with my husband, it was a struggle because Hispanic people are used to seeing a male as the pastor. But over the years it has gotten easier as I have been accepted as a pastor on my own. I work especially with Hispanic women, trying to help them see that there is a place for women at all levels of the church. I am praying and asking God to help me help the Hispanic women I work with to realize how much they are really capable of doing."

SOUTH INDIANA ANNUAL CONFERENCE

 *Sandra Frances Hoke*

 *Vanessa Allen Brown*

(EUROPEAN AMERICAN)
First Woman to Be Received into Full Connection

Received on Trial, Western North Carolina – 1966
Ordained Deacon, Western North Carolina – 1966
Received into Full Connection – 1969
Ordained Elder – 1969
Deceased – 2005

SANDRA FRANCES HOKE, better known as "Sandy," was born August 14, 1939, in Williamsburg, Kentucky. Sandy graduated from Charlotte Central High School, where she was noted for her artwork as well as for her academic skills. She attended the University of Utah for two years, majoring in architecture and mathematics, then transferred to the University of North Carolina at Chapel Hill. She graduated Phi Beta Kappa in 1962, with a double major in mathematics and religion. From UNC, she went on to Union Theological Seminary in New York City, where she earned the MDiv degree.

She was ordained deacon in 1966, the first woman ordained in the Western North Carolina conference, and served as assistant minister in the Burnt Hills Methodist Church in Burnt Hills, New York, in her intern year (1964–65). During her ministry Sandy served as associate minister at Fletcher Place United Methodist Church and Community Center in Indianapolis, Indiana; at the Smoky Hollow Neighborhood Ministry in Youngstown, Ohio; as the first woman pastor of the Parish of the Holy Covenant UMC in Chicago, Illinois; as visiting professor of church administration in 1978, and as an adjunct field education staff member for several years at Garrett-Evangelical Theological Seminary; as pastor of Edison Park UMC in Chicago, Illinois; as district superintendent of the Elgin District of the Northern Illinois Conference; as senior pastor of the First UMC in LaGrange, Illinois; and as senior pastor of Court Street UMC in Rockford, Illinois, a position she held until illness forced her to leave the active ministry.

Among other positions she held, Sandy also was elected as a delegate to Jurisdictional Conference and General Conference, and was a director of the General Board of Global Ministries and the General Board of Discipleship. Sandra Hoke died April 12, 2005, at age sixty-five.[9]

First African American Woman to Serve in Full Connection

Ordained Deacon, AMEZ Church – 1978
Ordained Elder, AMEZ Church – 1980
Transferred into Full Connection, South Indiana Conference – 1982
Current Appointment – Extension Ministries, Professor, University of Cincinnati; Part-time Pastor, York Street UMC, Cincinnati, Ohio (West Ohio Conference)

VANESSA ALLEN BROWN was born in New Bern, North Carolina.

"I was always active in my local church, Jones Chapel AME Zion Church. When I accepted Jesus into my life, I knew I had to be obedient to what I understood his will was for me. While a junior in college, I accepted a call into the ministry.

"I know I would have answered the question for this biographical statement entirely differently if it had been posed to me fifteen to twenty years ago. So, I tried to set my mind back to those years. I remember the discussions and arguments with fellow clergy and district superintendents on the role of women, and particularly black women, in the ordained ministry. I always felt 'they' did not know what to do with me. I always felt 'they' did not think I would ever be qualified or experienced enough.

"Today, I do not spend much time thinking about those days. I have moved so much closer to God and understand that people make decisions and formulate questions and concerns out of fear–fear that they will be left out or that the things they were taught about women and about black people since childhood could be wrong. Today, just as I struggled to do in the early years of my ministry, I look more to God for direction and acceptance as I continue to understand his call on my life."

Ida E. Easley

First African American Woman to Be Received into Full Connection

Received on Trial – 1984
Ordained Deacon – 1984
Received into Full Connection – 1987
Ordained Elder – 1987
Current Appointment – District Superintendent Rushville District

IDA E. EASLEY was born June 7, 1946, in Galax, Virginia.

"I first experienced my call when I was twelve years old at a youth retreat, although at the time I didn't know that it was a call. I did not know any woman ministers then. I went on to other things and it wasn't until I was in the midst of a divorce that I sought reassurance from God as to how I could be a faithful Christian as a single parent. I heard the call again and during that time I realized that it was a call to pastoral ministry. I went to my senior pastor to see if he would affirm my call–and he did! It was my first amazing moment.

"After I graduated from seminary and was ready for my first church, I received a letter from my D.S. saying that the town where they wanted to appoint me had a trailer park where the pastor was supposed to live. But the park did not want a single, black woman with a child (my son was eleven), and so they proposed putting a trailer out behind the church! I said, 'I don't think so' and refused the appointment.

"In many ways, my journey has been a struggle as I have tried to be patient with where people are but also feeling the need to speak prophetically and to say what needs to be said in a way people can hear it. I hear folks on the district say 'We've had our one woman, now we want a man.' I tell them that that is not the way it works. 'You have also had your one man.'

"Ministry is not a career choice; it is a call. Otherwise, women would never be able to put up with all that they've had to put up with."

Yvonne Cuenca Oropeza

First Hispanic/Latina Woman to Be Received into Full Connection

Received on Trial – 1985
Ordained Deacon – 1985
Received into Full Connection – 1988
Ordained Elder – 1988
Current Appointment – Extension Ministries, Clinical Pastoral Psychotherapist with HealthNet, Indianapolis, Indiana

YVONNE CUENCA OROPEZA was born in 1953 in San Jose, California. "My call to ministry came from the first days of my life when my mother, who was born and raised Roman Catholic, vowed to God that all of her children would be raised in the Methodist Church. She told me that God would never leave me and that the greatest thing a person could do is to serve the Lord full time."

Eventually, Yvonne signed on to the US-2 program and headed to Dayton, Ohio.

"This would be my home for the next four years. I worked with two local churches and with a wide variety of social service agencies. After my two-year term was up, I became involved with a volunteer chaplaincy program at Miami Valley Hospital. It was there that my specific call to pastoral counseling was born. The process of ordination was a natural progression; however, I never felt a call to preach. My first interview with a visiting committee from the Board of Ordained Ministry almost ended my call before it ever started. I shared with them my passion to specialize in counseling and therapy. They were concerned that I was too specific about how God would use me. I was told to 'spend time in the trenches' (i.e., local church) before I would ever be considered for an appointment beyond the local church. At my ordination as elder, I knelt as my bishop, superintendent, assistant to the bishop, and my husband 'laid hands' on me. When my husband came to the kneeling rail, he tripped and, with all of his weight, and hands forward, he (along with the other three men) pushed all their weight on my head. As I was fighting to lift up my head, the weight of their hands pressed my face into the veneer finish of the kneeling rail. The event became somewhat symbolic of the next fifteen years of pushing and pulling, of resistance and acceptance, of leaving and staying.

"Within my seventeen years of serving the church, I have found my niche in counseling. I finally made the total leap to go into private practice and eventually to my present position. I guess if I had a statement about my ministry thus far it would be to live out God's mission. It didn't seem like it would come together, and there are times even now when I wonder. But the bottom line is, my mother was right. God has been with me every step of the way."

In Suk Hong Peebles

First Korean Woman to Be Received into Full Connection

Received on Trial – 1991
Ordained Deacon – 1991
Received into Full Connection – 1996
Ordained Elder – 1996
Current Appointment – Clinton First UMC, Clinton, Indiana

IN SUK HONG PEEBLES was born February 20, 1959.

"I began my journey toward ordained ministry in 1986 during the World Methodist Religious Convocation in Louisville, Kentucky. I joined the U.S. Air Force on April 3, 1998, and I am currently a chaplain with the 183rd Fighter Wing in Springfield, Illinois, Air National Guard at the rank of captain.

"My journey has been like the little toy train and the little blue engine that could from the children's book, *The Little Engine That Could*. My little train stopped many a times, only to have the little blue engine show up at each stop and hitch me along up and down the mountain. I never was alone. God was always there in my journey. Moreover, God is good all the time."

WEST MICHIGAN ANNUAL CONFERENCE

Marjorie Swank Matthews

(EUROPEAN AMERICAN)
First Woman to Be Received into Full Connection
First Woman to Be Elected to the Episcopacy in 1980
Ordained Deacon – 1963
Ordained Elder – 1965
Received on Trial – 1968
Received into Full Connection – 1970
Retired – 1984
Deceased – 1986

MARJORIE SWANK MATTHEWS was born July 11, 1916, in Onaway, Michigan.

There was never any wavering in her elemental commitment to Christ and to the parish ministry. There were hard decisions along the way, obviously, and she never backed away from a tough decision or from the consequential demands they placed upon her. Early on I learned that she faced hardship and self-sacrifice with a chuckle or a low-keyed laugh, but never in tears and torment, complaining or blaming. Her life vibrations were always positive. "God did not give Marjorie the spirit of timidity, but of power, love and self-control."

From 1959, when she had her first appointment as a lay pastor, until she became a district superintendent in 1976, she served seven different parishes. Some of them were parishes that would try the soul and purpose of a saint, but she was never forced to move except by circumstances of schooling. The members of each parish she served wanted her to continue on with them when it became necessary for her to leave.

On September 1, 1976, Bishop Edsel Ammons became her bishop, and she served the rest of the Cabinet years under his leadership.... Recently, he said of her, "She was a woman with an indomitable spirit. She took on any job in the most gracious way with a capacity mentally and spiritually to overcome any and every difficulty. She had a tremendous grasp of the Church. She did her work in a manner that facilitated growth in other persons and challenged them to respond to life with generosity. I shall always cherish the memories that I have of working with her."[10]

And in 1980, Marjorie Matthews became the first female bishop not only in The United Methodist Church but in any denomination. Bishop Dwight Loder quotes Bishop William Cannon: "But now the election of Marjorie Matthews is a watershed in Ecclesiastical history. There is no other instance in the whole of Christiandom where a major world communion has opened its Episcopal ranks to a woman. By divine providence the United Methodist Church in this way has given validity to the New Testament claim: 'there is Jew or Greek, there is no longer slave or free, there is no longer male or female: for all of you are one in Christ Jesus'" (Gal. 3:28).[11]

Marjorie Swank Matthews died June 30, 1986, at age sixty-nine.

Joy Jittaun Moore

First African American Woman to Be Received into Full Connection

Received on Trial – 1989
Ordained Deacon – 1989
Received into Full Connection – 1991
Ordained Elder – 1991
Current Appointment – Extension Ministries, Assistant Professor of Preaching, Asbury Theological Seminary, Wilmore, Kentucky

JOY JITTAUN MOORE was born in Chicago, Illinois.

"My grandmother was ordained in the Baptist church and I began attending a community church when I was five years old where the pastor was a woman. When I was thirteen, in reading Isaiah 6, I responded, 'Here am I, Lord, send me. I'll go.' Of course, as a teenager, I realized that being a Holy Spirit-filled preacher would not make me popular in high school. So I immediately informed God he meant for me to teach, not preach. It took four years of teaching math, six years in campus ministry and seven years in the local church to understand God had been saying 'Teach preaching!'

"I seek to offer testimony about God that rehearses who we are as the community God is forming to be a people with whom he so evidently abides–that we bear witness to his glory to facilitate a glimpse of his kingdom so the world might know that the God of Israel, made known in the life, death, resurrection and ascension of Jesus of Nazareth, is the one and only Creator, Redeemer, and Sustainer of the universe. I aspire to remind others that God's action in history is not to provide simple principles for happiness, but to restore humanity to holiness that we might fulfill our created purpose to reflect the image of God. I seek to remind others that God has created this countercultural community called church that is diverse in participants but unified in participation. My commitment to the next generation of Christians is reflected in living out God's calling as a seminary professor, ordained Christian minister, and speaker around the world. Believing that God's justice and love are the sources of power vital to the tasks of human liberation and community formation, I hope to share the incarnation of God's power, understanding the world through the Word."

WEST OHIO ANNUAL CONFERENCE

Jane Ann Stoneburner Moore

(EUROPEAN AMERICAN)
First Woman to Be Received into Full Connection in 1958

(See chapter 2, 56)

Joethel Jeannette' Cooper Dicks

First African American Woman to Be Received into Full Connection

Received on Trial, North Georgia – 1977
Ordained Deacon, North Georgia – 1977
Received into Full Connection – 1980
Ordained Elder – 1980
Transferred to South Carolina – 1997
Current Appointment – Cumberland UMC, Florence, South Carolina

JOETHEL JEANNETTE' COOPER DICKS was born February 13, 1947, in Mullins, South Carolina, in the parsonage where her father was serving.

"I first began to experience my call during the 1974–75 school year, while teaching high school English and coaching cheerleading in a predominately white/Jewish community. The few blacks there were the precocious group and included future celebrities like Jasmine Guy and Ralph Abernathy, Jr. I experienced my call trying to articulate morals and values within an academic setting. I received my license to preach in April 1976 and entered seminary in August 1976.

"My ministry has been fulfilling but challenging every step of the way. I was the 'first' in every appointment in which I served. I was the first black woman in North Georgia going into elder's orders while working toward a PhD at Emory University. Out of the blue, I received a call from Bishop Loder from the West Ohio Conference and moved there. Here too I was a pioneer: the first black woman to be ordained in West Ohio; the first black woman to serve as an executive staff member of the West Ohio Conference Council on Ministries; the first black woman district superintendent to serve in the UMC (appointed by Bishop Ammons

to begin June 15, 1990); the first black woman to serve as senior pastor of a large cross-racial appointment; the first woman to serve all of the three other parishes in which I have served. I was the first black woman who was not a bishop to chair the North Central Jurisdiction Council on Ministries.

"I do believe in miracles, because God has performed many for me through this sometimes treacherous and lonesome valley."

Eunhae Kee

First Korean Woman to Be Received into Full Connection

Received on Trial – 1989
Ordained Deacon – 1989
Received into Full Connection – 1991
Ordained Elder – 1991
Disability Leave – 1993
Deceased – 1994

EUNHAE KEE was born March 11, 1953, in Seoul, South Korea.

"At the time, my father was a Presbyterian pastor in a country church and taught in a Bible college. I had excellent Sunday school teachers who told me exciting stories about the lives of the Bible characters and made me proud to be a Christian. I came to the United States in 1981 to study, accompanied by my son. While a student at Indiana University, I happened to be active in a Korean Methodist church on campus, consisting of students and their families. As I served as a volunteer Christian education director, I realized the joy of working for the people at church. So I started exploring the possibility of being in the ministry. I enrolled at United Theological Seminary, majoring in Christian education. I never dreamed of being a clergywoman; but with the encouragement of friends and professors, I began to seriously think, pray, and to explore the talents and grace that I could bring into the ministry.

"After ordination I was an associate pastor of Community United Methodist Church in Circleville. My experience was somewhat different and unexpected. It was a period of struggling, adjusting, and learning. In my first year under appointment, it occurred to me that I really needed time to test my skills and talents in a different parish and find out whether

I could function as a pastor. So far, my experience at Grand Rapids Calvary UMC has been good. I love the congregation, and I am pleased to be here and serve the people. I am excited about the potential that the congregation has and am looking forward to seeing its growth in coming years."[12]

Eunhae served for two more years at Grand Rapids, then served for a year-and-a half at Pomery UMC before taking disability leave. She died September 24, 1994, at age forty-one.

 *Linda Chamberlain Jones*

First Native American Woman to Be Received into Full Connection

Received on Trial – 1999
Ordained Deacon – 1999
Received into Full Connection – 2000
Ordained Elder – 2000
Current Appointment – Linden Community UMC, Columbus, Ohio

LINDA CHAMBERLAIN JONES was born in Knoxville, Tennessee.

"I first became involved in ministry in Tennessee–prison ministry, as a matter of fact. I decided to return to the University of Tennessee, where I graduated with a major in Greek. My husband, Jesse, and I moved to Columbus, Ohio, so that I could attend Ohio State University. During my years as a graduate student, I became very active in Native American groups but also felt the frustration of being both Indian and Christian. I felt a special burden for other Native American Christians like myself. It was here that I first felt the call to ordained ministry. I began the ordination process at the same time I began work on my dissertation in Latin paleography (on a Jesuit manuscript written about their mission work among the Illinois Indians in the St. Louis area). I also began taking classes at the Methodist Theological School in Ohio. It took me five years to complete both the dissertation and the course work in seminary. I had been working for the previous three to four years as a student with Native Americans at Linden UMC in Columbus, but after my ordination, I was appointed to another United Methodist congregation in Ohio. This congregation was not open to any kind of Native American ministry. I became very frustrated during this time and even contemplated leaving the ministry when I received a call asking if I would consider returning to Linden UMC in Columbus as their pastor. I returned in July 2001. However, I have been unable to regroup the original members of the Native American ministry and to my knowledge there is no such ministry within the West Ohio Conference.

"The journey of ministry has indeed been very difficult and often frustrating. Yet 'I can do all things through Christ who strengthens me.' I know without the Lord Jesus I would have thrown in the towel long ago. Yet I do have peace that I am where the Lord wants me to be for right now; and so I can say 'It is well with my soul.'"

WISCONSIN ANNUAL CONFERENCE

 *Chomingwen D. Pond*

 *Mary Council Austin*

(EUROPEAN AMERICAN)

First Woman to Be Received into Full Connection

Received on Trial – 1962
Ordained Deacon – 1962
Received into Full Connection – 1964
Ordained Elder – 1964
Retired – 1998

CHOMINGWEN D. POND was born September 1, 1927, in Madison, Wisconsin.

"It's been a great 'ride.' I worked in recreational clubs for the U.S. Army in Germany, which got me used to being one of a few women in an overwhelmingly male society. I was also part of a team ministry in the inner city and participated in the civil rights movement in the 1960s. In the mid-1970s, I taught in a black seminary, pastored small-town parishes and an Ojibwe church, and worked intermittently on a PhD for over eighteen years. I taught in African seminaries, first in Sierra Leone and then on the faculty of theology of Africa University in Zimbabwe. It was not always clear what the Good Lord had in mind! (And I was not always obedient when it was reasonably clear!)

"I suspect I have exemplified more than I have met the challenges of women moving into full clergy rights. So the courage has been on the part of the district superintendents and the congregations who were willing, however reluctantly, to take a chance on me. But perhaps just being there helped people get used to the idea and eventually accept the changes necessary.

"It has been years since I last heard the words, 'You're the first lady pastor I've ever seen.' I remember being the only woman in clergy meetings and being largely ignored. Then, perhaps because I was there, a few Roman Catholic sisters began to attend. Today clergywomen are common and active in such gatherings, often leading them. Today, I'm 'history.'"

First African American Woman to Be Received into Full Connection

Ordained Deacon, AMEZ Church – 1978
Ordained Elder, AMEZ Church – 1980
Transferred to Wisconsin UMC – 1981
Received into Full Connection – 1981
Current Appointment – Extension Ministries, Special Assistant to the President for Diversity, Marian College, Fond du Lac, Wisconsin

MARY COUNCIL AUSTIN was born January 4, 1953, in Wilson, North Carolina.

"My grandmother and mother were born into the Missionary Baptist tradition. From this cradle of care, they grew up with clear lines drawn in the sand regarding what the appropriate and acceptable roles were for women in the church. My mother and father accepted the call to preach at the same time. The local Free Will Baptist church embraced my father and set up a hearing to determine the validity of his call. Before too long, my dad was affirmed and certified as a candidate by our church family. My mother stood before the same group and was denied a hearing. My father decided that the whole family should withdraw from this church and unite with the AMEZ Church. [My mother eventually became] one of the first women ordained in the Cape Fear Conference of the AMEZ Church.

"Watching the lives of these 'women of thunder' from the sidelines, I made up my mind that the last thing I wanted to do was to answer the call to ordained ministry. During my freshman year of college, I called my mother (who, at that time, was my pastor) to tell her I felt God was calling me to be a minister. Even before I could finish the statement, she said, 'You have to preach, don't you?' Fellow students, faculty, staff, and the college chaplain recognized what I tried so hard to deny."

After being ordained in the AMEZ Church and waiting two years for an appointment, Mary transferred her membership to the Wisconsin Conference where she had been serving on loan. She has served local churches, in the conference office, at the General Board of Church and Society, as director of the Wesley Foundation at Howard

University and in her current appointment as special assistant for diversity at Marian College.

Kyunglim Shin Lee

First Korean Woman to Be Received into Full Connection

Received on Trial – 1987
Ordained Deacon – 1987
Received into Full Connection – 1990
Ordained Elder – 1990
Current Appointment – Extension Ministries, Vice President for Church Relations and Student Development, Wesley Theological Seminary, Washington, DC

KYUNGLIM SHIN LEE was born November 12, 1953, in Pusan, South Korea. Kyunglim's journey to ministry began with her mother who was a refugee from North Korea. At the age of thirty-five, Kyunglim's mother was still childless, which, in her culture, brought great shame. Like Hannah in the Old Testament, she prayed that if she were given a child, she would dedicate the baby to God. She assumed God would give her a son to become a minister. Instead, a girl was born. Kyunglim had an ordinary childhood until she was a sophomore in high school, when she became ill. The doctors could do little except prepare her for death. She prayed that if she recovered, she would do the most valuable thing she could with her life.

Later she attended Methodist Theological Seminary in South Korea. It was here that she remembered her mother's prayers and felt that God had opened her eyes to see the great needs of people. As a traditional Korean woman, however, she decided that she could help best by assisting her husband in his ministry. To her surprise, a few years later, she was asked to serve as campus chaplain at Ewha Girls High School. She then traveled with her husband to Toledo, Ohio, for graduate studies. It was during this time that Kyunglim first felt a call to ordained ministry. It would be a number of years, however, before she would finally graduate from seminary and be ordained. She then relocated with her husband to the Baltimore-Washington Conference. Though the conference could not find an appointment for her, she was hired as dean of community life at Wesley Theological Seminary and today serves as vice president for church relations and student development.[13]

Notes

1. Information on Karen Vo-To appears on the Web site for the General Board of Global Ministries, UMC, http://gbgm-umc.org//who_we_are/_mp/print_version.cfm?id=694.
2. Information for this biography was provided by Gloria Roach Thomas. Since it was written in the third person, it has been presented in this way.
3. Information for this part of the biography is taken from Constance Elmes's memoir, written by her daughter Mrs. Joseph F. (Catherine) Kelbacher, published in the 1970 Journal of the Northern Illinois Conference, UMC, 299.
4. Donna Atkinson, "A Journey Just Begun," *The History of Clergy Women in Northern Illinois Conference* (original script 1980, updated in 1982), 2.
5. The above information is taken from an obituary appearing in the bulletin for Barbara McEwing's funeral on April 9, 1981.
6. Atkinson, "A Journey Just Begun," 4.
7. E-mail from Barbara Isaacs, chairperson of the Northern Illinois Conference Commission on Archives and History, to the author, April 4, 2005.
8. "Filipina Is 1st Asian Woman to Receive Conference of United Methodists Membership," *Philippine News: Chicago/Toronto Edition*, July 14-20, 1982.
9. Information for this biography was provided by Sandra Hoke's sister, Jane Hoke Bultman, May 8, 2005.
10. Information for this biography is taken from Marjorie Matthews's memoir, written by Bishop Dwight W. Loder, published in the 1987 Journal of the West Michigan Conference, UMC, 295-96.
11. Ibid., 294.
12. Information for this biography is taken from a report to the West Ohio Board of Ordained Ministry, 1990 (from statements made in the report, though there is no date attached), "Question 1. Personal History" and from Eunhee Kee's Pension Record provided by the West Ohio Conference, UMC.
13. Information for this biography was provided by the Wisconsin Annual Conference.

Chapter 8

First Women of the Western Jurisdiction to Receive Full Clergy Rights

THERE ARE EIGHT CONFERENCES IN THE WESTERN JURISDICTION WITH THIRTY-FIVE "FIRST" WOMEN. Eleven of the women, or 29 percent, are now deceased, and seven, or 21 percent, are retired. Seven women, or 21 percent, are serving local churches. Seven women–including one D.S.–or 15 percent, are serving in extension ministries, including two Resident Bishops. Two women are on Honorable Location, and one woman has withdrawn. Three of the women–Minerva G. Carcaño, Grace Weaver, and Carol Youngbird-Holt–are each the "first" in two different conferences in the Jurisdiction.

Twelve of these women, or 34 percent, are European/American. There are five African Americans, two Korean women, two Chinese women, five Japanese women, two Hispanic/Latina women, three Native Americans, one Filipina woman, one Pakistani woman, and two Tongan women. The Western Jurisdiction has the first Korean woman, the first Japanese woman, the first two Chinese women, the first Filipina woman received into full connection in the United States, the first Pakistani woman, the first Tongan woman, and the first Native American woman to be received into full connection in the UMC.

ALASKA MISSIONARY CONFERENCE

This Conference Does Not Receive Members at the Present Time

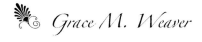 *Grace M. Weaver*

(EUROPEAN AMERICAN)
**First Woman in Full Connection to Serve in the Conference
While a Member of the Idaho Conference**

(See chapter 2, 35)

CALIFORNIA-NEVADA ANNUAL CONFERENCE

First Three Women to Be Received into Full Connection in 1958

(See chapter 2, 51, 52, 53)

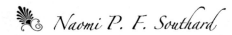

First Japanese Woman to Be Received into Full Connection in the Annual Conference and the UMC

Received on Trial – 1980
Ordained Deacon – 1980
Received into Full Connection – 1982
Ordained Elder – 1982
Current Appointment – Berkeley UMC, Berkeley, California

NAOMI P. F. SOUTHARD was born October 14, 1951, in San Francisco, California.

"I began my journey toward ordained ministry after beginning an MA degree in biblical studies at the Graduate Theological Union in 1975. After a year or so in that program, I began to explore the path to ordained ministry and, in 1978, switched to an MDiv degree at Harvard Divinity School, which I completed in 1980.

"From 1980 through 1982, I served as pastor of Lake Park United Methodist Church, Oakland, California. Then from 1982 through 1985, I was associate general secretary, General Commission on Christian Unity and Interreligious Concerns, New York City. In 1985 I was appointed as the executive director, National Federation of Asian American United Methodists in San Francisco, where I served until 1990. From 1991 through 1997 I was (part-time) administrative assistant to the secretary of the Council of Bishops, UMC. In this period, I also began a PhD program at the Graduate Theological Union, which I completed in 2004.

"The journey has been full of God's surprises. Most of my ministry has been 'beyond' the local church. Actually, I think it happened the 'right way'–this is a good time of life for me to be in pastoral ministry."

First Chinese Woman to Be Received into Full Connection
One of the First Two Chinese Women to Be Received into Full Connection in the UMC

Received on Trial – 1980
Ordained Deacon – 1980
Received into Full Connection – 1982
Ordained Elder – 1982
Retired – 2004

MOCHI LAM was born November 11, 1939, in Hong Kong.

"I heard the call in 1959 in Hong Kong and completed seminary in 1964 in Singapore. I served five years in Hong Kong as an associate and also as pastor. I served as a volunteer with the Ecumenical Institute for ten years.

"I came to the United States in 1972 and am grateful for the openness of the UMC. It accepted me as a foreign-trained pastor and later ordained and received me as a full member of the annual conference. During the twenty-five years of my ministry in the California-Nevada Conference, I have served three times as an associate pastor, and three times as pastor for bilingual, English, and Chinese congregations, in urban, suburban, rural, large, and small congregations. I love every one of them. They nurtured and challenged me to grow as the person I am today. It was interesting, enriching, and fulfilling. Each day I experienced the love and grace of God anew. It was a great ministry."

Although Mochi is retired, she is currently serving as a mission volunteer in Yunnan, China, through World Vision International. Along with Mamie Ko in the California-Pacific Conference, Mochi Lam is one of the first two Chinese women to be received into full connection in the UMC.

Dorothy Mae Williams

First African American Woman to Be Received into Full Connection

Received on Trial – 1982
Ordained Deacon – 1982
Received into Full Connection – 1985
Ordained Elder – 1985
Retired – 1992

DOROTHY MAE WILLIAMS was born October 23, 1925, in Houston, Texas.

"I began my journey toward ordained ministry in 1980. The call came as the result of a profound experience. I was engaged in a guided meditation, when, suddenly, I became aware of a small inner voice that said, 'There is nothing real in the world except love.' Inspired beyond my wildest imagination, I realized that this was a message I was being compelled to carry into the world. Hence my journey toward ordination began.

"My first appointment was to a cross-cultural setting. The people and I wanted to minister together and did not know how. In the five years as pastor and congregation we grew to love each other. Currently I am retired. Retirement, however, has not diminished my passion for the call to carry the message of love into the world. Presently, love weaves my life together with the lives of a wide range of persons. Through the founding of my own nonprofit organization, Spirit Weaving, Ltd., I serve as spiritual director to various pastors, seminarians, and laity. Also, I serve as a retreat leader and a counselor/mentor to women who are in recovery from drugs and alcohol.

"As St. John of the Cross proclaims, 'You [the Beloved] wake in my heart, where in secret You dwell alone; and in Your sweet breathing, filled with good and glory how tenderly You swell my heart with love.' This flame of love continues to lead me forward along the journey."

'Ana Moala Tiueti

First Tongan Woman to Be Received into Full Connection in the Conference and in the UMC

Received on Trial – 1990
Ordained Deacon – 1990
Received into Full Connection – 1992
Ordained Elder – 1992
Deceased – 2003

'ANA MOALA TIUETI was born November 1, 1953, in Tonga–the daughter of a pastor in the Free Wesleyan Church.

After she graduated from the University of Hawaii in 1984, she was preparing to return to Tonga. But many Tongans were coming to the U.S. for economic reasons, and she heard a call to help them adjust to their new culture and to a new Methodist system here....

As a teacher and immigration counselor, she led the way for Tongan women to be ordained into the UMC. ['Ana] was a mentor to many Tongan candidates for ministry and was a valued spiritual leader in that community and beyond. She was associate pastor for Tongan Ministries in San Bruno in 1998–90. Later she presided over a chartering ceremony for First Tongan UMC in San Bruno in 1990 and became its pastor through 1997. When she went to Hamilton UMC in San Francisco in 1997, many Tongans followed.

She had a quickly spreading cancer that had begun as a stomach tumor. Tongans had surrounded her in an earlier hospital stay in November 2003. Family and leaders of her church were with her at the time of passing. She enjoyed a pleasant Thanksgiving on November 27, but died the next day, Friday, November 28, 2003 [at age fifty].[1]

Carol Youngbird-Holt

First Native American Woman to Serve in Full Connection
Received into Full Connection in the Oregon-Idaho Conference in 2000

(See below, 185)

CALIFORNIA-PACIFIC ANNUAL CONFERENCE

 *Alice Weed*

 *Faith Joanne Conklin*

(EUROPEAN AMERICAN)
First Woman to Serve in Full Connection in the Former Southern California-Arizona Conference

Ordained Deacon, Szechwan Conference – 1940
Received into Full Connection, Costa Rica – (no date available)
Ordained Elder, Costa Rica – (no date available)
Transferred to Southern California-Arizona Conference – 1972
Deceased – 1992

ALICE WEED was born May 25, 1909, in Rye, Colorado. A missionary worked at Alice's church during her sophomore year in high school. "Alice was so stirred that she decided she would dedicate her life to try to meet those needs."[2] She resolved to spend her life in foreign lands.

At the end of her second year in seminary, Alice was told that she had been accepted as a missionary. Less than a week later, she left for China. "The first Annual Conference after [her] arrival in Kien Yang was a milestone. Alice, another missionary, and two Chinese were the first women to be ordained as deacons in Szechwan."[3] Alice spent ten years in ministry in China and then went to Costa Rica where she spent seventeen years.

She started her ministry in Costa Rica in the town of Ciudad Quesada. The pastor, who was American, indicated in no uncertain terms his disappointment in having a woman instead of a man as a co-worker. Alice was a fully ordained minister, but had to deal with the fact that women were not yet accepted readily among the ranks of the clergy.[4]

> She left Costa Rica to return to the United States as a pastor in Hispanic churches in Los Angeles.... But here in her own native land she met prejudice, even hostility, toward women in the clergy profession. The bishop reluctantly wrote to Costa Rica and learned that she had full clergy rights there. After three years of vague excuses, the Conference finally admitted her to full membership...the first woman to achieve such status in the Southern California-Arizona Conference.[5]
>
> She wrote, 'Each person living has a story to tell of the victories over difficulty and evil.... If this story of a life lived for a purpose can help someone realize the value of meeting obstacles, conquering defeats and discouragement, then it is worth writing.[6]

Alice Weed died June 7, 1992, at age eighty-three.[7]

(EUROPEAN AMERICAN)
First Woman to Be Received into Full Connection in the Former Southern California-Arizona Conference

Received on Trial – 1971
Ordained Deacon – 1971
Received into Full Connection – 1973
Ordained Elder – 1973
Current Appointment – Senior Pastor, Escondido First UMC, Escondido, California

FAITH JOANNE CONKLIN was born February 17, 1943, in Flushing, New York.

"My call was a gradual unfolding that began in my youth group. (I became a Methodist at fifteen after a journey through various churches.) The call was part of a sense of knowing I belonged in the church and partly a pulling forward at each step of the way. It culminated in a question at seminary when one of the deans asked me, 'Why aren't you getting ordained?' John [my husband] and I struggled with that question and what it would mean. (His sister was already in the ministry as was her husband.) John became the first nonclergy person to be married to a woman clergy in this conference.

"The bishop who ordained me didn't want to appoint women. So he placed me in the supernumerary category (for those mentally, physically, or emotionally unable to serve). That year I volunteered at two churches and had our first child. I was officially appointed to Church of the Good Shepherd as an associate and served from 1972 through 1974. I had my second child while serving there. I was appointed to Woodland Hills First UMC in 1976 as the first woman pastor in charge. I was appointed as the first woman superintendent in 1983 and served the San Diego District for six years. I was appointed to Whittier First UMC in 1989–the first time a woman was the senior pastor at a multiple-staff church. I served there for ten years. I am currently in my sixth year as the senior pastor of Escondido First UMC.

"My journey has been marked by a sense of deep joy and deep struggle. There have been, and still are, moments of 'amazing grace' and profound discouragement."

Mamie Ming Yan Ko

First Chinese Woman to Be Received into Full Connection
One of the First Two Chinese Women to Be Received into Full Connection in the UMC

Received On Trial – 1980
Ordained Deacon – 1980
Received into Full Connection – 1982
Ordained Elder – 1982
Current Appointment – Senior Pastor, Shepherd of the Hills UMC, Monterey Park, California

MAMIE MING YAN KO was born November 25 in Hong Kong. "In 1975, when I had almost finished my bachelor's degree, I started wondering whether I should be in the ordained ministry as a pastor of a local church. There were not too many women in ministry. I entered seminary in September 1976 and began my journey into the ordained ministry. I found myself being attracted to the ministries of the church, especially to preach.

"My ministry so far has been exciting, challenging, miraculous, and wonderful." Along with Mochi Lam in the California-Nevada Conference, Mamie Ko is one of the first two Chinese women to be received into full connection in the UMC.

Carmen Utzurrum Pak

First Filipina Woman to Be Received into Full Connection in the Conference and in the United States

Received on Trial – 1980
Ordained Deacon – 1980
Received into Full Connection – 1982
Ordained Elder – 1982
Retired – 1995

CARMEN UTZURRUM PAK was born March 13, 1926, in Dumaguete City, Philippines.

My original call was not to church-centered ministry–to spend my life professionally in the church–but rather to radical discipleship and a growing awareness of God's activity in what was happening around me as I was growing up. Then came the conviction that teaching was the area in which faith was made concrete: God caught my attention in and through my students. I loved teaching with every facet of my being. After I got married, my husband and I served in Hawaii as "home missionaries" and I assisted in the parish while bringing up two children. I remember Georgia Harkness's words to me "Don't forget who you are and what you can do, on your own. You are not simply Harry's wife and helper; you have your own unique gifts for ministry." A strong sacramental view of the church finally convinced me that I should be ordained.

The bishop at the time didn't think I should be ordained. He said, "I can't send you one place and Harry to another." I guess clergy couples were rather rare in those days.

Right down to the wire [Carmen] was asked, "What will you do with your children?" (Nathaniel and Marie [were] almost ready to graduate from high school.) "Are you sure this is what you want to do?" (Of course.) "You already have one ordained person in the family, why another?" (I want to expand the area of my ministry, to be able to serve the sacraments, to be more available.)[8]

And so, Carmen was finally ordained and served churches for several years in Hawaii. She also served on several conference boards and agencies before retiring from full-time ministry in 1995.

Colleen Kyung Seen Chun

First Korean Woman to Be Received into Full Connection in the Conference and the UMC

Received on Trial – 1979
Ordained Deacon – 1979
Received into Full Connection – 1983
Ordained Elder – 1983
Current Appointment – Senior Pastor, Trinity UMC, Pearl City, Hawaii

COLLEEN KYUNG SEEN CHUN was born March 15, 1949, in Honolulu, Hawaii.

"It was in church that I received my call at the age of thirteen. Reverend Harry Pak was leading the moments of prayer. During the silent prayer, I marveled at how precious life is and asked God what my purpose in life might be. There came a small voice within me telling me to look up. I did and saw Rev. Pak as he began to pray aloud. I knew God was asking me to be like Rev. Pak. The problem was that I didn't know if women could be ministers. Later, I asked my mother if women could be ministers. She thought about it and said she had never known one, so she believed women could not be ministers.

"Thus began a decade of floundering about trying to find myself. Was God so out of touch with humanity that God could direct me toward something that was impossible? Perhaps it was by God's hand that I was kept under the Methodist umbrella, because I graduated from the University of Puget Sound in 1971. Then came years of wandering as I lived in St. Louis and then in Idaho. When my sister suddenly died, leaving four children, I returned to Hawaii from my sojourn and joined Wahiawa United Methodist Church. There I learned it was possible to answer God's call.

"I returned to pastoral ministries in 2002 after seven years on family leave. In terms of firsts, I was the first single clergywoman to adopt three children. My favorite biblical passage is Mark 10:27, 'Jesus looked at them and said, "For mortals it is impossible, but not for God; for God all things are possible."' Through God, my life has been a miracle."

Miyeko Uriu

First Japanese Woman to Be Received into Full Connection in the Former Pacific-South Western Conference

Received on Trial, Troy Conference – 1976
Ordained Deacon, Troy Conference – 1976
Transferred to Pacific-South Western Conference – 1981
Received into Full Connection – 1983
Ordained Elder – 1983
Retired – 1989

MIYEKO URIU, known as Mickey, was born April 20, 1924, in Delano, California. She graduated from the University of Southern California with a bachelor of music degree in 1948. She studied organ at the American Conservatory of Music and did graduate work at the University of California. She taught school in California and was a church organist and director prior to attending Boston University School of Theology.

After being ordained deacon in the Troy Conference in 1976, Mickey completed her master of divinity degree at Boston University School of Theology and transferred to the Pacific-South Western Conference in 1981 where she served for a year as associate at St. Paul's in Oxnard. In 1982, she again was appointed to attend school. In 1983 she served Nozomi UMC in Santa Ana, and in 1984 was appointed to Chinese UMC in Los Angeles. Mickey retired from full-time ministry in 1989.

Mickey is married and has five children. Her interests include playing the organ, listening to serious music, coin collecting, and cooking.[9]

Beverly J. Shamana

First African American Woman to Be Received into Full Connection

Received on Trial – 1979
Ordained Deacon – 1979
Received into Full Connection – 1984
Ordained Elder – 1984
Current Appointment – Resident Bishop, San Francisco Area

BEVERLY J. SHAMANA was born November 4, 1939, in Los Angeles, California.

"I began my journey to ministry while serving as a staff member for the Commission on the Status and Role of Women in the annual conference during 1975–76 and while a member of the General Commission on the Status and Role of Women.

"The journey in ordained ministry has stretched me in ways I could have never imagined. What has been amazing is how God has resurrected and returned to me the many 'pasts' of my life that I thought were through wiggling. Now I use them in new ways that are fresh for me and useful to the church. Who would have thought? I give thanks for the gift of seeing the church universal from the perspective of the episcopal office and am renewed even when I am bone tired."

Cynthia Jean Abrams

First Native American Woman to Be Received into Full Connection

Received on Trial – 1993
Ordained Deacon – 1993
Received into Full Connection – 1995
Ordained Elder – 1995
Current Appointment – Extension Ministries, General Board of Church and Society, Director of Alcohol, Other Addictions, and Health Care Work Area

CYNTHIA JEAN ABRAMS was born October 11, 1960, in Buffalo, New York.

"I jokingly say that God's call was to drag me, kicking and screaming, digging my heels in, all the way into the ministry. I am a preacher's kid. So, as a teenager, being in the ministry didn't seem at all glamorous. In fact, I used to proclaim I would never marry a minister or be a minister. For most of my father's ministry, our family was fairly poor. As a teenager, I really disliked the church when I had to move to another high school for my junior and senior years when my father changed appointments, and then when we moved all the way across the country to California away from our extended families in New York.

"God began calling me through many people over an eight-year period in my twenties but I turned a deaf ear. But God has a way of never giving up on us, even when we don't listen. One day while at a meeting out of town, God got my attention in dramatic fashion: A woman came up to me in the lobby, sat down next to me, and said, 'Something told me to come over and sit down with you and let you know you should go into the ministry.' I trembled all the way home on the plane. I think it was the only way God could have gotten my attention. When I started my first semester of seminary at Claremont School of Theology, it felt like everything had fallen into place, just like a perfectly fitted glove. That's when I knew.

"Ministry hasn't been easy. I have had failures and successes. It is indeed a career and a call of blessings and sacrifices. Being an ethnic clergywoman is a unique path in life that has a way of humbling you. Sometimes I felt helpless and the only action I could take was to fall on my knees and turn to God to guide my path.

"I feel truly blessed to have been mentored by my mother, Melba, and wonderful clergy sisters Mamie Williams, Mary Elizabeth Moore, Linda Pickens Jones, Faith Conklin, Marilynn Huntington, Sharon Rhodes Wickett, and Bishop Mary Ann Swenson. Each of these strong women has inspired and nurtured me into ministry and I thank them for their continued support."

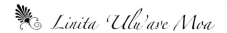 *Linita 'Ulu'ave Moa*

First Tongan Woman to Be Received into Full Connection

Received on Trial – 1998
Ordained Deacon – 1998
Received into Full Connection – 2003
Ordained Elder – 2003
Current Appointment – Ewa Beach UMC, Ewa Beach, Hawaii

LINITA 'ULU'AVE MOA was born November 14, 1962, in 'Eua, Tonga.

"I experienced my call in April 1993 while I was working at the Bank of Hawaii. One day, while eating lunch at a nearby Chinese restaurant, I met a homeless lady. She saw me reading the book *The Christian as Minister* and asked if I wanted to be a minister. At that moment I said to myself, 'This is the sort of question I was expecting from my minister or superintendent or bishop. Instead, in the midst of my struggle with my call it came from this homeless lady.' Saying yes to ministry was not easy. I felt that the word yes did not express adequately my willingness to say, 'Yes, here I am.'

"The person who most encouraged me in this journey was my mother. She was the person who introduced me to and walked with me in this journey of faith. She was a person of faith and commitment. Prayer and Bible study were regular habits, especially in the morning and in the evening before bedtime. From Monday through Sunday, she woke us up at five in the morning and again gathered us in the evening for Bible study and prayers. According to John Wesley's *Journal* this was one of the methods his mother Susanna used to teach her children the faith. John Wesley's theology and life, along with a deep knowledge of scripture, have been great gifts to me. I thank God for guidance and support every single moment in this journey helping me be one of his instruments in this world."

DESERT SOUTHWEST ANNUAL CONFERENCE

 *Beth Carey*

 *Tweedy Evelene Navarrete Sombrero*

(EUROPEAN AMERICAN)
First Woman to Be Received into Full Connection

Received on Trial, California-Pacific Conference – 1982
Ordained Deacon, California-Pacific Conference – 1982
Received into Full Connection – 1985
Ordained Elder – 1985
Honorable Location – 1994
Withdrew – 1998

BETH CAREY was born August 24, 1956, in Akron, Ohio.

"I experienced a call to the ministry while a college student active in campus ministry, in my local church and in my community.

"After graduating from Boston University School of Theology and serving nine years in parish ministry, I was granted a leave of absence in 1991 in order to step out of pastoral ministry and reflect on the integrity of my relationship with the church, particularly with regard to the itinerancy and The United Methodist Church's discriminatory exclusion of gay and lesbian clergy. I moved to Honorable Location status in 1994. In 1998, twenty-one years after answering the call to ministry, I accepted the call out of ordained ministry in the UMC and voluntarily surrendered my orders to the bishop.

"My current work is as director of client services for the Southern Arizona AIDS Foundation in Tucson, Arizona. Since leaving the church in 1991, my work has been in non-profit human service organizations working in areas related to homelessness, sexual violence, and HIV/AIDS. I am thankful for my long relationship with The United Methodist Church. Throughout the years, my soul was nurtured and my spirit strengthened. I continue my vocation now outside of the confinement of the UMC where I can be all that I am without discrimination and judgment–lesbian, feminist, activist, lover, partner, friend, daughter–whole, loved, and free."

First Native American Woman to Be Received into Full Connection in the Conference and the UMC

Received on Trial, New Mexico – 1985
Ordained Deacon, New Mexico – 1988
Received into Full Connection – 1992
Ordained Elder – 1992
Current Appointment – Winslow First UMC, Winslow, California; and Holbrook UMC, Holbrook, California

TWEEDY EVELENE NAVARRETE SOMBRERO was born December 22, 1953, in Red Lake, Arizona.

"I first began to experience my call in 1978. I knew in my heart that God was calling me to something bigger than myself. The more I experienced the church and its people, the more convinced I became of the calling. However, it wasn't until 1980 that I finally decided to pursue the ministry. It seems I had to climb a mountain in order to achieve the goals God had set out for me.

"The journey has been a long, hard road to travel but, for the most part, it has been worth it. Currently, I serve in a cross-cultural appointment in two towns near the Navajo reservation. There is a lot of racism in these towns. I have experienced racism inside as well as outside the church. My primary role is to educate people about Indian people and their life. My second role is spiritual leader, not only for the Navajos who have been discriminated against but also for the whites who don't realize that they rob themselves of a better way of life of love and Christ.

"It is funny how things come full circle. When I joined the church and decided to be a full-time minister, my family disowned me, kept me away from ceremonies, and held me apart at arm's length. The so-called 'Indian' Christians yelled at me and told me that I did not belong in their church because I wanted to continue to embrace my culture. And the so-called 'white' Christians said that I would not amount to much. Since then, my family has taken me back and has even embraced me. I am somebody in the church because of Christ Jesus. He died for me too. As I have always said, 'In the midst of my spirituality is my struggle and pain and in the midst of my struggle and pain is my spirituality. They cannot be separated.' One more thing I have learned on this journey, and that is that 'I'd rather stand with God against people than with people against God!' I have come full circle."

 *Minerva G. Carcaño*

First Hispanic/Latina Woman to Serve in Full Connection
Received into Full Connection in the Rio Grande Conference in 1980

Currently Serving as Resident Bishop Phoenix Area

(See chapter 6, 146)

Grace M. Weaver

(EUROPEAN AMERICAN)
First Woman to Be Received into Full Connection in the Former Idaho Conference in 1958

(See chapter 2, 35)

Ernestine Hitchcock

(EUROPEAN AMERICAN)
First Woman to Be Received into Full Connection in the Former Oregon Conference

Ordained Deacon – 1948
Ordained Elder – 1950
Received on Trial – 1958
Received into Full Connection – 1960
Voluntary Location – 1967
Honorable Location – 1977
Retired – 1982
Deceased – 1998

ERNESTINE HITCHCOCK was born April 11, 1917, in Portland, Oregon. Ernestine grew up in Montana and graduated from college with a double major in Christian education and sociology.

At the urging of the pastor of the church she then attended, Ernestine attended Scarritt College for Christian Workers in Nashville, Tennessee. While she was there, one of her professors pointed her toward the ministry. "She had had leanings in this direction even as a child but never really seriously considered it. It was just something that was not done. She had written sermons in her journal and rehearsed them as a child but it was a very private thing and not to be taken seriously."[10]

Although Ernestine was eventually ordained and received into full connection in the former Oregon Conference, she referred to the 1960s as an unpleasant time for women in the church. The Board of Ministry rejected a large number of women who felt a call to ministry.[11] The first church to which Ernestine was appointed was not prepared to have a woman minister. They brought charges against her; and though there was no truth to the charges, with no warning, Ernestine was left without an appointment at the next annual conference.

She did not appeal the decision at the time because she felt that she would not receive a fair hearing. It was not until Bishop Jack Tuell was assigned to the area that she finally appealed and was exonerated of the charges. She served one more small, rural church that was on the verge of closure. She said, "They did not think I could do any harm there."[12] She stayed only a short while and then left the ministry altogether.

Ernestine died February 9, 1998, at age eighty. "The brief obituary in the *Eugene Register Guard* did not mention that she was an ordained minister of the United Methodist Church even though she is listed in the Journal of the Oregon-Idaho Conference as a member of the clergy."[13]

Janice Kageta Haftorson

First Japanese Woman to Be Received into Full Connection

Received on Trial – 1986
Ordained Deacon – 1986
Received into Full Connection – 1991
Ordained Elder – 1991
Current Appointment – Extension Ministries, Village Christian Preschool, Sierra Vista, Arizona

JANICE KAGETA HAFTORSON was born July 26, 1958, in Auburn, California.

"I used to get *Campus Life*, a Christian magazine, when I was in high school. Once I saw an advertisement about mission work in the magazine that read 'Get Dirty for God.' So I wanted to be a missionary. However, my parents had different ideas for me. I enrolled at the University of California Berkeley as a French major. Three months before I graduated, I got down on my knees one Sunday morning and prayed, 'God, I don't want to be a French teacher and all other doors have been slammed in my face. Please help me! Give me an opening to talk to my pastor, if it is your will. If not, please don't let me make a fool of myself!' I went to church, but instead of my pastor, we had a guest speaker from San Francisco Theological Seminary speaking on the topic of missions. A light went on inside me that I thought had been long extinguished. When I got to the campus, I asked some of the other women, 'Are you going to become missionaries too?' 'No,' was the reply, 'we're going to become ministers.' And the rest is history.

"My journey has been rewarding and challenging,

fulfilling and unsatisfying. During one appointment, the staff-parish relations committee crushed my spirit. I left that church broken, reeling, and wounded. I was appointed to a small church in Portland, Oregon, and over the next seven years, healed and received healing from the local church. [My husband and I] adopted our first daughter from China in 1996. I said good-bye to the church and became a full-time mom. I've been struggling with my call to ministry ever since I left the church in June 1997. Some clergywomen may be disappointed that I am no longer serving the local church. Some ask me when I'm coming back. I am still searching for the balance and right now, and the scales are tipping toward my family."

Sandra D. Daniels

First African American Woman to Be Received into Full Connection

Received on Trial – 1989
Ordained Deacon – 1989
Received into Full Connection – 1991
Ordained Elder – 1991
Leave of Absence – 1995-1996
Served in California-Nevada – 1996-1997
Honorable Location – 1999

SANDRA D. DANIELS was born August 15, 1953, in Liberty, Texas.

"Around 1982 I knew I wanted to go back to school and work on a master's degree in computers. In 1983, while walking on the beach during a retreat, I heard God say, 'You're going to seminary.' I accepted. Upon returning home, I did a reality check with my friends and my pastor. Everyone was very affirming. By the summer [of 1984] I was off to Ohio where I attended United Theological Seminary.

"I served for about eight years in the Oregon-Idaho Conference. I was a trailblazer in every sense of the word—an African American woman in a predominantly white conference. I felt I did some good work in the churches I served, but I couldn't end racism and sexism and was considered a 'failure' (yes, I was told that) by the cabinet. I got tired of fighting the cabinet, took a leave of absence, and moved back to California. After two years I received a call and took an appointment in the California-Nevada Conference. The first church I served told the D.S. I had too much power as a pastor and they refused to work with me. I was placed in my first African American church as the first woman pastor but inherited a lot of problems created by the previous pastor and the D.S. The majority of the people wanted me to stay. They literally fought for me…but to no avail. With that I decided I was tired of fighting. I was tired of death threats, threats, and backstabbing and told God, 'I'm not closing the door to pastoring but I'm not going to actively seek an appointment. If I'm to serve, the position is going to have to come to me. I can't keep on fighting a senseless fight.' I'm currently on Honorable Location, living in California, have completed a master of arts degree in

counseling psychology and am working on a doctorate in psychology. I am also working on my hours to become a licensed marriage and family therapist. Currently, I am working for a domestic violence agency as a counseling intern. I also oversee the Batterers Intervention Program."

First Native American Woman to Be Received into Full Connection

Received on Trial – 1996
Ordained Deacon – 1996
Received into Full Connection – 2000
Ordained Elder – 2000
Deceased – 2003

CAROL YOUNGBIRD-HOLT was born October 3, 1949, in Bend, Oregon. Carol completed a master of social work degree in 1973 and worked as a counselor at Portland State University and at Willamette University. She was very active in her local United Methodist congregation, in the conference, and in church activities on the national and global levels. She was a delegate to the 1984 and 1992 General Conferences. She was also instrumental in building a coalition of delegates that helped elect persons of color to the episcopacy. She served as a member of the board of directors of United Methodist Communications, was on the Inter-faith Commission of the National Council of Churches, and was a delegate to the World Council of Churches General Assembly in Canberra, Australia, in 1991.

In the mid-1980s Carol answered a call to the ministry and graduated from Wesley Theological Seminary in Washington, DC, in 1987. Carol served the UMC in Toledo, Oregon, for four years before moving to Berkeley, California, to pursue a PhD at the Graduate Theological Union. She completed her course work in May 2003 and planned to begin work on her thesis in the fall. In July 2003 Carol accepted a one-fourth time appointment as pastor of the Round Valley UMC, the first fully credentialed Native American pastor in the 131-year history of the church. She served only five weeks before her untimely death due to complications arising from dehydration and a diabetes medication, on August 11, 2003, at age fifty-three.[14]

First Hispanic/Latina Woman to Serve in Full Connection
Received into Full Connection in the Rio Grande Conference in 1980
Served as District Superintendent from 2001 through 2004
Currently Serving as Resident Bishop Phoenix Area

(See chapter 6, 146)

PACIFIC NORTHWEST ANNUAL CONFERENCE

Ruth M. Lortz

(EUROPEAN AMERICAN)
First Woman to Be Received into Full Connection
Ordained Deacon – 1935
Ordained Elder – 1942
Received on Trial – 1957
Received into Full Connection – 1959
Retired – 1965
Deceased – 1985

RUTH M. LORTZ was born November 2, 1898, in Gypsum, Kansas.

It all began with my acceptance of Christ as my Savior at the age of thirteen years. On rainy days we children would often gather in the upstairs room and play Sunday school and church. We sang hymns and recited the memory verses and read some Bible stories....

One summer I found work in a large potato field, hoeing the weeds between the hills. At noon I went into a nearby woods to eat my lunch. During the time I was sitting and resting, I became aware of a voice within me saying, "I want you to preach the gospel." I remember protesting that it would be impossible to do that. I was without the means to prepare myself and besides that I didn't know any women preachers.

I never mentioned this experience to anyone. As time passed I kept remembering that voice.... One evening on my way to the rooming house where I was staying, I felt I could no longer fight the call I had heard. I said, "Yes, Lord, I will preach. I will go to Bible school and prepare." Two years later I graduated from The Northwest Training School for Deaconesses and Christian Workers. The Teachers in that School encouraged me to follow the Calling of the Lord. An opportunity came to attend Taylor University in Upland, Indiana, and work my way through School.[15]

Ruth graduated in June 1926 and returned to her home in Kennewick, Washington. She began to serve churches and eventually completed the conference course of study so that she could be ordained as a local deacon and elder, eventually becoming the first woman to be received into the conference as a full member. Ruth M. Lortz died July 3, 1985, at age eighty-six.[16]

Marilyn J. Littlejohn

First African American to Be Received into Full Connection
Received on Trial – 1977
Ordained Deacon – 1977
Received into Full Connection – 1981
Ordained Elder – 1981
Leave of Absence – 1984
Honorable Location – 1995

MARILYN J. LITTLEJOHN was received on trial and ordained a deacon in 1977, the first African American to have been ordained in the conference. She was appointed to attend school. In 1979, Marilyn was appointed as the associate pastor of Des Moines United Methodist Church in DesMoines, Washington. She was received into full connection and ordained an elder in 1981. In 1982 Marilyn was appointed to the Ridgefield UMC. After serving for two years, Marilyn took a leave of absence and went on Honorable Location in 1995.

Marilyn is currently active and involved in Seattle First UMC.[17]

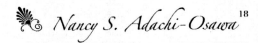
Nancy S. Adachi-Osawa [18]

First Japanese Woman to Be Received into Full Connection
Received on Trial – 1979
Ordained Deacon – 1979
Received into Full Connection – 1983
Ordained Elder – 1983
Retired – 1999

NANCY S. ADACHI-OSAWA was born April 7, 1936, in Seattle, Washington.

"In the early 1970s, while working as a medical social worker in a hospital in Doylestown, Pennsylvania, I developed an awareness that for maximum healing, it was important to be attentive to body, mind, and spirit. [Later] in my counseling ministry at a medical clinic, I noted that those who had a problem in their relationships with people also seemed to have a problem with their relationship with God. I found myself inadvertently counseling with them in this area. I then decided that, to do this with professional integrity, I should go back to school.

"On the intuitive level, I was feeling nudges from God to become an ordained minister. I went on a retreat to the ocean for personal reflection. When I returned, I consulted with my pastor as well as my family with what I felt was a call from God. I was now experiencing a desire to respond in a positive way. I received support from my community; so I decided to go back to school, complete my undergraduate degree, and then go on to seminary.

"My journey through theological school and ministry was both exhilarating and challenging. It was not easy to be a pioneer. I was among the first generation of Asian American women in the UMC to become ordained, and the first in my conference. Starting a new career in midlife was challenging enough. To find a place for myself in roles traditionally held by Euro-American males was not easy. To deal with the oppression of racism and sexism in the systems of school, church, and society was an added burden. My call was strong enough to sustain me in the struggles and hardships. I decided to become a local pastor instead of hospital chaplain because I wished to be in a position of dealing with the whole of persons' lives, not only in times of illness. Also I had the idea that the church could make an impact on society to reflect love, justice, and peace. My passion to help transform systems–within theological school, the UMC, and society–never ceased. I was willing to invest time and energy in this endeavor. When I retired in 1999, I figuratively 'passed the baton' to work for justice to younger generations."

ROCKY MOUNTAIN ANNUAL CONFERENCE

 *Frances W. Bigelow and Margaret Scheve*

(EUROPEAN AMERICAN)
First Two Women to Be Received into Full Connection in the Former Colorado Conference in 1958

(See chapter 2, 49, 50)

 *Christine Xavier*

First Pakistani Woman to Be Received into Full Connection in the Conference and the UMC

Received on Trial – 1982
Ordained Deacon – 1982
Received into Full Connection – 1985
Ordained Elder – 1985
Current Appointment – Pastor, United Methodist congregations in Springfield, Walsh, Two Buttes, Colorado

CHRISTINE XAVIER was received on trial and ordained a deacon in 1982 and was appointed to attend school in 1982 and 1983. She served Englewood UMC as associate pastor (three-fourths time) during 1983 and 1984. Christine then served as associate pastor at Parker UMC from 1984 through 1988. In 1988 she was appointed to Brush UMC and served there until 1992 when she was appointed to Lafayette UMC. Christine served Lafayette from 1992 through 1995 and was then appointed to Hygiene UMC, where she served until 2003 before moving to her current appointment.[19] Christine is the only Pakistani woman to be reported for this project.

 *Nobuko Miyake-Stoner*

First Japanese Woman to Serve in Full Connection

Received on Trial – Pacific Southwest – 1985
Ordained Deacon, Pacific Southwest – 1981
Received into Full Connection, Pacific Southwest – 1985
Ordained Elder, Pacific Southwest – 1985
Transferred to Rocky Mountain – 1992
Current Appointment – District Superintendent Metropolitan District

NOBUKO MIYAKE-STONER was born February 10, 1953, in Hiroshima, Japan.

"In 1978, when I was taking an internship in a United Methodist church in Kailua, Hawaii (as part of my master of religious education program at Iliff School of Theology), I sensed the Spirit of God guiding me to bring the good news to those who are silenced and disenfranchised by oppressive systems.

"In every appointment, I was the first foreign-born clergywoman ever. I experienced numerous challenges, being tested by the congregations. But equally powerful was the undergirding grace of God and the support and caring of people. Thus, my ministry is my grateful response to the goodness of God and to people who inspired me to discern God's unfailing presence on my journey."

Nobuko may be the first Japanese woman to serve as a district superintendent.

 *Edwina Madison Ward Burton*

First African American Woman to Be Received into Full Connection

Received on Trial – 1990
Ordained Deacon – 1990
Received into Full Connection – 1992
Ordained Elder – 1991
Retired – 1999

EDWINA MADISON WARD BURTON was born March 19, 1937, in Welch, West Virginia.

"I was born in the Methodist Church in the East Tennessee Conference of the Central Jurisdiction and grew up as an active participant in all of the activities of the church. I first felt called to the ministry when I was sixteen years old but did not know how or what to do to follow through.

"Upon graduation from Iliff School of Theology, I was appointed to Niwot UMC. I was the last person in my class to receive an appointment, but when the appointment was made, it was a good match. I stayed in that cross-racial appointment until I retired ten years later."

Youngsook Charlene Kang

First Korean Woman to Be Received into Full Connection

Received on Trial – 1991
Ordained Deacon – 1991
Received into Full Connection – 1993
Ordained Elder – 1993
Current Appointment – Extension Ministries, Deputy General Secretary, Mission Contexts and Relationships/Mission Education Units, General Board of Global Ministries

YOUNGSOOK CHARLENE KANG was born September 3, 1952, in Inchon, South Korea.

"I began to experience my call to ministry in August 1987 while attending an international United Methodist Clergywomen's Consultation in New Jersey. I sensed a call to ordained ministry, being empowered by the presence of over 1,000 clergywomen and seminary students. I felt the Spirit giving me an assurance that I was called to be part of the ordained ministry.

"My appointments have been cross-cultural. Serving predominantly white suburban congregations as a Korean American woman was a challenge. However, more difficult was to relate to the Korean American community as a woman clergy. I felt that I had to tread through serious roadblocks in order to work in a community where male leadership is more appreciated. However, in general, my ministry has been most fulfilling. I feel grateful that I have been able to contribute to making a difference at various levels of the church, including the annual conference, the jurisdiction, and the general church. Now I am grateful for the opportunity to serve the church and the global community through the General Board of Global Ministries.

"It took a tremendous amount of courage to keep going through hurdles and roadblocks. But trusting that it is God who moves us through history, both individual and community, I continue to take a step into the future with courage and boldness."

Lucia Guzman

First Hispanic/Latina Woman to Be Received into Full Connection

Received on Trial – 1989
Ordained Deacon – 1990
Received into Full Connection – 1992
Ordained Elder – 1992
Current Appointment – Extension Ministries, Executive Director of Agency for Human Rights and Community Relations, City and County of Denver, Colorado

LUCIA GUZMAN was born in 1945 in Katy, Texas, to a Mexican father and Mexican American mother, who were farm workers and railroad laborers.

"My call to ministry came at an early age, born out of the pain of witnessing the racial and other injustices toward my grandparents and parents. I knew it was not right under God. So I became fixed on righting wrongs to poor and undocumented men, women, and children. Because my father also worked for the railroad, he worked with many Japanese Americans and Jewish people who had been either interned in camps during World War II or had been discriminated against based on their race, culture, or national origin.

"My journey toward and through ministry has strong foundations in liberation theology. I have never compromised my prophetic witness. This has been true throughout seminary, my route to ordination, and my ministry. Parish ministry is a wonderful opportunity to walk with persons through their life journeys. But the ministry of presence, extension ministry, nontraditional ministry, and the public ministry in which I am currently involved place me at the crossroads of people's struggles with despair and hope. It continues to be my calling.

"I serve as an elected school board member of the Denver Public Schools where I constantly work on behalf of Latino and African American kids and families. I also continue to work as the executive director of the Agency For Human Rights and Community Relations for the City and County of Denver."

YELLOWSTONE ANNUAL CONFERENCE

 *Ellen Rose*

(EUROPEAN AMERICAN)

First Woman to Be Received into Full Connection in the Former Montana Conference in 1958

(See chapter 2, 54)

To date, the Yellowstone Conference has received no women of color in their conference.

Notes

1. Information for this biography is taken from 'Ana Tiueti's memoir, published in the 2004 Journal of the California-Nevada Conference, UMC, 266-67.
2. Evelyn Miller Berger, *This One Thing I Do* (Lima, OH: Fairway, 1983), 9.
3. Ibid., 104.
4. Ibid., 157-58.
5. Ibid., 172-73.
6. Ibid., 176.
7. Information for this biography was prepared by Gwen Jones-Lurvey, a member of the California-Pacific Conference.
8. Nadine W. Scott, "Methodist Minister's Wife Is Ordained," *Honolulu Star Bulletin*, July 19, 1980.
9. Information for this biography–including a description of Probationary Candidates and service records from the 1981 Journal of the Troy Conference, 620–is taken from material sent by the Troy Annual Conference, and service records from the California-Pacific Conference, provided by Nan Grissom Self, member of the California-Pacific Conference and the 50th Anniversary Task Force.
10. Undated interview with Ernestine Hitchcock by Janice Barclay, a member of the Oregon-Idaho Commission on Archives and History, UMC, 1.
11. Ibid., 1-2.
12. Ibid., 2.
13. Ibid, 4.
14. Information for this biography was taken from Carol Youngbird-Holt's memoir, written by her husband, John Youngbird-Holt, published in the 2004 Journal of the California-Nevada Conference, UMC, 269-70.
15. Ruth M. Lortz, "The Story of My Ministry in the Methodist Church" (from her manuscript, copied by Ruth L. Steach), 6.
16. Ibid., 6-9. See also "Northwest United Methodist," September 1985.
17. Marilyn Littlejohn's service record was provided by Wesley Stanton, member of the Pacific-Northwest Conference, UMC.
18. Formerly Nancy S. Yamasaki.
19. Christine Xavier's service record was provided by Kim James, member of the Rocky Mountain Conference, UMC.

Chapter 9

First Women of the Central Conferences to Receive Full Clergy Rights

GATHERING INFORMATION ON THE "FIRST" WOMEN OF THE CENTRAL CONFERENCES has been somewhat of a challenge. In the summer of 2004, the General Board of Higher Education and Ministry contacted all the bishops in the central conferences, seeking information on the "first" women in each of their annual conferences. Some of them replied relatively quickly while others were not able to gather the information until the spring of 2005. This has made it difficult to follow up with the women to obtain biographical information. In addition, some of the women do not speak and write English. The central conferences do not routinely publish memoirs for their deceased clergy, so there are no biographies for these first women for us to refer to. Efforts were made to contact as many women as possible and their stories are being told in this chapter. All the names that have been received are included here. However, it should be noted that all of the information provided has not been uniform; and there are instances where the location of the appointment has not been specified.

CENTRAL AND SOUTHERN EUROPE EPISCOPAL AREA

Due to unstable conditions in Central Europe during the mid- to late- 1950s, some of the early women in this episcopal area never had the opportunity to be ordained as elders. Therefore, in responding to the request for names of the first women to serve in full connection, Bishop Heinrich Bolleter noted, "To name the first ordained female elder of every annual conference only would not do justice to the very important role the ordained female deacons played in the church and the society."[1] Thus, I decided to include the names of both deacons and elders.

 *Ewa Dolej*

First Ordained Woman in the Poland Annual Conference

Date of Birth – April 16, 1901
Ordained Deacon – June 29, 1972
Deceased – January 4, 1987

 *Paula Mojzes*

First Ordained Woman in the Serbia-Montenegro/ Macedonia Provisional Annual Conference
First Woman in United Methodism to Be Appointed as District Superintendent

Ordained Deacon – September 1, 1957
Deceased – 1970

PAULA MOJZES was born January 18, 1906, in Magyarboly, Austria-Hungary (now Hungary).

> She was raised an Evangelical-Lutheran in the pietist branch of that church. From an early age (about 14 or 15) she went to evangelize in taverns, telling the men to stop drinking, go home to their families, repent of their sins, and accept Jesus Christ. She herself was "born again" at an early age. Later, she became dissatisfied with what she considered a too-worldly Lutheranism and joined several more Evangelical/Pietist denominations, until, finally, she found her permanent home in the Methodist Church.[2]
>
> While Reverend Georg Sebele was the District Superintendent of the Yugoslav Methodist provisional conference (not officially an annual conference because it was too small, but with two districts: north, Vojvodina; and south, Macedonia) he employed Paula Mojzes as the church secretary. Reverend Sebele was the only ordained minister in the north…. In the south there were five ordained ministers…. Paula Mojzes and a small group of women from both Vojvodina and Macedonia were called "church sisters" but they performed almost all the duties of an ordained minister except the sacraments…. When he [Rev. Georg Sebele] died suddenly in the fall of 1955, the church experienced its heaviest loss. Besides the loss of personal friendship, the death of a capable, almost irreplaceable leader in Yugoslavia, Rev. Georg Sebele [had] also created a problem of administration. The Bishop then appointed Mrs. Paula Mojzes to serve as the acting superintendent in addition to her duties as the secretary of the church administration. This she did until Bishop [Ferdinand] Sigg could come to the Annual Conference in 1957 to appoint pastor Krum Kalajlijev as the new superintendent of Yugoslav Methodism. Mrs. Mojzes was on that occasion ordained a deacon of the Methodist Church along with three men…. She was then appointed the supervising pastor of the Northern District.[3]

When she was ordained deacon, Paula Mojzes became the second woman in Central European Methodism to be ordained. "On several occasions [Paula] stated that she was doing the pastoral work only because there were no men to do it, and if there had been enough men she would have pulled back. She encouraged and trained both men and women for the ministry. Her motto was that she would do anything the Lord asked her to do."[4] She retired in the late 1960s and died in the winter of 1970 at age sixty-four.

 *Eleonore Meier*

First Woman to Be Ordained in the Switzerland/France Annual Conference

Date of Birth – September 16, 1932
Ordained Deacon – April 9, 1967
Deceased – April 24, 1996

Margarita Todorova

First Woman to Be Received into Full Connection in the Bulgaria Annual Conference

Received on Trial – 1998
Ordained Deacon – 1998
Received into Full Connection – 1999
Ordained Elder – 1999
Current Appointment – Shumen UMC, Shumen, Bulgaria

MARGARITA TODOROVA was born February 22, 1962.

"I never imagined that I would be a pastor. My greatest desire and constant prayer have been to serve God. In the late 1980s I had a dream in which God told me that everything was ready. I saw myself queuing up with a bunch of brides dressed in white, kneeling one after the other. When I looked more carefully, I noticed they were all men–I was the only woman. At the time I thought my dream meant these people represented the church, the Bride of Christ. So I connected the dream with the 'last days.' One day, without planning to, I asked my retired pastor (who had taken over the pulpit while the young pastor was on vacation) to let me preach. The moment I asked the question I was ready to kill myself for asking something like that. When he agreed without hesitation, I told myself, 'Now you've done it, haven't you? There is no way now to pull out. You'll have to preach.' Later I was approached and asked whether I would like to be trained for the ministry. I agreed.

"My ministry has been marked by both tremendous difficulties and great blessings. Some of the preachers and old, untrained pastors in the annual conference have found it difficult to accept a woman minister. One observed that he wouldn't mind accepting a woman minister, but 'why start with this one–she is too strong.' The reasons for the hardships I had to face were due partially to the strong patriarchal views in the Balkans and, to a great extent, to the older generation of untrained pastors and preachers who were afraid that younger, better-trained people would replace them. Much of the negativity toward me reflected this fear. Another difficulty I face is shared by women in ministry everywhere: I am expected to work much harder than male ministers. As for the many difficulties I have had to overcome, I don't like dwelling on them and let them pass."

Antonia Wladar

First Woman to Be Ordained in the Hungary Annual Conference in 1956
First Woman to Be Ordained in the Central European Conferences

(See chapter 2, 59)

Marta Buresova

First Woman to Be Ordained in the Czech Republic/Slovak Republic Annual Conference

Date of Birth – July 31, 1903
Ordained Deacon – October 7, 1962
Deceased – December 13, 1985

Helga Johanna Schwarzinger

First Woman to Be Ordained in the Austria Provisional Annual Conference

Date of Birth – August 3, 1954
Ordained Deacon – April 15, 1984
Current Appointment – Roman Catholic Church, Linz, Austria

EURO-ASIA EPISCOPAL AREA

 *Ludmila P. Garbuzova*

First Woman Received into Full Connection in Central Russia Annual Conference

Date of Birth – September 9, 1948
Received on Trial – 1995
Ordained Deacon – 1995
Received into Full Connection – 1998
Ordained Elder – 1998
Current Appointment – First UMC, Moscow ("The Singing Methodists")

 *Elena A. Stepanova*

One of First Two Women Received into Full Connection in the Eastern Russia-Central Asia Provisional Annual Conference

Received on Trial – 1995
Ordained Deacon – 1995
Received into Full Connection – 1998
Ordained Elder – 1998
Current Appointment – "Return to Christ" UMC, Ekaterinburg and chair of the Board of Ordained Ministry of Russian UMC Annual Conference

ELENA A. STEPANOVA was born August 24, 1956, in Sverdlovsk (now Ekaterinburg), Russia.

"I have been involved in ministry since 1992 as the local pastor of one UMC in Ekaterinburg, Russia. I was then ordained as deacon in 1995, and as elder in 1998. In 1992 the UMC in Russia was just two years old, and I was very much attracted by the church and the possibilities for ministry–especially prison ministry, which has been going since 1991.

"My ministry in the church has changed my life completely. I have several responsibilities in The Russian United Methodist Church–D.S. from 1996 through 2002; chair of the Board of Discipleship since 2002; and member of the Board of Directors of the General Board of Higher Education and Ministry (1996–2004). At present, I serve as a member of the Board of Directors of the General Board of Discipleship. I was a delegate to the 2004 General Conference, and also to the Central Conference of Northern Europe in 2001 and 2005."

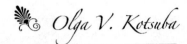 *Olga V. Kotsuba*

One of First Two Women Received into Full Connection in the Eastern Russia-Central Asia Provisional Annual Conference

Date of Birth – September 25, 1960
Received on Trial – 1995
Ordained Deacon – 1995
Received into Full Connection – 1998
Ordained Elder – 1998
Current Appointment – First UMC, Yekaterinburg, and District Superintendent Urals District

 *Nelya A. Mamonova*

One of First Two Women Received into Full Connection in the Northwest Russia Provisional Annual Conference

Date of Birth – March 9, 1952
Received on Trial – 1995
Ordained Deacon – 1995
Received into Full Connection – 1998
Ordained Elder – 1998
Current Appointment – First UMC Pskov, and District Superintendent West District

 *Oxana R. Petrova*

One of First Two Women Received into Full Connection in the Northwest Russia Provisional Annual Conference

Date of Birth – June 23, 1958
Received on Trial – 1995
Ordained Deacon – 1995
Received into Full Connection – 1998
Ordained Elder – 1998
Current Appointment – Trinity UMC, St. Petersburg

 *Irina Mitina*

**First Woman Received into Full Connection in the South
Russia-Ukraine-Moldova Provisional Conference**

Received into Full Connection – 2001
Ordained Elder – 2001
Current Appointment – Resurrection UMC, Voronezh, Russia

IRINA MITINA was born October 19, 1960, in Kursk, Russia.

"For thirty-three years I was an atheist. We were brought up to be atheists. After graduating from secondary school, I wanted to become an actress. But my mother strongly opposed the idea and insisted that I enter Voronezh State University to study foreign languages. When foreign delegations came to the university, I was invited to help with interpretation. In 1993 a group of Americans from Oklahoma visited Voronezh. They were Methodists. I interpreted the lectures in the evenings (I didn't know it at the time, but they were sermons). I heard about Christ and salvation. That was God's plan for me–to hear the gospel in English! I accepted Christ in my heart in 1993 at age thirty-three.

"I and five other people from the University started a Bible study group. The Bible was new to us. Every week we gathered to read the Bible and sing Christian songs in English. We learned these songs from our friends from Oklahoma. We didn't know any Christian songs in Russian. In 1994 three of us went to Oklahoma to study the fundamentals of Methodism at Oklahoma City University's Wimberly School of Religion.

"Upon my return to Voronezh, I started a Sunday school for children. Eventually, their parents came and we started worship services. In 1994 Vyacheskav Kim was appointed as pastor to our church. For two years I helped Vyacheskav. Then, in 1996, I was called by God to start another United Methodist congregation in Voronezh.

"Becoming a pastor was not an easy decision. I argued with God. I told him that I was only a woman. It was a painful decision, but God placed me in a situation that put me before a choice–leave the church or start a new one. I went to Moscow and talked to Bishop Ruediger Minor. I got his blessing and I started the Resurrection UMC with leukemia children and their parents. Barely three years after becoming a Christian, I became a lay pastor. I had no theological education and knew almost nothing about Methodism. However, one thing helped me: my heart was open to God, I felt loved by the Lord, I found meaning and joy in my life, and I wanted to share this joy with other people! I was ordained in May 2001 in Druzba at our central conference. I was ordained without having finished my seminary training. However, I completed seminary three years later in May 2004."

GERMANY EPISCOPAL AREA

First Woman to Be Received into Full Connection in the Former Northeastern Germany Annual Conference and in German Methodism

Received into Full Connection – 1959
Ordained Elder – 1959
Member of the North Indian Methodist Conference – 1964
Retired – 2001

HILDEGARD GRAMS was born November 28, 1920, in Schneidemühl, Germany. She finished the German *Abitur* (the highest school education that allows one to go to university) in 1939, but because of the war was unable to go for further studies. She did, however, do social work. When Berlin was bombed, she helped to build up her congregation–a Methodist Church. The minister asked her to become a *Gemeindehelferin* (church assistant). After some inner struggle, she became a church assistant in the Elim congregation in East Berlin. At the end of 1940, Hildegard heard a lecture by a missionary from China, who concluded with the question, "Who is ready to do such work in another land?" Upon receiving the call to be a missionary, she discussed it with several people, including Luise Scholz, president of the *Frauendienst* (Methodist women's association). Scholz recommended that she study at the seminary at Frankfurt-am-Main. Hildegard entered the seminary in 1950 as the only woman, along with fifty-six men. She studied there for two years, after which she went to England for three months to practice her English. In 1953, the German Methodist women's association sent her to Punjab in northern India and supported her financially.

In 1958, Hildegard returned to Germany for vacation and also to study further, since she wanted to organize a school for poor Indian girls to qualify them for teaching in nursery schools, children's homes, and other institutions. She studied for another two years in a special program for social education. However, because of the political situation, Hildegard was not allowed to return to India until 1964. In the years that followed, Hildegard fulfilled her vision of building a training school for hostel workers. She also directed a Methodist coeducational school in Batala, as well as a boarding school. She organized a system with

godmothers and godfathers for poor children to help them receive an education.

Hildegard Grams returned to Germany in 2001 and lives near Hanover, Germany.[5]

First Woman to Be Received into Full Connection in the East Germany Annual Conference

Date of Birth – March 24, 1943
Received into Full Connection – 1970 (There is no deacon's order in Germany)
Ordained Elder – 1970
Retired – Date not provided

First Woman to Be Received into Full Connection in the Former Southwest Germany Annual Conference (Since 2003: South Germany Annual Conference)

Date of Birth – March 24, 1944
Received into Full Connection – 1976
Ordained Elder – 1976
Current Appointment – Simmern, Germany

First Woman to Be Received into Full Connection in the North Germany Annual Conference

Received on Trial – 1965
Received into Full Connection – 1969
Ordained Elder – 1969
Current Appointment – Wuppertäl

CHRISTEL POHL GRUENEKE was born November 7, 1941, in Schoeppenfelde/Ostpreussen, Germany.

"I had worked for two years as an interpreter for English and Spanish on the Canary Islands (Spain). When I returned to Bremen in 1962, I was invited by a friend to join the Methodist youth group (I was Lutheran but not a Christian or an active member of that church). Three months later, during an evangelistic outreach, I experienced God and received Jesus Christ as Savior. Another three months later, I took part as delegate in a Methodist Youth Conference in London. Listening to a sermon I came to know that God was calling me to serve him in a full-time appointment in the church. I had no idea how this could happen. There were no clergywomen in The Methodist Church in Germany. But my local pastor and the president of the Women's Fellowship in Germany, Maria Wunderlich (she was the spouse of Bishop Wunderlich), encouraged me to start my studies in theology.

"My first appointment was as part of a pastoral team at Luebeck, where I was very well accepted. In 1977 I married Pastor Karl Heinz Grueneke, who had become a widower while serving First German United Methodist Church in Los Angeles. From 1977 to 1982 I worked with my husband at First German UMC in L.A. and in a German American congregation of the United Church of Christ in L.A. In 1982 we returned to Germany. In 1983 the second clergywoman was ordained, and many more followed. I experienced much encouragement from my church and my colleagues. For twenty years I served on the Board of Ordained Ministry of the North German Conference. From 1977 to 1997 I was a delegate to the Central Conference, and in 1996 to the General Conference in Denver, Colorado. My church has offered me many interesting challenges on my journey in ministry. But most of all I love my work in the local church. I am grateful for God's blessing. After thirteen years in Wuppertäl, I will retire in 2006."

Sabine Schober

First Woman to Be Received into Full Connection in the South Germany Annual Conference

Received on Trial – 1987
Received into Full Connection – 1989
Ordained Elder – 1989
Current Appointment – Pastoral Counselor

SABINE SCHOBER was born March 22, 1960, in Stuttgart, Germany.

"I was part of a Methodist church in Stuttgart since childhood. Growing up, I never saw a woman in the pulpit. That is why the calling of a clergywoman had never come to my mind, even though participating in the local church was a great pleasure and church played an important role in my life. I had one clear aim for my choice of career: I wanted to have contact with people in my job. I enrolled in theology and Latin at the University of Tübingen. During the first year at university, I became so fascinated with theology that I switched to theological studies.

"A clergy member of our church, Rev. R. Stahl, approached me several times asking if I could conceive of a ministry in the UMC. Toward the end of my studies I prayed a lot about this and talked to friends and my family. For me, the central question was this: Where does God need me? At the end of an intensive process of prayer and of seeking God's will, I was sure the Lord would accompany me on my way as a clergywoman in the UMC.

"The majority of the members of the congregation I served looked forward to my ministry. But there were some people who disapproved of me as a clergywoman, not as a person. They were convinced that women should not become ordained elders. Dealing with this opposition was not easy. Early on, I still believed I would be able to convince opponents of clergywomen through Bible lessons, arguments, and attention. But my efforts were unsuccessful. That was one of greatest and most painful disappointments in the first years of my professional life.

"After six years of ministry in a local church God gave me a wonderful opportunity: The leaders of my church asked me if I would be willing to set up the ministry of pastoral care in the Methodist Martha Maria Hospital at Nürnberg. I have been working full-time in pastoral care since 1993. So today I can honestly say I am in the right place in my church."

NORDIC AND BALTIC EPISCOPAL AREA

 *Charlotte Thaarup*

First Woman to Be Received into Full Connection in the Denmark Annual Conference

Received on Trial – 1979
Ordained Deacon – 1979
Received into Full Connection – 1981
Ordained Elder – 1981
Current Appointment – Copastor with husband, Jergen, at Strandby UMC, Strandby, Denmark

CHARLOTTE THAARUP was born June 21, 1956, in Denmark.

"Growing up in a loving and supporting family as the daughter of a minister (Fletcher Thaarup) in the Methodist Church in Denmark, I experienced how a young woman (Aase Johnsen) of our congregation began her way to ministry. She was taken in as a probationary member in the annual conference in 1967 but left the ministry before ordination. Looking back, I can see it made an influence on me as a little girl. It never crossed my mind that anyone might have anything to say against women in ministry. When I was fourteen years old, a schoolteacher asked the class if we had any idea what we would like to do for a living. Only a few answered. For the first time in my life I spoke out loud about being a pastor. In my late teens, I struggled with the call and with the struggles and conflicts I feared my response to the call would cause. But I carried on, became a lay preacher, and was accepted as a candidate for ordination.

"Of Denmark's 5.5 million inhabitants, almost 85 percent belong to the Evangelical Lutheran Church. The annual conference of the Danish UMC has 27 pastors serving 2,261 baptized members, with 1,293 in professing membership. We have no staff, and being a pastor is a challenge of one's skills. The most difficult challenge has been combining the duties of being a pastor of a very small church with responsibilities at the annual conference level. I share the leadership of the congregation with my husband and colleague, as well as a number of very gifted laypersons. The Sunday service, pastoral care, meditations, and silent retreats are my favorite fields in ministry. In 2004 we celebrated my twenty-fifth anniversary as a pastor in the Danish UMC. It has been a great time with a lot of work and joy."

 *Eila Orvokki Pimiä*

First Woman to Be Received into Full Connection in the Finland Finnish Provisional Conference

Received on Trial – 1958
Ordained Deacon – 1958
Received into Full Connection – 1961
Ordained Elder – 1961
Deceased – 2004

EILA ORVOKKI PIMIÄ was born May 1, 1927. During her ministry she served churches at Ylistaro, Joensuu, and Lahti. Eila Pimiä died April 15, 2004, at age seventy-six.

 *Kerstin Ekholm*

First Woman to Be Received into Full Connection in the Finland Swedish Provisional Conference

Received on Trial – 1965
Ordained Deacon –1965
Received into Full Connection – 1969
Ordained Elder – 1969

KERSTIN EKHOLM moved to Sweden and withdrew from the UMC.

 *Jorunn Wendel*

First Woman to Be Received into Full Connection in the Norway Annual Conference

Received on Trial – 1974
Ordained Deacon – 1974
Received into Full Connection – 1976
Ordained Elder – 1976
Current Appointment – Fredrikstad, Norway

JORUNN WENDEL was born April 5, 1943, in Halden, Norway.

"When I finished high school (called *Examen Artium* in Norway) in 1962, I felt it was the right thing to study theology and go into the ministry. But at that time I did not have the courage to be the first woman. Therefore, I started to study philology with the subjects Greek, Latin, and Knowledge of Christianity. After graduating as 'Cand mag,' I started working in high school, and did that for four years. It was the direct call from the church and my bishop that gave me courage to go into the ministry.

"The whole of my ministry has been in congregations, except the six years (1992–1998) as a district superintendent for the Eastern Norway District. I have had a very rich time as a minister and have not felt the need to be a teacher. I see my ministry as a way of teaching, especially through my sermons. When I moved to Bergen, however, it was quite hard, as I was the only female minister in the city. The local newspaper made a decision not to have anything to do with me. I had a lot of bad experiences there. But my bishop, Ole Borgen, and the congregation and others encouraged me not to give up. Now I consider it all as God's statement of his calling. In the beginning of 2006 I will have three months' sabbatical leave and will probably use the time to write my story. It might be of interest for my church."

Inese Budnika

First Woman to Be Received into Full Connection in the Latvia Annual Conference
Received on Trial – 2000
Ordained Deacon – 2000
Received into Full Connection – 2003
Ordained Elder – 2003
Current Appointment – Pastor, Liepaya and Kuldigas, and Youth Coordinator for the Annual Conference

INESE BUDNIKA was born November 1, 1974, in Riga, Latvia.

"My first training is as a music teacher. I graduated in 1995 from the Music College of Liepaja, Latvia. I had plans to continue my studies in the Music Academy of Latvia, but it wasn't God's plan of my life. During the summer of 1995 God worked with me very deeply and my life was changed. I decided not to continue my music studies because God had called me to study theology. The decision was not easy, because my music teachers were sure that I would be a very good music teacher and historian. I was a little bit confused, but God showed me the way. I enrolled in theological studies at the University of Latvia in 1995. Even though I did not receive an appointment the following year, I was sure I was in the right place. Two years later, I received a call to be a pastor and discussed my call with our bishop at the time, Hans Vaxby. We prayed together and he encouraged me to continue my studies.

"I was married in 1997. In the summer of 2004 God called my husband also to be a pastor. He enrolled at the Baltic Methodist Seminary. Now we feel we are real family. We have more time to spend together. God totally changed our lives. It is very important for the UMC in Latvia to have full families in ministry. There is a significant problem in our congregations. Our churches have lots of elderly people, children, and young people, but we miss persons between twenty-five and fifty years of age. This problem is rooted in Soviet times when people weren't allowed to go to church if they wanted to get a good education and a job. We see the results of such thinking today, as our churches are empty of people in this age group. I hope more and more families will join our congregations. I see our future in our young people. They are active in the congregations now and I hope it will be so in the future as well. There will be new families who are disciples of Jesus Christ. I think the UMC in Latvia is growing because God never makes mistakes. God has plans for The United Methodist Church in Latvia! And my family and I are like the pieces of a puzzle in God's wonderful picture of creation."

Maire Ivanova

One of the First Two Women Received into Full Connection in the Estonia Annual Conference
Received into Full Connection – 2005
Ordained Elder – 2005
Current Appointment – Estonian Fellowship of Evangelical Students, Tartu, Estonia

MAIRE IVANOVA was born February 28, 1978, in Pärnu, Estonia.

"God's call has been in my heart for several years. It probably started in the tenth grade, while studying history of philosophy and religious education, and doing a major project on the Jews in the Roman Empire. My call has not been dramatic but rather a silent conviction that God wants to use me. When I started my theological studies in 1996, first at Cliff College in England, and then at the University of Tartu in Estonia, there were no women clergy in Estonia. Nor did I expect anything to change in the near future. At that time, I thought it might take another twenty to twenty-five years before someone would step out to be the first brave one. Nevertheless, I took subjects necessary for practical church work. When my senior minister, Üllas Tankler, suggested I might consider going into ministry, the main obstacle was my doubt that I would be accepted as a woman in the church.

"During my time as a probationary member, I served in Pärnu as a youth minister. Pärnu has been my congregation since my childhood; so it took time to get used to a new role. The fact of a woman minister has not caused any major problems in my church. However, the 'identity crisis' has come up every year at annual conference, when the issue of women clergy is debated. I am at the beginning of my road with God, hoping and praying that God will guide me further. This is the only way any ministry can bear fruit."

Ele Paju

One of the First Two Women Received into Full Connection in the Estonia Annual Conference
Received into Full Connection – 2005
Ordained Elder – 2005
Current Appointment – Pastor, Voru, Estonia

PHILIPPINES-DAVAO EPISCOPAL AREA

 *Belen Sombilon*

First Woman to Be Received into Full Connection in the Northwest Mindanao Philippines Annual Conference

Date of Birth – December 15, 1965
Received into Full Connection – May 1991
Current Appointment – Local Church Pastor

 *Fernandita J. Miguel*

First Woman to Be Received into Full Connection in the Visayas Philippines Annual Conference

Date of Birth – June 12, 1959
Received into Full Connection – 1997
Currently on Leave of Absence

 *Erlincy Cayod-ong Rodriguez*

First Woman to Be Received into Full Connection in the East Mindanao Philippines Annual Conference

Ordained Deacon – 1993
Received into Full Connection – 1994
Ordained Elder – 1995
Current Appointment – Special Appointment to Community-Based Primary Health Care in the Compostela Valley

ERLINCY CAYOD-ONG RODRIGUEZ was born April 24, 1954, in Usocan, Plaridel, Misamis Occidental, Philippines.

"According to her mother, when Erlincy was ten months old, she was so ill that she was near death. Her mother promised God that if Erlincy survived, she would offer her to God. Miraculously, Erlincy survived!

"Never in her life did she dream that she would become a deaconess. Her desire was to become a missionary midwife. In fact, during their seniors' night in her fourth year in high school, she portrayed the role of a midwife in a play. After graduating from high school, however, she was sent to Harris Memorial College to be trained to become a deaconess. Erlincy was very hesitant because she felt she lacked the necessary talent. But she was obedient to her mother and

it was probably the Lord's will. After four years of studying at Harris Memorial College, she finished her course.

"On May 17, 1975, following the session of the Mindanao Annual Conference, she was assigned as a deaconess to Bantacan United Methodist Church, Bantacan, New Bataan, Davao, Philippines. No pastor was assigned to the church at that time, so Erlincy did the duties of a pastor. She baptized children, officiated at Holy Communion, and preached–all things a deaconess does not usually do. Bantacan was a remote village of New Bataan at that time.

"From 1978 through 1988, she was employed at the Department of Education as a public school elementary teacher. In 1989, she resigned the post, applied as a local pastor, and was accepted in the annual conference. Her calling was becoming intense and very much alive in her heart. She loves to work in the far-flung areas among the poorest of the poor. She is not only a deaconess, a pastor, and a teacher but also a committed community organizer.

"'Serving the Lord is not a bed of roses,' she says. There are frustrations, hardships, and obstacles but her love of the Lord and love for the people have moved her to go on with her journey in serving the Lord to the present. It is God who called her when He said, 'You have not chosen me but I have chosen you.' At every moment, God was directing her, preparing people and places. All she had to do was follow."[6]

 *Munda V. Dablo*

First Woman to Be Received into Full Connection in the Palawan Philippines Annual Conference

Date of Birth – June 24, 1959
Received into Full Connection – April 1999
Current Appointment – Local Church Pastor

 *Crispina Estaris*

 *Luzminda Pablo*

First Woman to Be Received into Full Connection in the Mindanao Philippines Annual Conference

Date of Birth – January 1, 1931
Received into Full Connection – 1972
Retired – Date not provided

First Woman to Be Received into Full Connection in the Southwest Philippines Annual Conference

Date of Birth – March 12, 1941
Received into Full Connection – 1988
Current Appointment – Local Church Pastor

PHILIPPINES-MANILA EPISCOPAL AREA

Paz Macaspac

First Woman to Be Received into Full Connection in the Pampango Philippines Annual Conference

Entered the Pastorate – 1957
Entered Itinerancy – 1973
Received into Full Connection – 1974
Retired – 1985

Cornelia Mauyao

First Woman to Be Received into Full Connection in the Middle Philippines Annual Conference
The First Filipina UMC Pastor to Be Ordained in the Philippines

Entered the Pastorate – 1961
Entered Itinerancy – 1967
Received into Full Connection – 1971
Retired – 1993
Deceased – 2004

Mila Bawan

First Woman to Be Received into Full Connection in the West Middle Philippines Annual Conference

Entered the Pastorate – 1963
Entered the Itinerancy – 1978
Received into Full Connection – 1979
Current Appointment – Faculty Member at Wesleyan University-Philippines, Cabanatuan City

Elizabeth S. Tapia

First Woman to Serve in Full Connection in the Bulacan Philippines Annual Conference

Ordained Deacon, California-Nevada – 1976
Entered the Itinerancy – 1977
Received into Full Connection, Middle Philippines – 1979
Ordained Elder, Middle Philippines – 1979
Current Appointment – Faculty Member, Bossey Institute, Geneva, Switzerland

ELIZABETH S. TAPIA was born April 19, 1950.

"I am a woman of color (from the Philippines) and my ministry is like a rainbow of colors, of different ways of service, touching different locations. A big portion of my ministry has been in the area of theological education and deaconess formation, now in ecumenical formation at Bossey Ecumenical Institute of the World Council of Churches, near Geneva, Switzerland. I experienced the call to ministry as I was completing my high school education. My journey as a deaconess, pastor, theologian, church organizer, and leadership developer has been very inspiring and challenging, amidst patriarchal and economic difficulties encountered along the way. But I can say I am very happy in the full-time ministry, and I feel I grow as each challenge and opportunity of service arises. It is a great privilege to be able to participate in God's mission today."

Minerva Amable

First Woman to Be Received into Full Connection in the Philippines Annual Conference East
Entered the Pastorate – 1993
Entered the Itinerancy – 1994
Received into Full Connection – 1999
Current Appointment – Associate Pastor of Angono UMC, Angono, Rizal, Philippines

 *Thelma Colorado Subramanian*

First Woman to Be Received into Full Connection in the Philippines Annual Conference

Received on Trial – 1973
Ordained Deacon – 1975
Received into Full Connection – 1977
Ordained Elder – 1980
Transferred to Iowa Conference, United States – 1991
Current Appointment – Riceville-McIntire UMC, Riceville, Iowa

THELMA COLORADO SUBRAMANIAN was born December 7, 1950, in Oriental Mindoro, Philippines.

"I am a pastor's kid and I lived and grew up in the church; the church is my community and my life. Members of the church believed I had some qualities for the ministry and began to pray and encourage me. A thousand times I said, 'I do not believe I am here for full-time ministry.' I had other plans for my future but I kept finding myself participating and seemed to have passion for church life and work, which I interpreted as God's way of calling me. When I responded and said yes to God's call, I was so afraid. Many others were scared, too, because I was the first woman to be ordained in the midst of clergymen in a patriarchal society. I persevered and prayed hard for my call because it is never easy to pioneer this new lifeline in the church.

"As the first woman clergyperson in the Philippines Annual Conference, I experienced rejection from many of the male clergy and church members. The real challenge came when I as appointed as associate pastor. I was treated unfairly. My salary was low compared with other associate pastors. I was not given the chance to administer the sacraments and made to feel second-class because I am a woman. One Sunday, Bishop Paul Locke Granadosin was the guest preacher in all the worship services. At the vespers worship service I put on the choir gown to sing with the choir. The bishop noticed it and asked, 'Why are you wearing a choir gown and not a ministerial gown?' I said, 'I am not allowed to celebrate the sacraments.' When the time came for celebrating Holy Communion, Bishop Granadosin told the congregation, 'I am inviting Pastor Thelma to join me in the celebration of Holy Communion. She is an ordained pastor of The United Methodist Church. She has the authority given by the Church and I am a witness to that. I was the one who ordained Pastor Thelma as an elder and nobody can take that away from her.' I cried and thanked the Lord for this liberation and freedom.

"In the Iowa Annual Conference, I have served several rural churches. Most members accepted me as I am, but there were those who resented my being a woman clergy and an ethnic person. One cannot survive the ministry as a woman ethnic clergy without the power of the Spirit. I could have given up a long time ago but the Lord kept telling me to keep going. Each trial became an opportunity to grow and I have become strong in the faith. I also learned to count my blessings and look at the glass as half full. I have learned to fight back with the truth. I also learned to choose my own battles. I may lose in one battle but I haven't lost the war."

PHILIPPINES-BAGUIO EPISCOPAL AREA

Rebecca G. J. Santiago

First Woman to Be Received into Full Connection in the Northern Philippines Annual Conference

Received into Full Connection – 1988
Current Appointment – John Wesley College, Tuguegarao City, Cagayan, Philippines

Aurea Talosig

First Woman to Be Received into Full Connection in the North Central Philippines Annual Conference

Received into Full Connection – 1991
Deceased – 2000

Luz Grospe Antonio

One of the First Two Women to Be Received into Full Connection in the Northeast Philippines Annual Conference

Received into Full Connection – 1985
Deceased – 2000

Luz Bungubong Dado

One of the First Two Women to Be Received into Full Connection in the Northeast Philippines Annual Conference

Received on Trial – 1983
Ordained Deacon – 1983
Received into Full Connection – 1985
Ordained Elder – 1985
Current Appointment – Person in Mission, Baguio Episcopal Area Ministry on Children and Poverty

LUZ BUNGUBONG DADO was born January 3, 1957, at Lamo, Dupax del Norte, Nueva Vizcaya, Philippines.

"During my third year in high school (1973) I often dreamed that I was teaching and that the setting was a church. That was also the time when decisions have to be made regarding what course a student will take after graduation from high school. I could not think of any course except the one that appeared in my dreams. So I decided to go to training school in 1976, which also appeared in my dreams.

"What a wonderful and amazing God we have! With words 'Come, follow me,' and 'Whom shall I send,' God quietly and gently called my name; and I responded with awe and a sense of responsibility. Jesus turned everything in me (John 20:11, 14, 16-17). With the nature of my work/ministry now, I have discovered what makes life work. Life works most perfectly when a shared love relationship is in place between God and me, and this, I believe, is also true for others. This does not guarantee an easy life or a life without suffering and trials. But when I seek and glorify God in all I do, God's love will carry me through any difficulty (1 Peter 5:6-7). I may not understand what God is doing in my life right now, but I know God loves me. With King David, I say, 'O God, you are my God' (Ps. 63:1)."

Lelita Pascua

First Woman to Be Received into Full Connection in the Central Luzon Philippines Annual Conference

Received into Full Connection – 1975
Current Appointment – UMC, Vargas, St. Ignacia, Tarlac (province), Philippines

Romana Olermo Madlangsakay

First Woman to Be Received into the Pangasinan Philippines Annual Conference

Received on Trial – 1992
Ordained Deacon – 1992
Received into Full Connection – 2005
Ordained Elder – 2005
Current Appointment – Burgos UMC, Poblacion, Pangasinan (province), Philippines

ROMANA OLERMO MADLANGSAKAY was born August 27, 1967, in Goyoden, province of Pangasinan, in the Philippines.

"I received my call to become a pastor when I saw the urgent need for leadership and the lack of workers of the gospel in our district. I became compassionate when I received Jesus as my personal Lord and Savior in 1986. I became more concerned about the spiritual needs of spiritually poor people in our district. Moreover, I discovered the perfect design of God for my life–to become a pastor and advocate for rights of women in God's ministry in the church.

"To become a pastor is a privilege. It is God's ordained grace for me. God called me into his ministry and I consider it the highest calling and service on earth. I am not after my personal glory and prestige. I am called to give glory to him alone and to be with him forever. My Lord Jesus is my perfect destiny. Because of Jesus I am willing to give up everything. He is the number one priority in my life. Nothing compares to my relationship with him. I have nothing to boast of, but I am very bold to say that I am a born-again believer and I am in love with Jesus."

(EUROPEAN AMERICAN)
First Woman to Be Received into Full Connection in the Northwest Philippines Annual Conference

Received on Trial, Kansas West, United States – 1964
Ordained Deacon, Kansas West, United States – 1964
Received into Full Connection – 1968
Ordained Elder – 1968
Transferred to Kansas East – 1971
Retired – 2001

JEAN MARIE GRABHER was born November 3, 1934, on her grandfather's farm near Paradise, Kansas.

"My first call to professional ministry in the church was at a senior high school camp. Because this was before ordination was an option for women, I felt called to overseas ministry in the field of Christian education. After serving there and in the Philippines, our family chose to remain in the United States. Serving as christian education director at Lowman UMC brought opportunities to do 'pastoral things' like preaching, calling, etc. It became clear that my talents were more as pastor than as Christian educator. I shall always be grateful to the persons at Lowman for allowing me a supportive community to make that change in direction in my ministry. I shall be grateful to Bishop Ernest Dixon for

pioneering by appointing me as a district superintendent when there were very few women clergy in The United Methodist Church in the United States. The year I was appointed, the number of women D.S.s grew from three to seven! Since retiring, I have served as interim pastor at five UM churches and began serving as interim for another beginning June 13, 2004. I am grateful to The United Methodist Church for providing support, challenge, and inspiration, especially in the areas of justice as well as openness to struggle."

First Filipina Woman to Be Received into Full Connection in the Northwest Philippines Annual Conference

Received on Trial – 1972
Ordained Deacon – 1974
Received into Full Connection – 1977
Ordained Elder – 1979
Retired – 2001

ROSALINA T. FRENDOL was born August 30, 1931, in San Manuel, Pangasinan, Philippines.

"It was March 1970 when I first experienced my call to the ministry. Before the service began, our pastor told the congregation of San Manuel United Methodist Church to attend the district conference, to be held at the United Methodist Church, San Nicolas, Pangasinan, especially those who would like to attend the district conference and apply as pastor. My husband asked me if I could make it and about my teaching appointment in the public school. I told him that God would take care of my plans. I believe God called me because I did not plan to be one among the workers in his vineyard.

"From 1970 to 1972 I served the UMC San Felipe, San Nicolas, Pangasinan. From 1972 to 1974 I attended Union Theological Seminary, Dasmarinas Cavite. In 1974 and 1975 I was appointed to the UMC Anulid, Alcala, Pangasinan. In 1983 I was assigned to UMC San Roque, San Manuel, Pangasinan but served UMC Labayug, Sison, Pangasinan. From 1984 to 1991 I served UMC Bantog, Asingan, Pangasinan, and in 1991 was appointed to UMC Villasis, Pangasinan. Then from 1992 to 2001 I served my home church of UMC San Manuel, Pangasinan. In 2001 I took mandatory retirement."

AFRICA CENTRAL CONFERENCES

 *Liatu J. Kane*

First Woman to Be Received into Full Connection in the Nigeria Annual Conference

Received on Trial – 1992
Ordained Deacon – 1995
Received into Full Connection – 1997
Ordained Elder – 1997
Currently Appointed to Attend School at Methodist Theological School in Ohio, Delaware, Ohio

LIATU J. KANE was born July 7, 1958, in Kwajji, a village in the northeastern part of Nigeria.

"I experienced my call into the pastoral ministry through a vision in 1982 while a student at the College of Education in Jalingo. I never understood that God was calling me to be a pastor. The fateful night God gave me a vision, I was asking him to show me what exactly he wanted me to do for him. God answered my prayers through the vision. However, it never occurred to me that the vision was, in fact, a calling and that I was going to spearhead the ministry of women in my church. In fact, I never believed women should be ordained.

"So in 1987 when I was handed an application form for seminary, I did not take it seriously. But the form haunted me. A voice continued to say, 'Fill out that form.' I decided to put God to the test, and in 1989 I went to the seminary. I was not convinced, but it was my way of testing God. God cleared my doubts in a very remarkable way. I graduated from the seminary fully convinced but did not know how my church would react to the fact of a woman being ordained. God has no incomplete plans. I was put on probation immediately following graduation in June 1992.

"Life and ministry as a pastor have been challenges, but in it all I see how God's gentle hand has been with me and continues to shape me for a better future. At first, it was not easy. I had to cope with pastoral work and at the same time be a mother and housewife in a culture where womanhood has secondary value. My late husband had to cope with the accusation of being weak and letting me 'control' him. People called us all kinds of names. Deep inside, my husband and I felt the direction of God; so his gentle presence was our comfort in the midst of all these challenges.

"Another big challenge was the fact that I had no role models with whom to share my struggles and who could encourage me. However, I always look forward to international travel. I was always eager to learn and experience how people–especially women leaders–went about ministry and solved their problems. Sharing their stories always renewed my spirit. Difficult as it might have seemed, ordained ministry has been the most satisfying and enjoyable experience of my life. Having a supportive husband by my side made it easier. Now, as a single woman and a widow, it is more challenging. However, the most reassuring reality that has become a part of me now is the fact that God, the Lord of the journey, is there with me and is in perfect control of every situation."

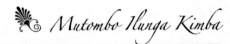 *Mutombo Ilunga Kimba*

First Woman to Be Received into Full Connection in the North Katanga Conference and the Entire Congo Area

Received on Trial – 1977
Ordained Deacon – 1977
Received into Full Connection – 1979
Ordained Elder – 1979
Current Appointment – Coordinator of United Methodist private schools; contact person for Volunteers in Mission Program, Pacific Northwest Conference, United States

MUTOMBO ILUNGA KIMBA was born June 4, 1955, in Kamina, Congo.

"When I was a young girl I was very active in my local church. I sang in the choir and was active in the youth group. In my fourth year in high school, I asked a question of one of our pastors, 'Is it possible for a woman to be a pastor?' He said it was possible but 'we don't have any in our country; but in America they do have women clergy.' Afterward, I kept asking the same question of different people. Many of them said that I was becoming crazy because they could not understand the reason for me to be interested in the ministry. But a very few people who very supportive of women did encourage me to go ahead and plan for it. It was not easy for me in this male-dominated society, but God remains God and when he calls, he does not care if you are a man or a woman. After I graduated from high school, I decided to go to seminary at Mulungwishi in the Congo. I told people who did not want me to go to seminary that I would take the entrance exam. If I failed the exam, then I would take that to mean God was not calling me into the ministry. However, if I passed, then I would say that that was where God wanted me to be and I would go.

"To my surprise, I passed the exam, and with the highest score! When it came time for me to go to Mulungwishi, some professors at the seminary said that it was not time for women yet. But Bishop Ngoi Kimba Wakadilo, director at the seminary at that time, told these professors, 'We must let this young lady come and study. God has said the time for women is now.' Finally, I was accepted and I went to study. Some of the professors said that if I did not do well in class, they would never accept another woman. So for me, being the first clergywoman was not an honor but a big responsibility. Today I am proud because there are many clergywomen in our country of Congo and in all our three episcopal areas in The United Methodist Church."

First Woman to Be Received into Full Connection in the Central Congo Conference

Received on Trial – 1981
Ordained Deacon – 1982
Received into Full Connection – 1983
Ordained Elder – 1983

"KOMBE ALUA was born September 22, 1955, in Wembo-Nyama. She attended the Institute of Higher Theology at Mulungwishi in Katanga from 1978 to 1981. She has served as senior pastor in several large parishes. She is president of the women pastors in the conference and represented the women pastors at meetings in Nairobi in 1986, in Liberia in 1988, and in Harare in 1989. She served as District Superintendent of Wembo-Nyama from 1993 through 1997. Kombe is married and is the mother of three boys and two girls."

First Woman to Be Received into the Southern Congo Conference

Received on Trial in 1983[7]

First Woman to Be Received into the West Angola Conference

Received into Full Connection – 1985
Current Appointment – Local Church Pastor

Notes

1. Bishop Heinrich Bolleter, letter to Dr. Marion Jackson, September 13, 2004.
2. Paul Mojzes, *A Short Biography of the Rev. Paula Mojzes* (Macedonia: United Methodist Church, 2004), 4.
3. Ibid., 6, 11.
4. Ibid., 18.
5. Information for this biography was provided by Ulrike Schuler in an e-mail to the author on December 19, 2005.
6. Information for this biography was sent by Erlincy Rodriguez, but since it was written in the third person, I have left it that way.
7. This woman's name was forwarded by Mutombo Illunga Kimba. She requested a biography but none was ever received.

Chapter 10

Claiming Our Bold Future

IN 2006 FIFTY YEARS WILL HAVE PASSED SINCE THE 1956 General Conference of The Methodist Church finally granted full clergy rights to women. Certainly the face of The United Methodist Church has not been the same since then. In many ways we have already begun living into that bold future we are anticipating. From the thirty women who served in 1956 as members of their annual conferences (along with the uncounted numbers of women who were then serving as supply pastors), the number of clergywomen has grown to over eighty-six hundred in 2002, serving at all levels—with 4,787 women serving in full connection.[1]

Every annual conference in the United States that receives members, with the exception of the Red Bird Missionary Conference, has women who have been received into full connection, as do a majority of the central conferences.[2] All of the annual conferences in the United States that have members, with the exception of the Yellowstone Conference, have had a least one woman of color in full membership.

Eleven years after the first woman was received on probation, one of those women—the Reverend Margaret Henrichsen—was appointed as the first district superintendent in American Methodism when she was appointed to the Bangor District of the Maine Annual Conference in 1967.[3] Even before that, however, there were women in the central conferences who had served in that capacity. The first woman who is known to have done so is Paula Mojzes from Yugoslavia. As mentioned earlier, while district superintendent of the Yugoslav Methodist Provisional Conference, the Reverend Georg Sebele employed Paula Mojzes as the church secretary. His sudden death in 1955 created a problem of administration. The bishop appointed Paula as acting superintendent, in addition to her duties as secretary.[4]

Paula Mojzes served in that capacity until the bishop was able to come for annual conference in 1957, when she was ordained as a deacon, along with three men.[5] Those were difficult and unstable times in Europe and they called for unusual—even bold—measures.

The first ordained woman in full connection to hold the position of district superintendent was Gusta Robinette, who spent her life in ministry as a missionary in the Far East—first in China and then in Sumatra in Indonesia. Gusta was ordained as a deacon in 1943 and as an elder in 1945. She became a probationary member of the Sumatra Conference in 1957 and a full member in 1959 when she was also appointed to serve as district superintendent of the Medan Chinese District in 1959 in Sumatra.[6] Since Margaret Henrichsen's appointment in Maine in 1967, many women have served and are currently serving as district superintendents as the biographies in this book indicate.

Then, twenty-five years after the historic 1956 decision, and twenty-one years after she became the first woman in the West Michigan Conference to be received on probation, Marjorie Swank Matthews became the first woman in post-Reformation history to be elected to the episcopacy, not only in the history of United Methodism but also in a major Protestant church.[7] She was elected by the North Central Jurisdiction and assigned to serve the Wisconsin area in 1980. In 1984, Leontine Turpeau Current Kelly became the first African American woman to be elected to the episcopacy in The United Methodist Church, when she was elected, not in the Southeastern Jurisdiction where she was serving but in the Western Jurisdiction. Judith Craig was elected in 1984 in the North Central Jurisdiction. In every quadrennium since, women have been elected to the episcopacy, bringing the total elected to twenty in 2004. This same year also saw the first Hispanic/Latina woman to be elected, with the election of Minerva G. Carcaño in the Western Jurisdiction. The year 2004 also witnessed the first Korean woman stepping forward in boldness to offer herself as a candidate for the episcopacy when Ha-Kyung Cho-Kim became a candidate in the Northeastern Jurisdiction. Then, in spring 2005, Rosemary Wenner was elected to the episcopacy in Germany, making her the first woman to be elected in the central conferences.

Women are now serving at all levels of the church—from small, rural churches to large-membership, urban churches. They serve not only as district superintendents but also as annual conference and general conference staff. Many women are serving in a variety of extension ministries.

With all these gains over the past fifty years, the question might well be asked, "What is there of the 'bold future' yet to be claimed?"

It is impossible to read the biographies in this book of the "first" clergywomen who had the courage to answer God's call without understanding that there is still much work to be done in claiming the bold future ahead. The pain that so many have openly expressed and the sacrifices that many clergywomen have had to make to answer their call are almost palpable at times.

Statistics for United Methodist clergywomen in 1992 show that nearly one-third of the clergywomen in full connection were not serving local churches. Some were on leave while others were serving in a variety of extension ministries. Staff from the Anna Howard Shaw Center at Boston University School of Theology began hearing remarks from clergywomen in the former Southern New England Conference that the number of clergywomen colleagues was diminishing. Thus, in 1993 the Shaw Center, with funding from the General Board of Higher Education and Ministry, launched The United Methodist Clergywomen Retention Study. The purpose of the study was "to identify reasons why large numbers of clergywomen were not serving local churches and to propose possible interventions by the connectional structure of the Church intended to retain clergywomen in the local church."[8] The findings of this study are informative for issues that are reflected in the biographies included in this book and that need to be addressed in order for United Methodist clergywomen to claim their bold future.

This study further notes the incredible amount of pain that many clergywomen have experienced in attempting to live out their call.[9] Chapter 1 of the study concludes with these words:

Hearing difficult voices is often hearing prophetic voices. The Church is both location of God's grace and a place of human responsibility, fallibility, and faith. Hearing the voices of clergywomen is not an ancient activity in the Church. Sometimes voices of clergymen have also been heard only as contradictions of the tradition or the dear status quo. Hearing openly and carefully voices of clergywomen offers an occasion for the Church itself to live more completely its vision of gracious, abundant life.

This is a vision for women and men, for children and adults, a vision for humans and the whole creation.[10]

Thus, part of claiming our bold future is not only having the courage to speak out boldly where that is required and to name the various "isms" that keep us from fulfilling the vision described above but also to be willing to listen with "bold" ears and not simply shut out those voices that we think are too painful to hear or with which we may not agree.

At the end of her book *The Leading Women*, in which Bishop Judith Craig chronicles the early stories of the then thirteen living women bishops, she also includes some open and forthright conversation eleven of the thirteen women bishops shared in January 2003. Interestingly, some of the comments address some of the same issues identified in the Clergywomen's Retention Study. Below, I draw on these comments, in conjunction with the study's findings, to describe some of the pain and frustration that is still evident as women at all levels boldly attempt to address issues facing not only clergywomen but the whole United Methodist Church today.

The Clergywomen Retention Study questionnaire and interview data show that

lack of support from the hierarchical system, being unable to maintain one's integrity in the system, rejection from congregations/parishioners, and the conflict of family and pastoral responsibilities are the major reasons clergywomen are leaving local church ministry.... Implicit in the questionnaire's phrase "lack of support from the hierarchical system" is the appointment system and process that are responsible for placing United Methodist clergy in local churches as well as in other positions. In the interviews the appointment system received an astounding proportion of negative comments (74%); such a large proportion indicates a negative experience with the appointment process, and subsequently, a distrust of the appointment system and its agents....The distrust among the United Methodist clergywomen in this study toward district superintendents, bishops, and cabinets as a whole has been the result of personal experiences with the system and its officials who have demonstrated a lack of support for clergywomen and their ministry. Women perceive a lack of support at the beginning of the appointment process when new appointments are made. Gender is made the defining factor in some cases where churches are being assigned women pastors.... A larger proportion of ethnic minority women are out of local church ministry than are white women, particularly among Black and Asian women. Particular attention must be paid to the reasons given by these women for leaving the local church.... Almost twice the proportion of ethnic minority women as white women list "lack of support from the hierarchical system" as their primary reason for leaving local church ministry.[11]

Bishop Charlene Kammerer and Bishop Susan Hassinger speak of their experiences in attempting to address some of these issues:

KAMMERER: I'm finding Vi's question and your

question just so painful, I think, because of what serving as an episcopal leader has cost me. The first system I needed to address as the new bishop in my conference was an informal system of appointment-making in which the large-membership churches call the shots and slip a list of preferred pastors to the bishop. Against generations of that system, I communicated to each district how we were going to do appointment-making and consultation. My cabinet and I have lived into that for six years now. Some of that has been at great cost as we treated churches and pastors equitably, bringing women up to senior pastorates, creating more opportunities for pastors of color in our conference, and working hard to create multicultural settings for people to serve in ministry.[12]

HASSINGER: I was reflecting on how my style of being prophetic is seldom through the spoken word. It has more often been expressed in action or in community. In terms of race, I have brought in required anti-racism training, as I know others of you have. I've been getting a lot of flack about that in the last several months. I've heard some say that it isn't the conference's issue, but rather the bishops' issue. But racism is growing in our country, and it's the right thing to do. So you go on. You try to build a critical mass for change in the climate. There were charges filed with the Religion and Race Commission, accusing me of racism, and charges filed with the college. Our cabinet will be six persons of color and four white. As that number of persons of color has grown—so that there is less white privilege within the cabinet itself— there have been cries among the clergy (primarily from white males) about being overlooked. Then there are cries about the appointment process because we have placed persons of color, men and women, in churches previously reserved for whites.[13]

We can certainly hope that with the presence of female bishops (among them women of color), along with a raised awareness of the issues of racism and white privilege in the twenty-first century, that the difficulties women—especially women of color—have faced in feeling a lack of support from their cabinets has already begun to change for the better and would continue to do so in the years ahead. But it is important to support our bishops and district superintendents—both female and male—when they speak out courageously on these issues and take bold steps to address them. Those in leadership positions may be the ones to address these issues, but if the church is going to change, it will take robust support from those of us in the trenches as well.

Even though the number of elected female bishops now stands at twenty-one, there are still issues of racism in episcopal elections. In the 2004 elections in the Southeastern Jurisdiction, even though two additional women were elected to the episcopacy, the Reverend Geraldine McClellan (first African American woman in full connection in Florida) "said racism was blatant at the conference, both in the balloting and in the way delegates interacted with each other." Dawn Hand, a lay delegate from Western North Carolina, said she does not like to make things into racial issues, but it is "painfully obvious it's not the will of this conference right now to support a Native-American person who is qualified, a black woman who is qualified."[14] It still remains for The United Methodist Church not to succumb to tokenism and quotas at any level of the church.

Another area addressed by the Clergywomen Retention Study arose in that body of women who had surrendered their credentials, as well as those who were no longer in local church ministry. "Among the women who had withdrawn from the ordination process or surrendered their credentials, few real differences (in some cases none at all) emerged between samples according to marital status, clergy partners, and ethnicity…. The only substantial difference was found among the women in committed relationships, in which 10% of those women had surrendered their credentials or withdrawn from ordained ministry."[15] There was also a noticeable difference in women who had identified themselves as being in committed relationships regarding where they were currently serving in ministry within the church.

> Analysis of the clergywomen who identified themselves in the questionnaire as being in a committed relationship and of their reasons for leaving local church ministry raises serious concerns. The proportion of women in committed relationships leaving the local church to follow a call to another ministry is lower than for the other groups. These women are more often found in other kinds of ministry; however, they are not necessarily leaving local church ministry because they feel called to another ministry situation. The primary reason they gave for leaving local church ministry was that they felt unable to maintain their integrity in the current system. Thirty-six percent of the women in committed relationships took this view.
>
> Some interview participants identified themselves as lesbian, so the overall study sample does include a lesbian population. However, given the design of the study, the size of that population cannot be quantified. Some women in the lesbian population in the study may have identified themselves with the committed relationship marital status category. For the women in committed relationships, then, the predominance of concerns over integrity in the reasons for leaving local church ministry may partially reflect the painful and controversial debate within The United Methodist Church regarding sexuality. "Unable to maintain my integrity in this system" can be interpreted as being unable to live authentically. All clergywomen are trying to live out their vocation in ordained ministry as authentic, whole human beings. Lesbian clergywomen may have a particularly difficult time living as authentic persons in a system that denies them that possibility.[16]

During the past decade it would seem that it is clergywomen who have courageously and boldly addressed the issue of gender preference in committed relationships within The United Methodist Church—Rosemary Denman, Jeanne Audrey Powers, Karen Dammann, and Beth Stroud, in particular. At least one of our "first" clergywomen has indicated this as the major reason for leaving the ordained ministry. Clergywomen choose different ways to live this out—some remain silent, others leave in order to "maintain their integrity," and still others have spoken out boldly.

COURAGEOUS PAST—BOLD FUTURE

Addressing issues of gender preference within annual conferences can be difficult to do in a fair and open manner. Bishop Hassinger continues her discussion of maintaining a prophetic stance within the conference:

> In another instance, a resolution came at the last annual conference to revitalize a congregation as open to gays, lesbians, bisexual and transgendered persons. Every month I get a variety of letters saying that that is wrong for me to have allowed the resolution to come on the floor, and threatening to take the matter to the judicial council. And that church is growing it's not huge–but it's clearly targeting a particular audience. I have not made any statements about where I am on that issue. But my job is to create a climate where those kinds of directions can happen, maintain that climate, and hope to stay self-differentiated enough not to break down in the face of reactivity.[17]

Regardless of which side of this issue any particular individual stands, this is clearly an issue in which there will continue to be dialogue in the years ahead. Being bold enough to name the issue *and* to work toward creating an atmosphere where open dialogue and discussion can be held so that all voices are able to be heard may be one of the most difficult issues clergywomen will face in the coming days–along with continuing to address the issues of sexism and racism in a church that often would prefer that the voices be silenced. Bishop Susan Morrison speaks to her struggle in the midst of those who would silence those voices:

> I can get really strong when I think the Council [of Bishops] has been silenced. I think we're not providing leadership. We're doing better than we ever have, but we're not providing the kind of leadership the Church needs, because the Church has silenced us. It has created an institutional ethos where people who speak out get beaten down and can't be authentic. I think that's also true with a lot of our clergy who aren't living inside what they're having to talk and be. In the end, I think the compromise helps folks lose the passion that they had at first. My struggle is to keep that passion when I feel as if it gets me in trouble. It may be my problem and how I deal with it. But it's been the biggest battle for me and obviously still is.[18]

Another development, addressed briefly in the study, may affect clergywomen and their role in the church. It has to do with the recent change in the "two-step" ordination system, which separates the tracks toward deacon's orders and elder's orders and creates a permanent order for these two forms of ministry.

> The new deacons' orders for ordination may also contribute to the disappearance of clergywomen from local church ministry. The new order potentially could provide a means for tracking women, particularly women with clergy and non-clergy partners, away from local church ministry. Another danger is that women who would prefer to be in local church ministry may seek deacons' orders because they are discouraged from entering an appointment system which appears unwilling to accommodate the challenges they present. Since the ordination changes have the potential to be

detrimental to clergywomen, the Church needs to be continually evaluating the effects these new changes in the appointment system are having on the presence of women elders in local church ministry.[19]

One final area addressed by the study that is important for the future of all clergywomen is the need for self-care and support in the process. It is easy to become so absorbed in meeting the needs of others in the local church or any other ministry setting that a pastor loses herself in the process. Therefore, establishing clear boundaries between, on the one hand, one's ministry with the local church, or whatever setting, in which a woman may serve and one's own needs for Sabbath rest and renewal, on the other, is crucial for clergywomen. One way to accomplish this is to establish a support network of clergywomen mentors, therapists, family members, or friends outside the church. This network needs to be nourished so that when a need arises, the clergywoman has a safe sanctuary to turn to for support and guidance. However, clergywomen also need to take responsibility for fostering this network and relationships if self-care is going to be an effective reality.[20]

Bishop Janice Huie addresses the importance of this kind of support within the circle of women bishops:

> There's something I treasure, something remarkable about this community gathered here and our sisters who are missing. I treasure each one of you. But I treasure all of us together even more. I think there is a sense in which each of us, though we may not know the particulars of the others' journey, know enough to know that nobody came here without paying a price, and that everyone continues to pay the price in her own way. There's a connection among us that's grace-filled and unique. I sometimes realize, you know, how quickly I get caught up in my own stuff. It is important to stay connected to one another.[21]

It is easy for any one of us to get caught up in "our own stuff" and fail to stay connected with the community that is our support when all is said and done. Bishop Sharon Rader, however, also points out the unique ability of women to cultivate that community and how important that is in surviving in the midst of answering the call. "I think that part of what women bring to the mix is the reliance on community and the hope for building a community that will continue to identify and nurture other people. I think men are acculturated to do it alone, and there's always the expectation that you're good enough, that you're going to be just fine. But it's different for women."[22]

At the same time, however, issues have sometimes arisen when women are placed in positions of authority over other clergywomen as district superintendents or bishops. In her article, "Honoring One Another with Our Stories: Authority and Mutual Ministry among United Methodist Clergywomen in the Last Decade of the Twentieth Century," Barbara Troxell observes that,

> several of the women recalled differences in attitudes, by some whom they considered friends, after they were elected or appointed to their position as bishop or superintendent. They tried to deal with such situations by

honestly confronting their own discomfort while holding to the awareness of their roles and offices. Their respect for the confidentiality of the cabinet came into conflict for some in their relationships with other clergywomen and clergymen.

One superintendent speaks appreciatively of the support given her by the other clergywomen of the conference, even as she has learned the difficult balance necessitated by her position.

There have been moments when I have felt there have been obstacles to nurturing friendship, partly because of the level and type of information I'm suddenly party to…. It's a continuing challenge to know how to shift the particular role that you are called to on any given day. Yet because it is important to me to be a friend, I do feel like it's possible…[though at times] it's really difficult.[23]

At the end of her article, Troxell comments further on the issue of the diversity of the clergywomen within The United Methodist Church–a fact that has certainly been reflected in the pages of this book. This diversity, however, which brings a great richness to the church, also presents its own problems.

As we move further into the new millennium, the diversity among clergywomen will only continue to grow. How, then, can we as ordained clergywomen address the differences and pain that exist among us in a way that is both authentic and that offers mutual support? One way is to take the time to listen to and honor each other's stories and to recognize the pain and sacrifice that many have experienced in order to survive the journey thus far. This book is one effort to begin to share these stories in a public arena. Further, it is important to remember how we came to be where we are today–having exercised our power for and on behalf of one another, while continuing to speak the truth in love and respect.

Part of the truth that must be spoken concerns a fresh exploration of the meaning of servant ministry and self-giving, as well as self-affirmation and empowerment. Jealousy and resentment of those who are in leadership is being felt among clergywomen. An apparent inability to hear others' stories without feeling threatened in one's own is evident. As one of the interviewees stated a year after the interview: "Surely I can make compassionate connections with the herstories out of which lack of trust, confusion about servanthood, and edges of selfishness are arising, but …I often feel a lack of hard, clear, mutually self-less searching that will be necessary for us [if we are to become] agents of change in the church."[24]

The Clergywomen Retention Study concludes with these words:

Decades have passed since The United Methodist Church first approved the ordination of women. The Church needs to ask itself the difficult questions about the underlying theology that reinforces and affirms a highly hierarchical and political power structure. The Church needs to develop and embrace a theology that would promote more equitable, cooperative, and respectful mentality among its clergy and laity. The Church also needs to articulate what kind of God is pleased when clergy must leave the local church, or ordained ministry altogether, in order to live authentically. These clergy-

women are calling the Church to be prophetic in its own way by seizing the opportunity to respond effectively to the painful experiences of these and other clergywomen. Acknowledgment that those painful experiences are actually symptoms of problems within the larger Church is an important place for the Church to begin.[25]

Surely a part of claiming our bold future will be the courage and willingness to ask some of the hard questions that face both United Methodist clergywomen and The United Methodist Church today, to be willing to name the pain and its sources, and to continue to be willing to live out the call that has led some eighty-six hundred women [and even more in 2006] into ministry in The United Methodist Church. Furthermore, we need to continue to do the hard work necessary to make The United Methodist Church a place where we truly can proclaim with certainty that we have "Open Hearts, Open Minds, and Open Doors."

But we cannot do it alone, nor should we want or expect to. For if one thing has become clear to me in writing this book, it is this: the strength of the faith of the women whom God has called to ministry in The United Methodist Church over the past 260-plus years and the sure knowledge that these women have had of the presence and faithfulness of God throughout the journey. Bishop Kelly says it this way: "In the long run, God reigns no matter what happens. When we plug into our own faith perspectives, we know that we couldn't have made it without our own faith, because there's certainly nothing in any of our backgrounds that made us feel we were destined to be bishops. But when God calls and that call is clear to you, then God also sustains. No matter how much the pain, there's somebody there for you in every situation."[26] These words are true not only for our "leading women"–our bishops–but also for all of us who have stayed the course. Over and over, the stories of the women included in the foregoing pages have witnessed to the mighty power of God and the presence of the Holy Spirit throughout the journey.

As God called and gave strength to the clergywomen whose stories are told in this book (and to countless women whose stories will never be told) to live out the call to ministry in The United Methodist Church in order that we can indeed "celebrate our courageous past," so God will continue to bless and give courage and strength to those women who will be the ones to go forth to "claim our bold future." Amen.

Notes

1. "Statistics," *WellSprings: A Journal for United Methodist Clergywomen* (Winter 2003): 39.
2. The Alaska Missionary Conference does not receive members at the present time.
3. For more information on Margaret Henrichsen, see chapter 2, 41.
4. Paul Mojzes, *An Extraordinary Woman: Paula Mojzes 1906–1970* (United Methodist Church in Macedonia, 2004), 6, 11.
5. Ibid., 11. For further information on Paula Mojzes, see chapter 9, 192.
6. Records from the North Indiana Conference. See also, General Commission on Archives and History and "Historical Firsts for Women Clergy–Part 2," (http://www.gcah.org/women_ministry2.htm).

7. Judith Craig, comp., *The Leading Women: Stories of the First Women Bishops of The United Methodist Church* (Nashville: Abingdon, 2004), 9. © 2004 Abingdon Press. Used by permission.

8. Margaret Wiborg and Elizabeth Collier, *The United Methodist Clergywomen Retention Study* (Anna Howard Shaw Center, http://www.bu.edu/sth/shaw/retention.html), 1:1.

9. Ibid., 1:2.

10. Ibid., 1:3

11. Ibid., 3:1-2; 2:7.

12. Craig, comp., *The Leading Women*, 263.

13. Ibid., 267.

14. "Delegates Say Racism Affected Southeast Jurisdictional Elections," UMNS News Feature, July 28, 2004.

15. Wiborg and Collier, *Clergywomen Retention Study*, 2:6.

16. Ibid., 2:10.

17. Craig, comp., *The Leading Women*, 268.

18. Ibid., 276.

19. Wiborg and Collier, *Clergywomen Retention Study*, 3:8.

20. Ibid., 3:16.

21. Craig, comp., *The Leading Women*, 273.

22. Ibid., 256.

23. Barbara B. Troxell, "Honoring One Another with Our Stories," in *Spirituality and Social Responsibility*, ed. Rosemary Skinner Keller (Nashville: Abingdon, 1993), 294-95.

24. Ibid., 297.

25. Wiborg and Collier, *Clergywomen Retention Study*, 3:17-18.

26. Craig, comp., *The Leading Women*, 281.

Suggestions for Further Reading

Chilcote, Paul Wesley. *She Offered Them Christ: The Legacy of Women Preachers in United Methodism.* Nashville: Abingdon, 1993.

Craig, Judith, comp. *The Leading Women: Stories of the First Women Bishops of The United Methodist Church.* Nashville: Abingdon, 2004.

Gorrell, Donald K., ed. *Woman's Rightful Place.* Dayton, OH: United Theological Seminary, 1980.

Henrichsen, Margaret. *Seven Steeples.* Boston: Houghton Mifflin, 1953.

Keller, Rosemary Skinner, ed. *Spirituality and Social Responsibility: Vocational Vision of Women in The United Methodist Tradition.* Nashville: Abingdon, 1993.

Keller, Rosemary Skinner, Hilah F. Thomas, and Louise L. Queen, eds. *Women in New Worlds: Historical Perspectives on the Wesleyan Tradition.* 2 vols. Nashville: Abingdon, 1981–82.

Kim, Jung Ha and Rosetta Ross, *The Status of Racial-Ethnic Minority Clergywomen in The United Methodist Church.* Nashville: General Board of Higher Education and Ministry, 2004.

Richey, Russell E., Kenneth E. Rowe, and Jean Miller Schmidt, eds. *Perspectives on American Methodism: Interpretive Essays.* Nashville: Kingswood, 1993.

Schmidt, Jean Miller. *Grace Sufficient: A History of Women in American Methodism 1760–1939.* Nashville: Abingdon, 1999.

Shaw, Anna Howard. *The Story of a Pioneer.* New York: Harper and Brothers, 1915; Cleveland, OH: Pilgrim, 1994.

Articles from *Methodist History*:

Cooney, Jonathan. "Maintaining the Tradition: Women Elders and the Ordination of Women in The Evangelical United Brethren Church," *Methodist History* 27, no. 1 (October 1988): 25-35.

Dayton, Lucille Sider, and Donald W. Dayton. "Your Daughters Shall Prophesy: Feminism in the Holiness Movement," *Methodist History* 14, no. 2 (January 1976): 67-92.

Gorrell, Donald K. "Ordination of Women by the United Brethren in Christ, 1889," *Methodist History* 18, no. 2 (January 1980): 136-43.

Irons, Kendra Weddle. "From Kansas to the World: M. Madeline Southard, Activist and Pastor," *Methodist History* 43, no. 1 (October 2004): 33-44.

Knotts, Alice. "The Debate over Race and Women's Ordination in the 1939 Merger," *Methodist History* 29, no. 1 (October 1990): 37-43.

Noll, William T. "Women as Clergy and Laity in the 19th Century Methodist Protestant Church," *Methodist History* 15, no. 2 (1977): 107-21.

——. "A Welcome in the Ministry: The 1920 and 1924 General Conferences Debate Clergy Rights for Women," *Methodist History* 30, no. 2 (1992): 91-99.

Shoemaker, Christopher M. "A Small Work: The Story of Helenor Alter Davisson, Methodism's First Ordained Woman," *Methodist History* 41, no. 2 (January 2003): 3-11.

Troxell, Barbara B. "Ordination of Women in the United Methodist Tradition," *Methodist History* 37, no. 2 (January 1999): 119-30.

Index of Names

Note: The list of names below is not exhaustive. It contains only the names of those "first" women whose biographies appear in the book, starting in Chapter 2.

Eastin, Carol Sue Lakota, 159
Edwards, Esther E., 68
Ekholm, Kerstin, 198
Ellis, Ruth Marion, 45, 78
Elmes, Constance Hasentab, 163
Esbenshade, M. Lucile, 68
Estaris, Crispina, 201

Fernandez, Julia Torres, 91
Finley, Ruthenia Helen, 87
Floyd, Madge Black, 95
Fosua, Abena Safiyah, 161
Franklin, Velma Hart, 139
Franks, Barbara Longyear, 106
Frendol, Rosalina T., 205

Garbuzova, Ludmila P., 194
Gitterman, Harriette M., 61, 158
Gleaves, Edith Lee, 112
Glory-Neal, Lois V., 145
Gonzales, Adele, 164
Grabher, Jean Marie, 205
Grams, Hildegard, 196
Greenwaldt, Karen Ann, 129
Grueneke, Christel, 196
Guzman, Lucia, 189

Haftorson, Janice Kageta, 184
Hakeem-Michael, Sukumari S., 110, 152
Hallman, Julieanne Sotzing, 83
Ham-Son, Suzy, 106
Hand, Vivian Joyce, 135
Han-Kim, Youngsook, 87
Harris, Gertrude Genevra, 38, 82
Harris-Scott, Elma Joyce, 130
Hart, Alice Townsend, 38, 39, 82
Hartman, Doris, 92
Haskard, Esther A., 38, 40, 82
Hassinger, Susan Wolfe, 70, 73, 76, 209-10
Hatchell, Sandra Hardin, 118
Hathaway, Lucy Campbell, 100
He, Huibing, 88
Henrichsen, Margaret Kimball, 38, 41, 82, 208
Henry-Crowe, Susan Thurston, 117
Hitchcock, Ernestine, 184
Hoke, Sandra Frances, 166
Hopkins, Felicia Pringle, 138
Horton, Hey Young Nam, 81
House, Hazel Jane Arnold, 141
Huck, Grace E., 34, 152
Hughes, Edna Beougher, 67
Hunter, Everne, 61, 127
Hwang, In-Sook, 158

Icaza-Willetts, Lia, 103
Ivanova, Maire, 199

Jackson, Marion Alberta, 80
Jackson, Perrie Joy, 149
James, Inez Yvonne, 82
Jensen, Maud Keister, 33, 75
Joiner, Lisa Michelle Scott, 157
Jones, Linda Chamberlain, 171
Jones-Lurvey, Gwen, 83, 133
Joyner, Lea, 60, 132

Kagiyama, Karen Miyoshi, 115, 124
Kammerer, Charlene Payne, 102, 209-10

Kane, Liatu J., 206
Kang, Youngsook Charlene, 189
Kasambira, Mercy Mwazviwanza Mujati, 75
Kee, Eunhae, 170
Kelly, Leontine Turpeau Current, 99, 121, 159, 208, 212
Kiboko, Kabamba, 207
Kim, Ai Ra, 79
Kim, Gina Moon, 156
Kim, Hea Sun, 73
Kim, Millie L., 115
Kim, Young, 83
Kimba, Mutombo Ilungu, 206
Kinard, Norma Jean, 66, 69
Kline, Marion, 48, 153
Ko, Mamie Ming Yan, 179
Kotey, Janette, 143
Kotsuba, Olga V., 194
Krisher, C. Maxine, 68
Kumar, Felicia Ethel Dorcas, 77
Kunjravia-Patel, Snehlata, 88
Kwon, Hee-Soon, 160

Lam, Mochi, 176, 179
Lambert, Carolyn Stokes, 132
Latimer, Portteus Helen, 131
Lee, Kyunglim Shin, 173
Littlejohn, Marilyn J., 186
Long, Mary Louise, 52, 176
Lopez, Elizabeth Ann, 137, 162
Lortz, Ruth M., 186

Macaspac, Paz, 202
MacNicholl, Mary, 46, 162
Madlangsakay, Romana Olermo, 204
Mamonova, Nelya A., 194
Mansfield, Marietta, 105
Marshall, Margaret Ann, 93
Martinez, Lydia Salazar, 148
Matthews, Marjorie Swank, 168, 208
Mauyao, Cornelia, 202
Maxwell, Eva Banton, 53, 176
McClellan, Geraldine Williams, 102, 210
McCrary, Maloie Bogle Lee, 123
McEwing, Barbara C., 163
McFadden, Vivian Patricia, 117
McNair, Emma Louise, 109
Meier, Eleonore, 192
Meinhold, Dorothea, 196
Meyer, Mary Ellen, 134
Michelmann, Gertrud, 196
Miguel, Fernandita J., 200
Milam, Lenn Harris, 107
Milton, Sadye Joiner, 123
Misal, Margaret, 158
Mitina, Irina, 195
Miyake-Stoner, Nobuko, 188
Moa, Linita 'Ulu'ave, 181
Mojzes, Paula, 192, 208
Montgomery, Carolyn J., 16, 79
Moon, SungJa Lee, 164
Moore, Jane Ann Stoneburner, 32, 56, 170
Moore, Joy Jittaun, 168
Moore, Kathryn Louise Bailey, 66, 69, 73
Moore-Colgan, Marion May, 92
Morgan, Allison Rhodes, 119
Morrow, Mae Charlotte, 155
Mowry, Elizabeth Suydam Foster, 89